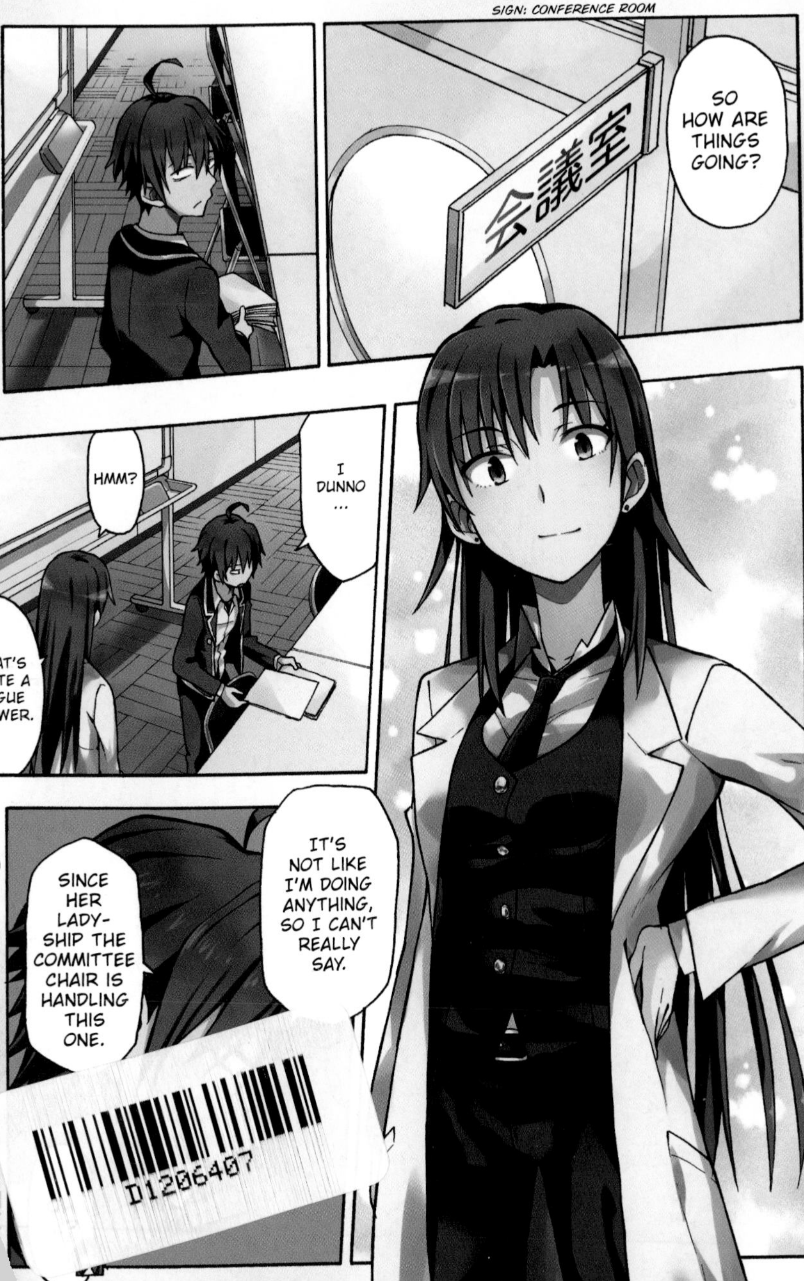
SIGN: CONFERENCE ROOM
会議室
SO HOW ARE THINGS GOING?
I DUNNO...
HMM?
THAT'S QUITE A VAGUE ANSWER.
IT'S NOT LIKE I'M DOING ANYTHING, SO I CAN'T REALLY SAY.
SINCE HER LADYSHIP THE COMMITTEE CHAIR IS HANDLING THIS ONE.

CHAPTER 48 ... AND NOW THE FINAL MEETI… BREAKS I

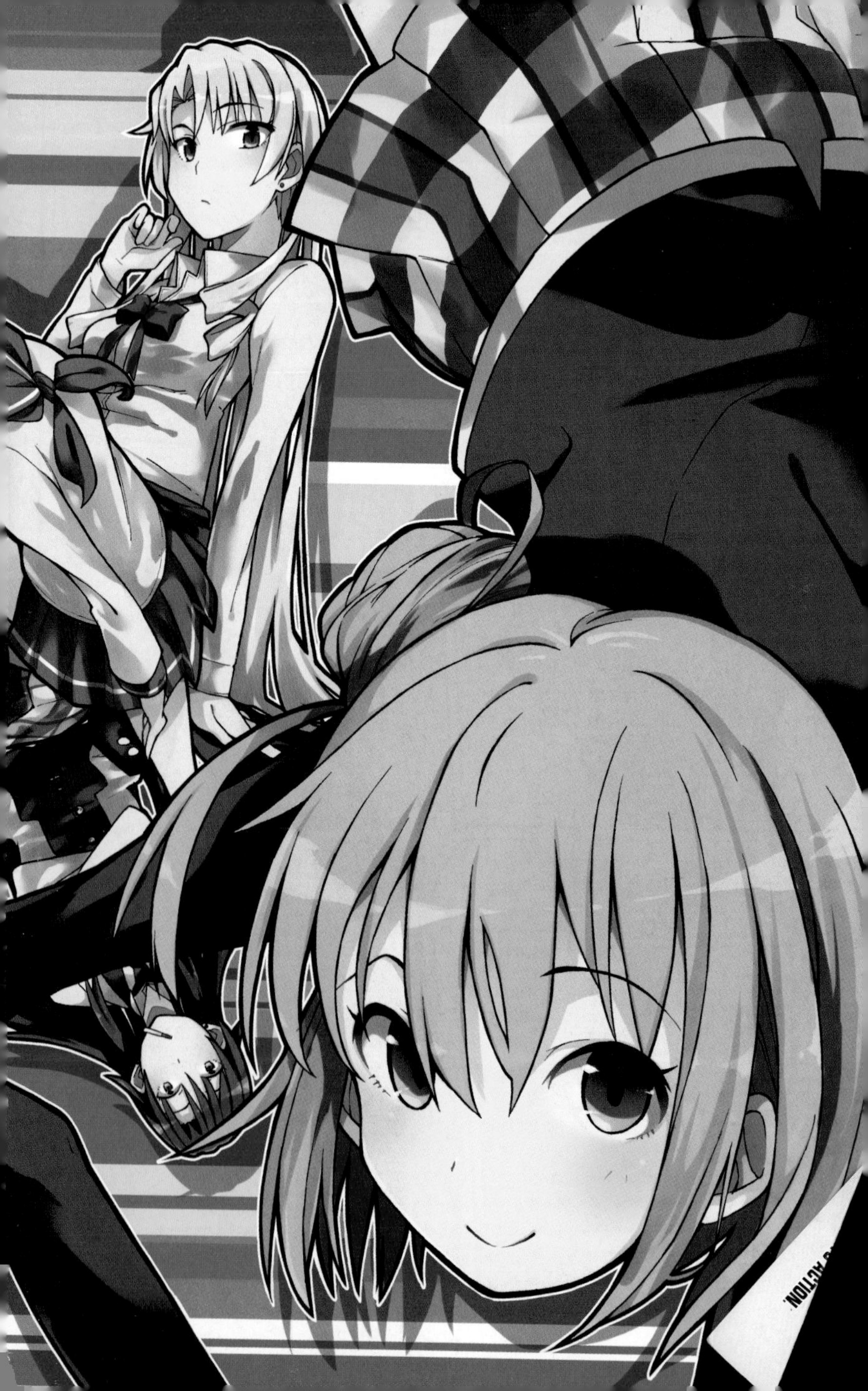

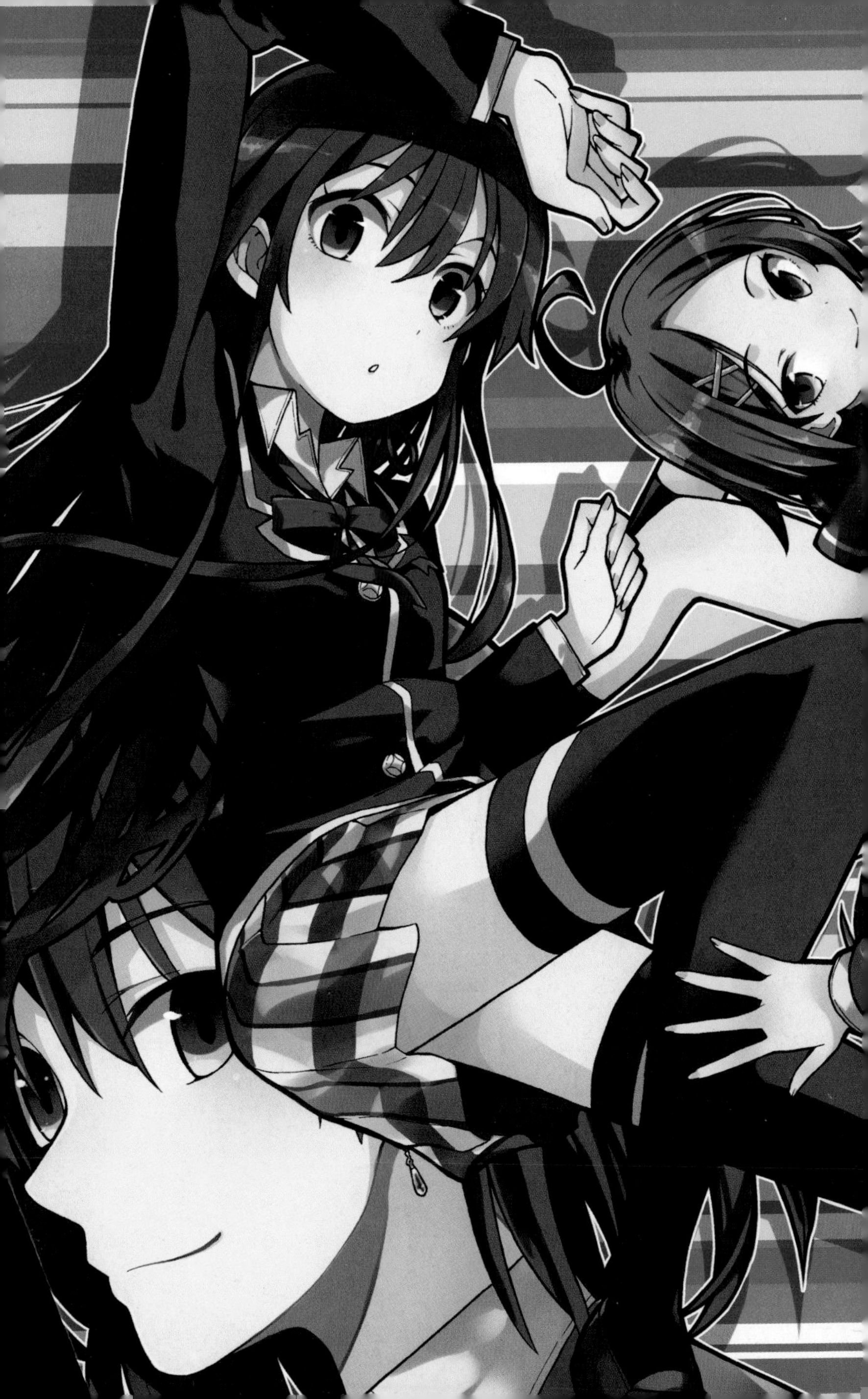

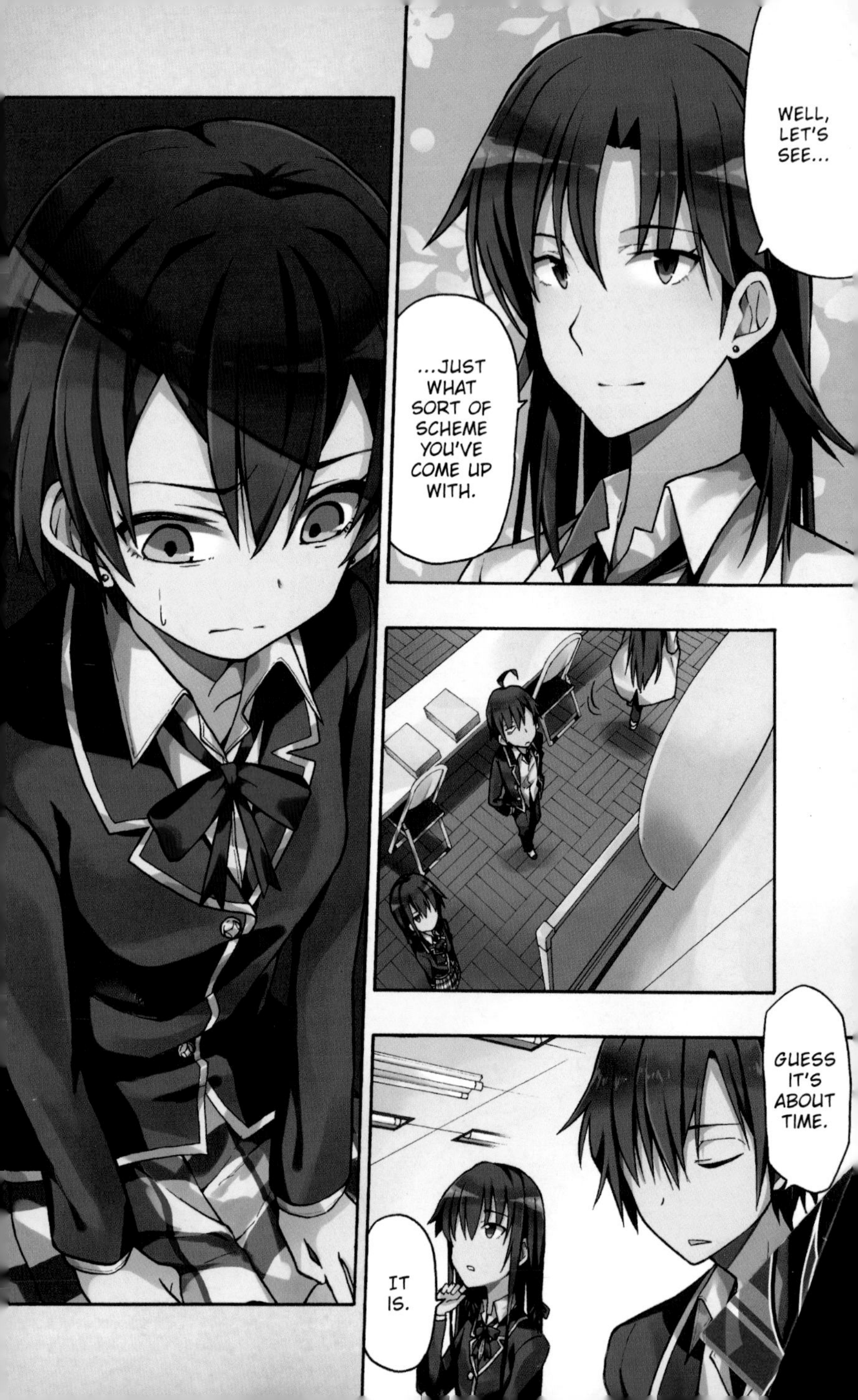
WELL, LET'S SEE...
...JUST WHAT SORT OF SCHEME YOU'VE COME UP WITH.
GUESS IT'S ABOUT TIME.
IT IS.

MY YOUTH RØMANTIC COMEDY is WRØNG, AS I EXPECTED @comic 09

▌Original Story
Wataru Watari
▌Art
Naomichi Io
▌Character Design
Ponkan⑧

MY YOUTH ROMANTIC COMEDY IS WRONG, AS I EXPECTED @COMIC

CHARACTERS + STORY SO FAR

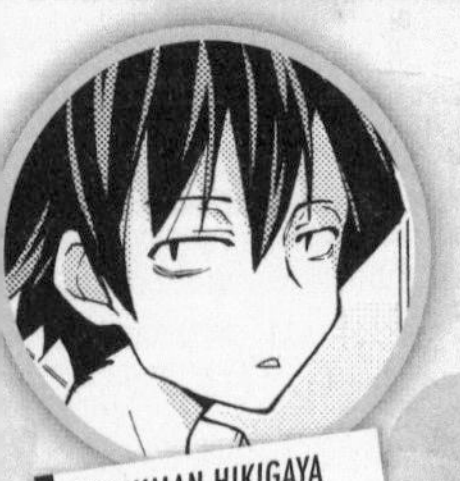

HACHIMAN HIKIGAYA

LONER AND A TWISTED HUMAN BEING. FORCED TO JOIN THE SERVICE CLUB. ASPIRES TO BE A HOUSEHUSBAND.

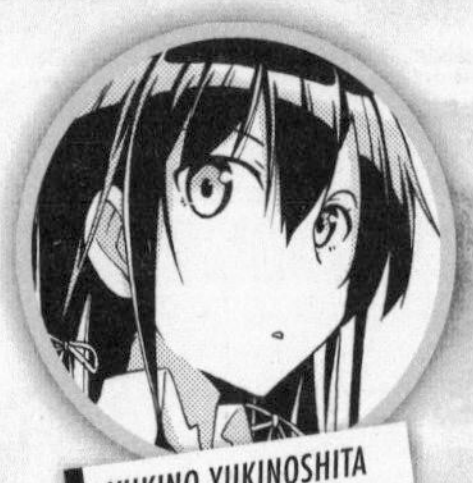

YUKINO YUKINOSHITA

PERFECT SUPERWOMAN WITH TOP GRADES AND FLAWLESS LOOKS, BUT HER PERSONALITY AND BOOBS ARE A LETDOWN. PRESIDENT OF THE SERVICE CLUB.

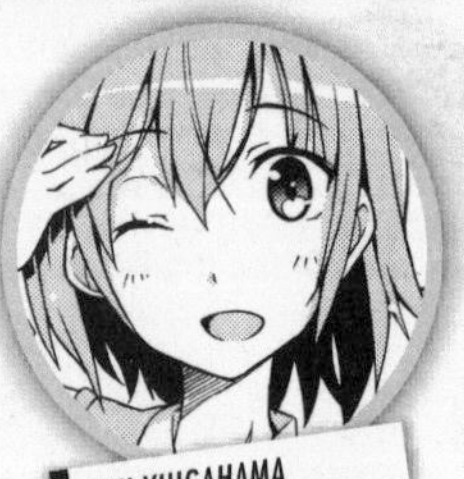

YUI YUIGAHAMA

LIGHT-BROWN HAIR, MINISKIRT, LARGE-BOOBED SLUTTY TYPE. BUT SHE'S ACTUALLY A VIRGIN!? MEMBER OF THE SERVICE CLUB.

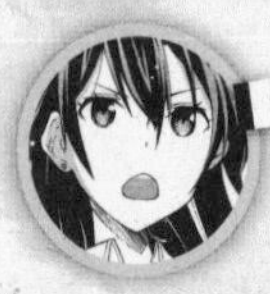

SHIZUKA HIRATSUKA

GUIDANCE COUNSELOR. ATTEMPTING TO FIX HACHIMAN BY FORCING HIM INTO THE SERVICE CLUB.

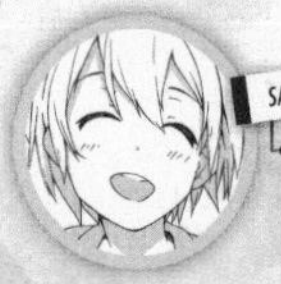

SAIKA TOTSUKA

THE SINGLE FLOWER BLOOMING IN THIS STORY. BUT...HAS A "PACKAGE."

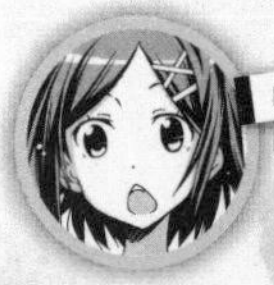

KOMACHI HIKIGAYA

HACHIMAN'S LITTLE SISTER. IN MIDDLE SCHOOL. EVERYTHING SHE DOES IS CALCULATED!?

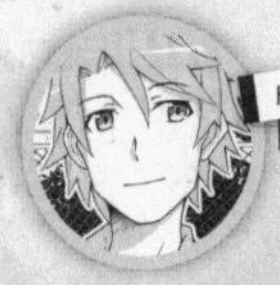

HAYATO HAYAMA

TOP RANKED IN THE SCHOOL CASTE. HANDSOME MEMBER OF THE SOCCER TEAM.

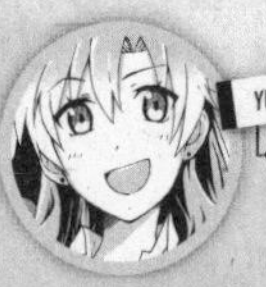

YUMIKO MIURA

THE HIGH EMPRESS NONE CAN OPPOSE.

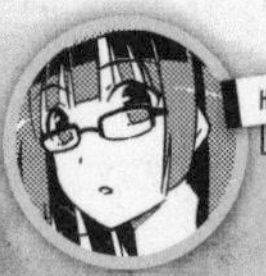

HINA EBINA

A MEMBER OF MIURA'S CLIQUE, BUT A RAGING FUJOSHI ON THE INSIDE.

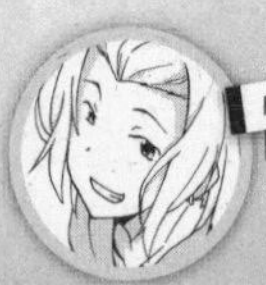

KAKERU TOBE

ALWAYS OVEREXCITED. MEMBER OF HAYAMA'S CLIQUE.

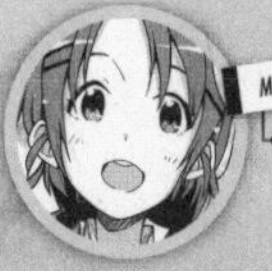

MEGURI SHIROMEGURI

THIRD-YEAR. THE PLEASANT AND GENTLE PRESIDENT OF THE STUDENT COUNCIL.

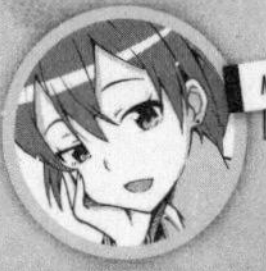

MINAMI SAGAMI

HACHIMAN'S CLASSMATE AND A MEMBER OF THE GIRLS' B-GROUP.

SO FAR

HACHIMAN HIKIGAYA, SECOND-YEAR AT CHIBA CITY MUNICIPAL SOUBU HIGH SCHOOL, IS A LONER. BUT EVER SINCE HE WAS FORCED INTO JOINING THE SERVICE CLUB, A MYSTERIOUS CLUB CAPTAINED BY THE MOST BEAUTIFUL GIRL IN SCHOOL, YUKINO YUKINOSHITA, HIS LONER LIFE HAS RAPIDLY BEEN VEERING OFF IN AN UNDESIRABLE DIRECTION. NOW, SAGAMI HAS BEEN INSTALLED AS THE CHAIRWOMAN OF THE SPORTS FESTIVAL MANAGEMENT COMMITTEE, WITH THE SERVICE CLUB SUPPORTING HER. BUT CONFLICT HAS ARISEN IN THE COMMITTEE BETWEEN THE EXECUTIVES AND THE CREW...

CONTENTS

MADE IN COOPERATION WITH THE CHIBA CITY LOCATION SERVICE

CHAPTER 48 ● AND NOW THE FINAL MEETING BREAKS INTO ACTION.

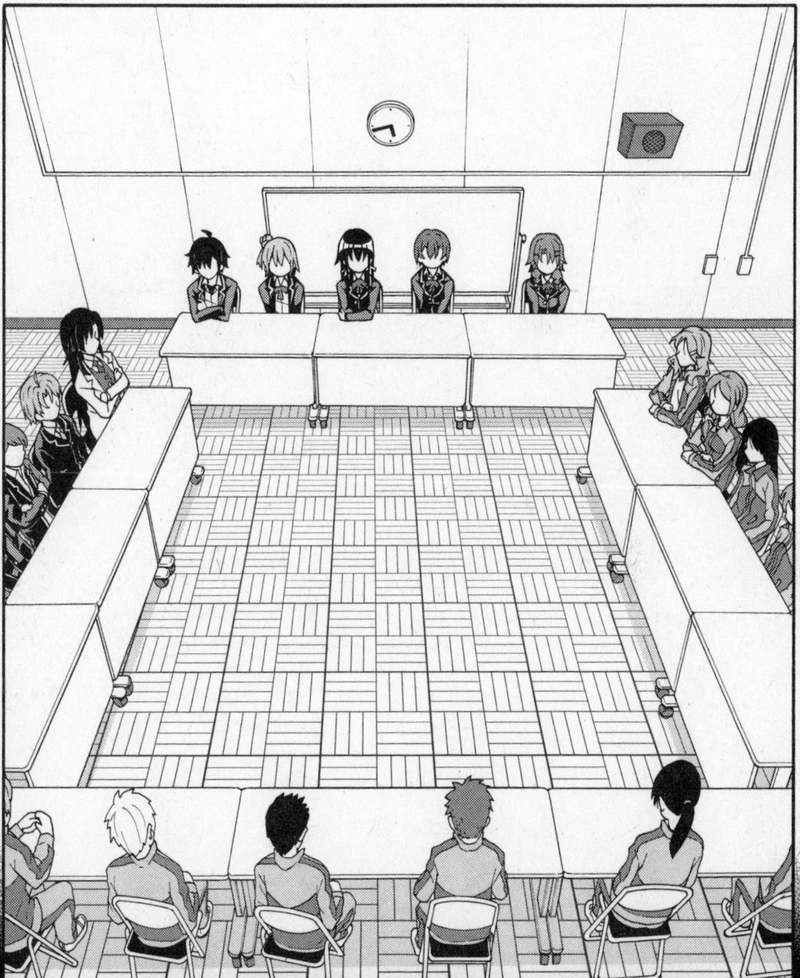

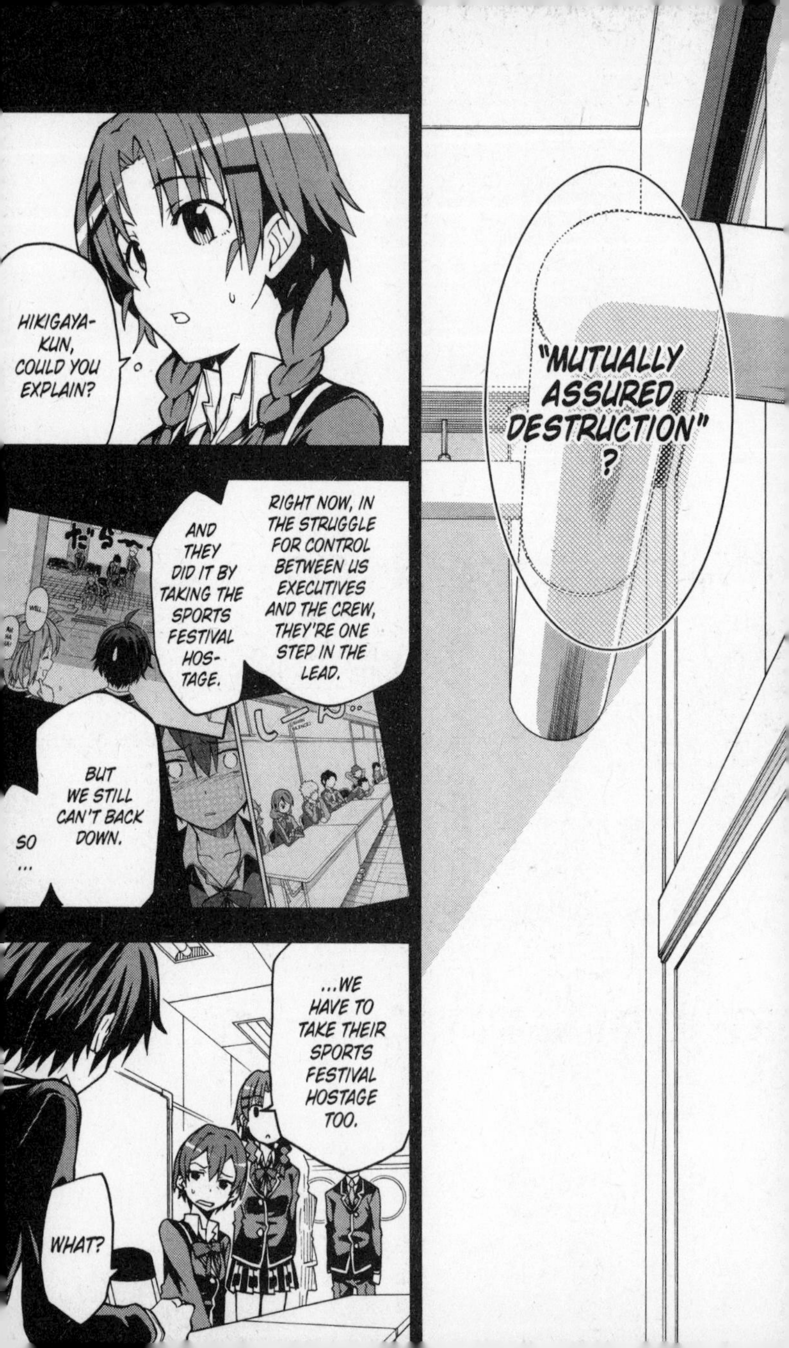
"MUTUALLY ASSURED DESTRUCTION"?
HIKIGAYA-KUN, COULD YOU EXPLAIN?
RIGHT NOW, IN THE STRUGGLE FOR CONTROL BETWEEN US EXECUTIVES AND THE CREW, THEY'RE ONE STEP IN THE LEAD.
AND THEY DID IT BY TAKING THE SPORTS FESTIVAL HOSTAGE.
BUT WE STILL CAN'T BACK DOWN.
SO...
...WE HAVE TO TAKE THEIR SPORTS FESTIVAL HOSTAGE TOO.
WHAT?

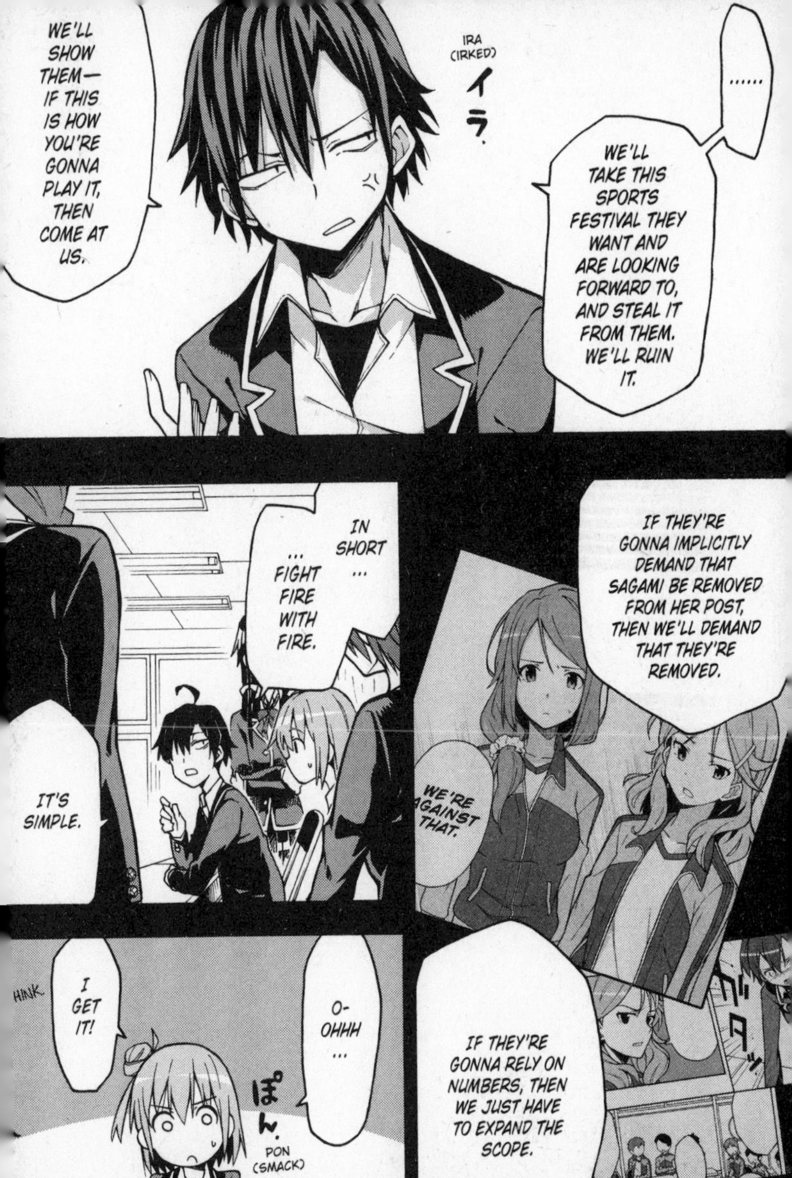
......
WE'LL TAKE THIS SPORTS FESTIVAL THEY WANT AND ARE LOOKING FORWARD TO, AND STEAL IT FROM THEM. WE'LL RUIN IT.
IRA (IRKED) イラ
WE'LL SHOW THEM—IF THIS IS HOW YOU'RE GONNA PLAY IT, THEN COME AT US.
IF THEY'RE GONNA IMPLICITLY DEMAND THAT SAGAMI BE REMOVED FROM HER POST, THEN WE'LL DEMAND THAT THEY'RE REMOVED.
WE'RE AGAINST THAT.
IN SHORT ...
... FIGHT FIRE WITH FIRE.
IT'S SIMPLE.
ガタッ
IF THEY'RE GONNA RELY ON NUMBERS, THEN WE JUST HAVE TO EXPAND THE SCOPE.
O-OHHH ...
ぽん。
PON (SMACK)
I GET IT!

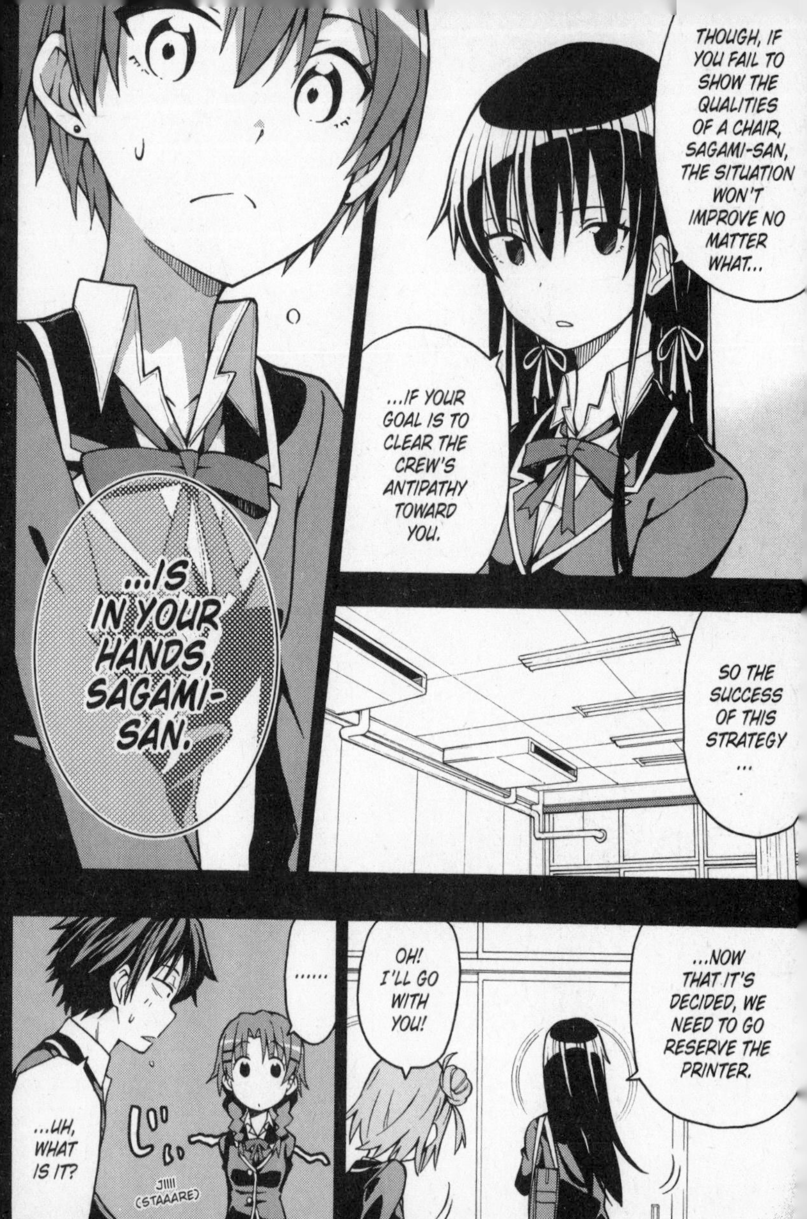
THOUGH, IF YOU FAIL TO SHOW THE QUALITIES OF A CHAIR, SAGAMI-SAN, THE SITUATION WON'T IMPROVE NO MATTER WHAT...
...IF YOUR GOAL IS TO CLEAR THE CREW'S ANTIPATHY TOWARD YOU.
SO THE SUCCESS OF THIS STRATEGY ...
...IS IN YOUR HANDS, SAGAMI-SAN.
...NOW THAT IT'S DECIDED, WE NEED TO GO RESERVE THE PRINTER.
OH! I'LL GO WITH YOU!
......
...UH, WHAT IS IT?
JIIII (STAAARE)

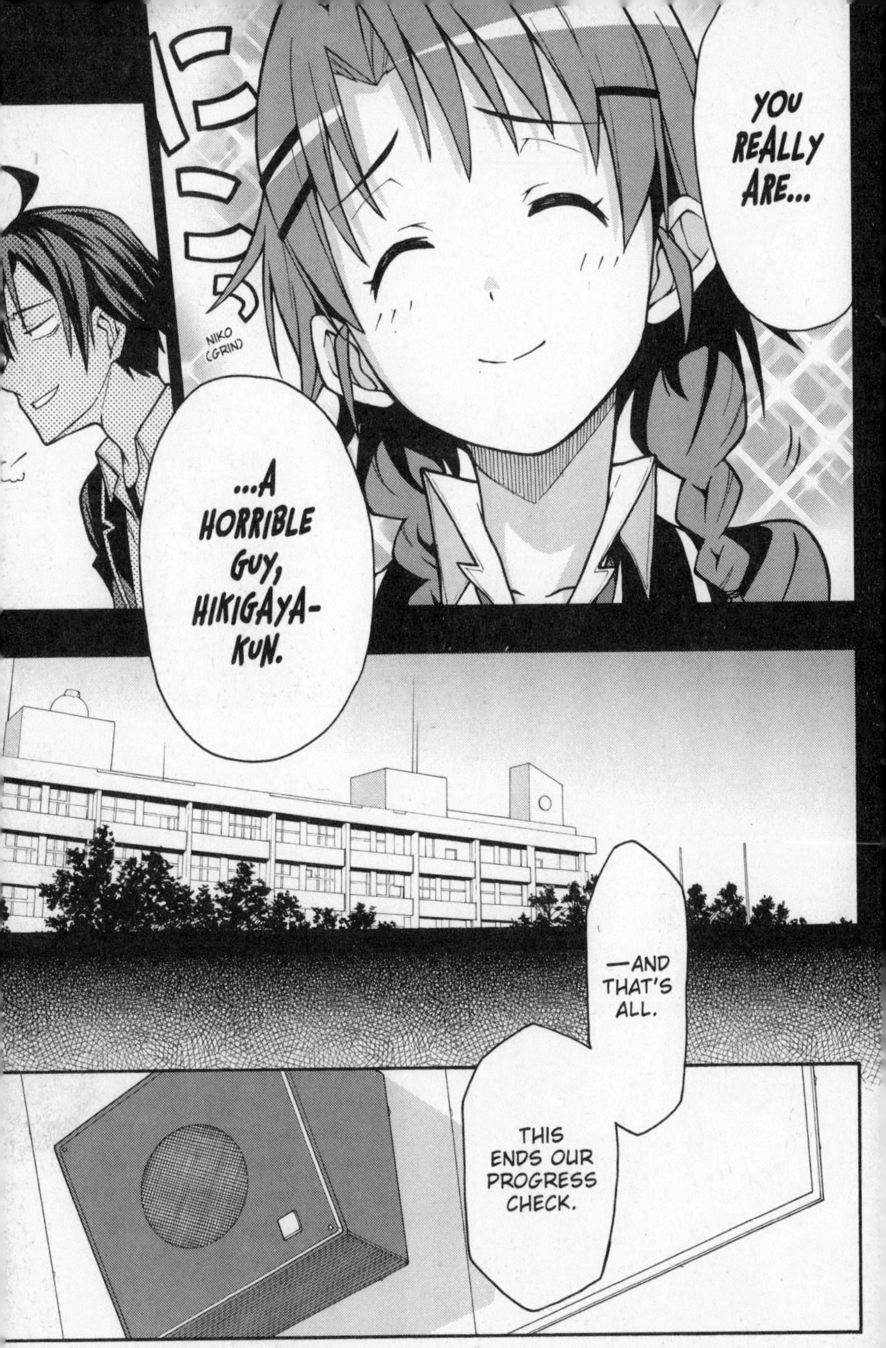
YOU REALLY ARE...
NIKO (GRIN)
...A HORRIBLE GUY, HIKIGAYA-KUN.
—AND THAT'S ALL.
THIS ENDS OUR PROGRESS CHECK.

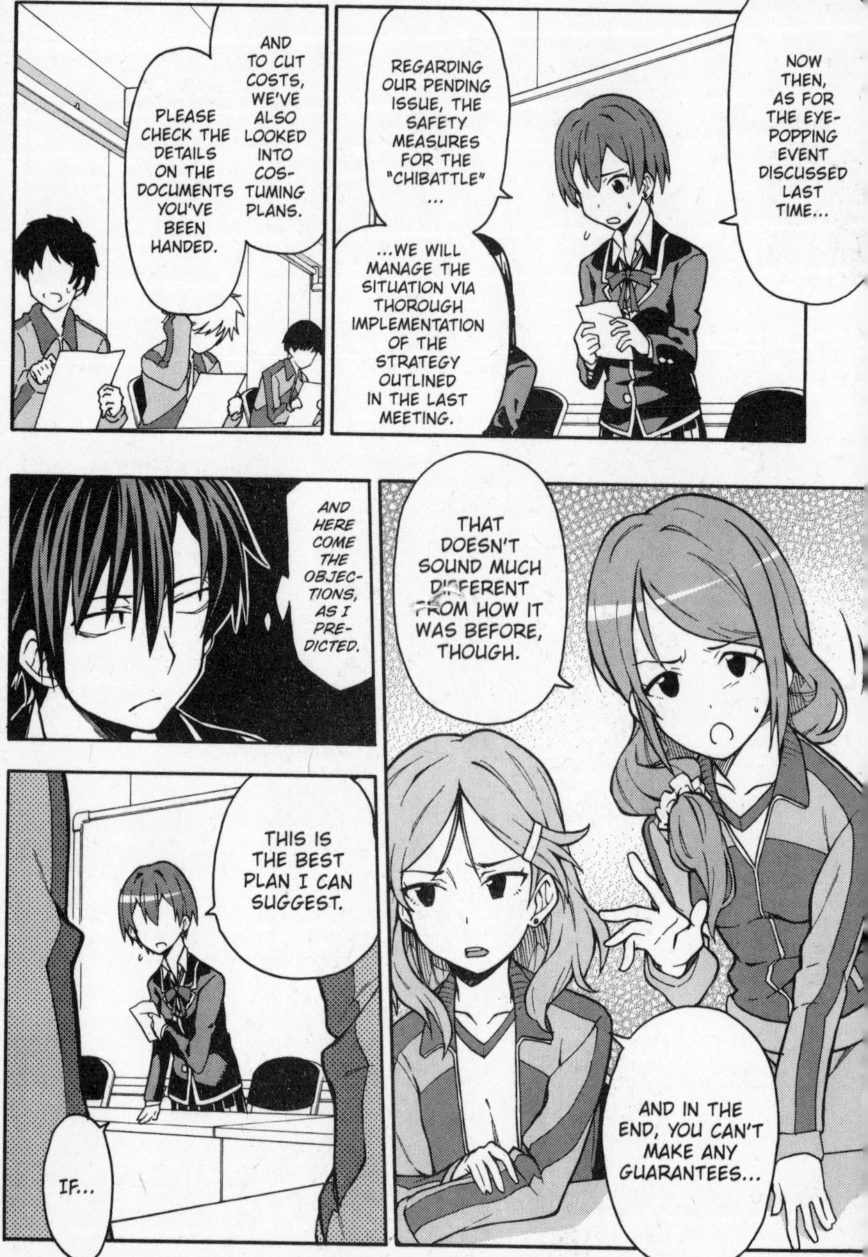
NOW THEN, AS FOR THE EYE-POPPING EVENT DISCUSSED LAST TIME...
REGARDING OUR PENDING ISSUE, THE SAFETY MEASURES FOR THE "CHIBATTLE"...
...WE WILL MANAGE THE SITUATION VIA THOROUGH IMPLEMENTATION OF THE STRATEGY OUTLINED IN THE LAST MEETING.
AND TO CUT COSTS, WE'VE ALSO LOOKED INTO COSTUMING PLANS.
PLEASE CHECK THE DETAILS ON THE DOCUMENTS YOU'VE BEEN HANDED.
THAT DOESN'T SOUND MUCH DIFFERENT FROM HOW IT WAS BEFORE, THOUGH.
AND IN THE END, YOU CAN'T MAKE ANY GUARANTEES...
AND HERE COME THE OBJECTIONS, AS I PREDICTED.
THIS IS THE BEST PLAN I CAN SUGGEST.
IF...

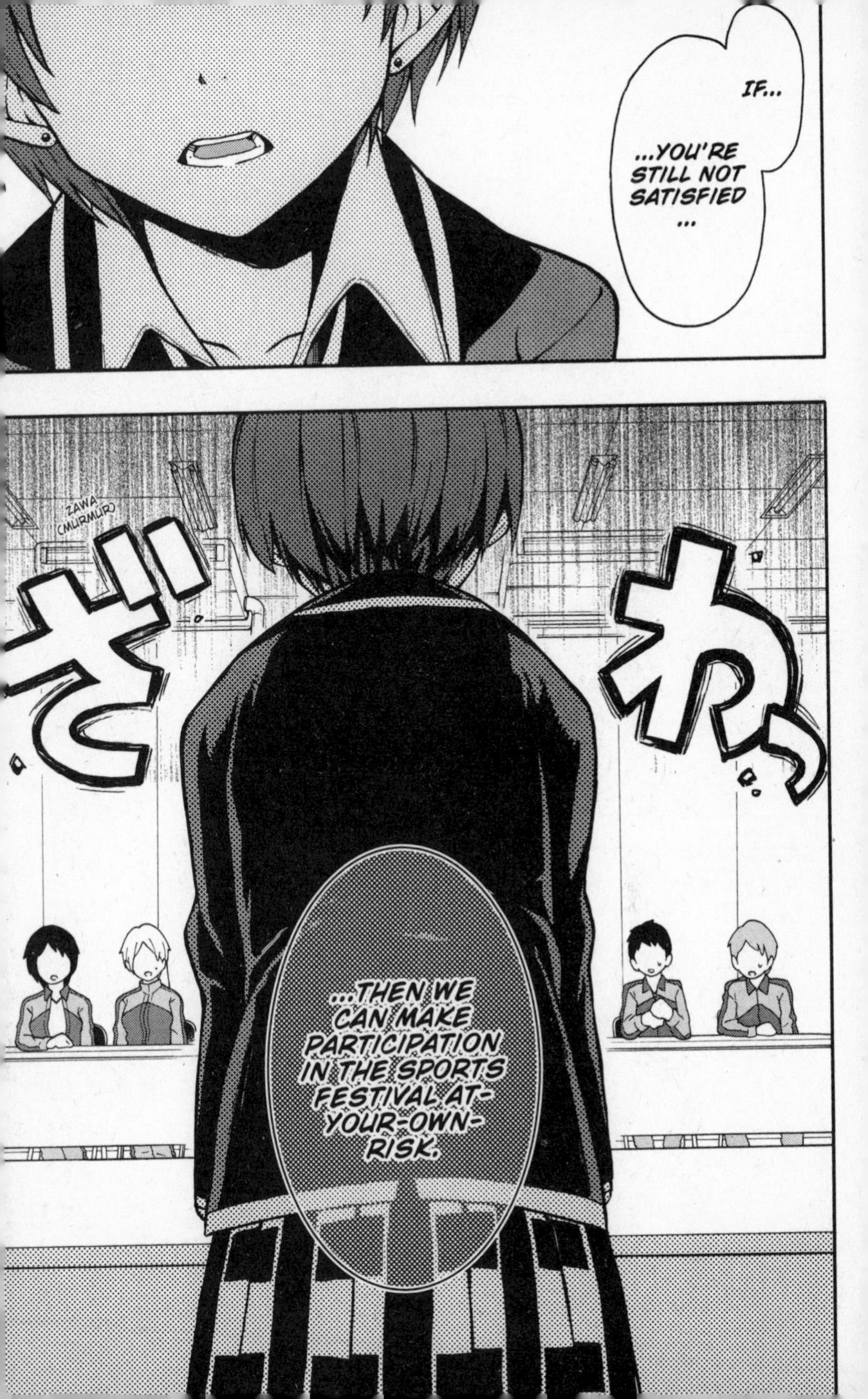
IF...
...YOU'RE STILL NOT SATISFIED ...
ざわっ
ZAWA (MURMUR)
...THEN WE CAN MAKE PARTICIPATION IN THE SPORTS FESTIVAL AT-YOUR-OWN-RISK.

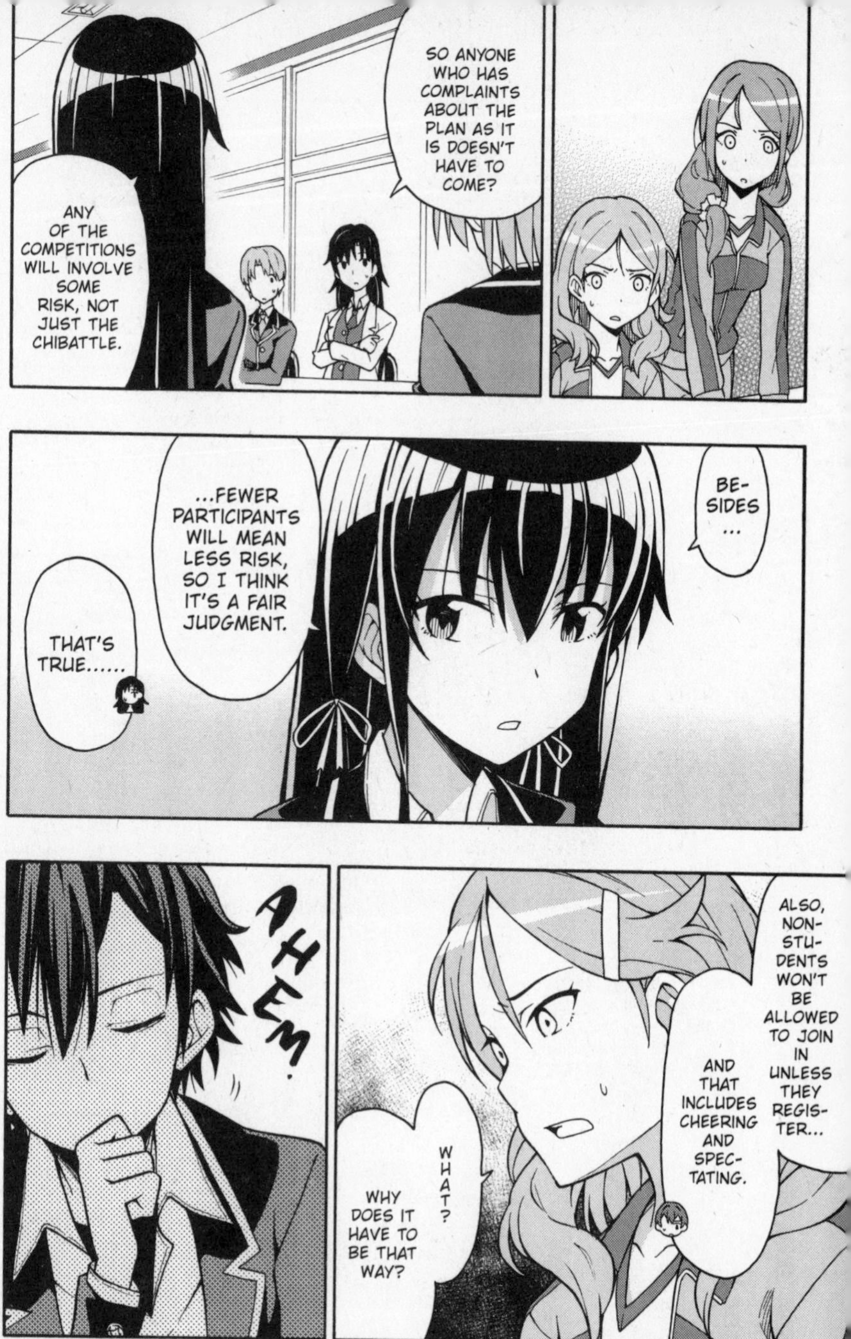
SO ANYONE WHO HAS COMPLAINTS ABOUT THE PLAN AS IT IS DOESN'T HAVE TO COME?
ANY OF THE COMPETITIONS WILL INVOLVE SOME RISK, NOT JUST THE CHIBATTLE.
BE-SIDES...
...FEWER PARTICIPANTS WILL MEAN LESS RISK, SO I THINK IT'S A FAIR JUDGMENT.
THAT'S TRUE......
ALSO, NON-STU-DENTS WON'T BE ALLOWED TO JOIN IN UNLESS THEY REGIS-TER...
AND THAT INCLUDES CHEERING AND SPEC-TATING.
WHAT?
WHY DOES IT HAVE TO BE THAT WAY?
AHEM.

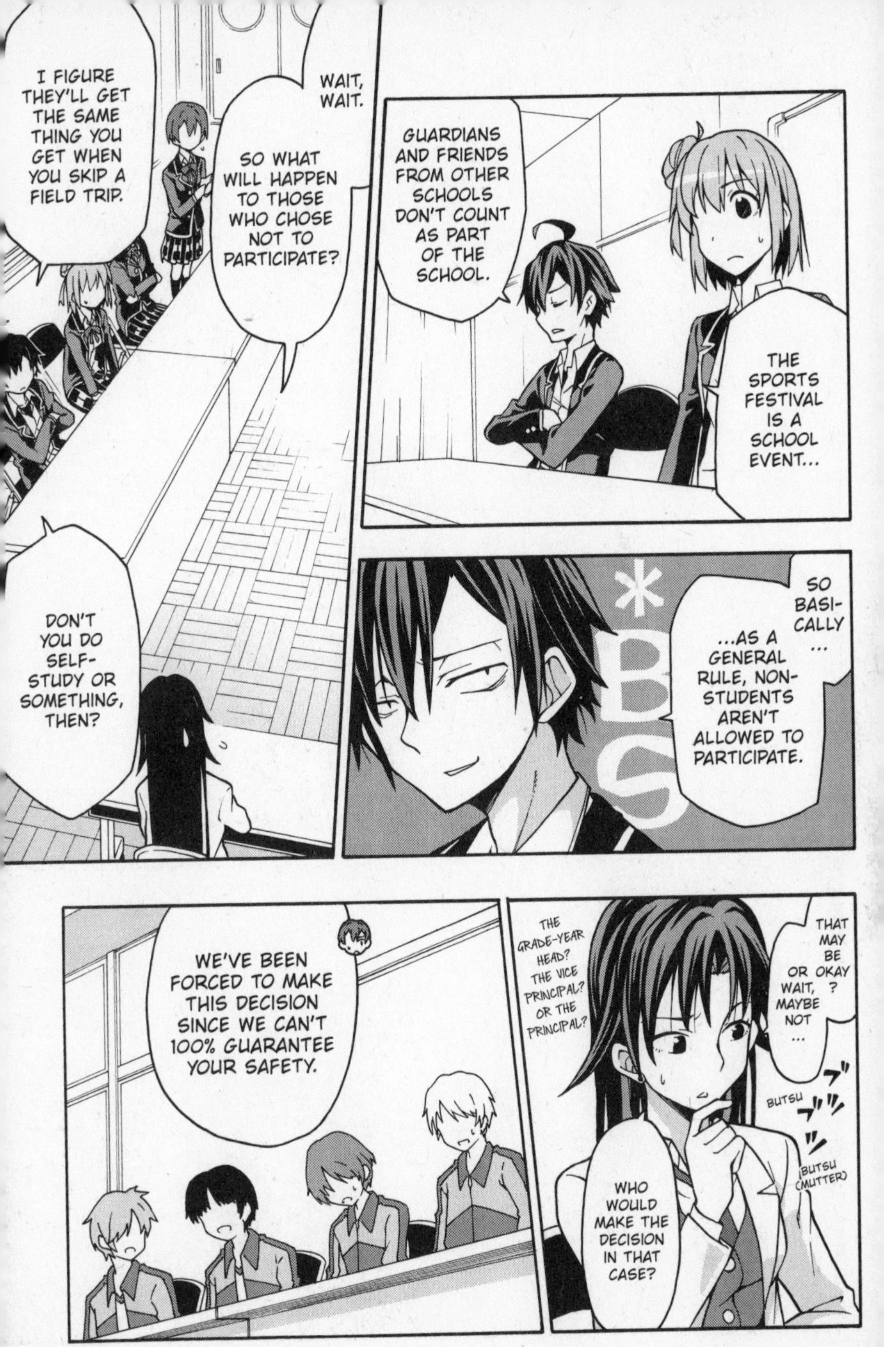
THE SPORTS FESTIVAL IS A SCHOOL EVENT...
GUARDIANS AND FRIENDS FROM OTHER SCHOOLS DON'T COUNT AS PART OF THE SCHOOL.
SO BASICALLY...
...AS A GENERAL RULE, NON-STUDENTS AREN'T ALLOWED TO PARTICIPATE.
WAIT, WAIT.
SO WHAT WILL HAPPEN TO THOSE WHO CHOSE NOT TO PARTICIPATE?
I FIGURE THEY'LL GET THE SAME THING YOU GET WHEN YOU SKIP A FIELD TRIP.
DON'T YOU DO SELF-STUDY OR SOMETHING, THEN?
THAT MAY BE OKAY? OR WAIT, MAYBE NOT...
THE GRADE-YEAR HEAD? THE VICE PRINCIPAL? OR THE PRINCIPAL?
BUTSU
BUTSU (MUTTER)
WHO WOULD MAKE THE DECISION IN THAT CASE?
WE'VE BEEN FORCED TO MAKE THIS DECISION SINCE WE CAN'T 100% GUARANTEE YOUR SAFETY.

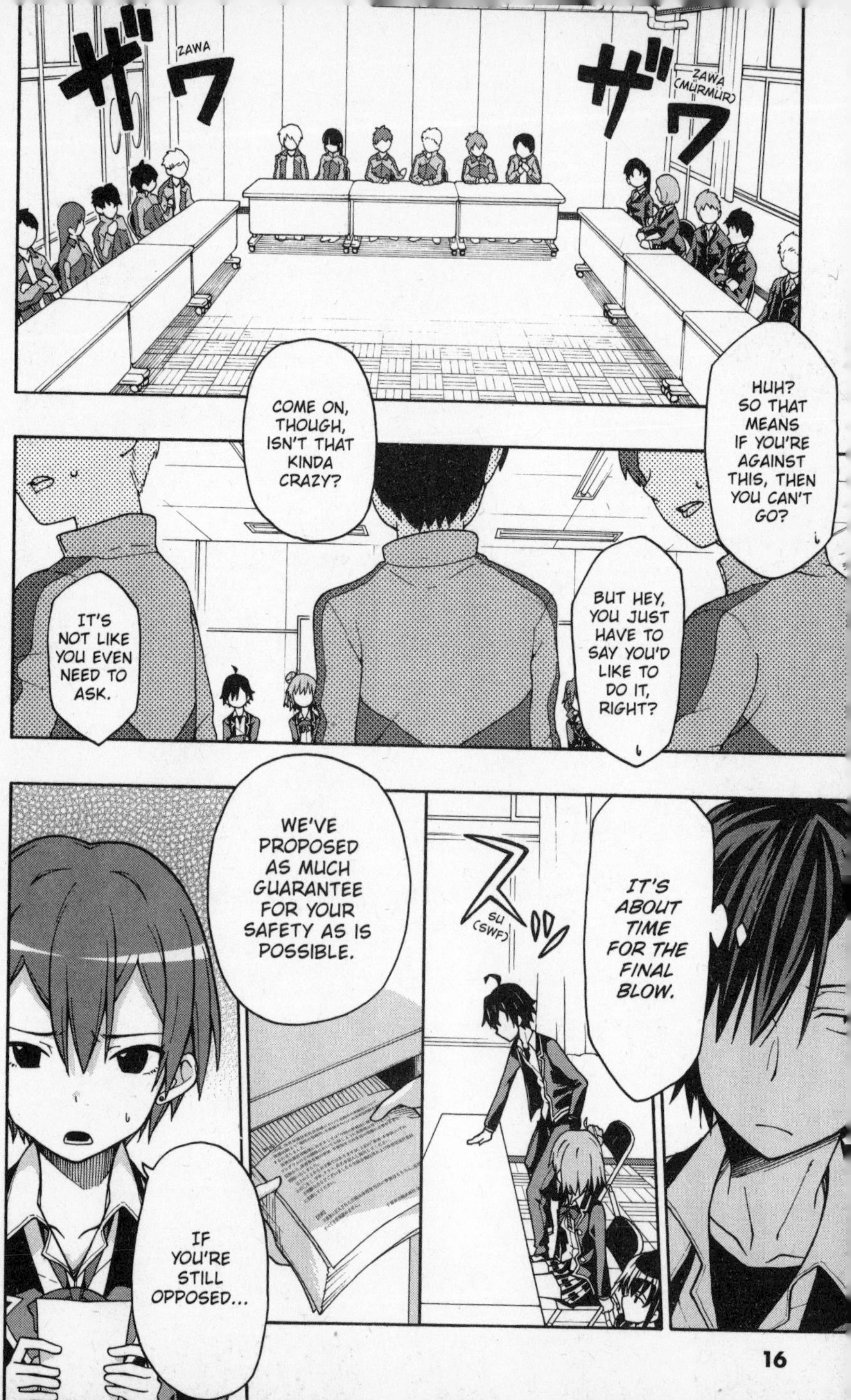
ザワ
ZAWA (MURMUR)
ザワ
ZAWA
HUH? SO THAT MEANS IF YOU'RE AGAINST THIS, THEN YOU CAN'T GO?
COME ON, THOUGH, ISN'T THAT KINDA CRAZY?
BUT HEY, YOU JUST HAVE TO SAY YOU'D LIKE TO DO IT, RIGHT?
IT'S NOT LIKE YOU EVEN NEED TO ASK.
IT'S ABOUT TIME FOR THE FINAL BLOW.
SU (SWF)
WE'VE PROPOSED AS MUCH GUARANTEE FOR YOUR SAFETY AS IS POSSIBLE.
IF YOU'RE STILL OPPOSED...

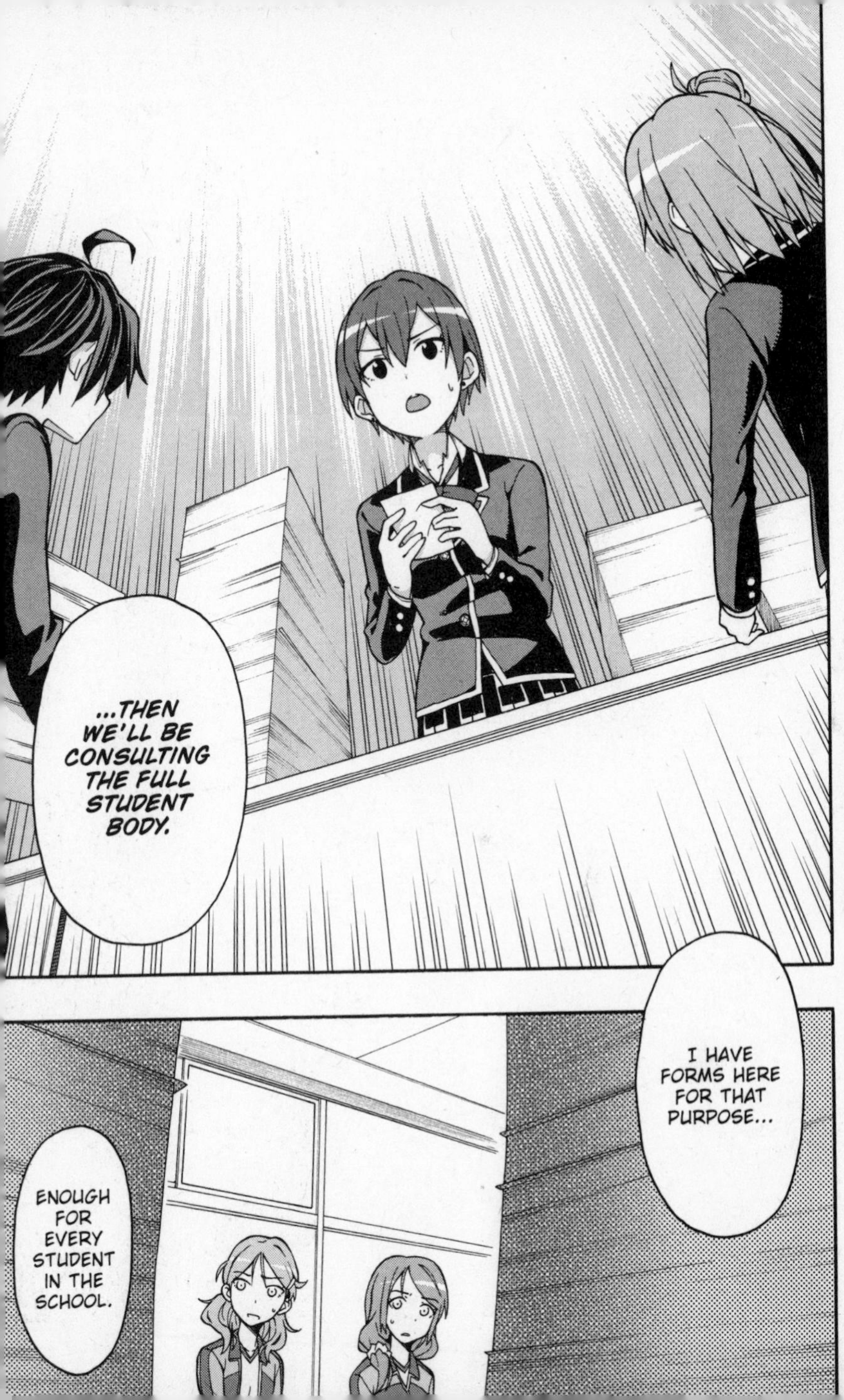
...THEN WE'LL BE CONSULTING THE FULL STUDENT BODY.
I HAVE FORMS HERE FOR THAT PURPOSE...
ENOUGH FOR EVERY STUDENT IN THE SCHOOL.

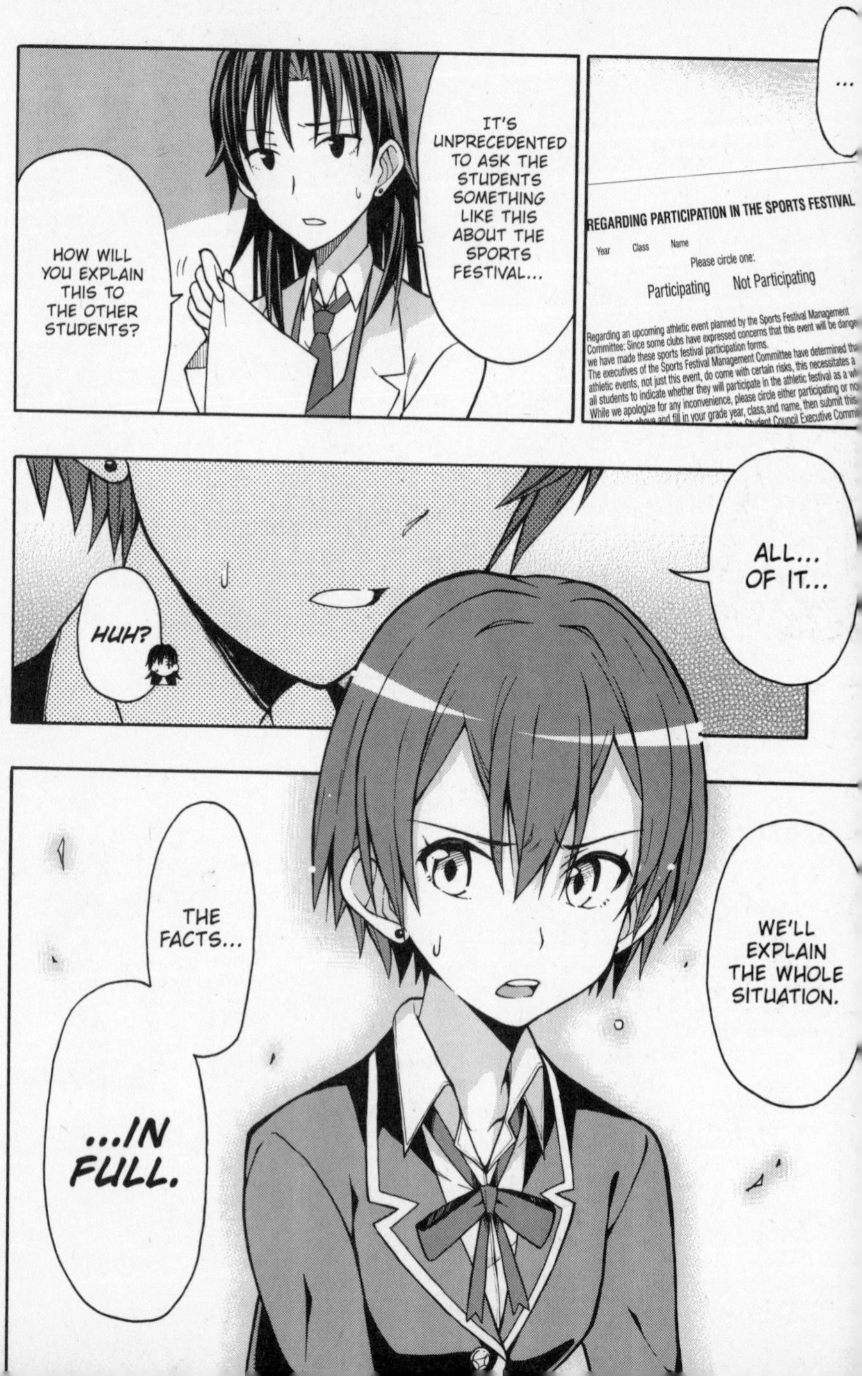
...
REGARDING PARTICIPATION IN THE SPORTS FESTIVAL
Year Class Name
Please circle one:
Participating Not Participating
Regarding an upcoming athletic event planned by the Sports Festival Management
Committee: Since some clubs have expressed concerns that this event will be
we have made these sports festival participation forms.
The executives of the Sports Festival Management Committee have determined
athletic events, not just this event, do come with certain risks, this necessitates a
all students to indicate whether they will participate in the athletic festival as a
While we apologize for any inconvenience, please circle either participating or
IT'S UNPRECEDENTED TO ASK THE STUDENTS SOMETHING LIKE THIS ABOUT THE SPORTS FESTIVAL...
HOW WILL YOU EXPLAIN THIS TO THE OTHER STUDENTS?
ALL... OF IT...
HUH?
WE'LL EXPLAIN THE WHOLE SITUATION.
THE FACTS...
...IN FULL.

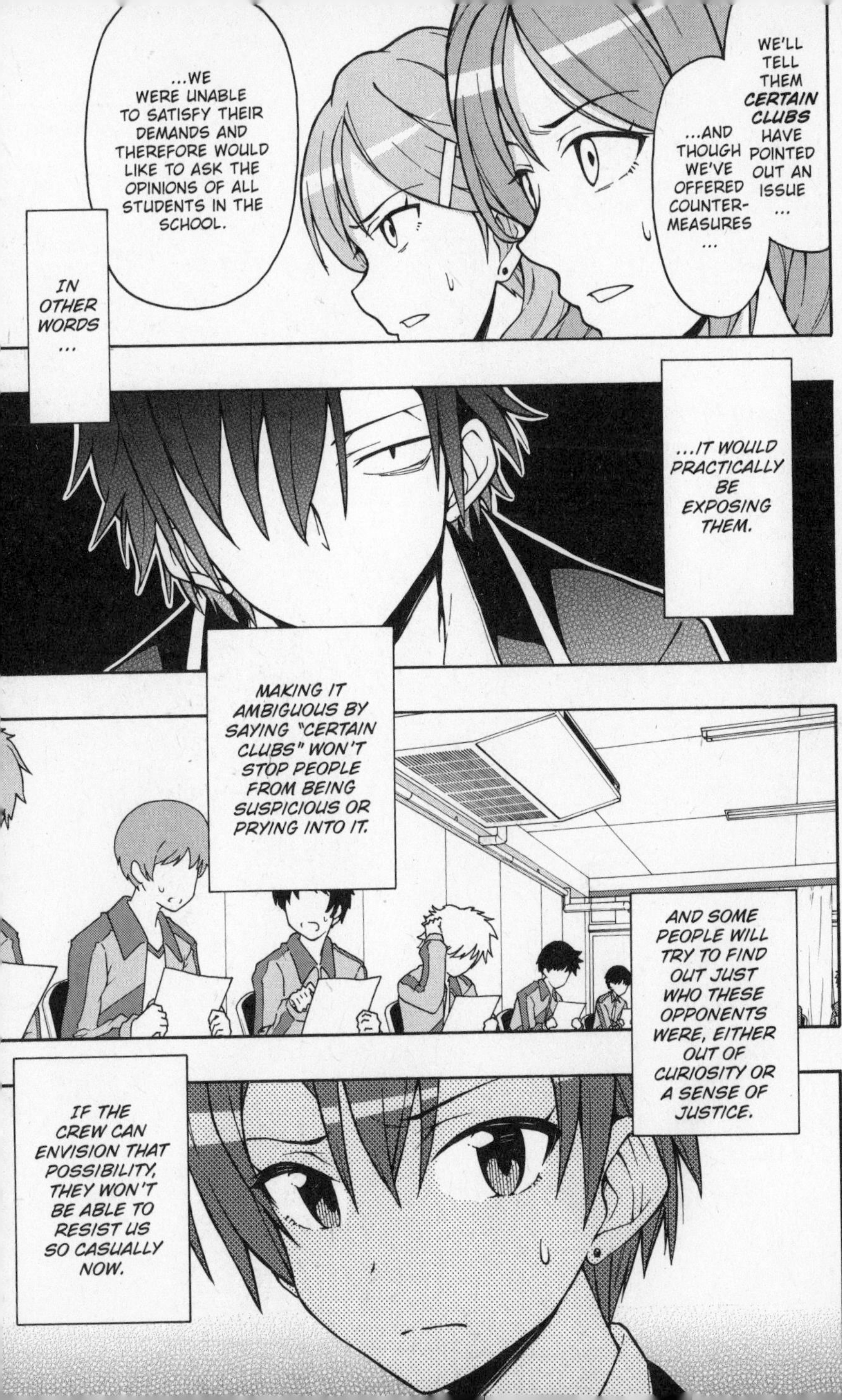
WE'LL TELL THEM CERTAIN CLUBS HAVE POINTED OUT AN ISSUE...
...AND THOUGH WE'VE OFFERED COUNTER-MEASURES...
...WE WERE UNABLE TO SATISFY THEIR DEMANDS AND THEREFORE WOULD LIKE TO ASK THE OPINIONS OF ALL STUDENTS IN THE SCHOOL.
IN OTHER WORDS...
...IT WOULD PRACTICALLY BE EXPOSING THEM.
MAKING IT AMBIGUOUS BY SAYING "CERTAIN CLUBS" WON'T STOP PEOPLE FROM BEING SUSPICIOUS OR PRYING INTO IT.
AND SOME PEOPLE WILL TRY TO FIND OUT JUST WHO THESE OPPONENTS WERE, EITHER OUT OF CURIOSITY OR A SENSE OF JUSTICE.
IF THE CREW CAN ENVISION THAT POSSIBILITY, THEY WON'T BE ABLE TO RESIST US SO CASUALLY NOW.

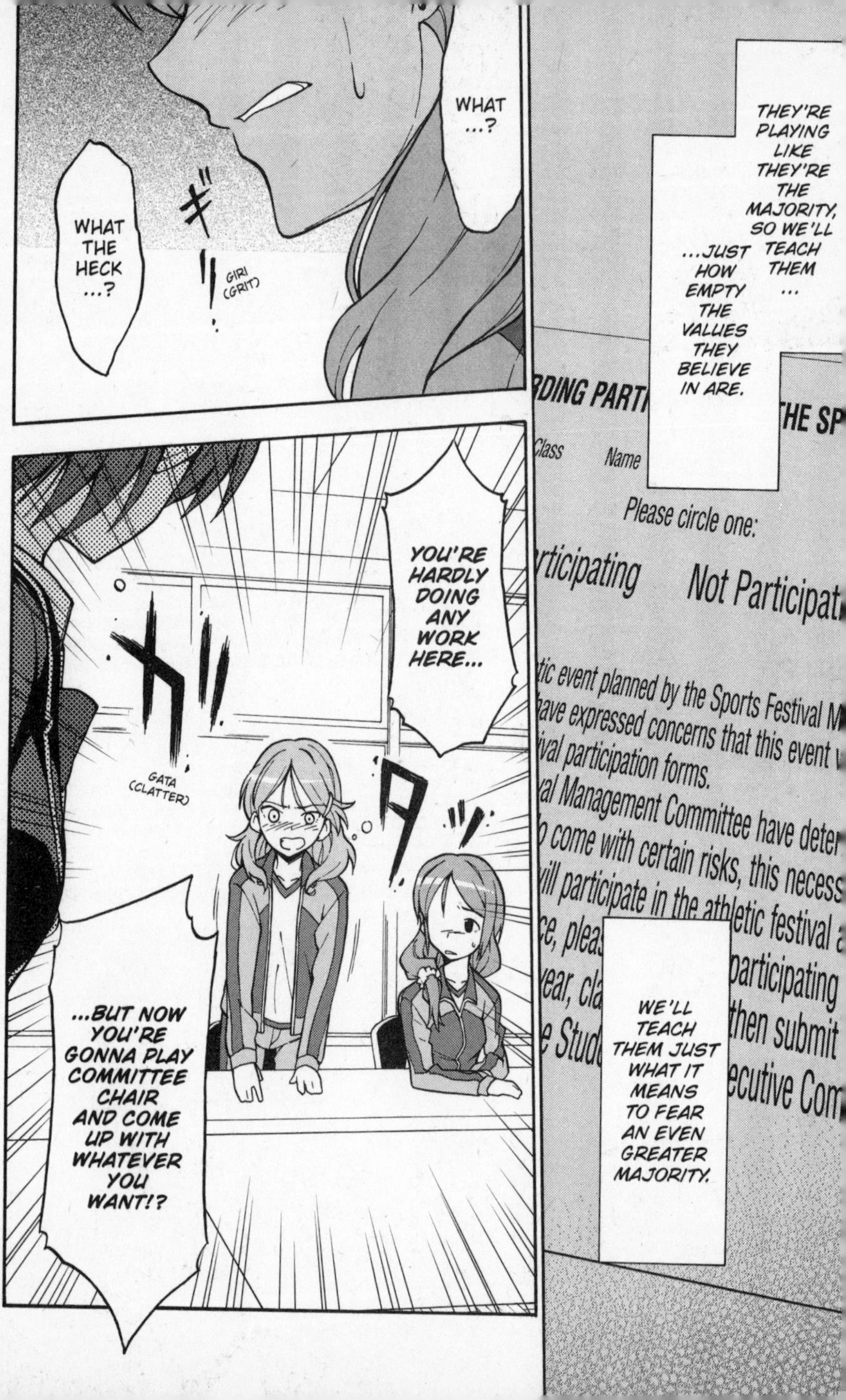
THEY'RE PLAYING LIKE THEY'RE THE MAJORITY, SO WE'LL TEACH THEM...
...JUST HOW EMPTY THE VALUES THEY BELIEVE IN ARE.
Class
Name
Please circle one:
WE'LL TEACH THEM JUST WHAT IT MEANS TO FEAR AN EVEN GREATER MAJORITY.
WHAT...?
GIRI (GRIT)
WHAT THE HECK...?
YOU'RE HARDLY DOING ANY WORK HERE...
GATA (CLATTER)
...BUT NOW YOU'RE GONNA PLAY COMMITTEE CHAIR AND COME UP WITH WHATEVER YOU WANT!?

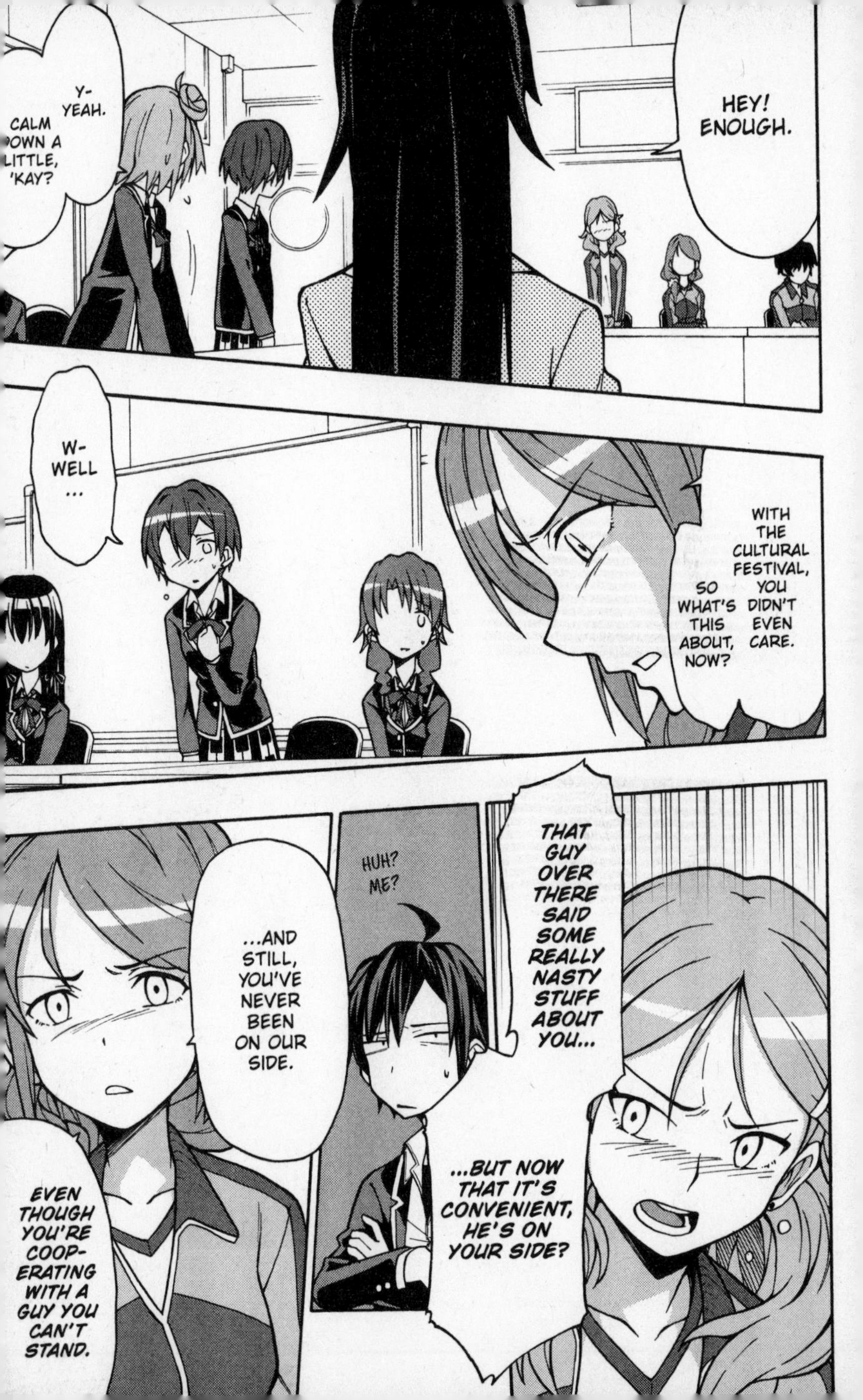
HEY! ENOUGH.
Y-YEAH.
CALM DOWN A LITTLE, 'KAY?
WITH THE CULTURAL FESTIVAL, YOU DIDN'T EVEN CARE.
SO WHAT'S THIS ABOUT, NOW?
W-WELL...
THAT GUY OVER THERE SAID SOME REALLY NASTY STUFF ABOUT YOU...
...BUT NOW THAT IT'S CONVENIENT, HE'S ON YOUR SIDE?
HUH? ME?
...AND STILL, YOU'VE NEVER BEEN ON OUR SIDE.
EVEN THOUGH YOU'RE COOP-ERATING WITH A GUY YOU CAN'T STAND.

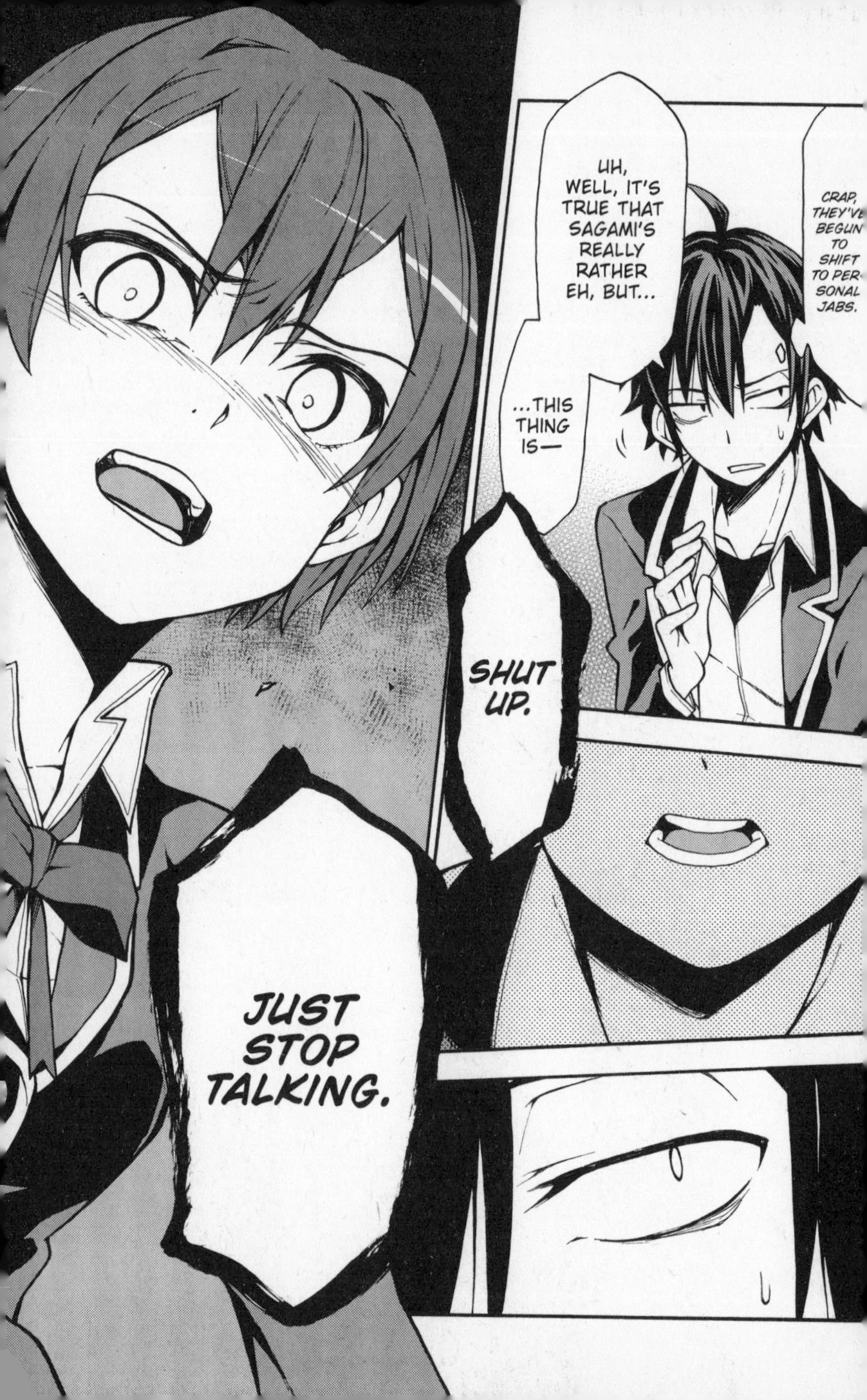
CRAP, THEY'VE BEGUN TO SHIFT TO PERSONAL JABS.
UH, WELL, IT'S TRUE THAT SAGAMI'S REALLY RATHER EH, BUT...
...THIS THING IS—
SHUT UP.
JUST STOP TALKING.

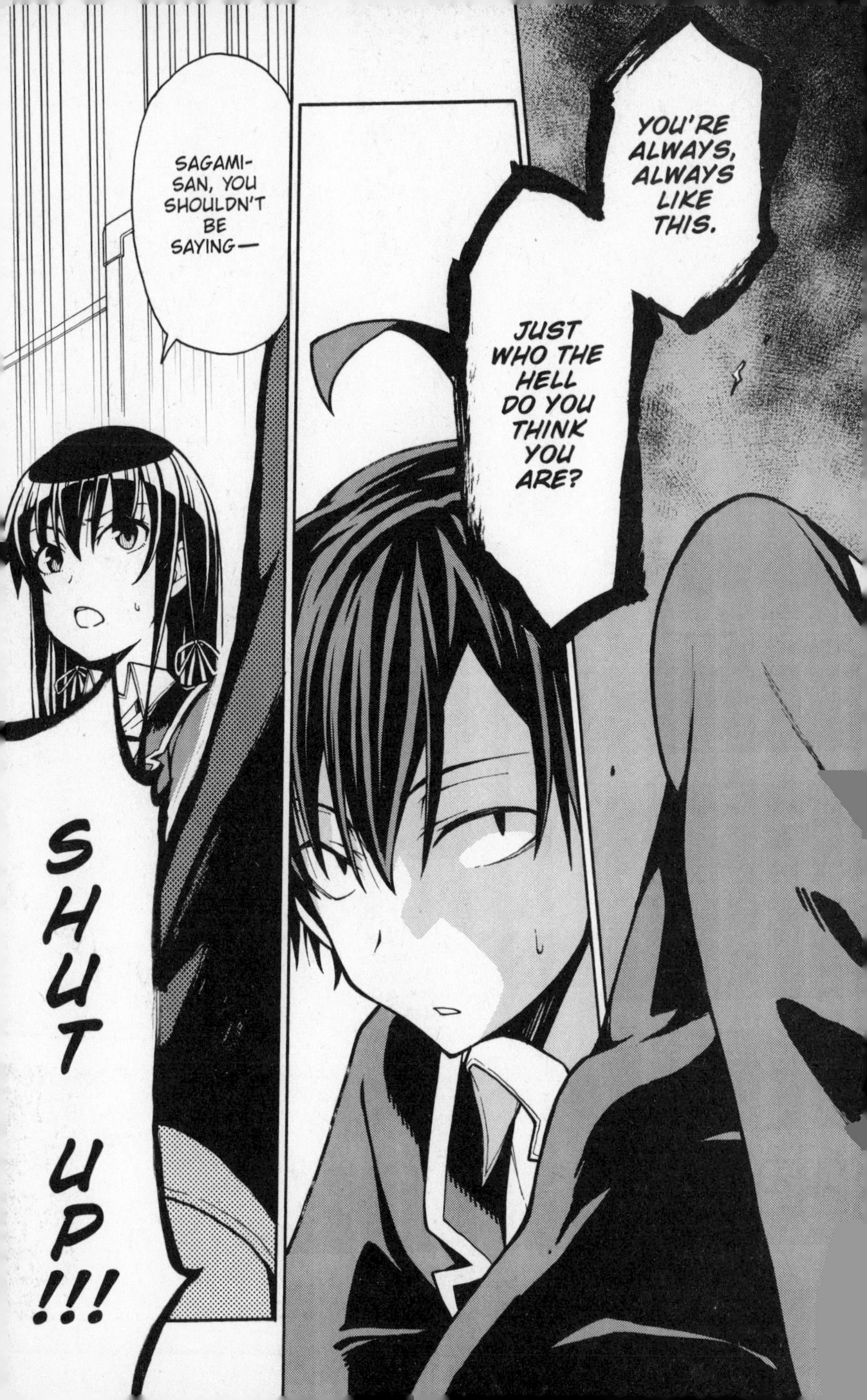
YOU'RE ALWAYS, ALWAYS LIKE THIS.
JUST WHO THE HELL DO YOU THINK YOU ARE?
SAGAMI-SAN, YOU SHOULDN'T BE SAYING—
SHUT UP!!!

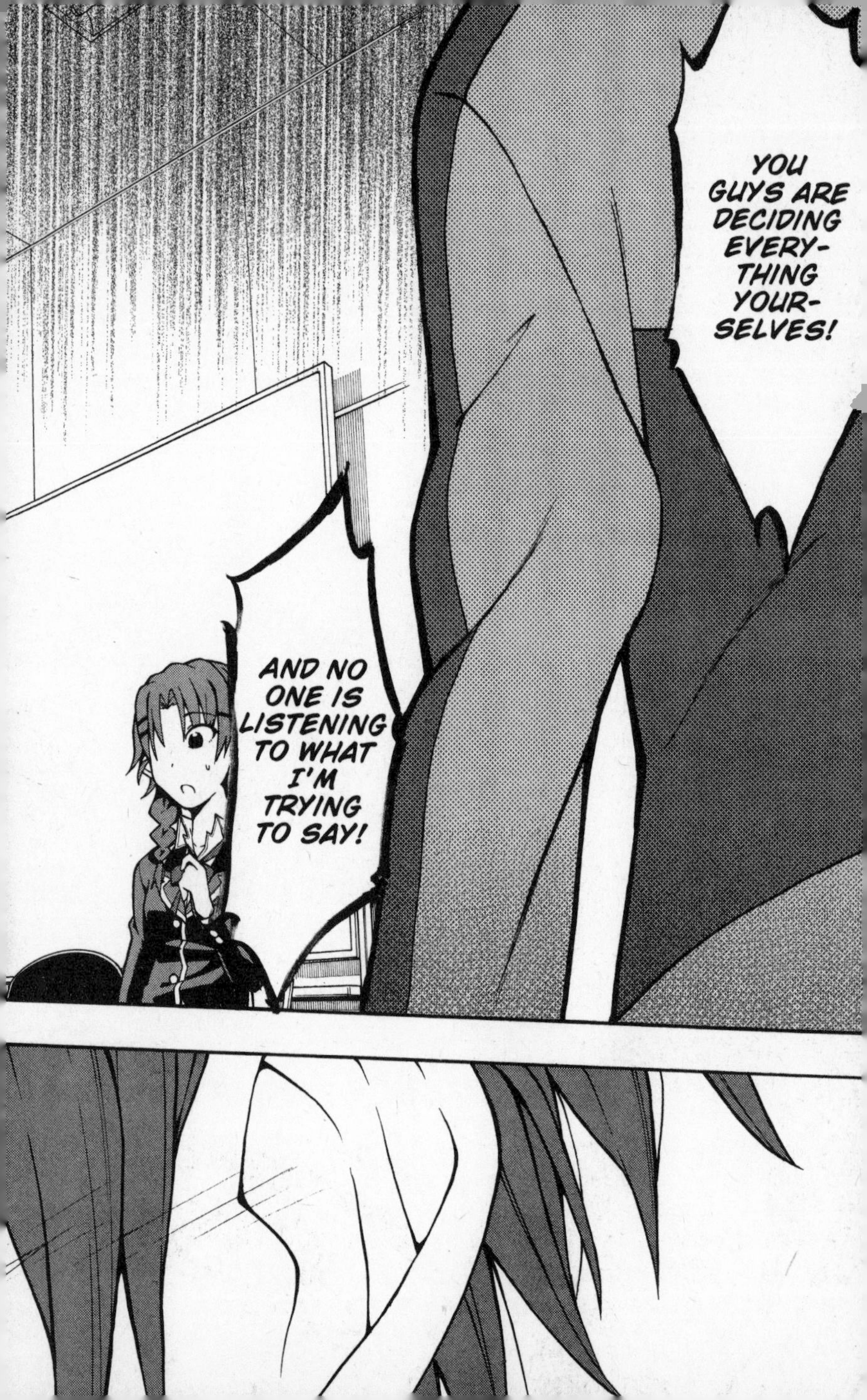
YOU GUYS ARE DECIDING EVERY-THING YOUR-SELVES!
AND NO ONE IS LISTENING TO WHAT I'M TRYING TO SAY!

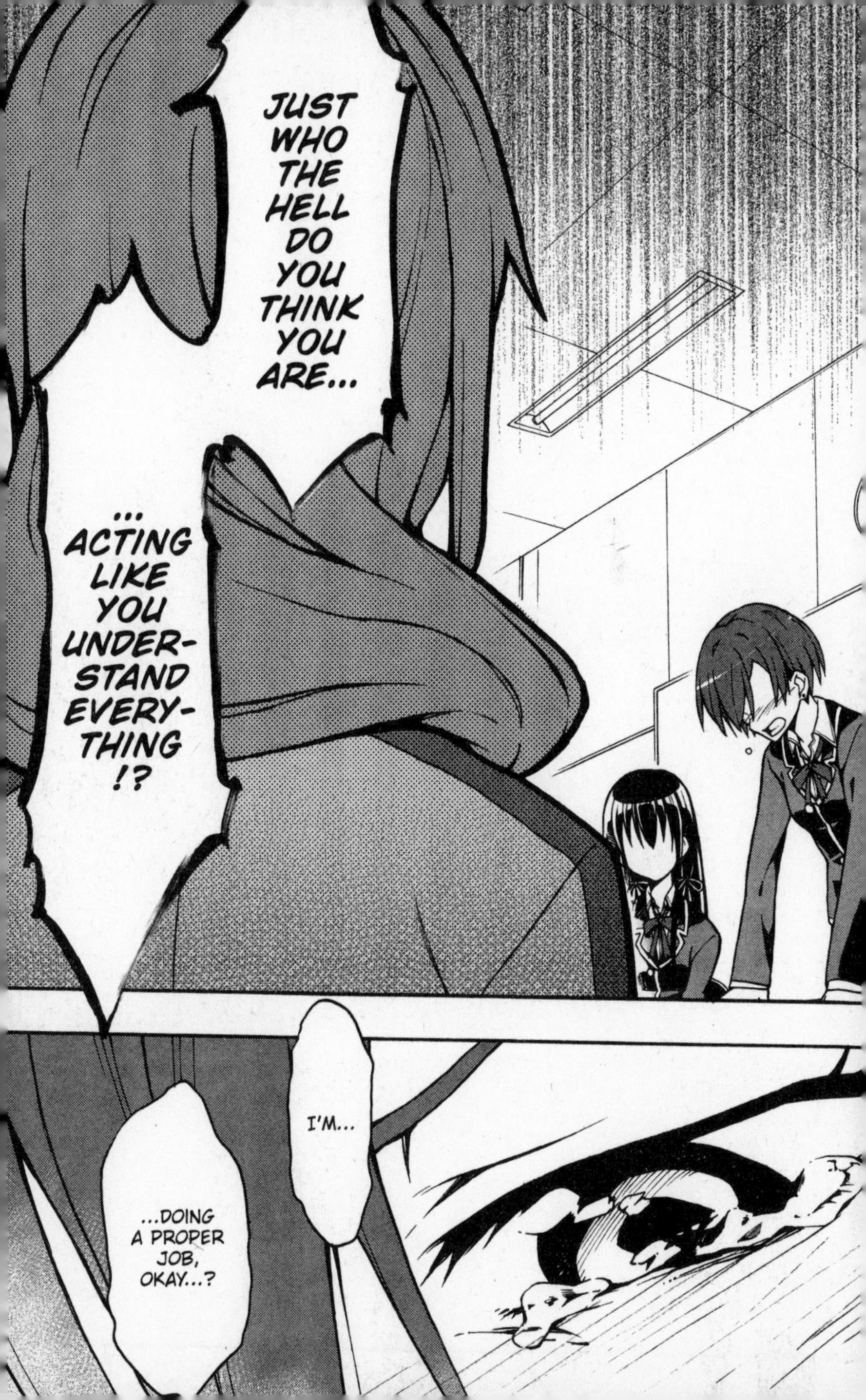
JUST WHO THE HELL DO YOU THINK YOU ARE...
...ACTING LIKE YOU UNDER-STAND EVERY-THING!?
I'M...
...DOING A PROPER JOB, OKAY...?

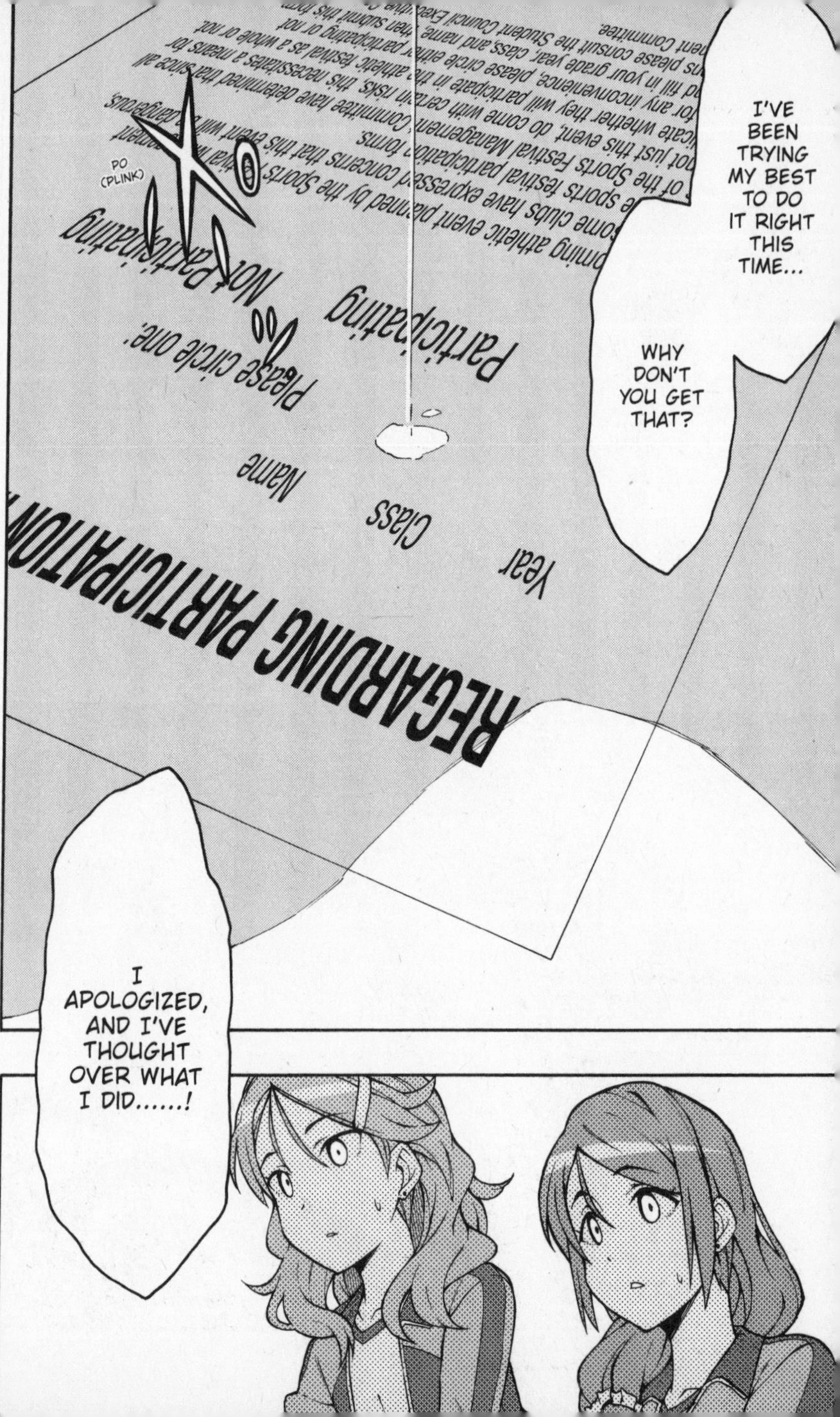
I'VE BEEN TRYING MY BEST TO DO IT RIGHT THIS TIME...
WHY DON'T YOU GET THAT?
REGARDING PARTICIPATION
Year
Class
Name
Please circle one:
Participating
Not Participating
PO (PLINK)
I APOLOGIZED, AND I'VE THOUGHT OVER WHAT I DID......!

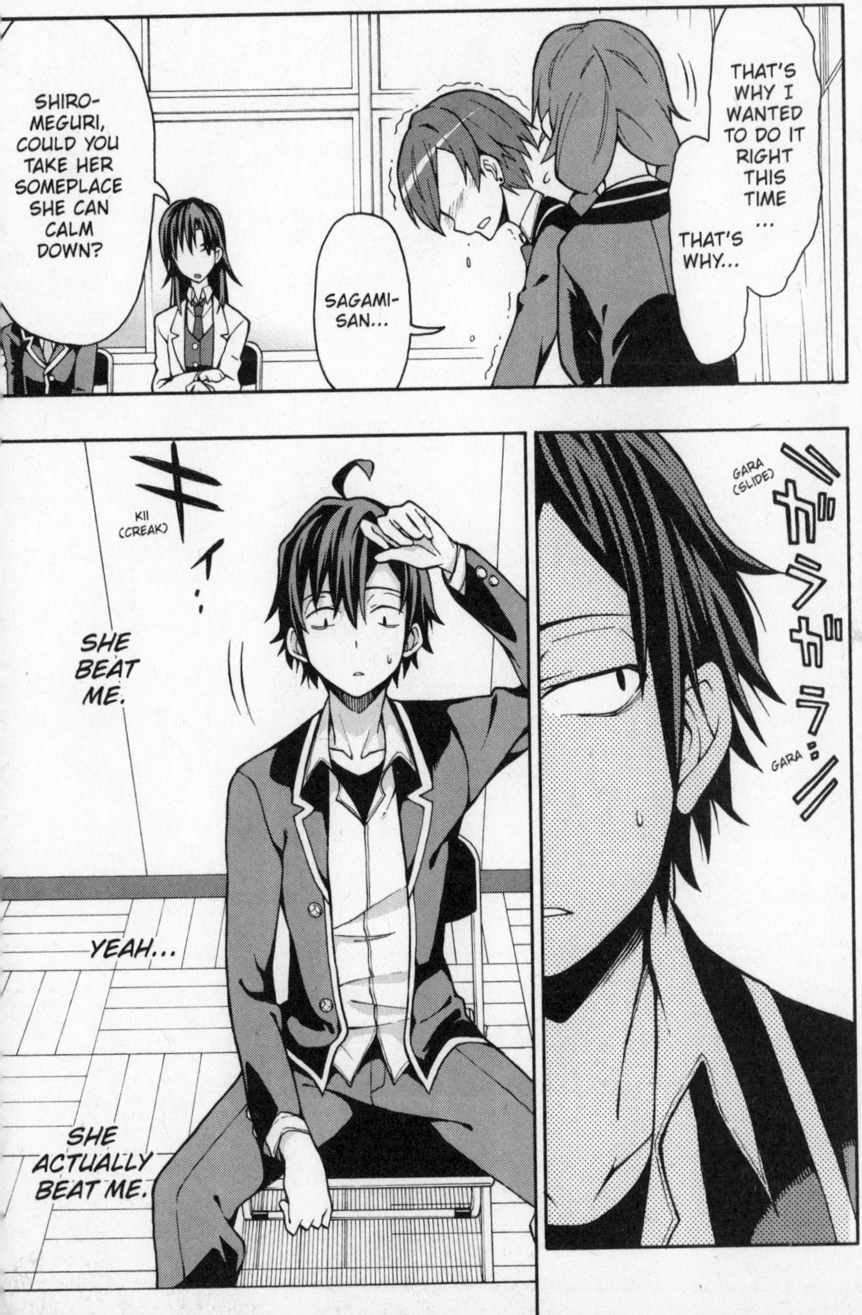
THAT'S WHY I WANTED TO DO IT RIGHT THIS TIME ...
THAT'S WHY...
SAGAMI-SAN...
SHIRO-MEGURI, COULD YOU TAKE HER SOMEPLACE SHE CAN CALM DOWN?
GARA (SLIDE)
GARA
KII (CREAK)
SHE BEAT ME.
YEAH...
SHE ACTUALLY BEAT ME.

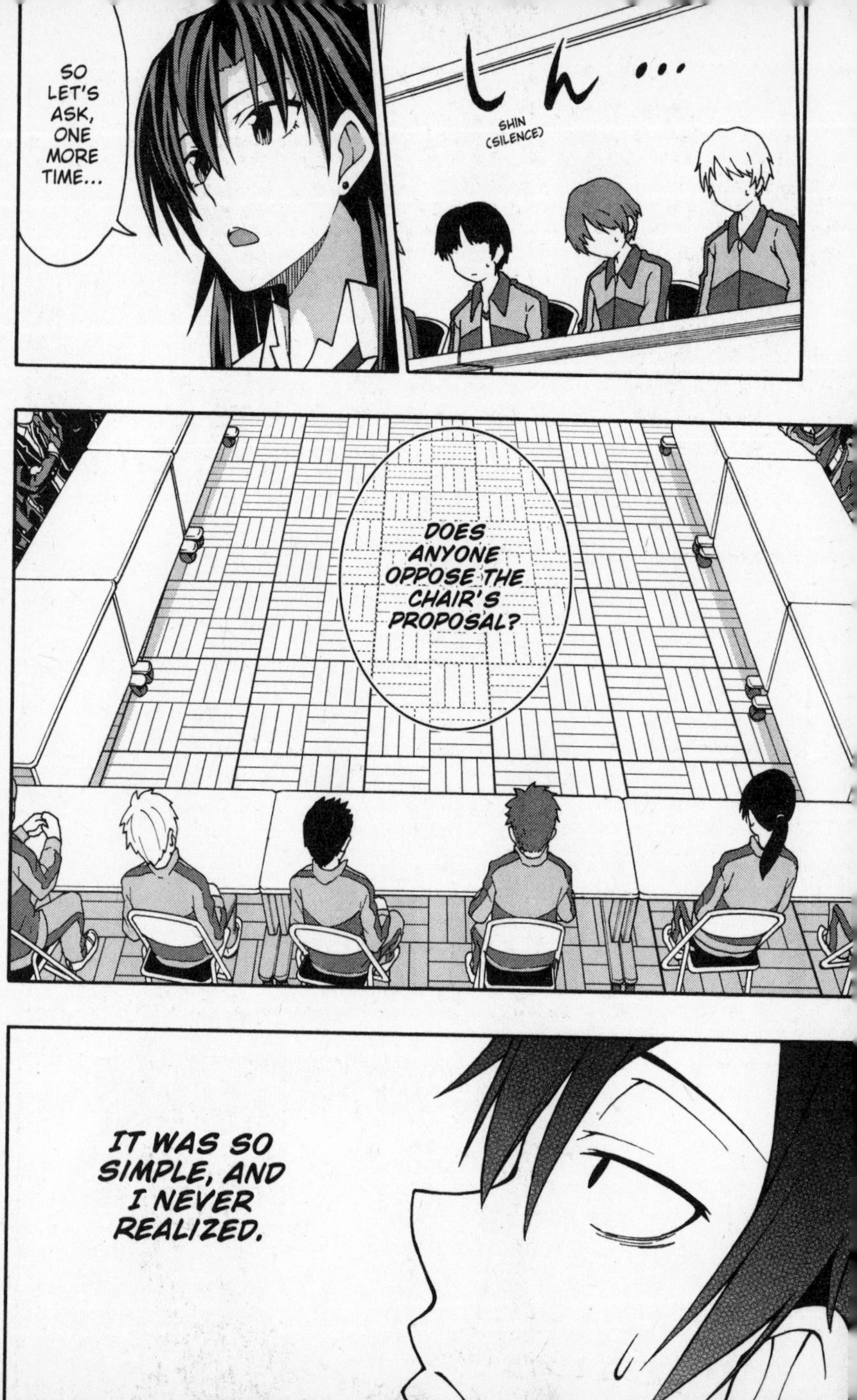
しん…
SHIN (SILENCE)
SO LET'S ASK, ONE MORE TIME…
DOES ANYONE OPPOSE THE CHAIR'S PROPOSAL?
IT WAS SO SIMPLE, AND I NEVER REALIZED.

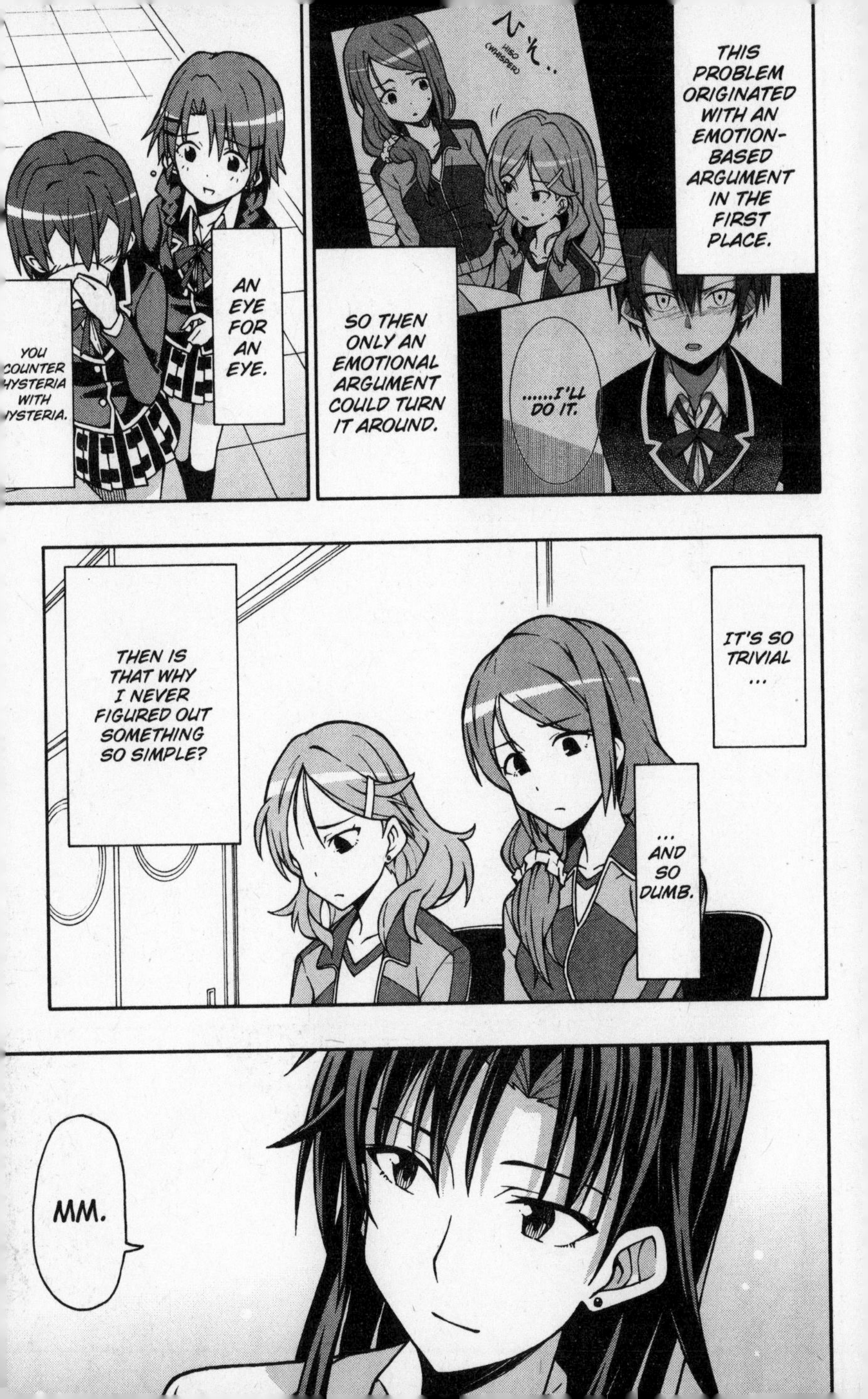
THIS PROBLEM ORIGINATED WITH AN EMOTION-BASED ARGUMENT IN THE FIRST PLACE.
……I'LL DO IT.
ひそ…
HISO (WHISPER)
SO THEN ONLY AN EMOTIONAL ARGUMENT COULD TURN IT AROUND.
AN EYE FOR AN EYE.
YOU COUNTER HYSTERIA WITH YSTERIA.
IT'S SO TRIVIAL …
… AND SO DUMB.
THEN IS THAT WHY I NEVER FIGURED OUT SOMETHING SO SIMPLE?
MM.

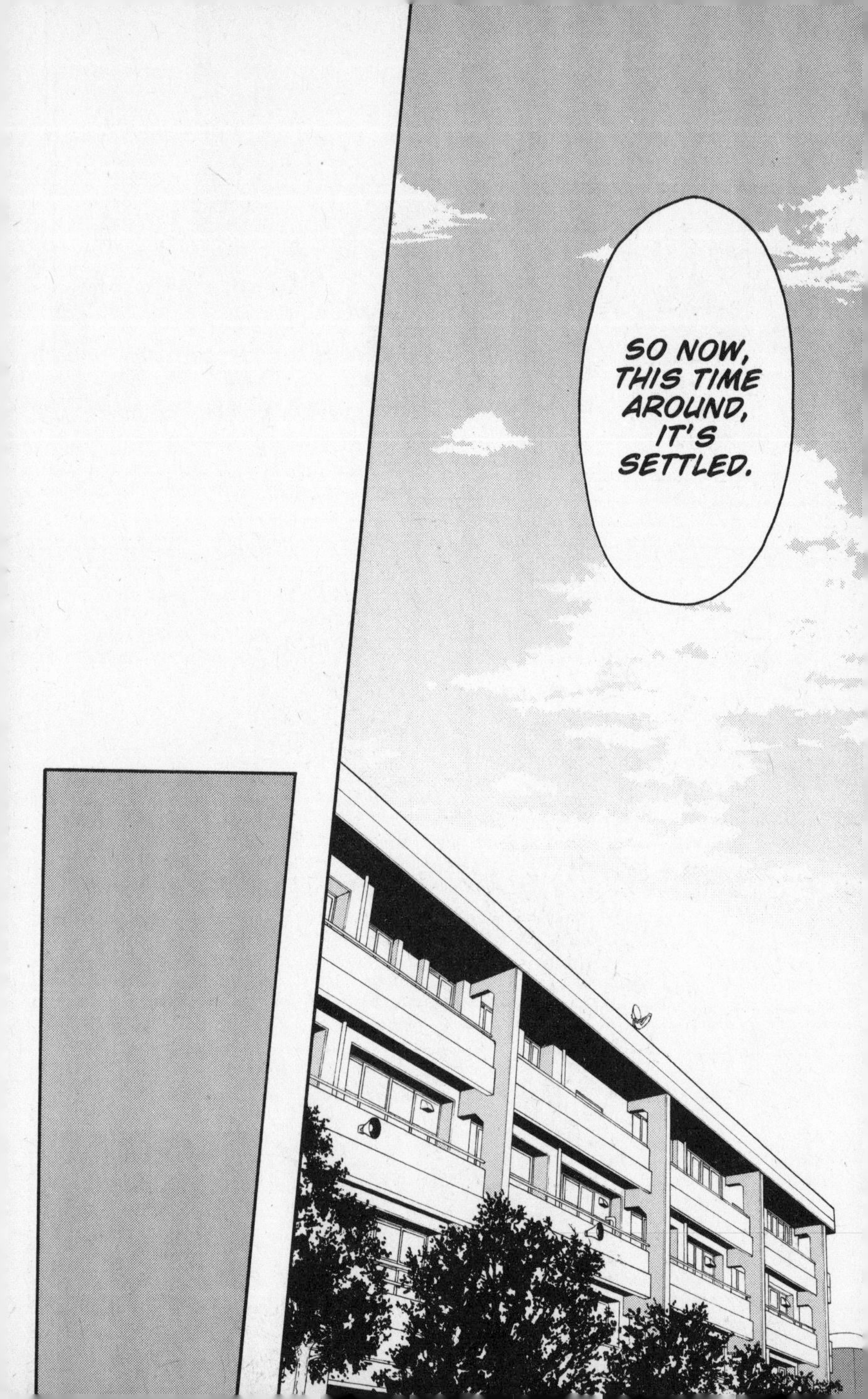
SO NOW, THIS TIME AROUND, IT'S SETTLED.

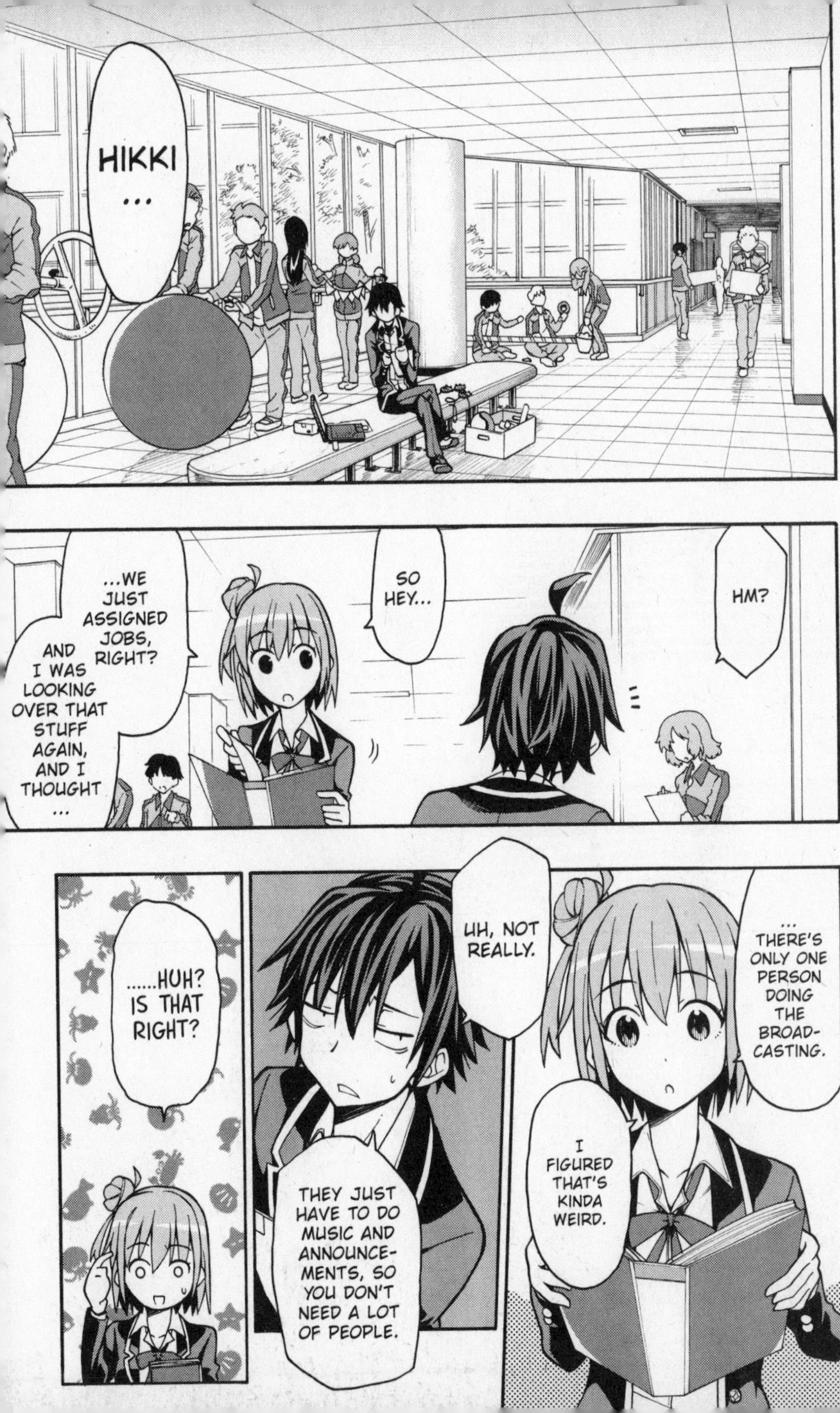
HIKKI...
HM?
SO HEY...
...WE JUST ASSIGNED JOBS, RIGHT?
AND I WAS LOOKING OVER THAT STUFF AGAIN, AND I THOUGHT...
...THERE'S ONLY ONE PERSON DOING THE BROAD-CASTING.
I FIGURED THAT'S KINDA WEIRD.
UH, NOT REALLY.
THEY JUST HAVE TO DO MUSIC AND ANNOUNCE-MENTS, SO YOU DON'T NEED A LOT OF PEOPLE.
......HUH? IS THAT RIGHT?

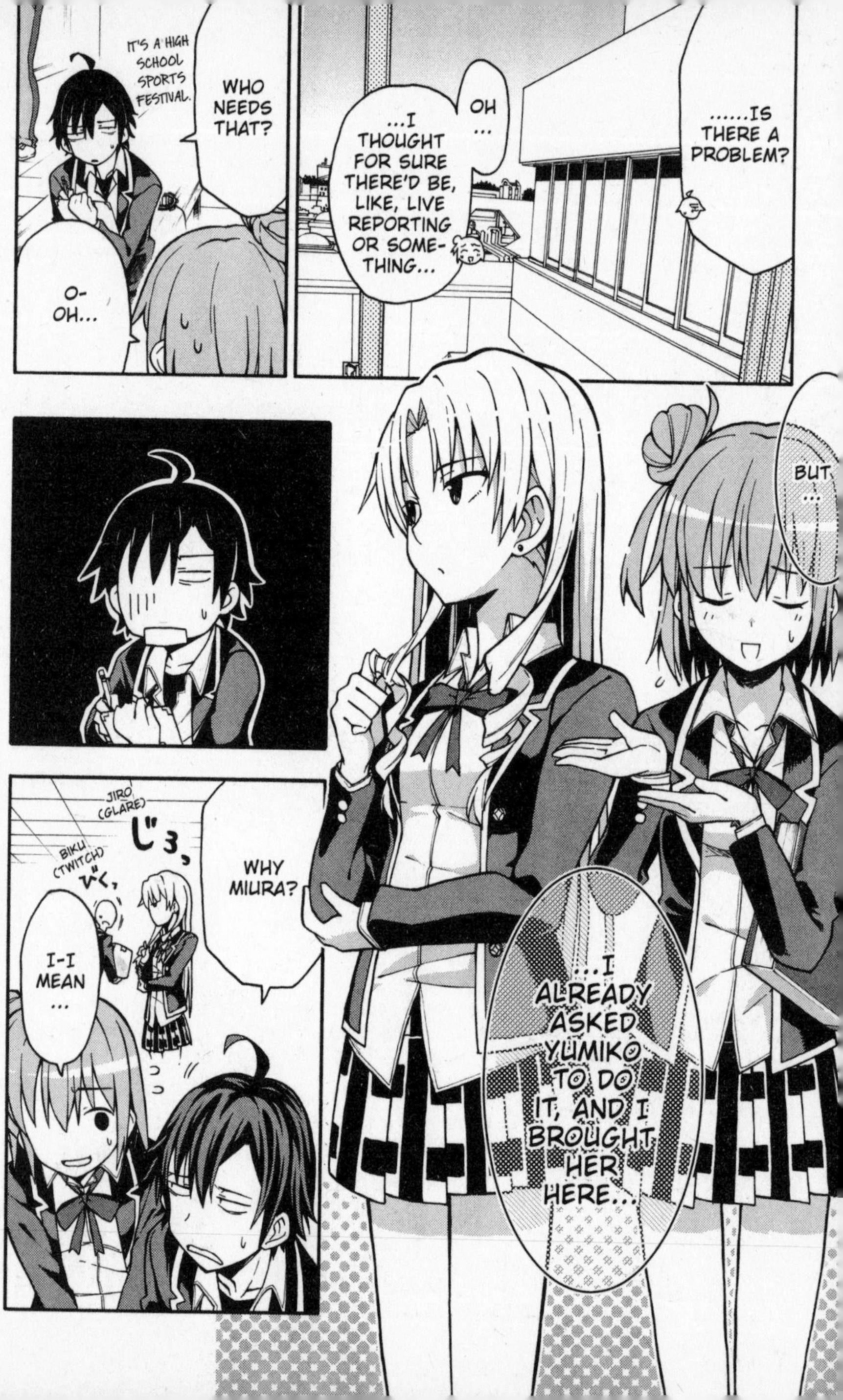

......IS THERE A PROBLEM?
OH ...
...I THOUGHT FOR SURE THERE'D BE, LIKE, LIVE REPORTING OR SOME-THING...
WHO NEEDS THAT?
IT'S A HIGH SCHOOL SPORTS FESTIVAL.
O-OH...
BUT ...
...I ALREADY ASKED YUMIKO TO DO IT, AND I BROUGHT HER HERE...
WHY MIURA?
JIRO (GLARE)
じろ
BIKU (TWITCH)
びく
I-I MEAN ...

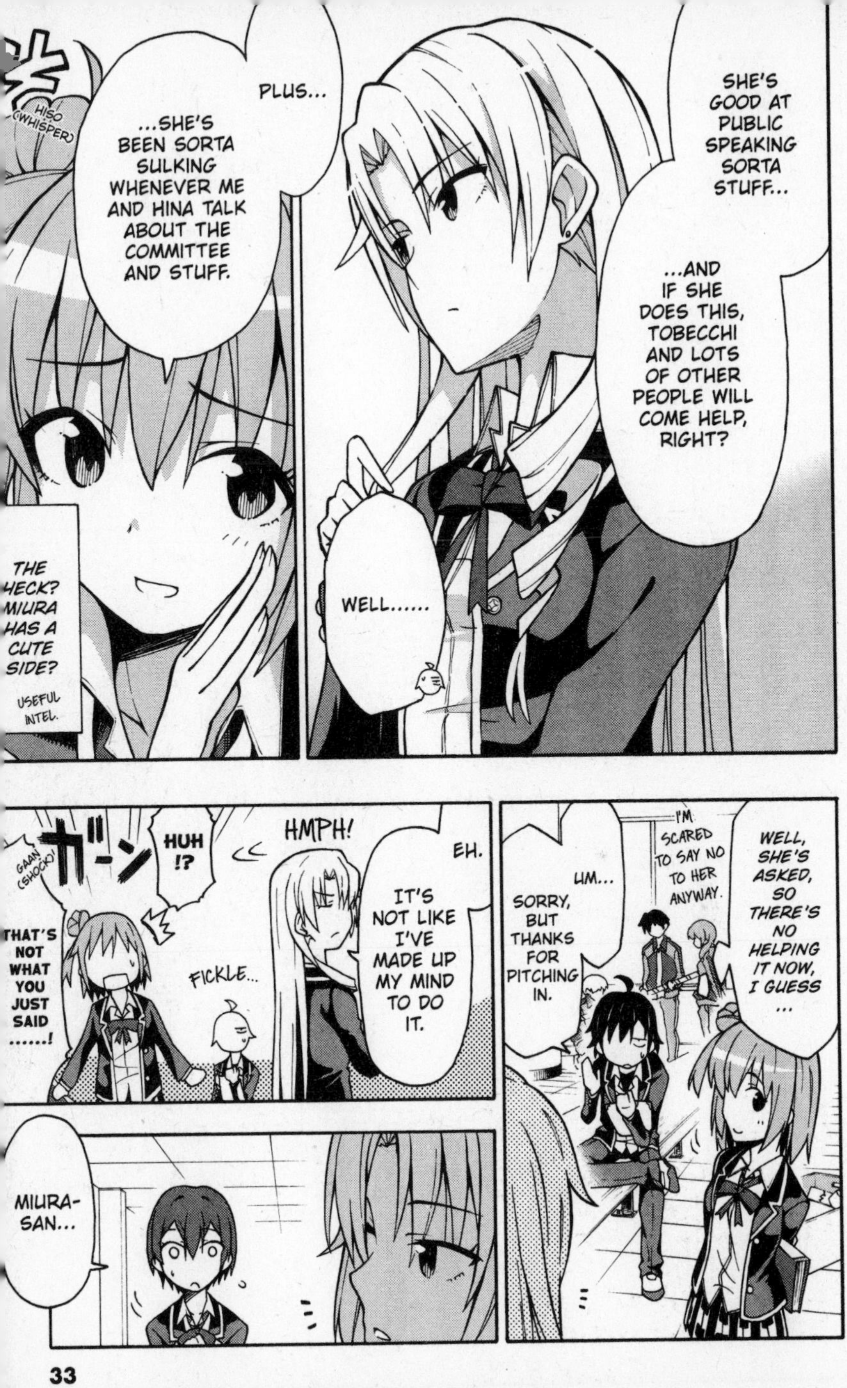
SHE'S GOOD AT PUBLIC SPEAKING SORTA STUFF...
...AND IF SHE DOES THIS, TOBECCHI AND LOTS OF OTHER PEOPLE WILL COME HELP, RIGHT?
WELL......
PLUS...
...SHE'S BEEN SORTA SULKING WHENEVER ME AND HINA TALK ABOUT THE COMMITTEE AND STUFF.
HISO (WHISPER)
THE HECK? MIURA HAS A CUTE SIDE?
USEFUL INTEL.
WELL, SHE'S ASKED, SO THERE'S NO HELPING IT NOW, I GUESS...
I'M SCARED TO SAY NO TO HER ANYWAY.
UM... SORRY, BUT THANKS FOR PITCHING IN.
EH.
IT'S NOT LIKE I'VE MADE UP MY MIND TO DO IT.
HMPH!
HUH!?
GAAN (SHOCK)
FICKLE...
THAT'S NOT WHAT YOU JUST SAID......!
MIURA-SAN...

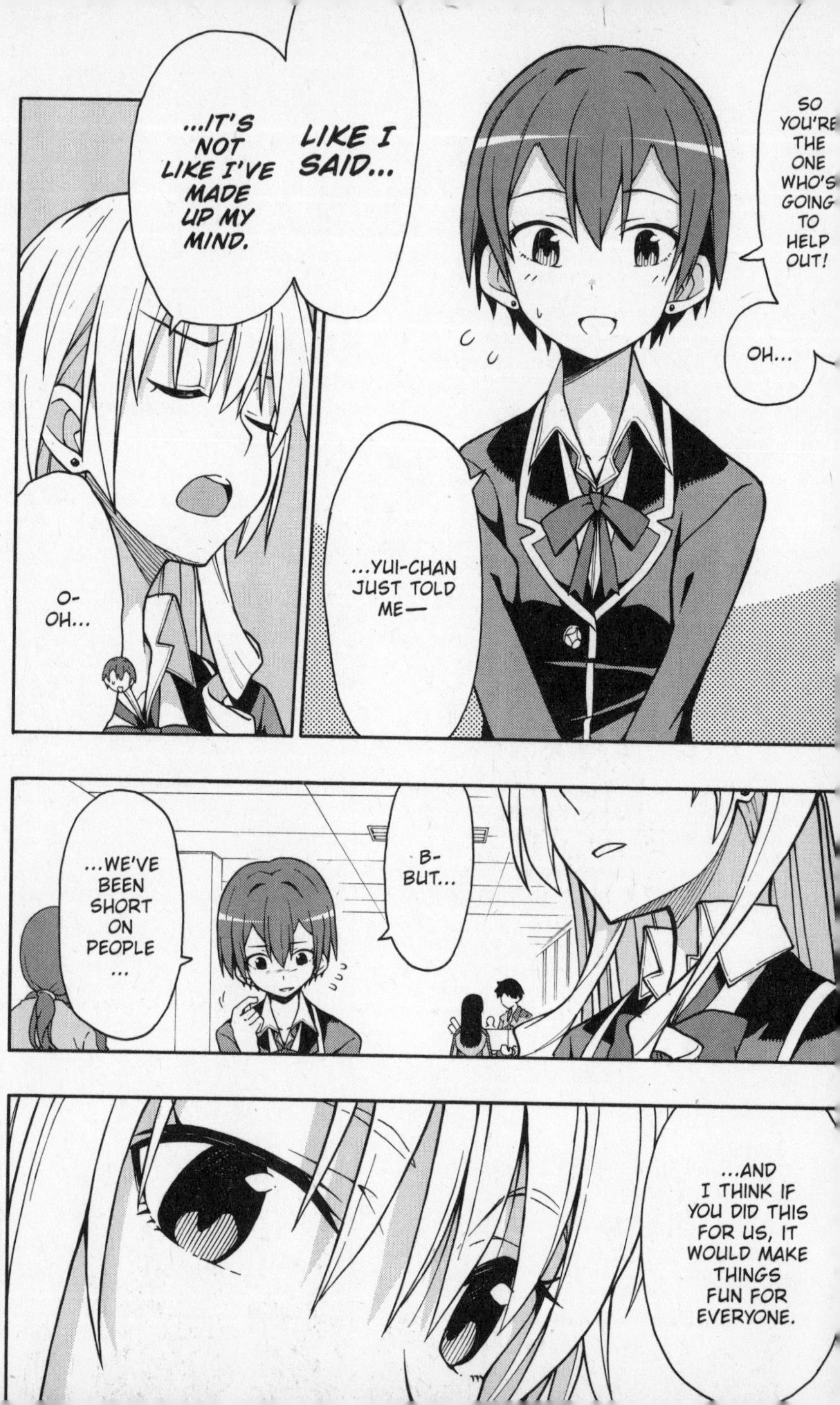
SO YOU'RE THE ONE WHO'S GOING TO HELP OUT!
OH...
...YUI-CHAN JUST TOLD ME—
LIKE I SAID...
...IT'S NOT LIKE I'VE MADE UP MY MIND.
O-OH...
B-BUT...
...WE'VE BEEN SHORT ON PEOPLE...
...AND I THINK IF YOU DID THIS FOR US, IT WOULD MAKE THINGS FUN FOR EVERYONE.

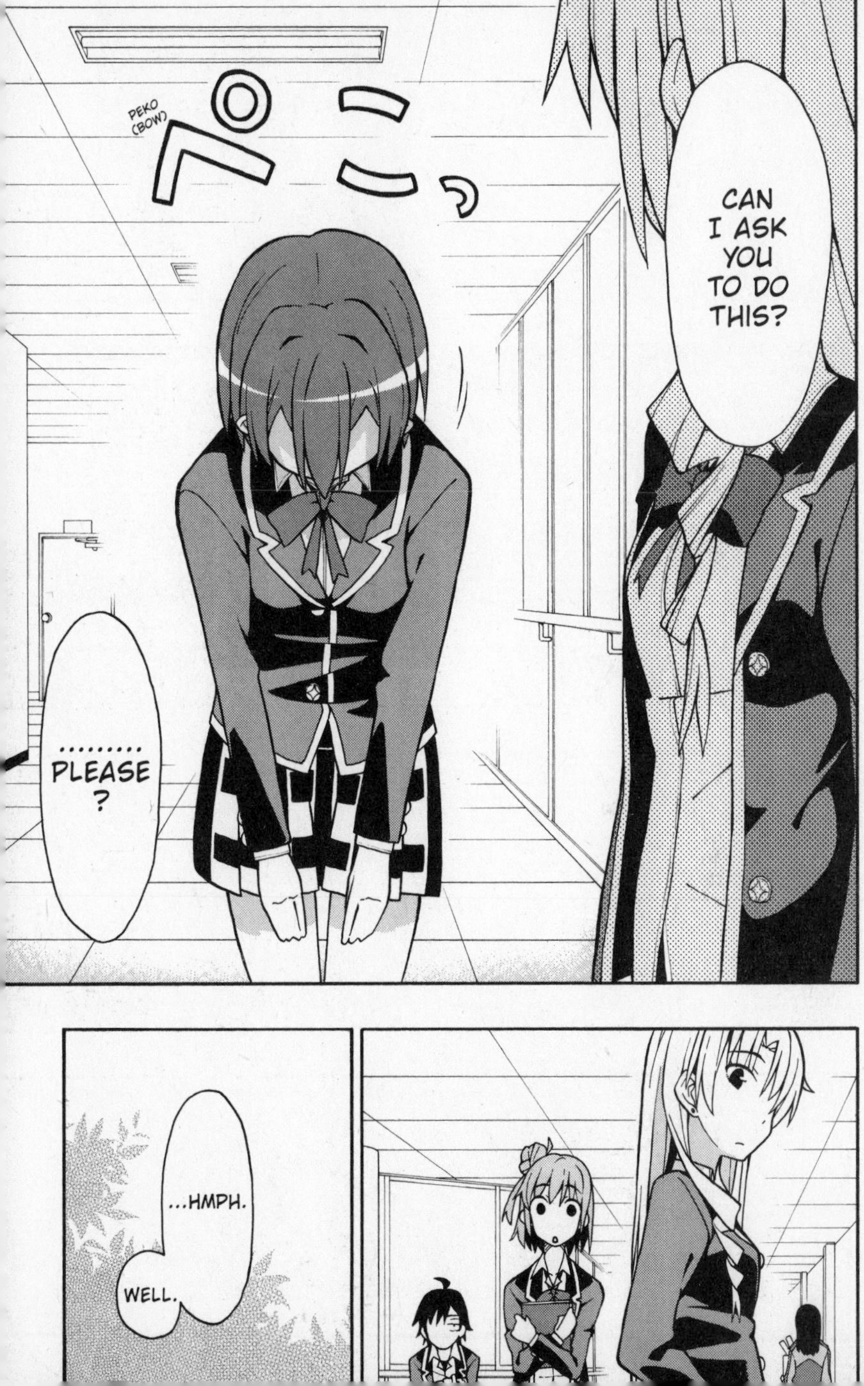
CAN I ASK YOU TO DO THIS?
PEKO (BOW)
.........PLEASE?
...HMPH.
WELL.

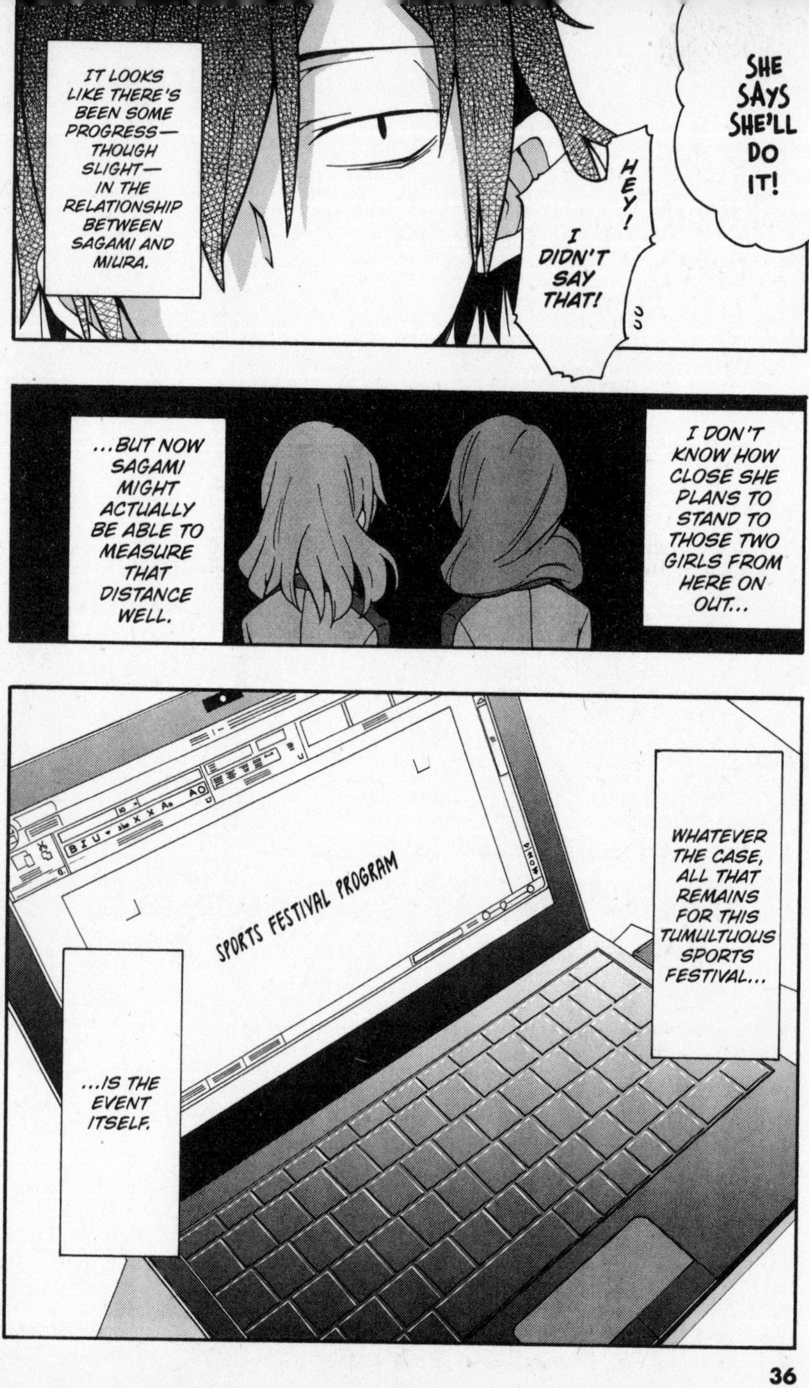
SHE SAYS SHE'LL DO IT!
HEY! I DIDN'T SAY THAT!
IT LOOKS LIKE THERE'S BEEN SOME PROGRESS—THOUGH SLIGHT—IN THE RELATIONSHIP BETWEEN SAGAMI AND MIURA.
I DON'T KNOW HOW CLOSE SHE PLANS TO STAND TO THOSE TWO GIRLS FROM HERE ON OUT...
...BUT NOW SAGAMI MIGHT ACTUALLY BE ABLE TO MEASURE THAT DISTANCE WELL.
WHATEVER THE CASE, ALL THAT REMAINS FOR THIS TUMULTUOUS SPORTS FESTIVAL...
SPORTS FESTIVAL PROGRAM
...IS THE EVENT ITSELF.

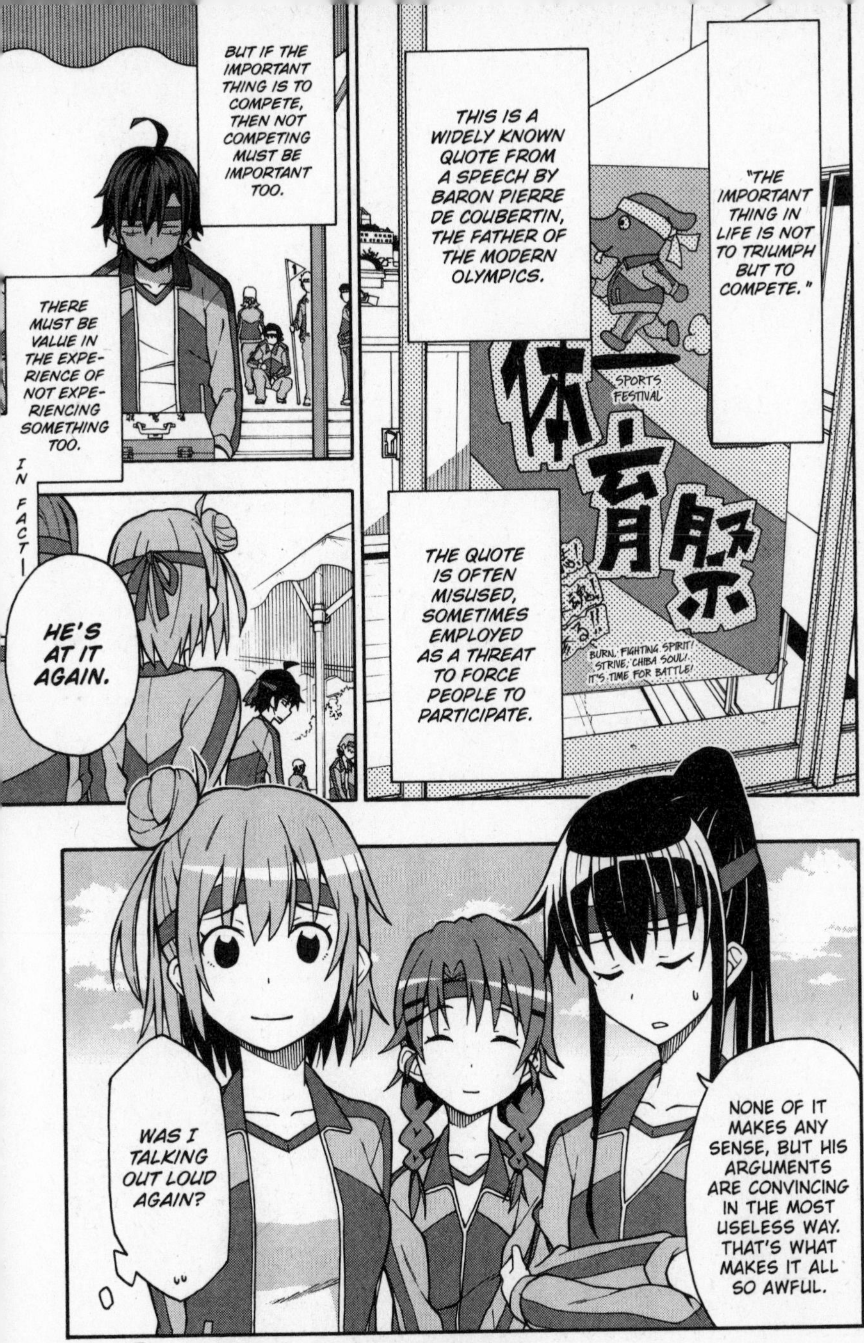
"THE IMPORTANT THING IN LIFE IS NOT TO TRIUMPH BUT TO COMPETE."
THIS IS A WIDELY KNOWN QUOTE FROM A SPEECH BY BARON PIERRE DE COUBERTIN, THE FATHER OF THE MODERN OLYMPICS.
体育祭
SPORTS FESTIVAL
BURN, FIGHTING SPIRIT! STRIVE, CHIBA SOUL! IT'S TIME FOR BATTLE!
THE QUOTE IS OFTEN MISUSED, SOMETIMES EMPLOYED AS A THREAT TO FORCE PEOPLE TO PARTICIPATE.
BUT IF THE IMPORTANT THING IS TO COMPETE, THEN NOT COMPETING MUST BE IMPORTANT TOO.
THERE MUST BE VALUE IN THE EXPERIENCE OF NOT EXPERIENCING SOMETHING TOO.
IN FACT—
HE'S AT IT AGAIN.
NONE OF IT MAKES ANY SENSE, BUT HIS ARGUMENTS ARE CONVINCING IN THE MOST USELESS WAY. THAT'S WHAT MAKES IT ALL SO AWFUL.
WAS I TALKING OUT LOUD AGAIN?

CHAPTER 49 ··· THAT'S WHY THEIR FESTIVAL WON'T END.

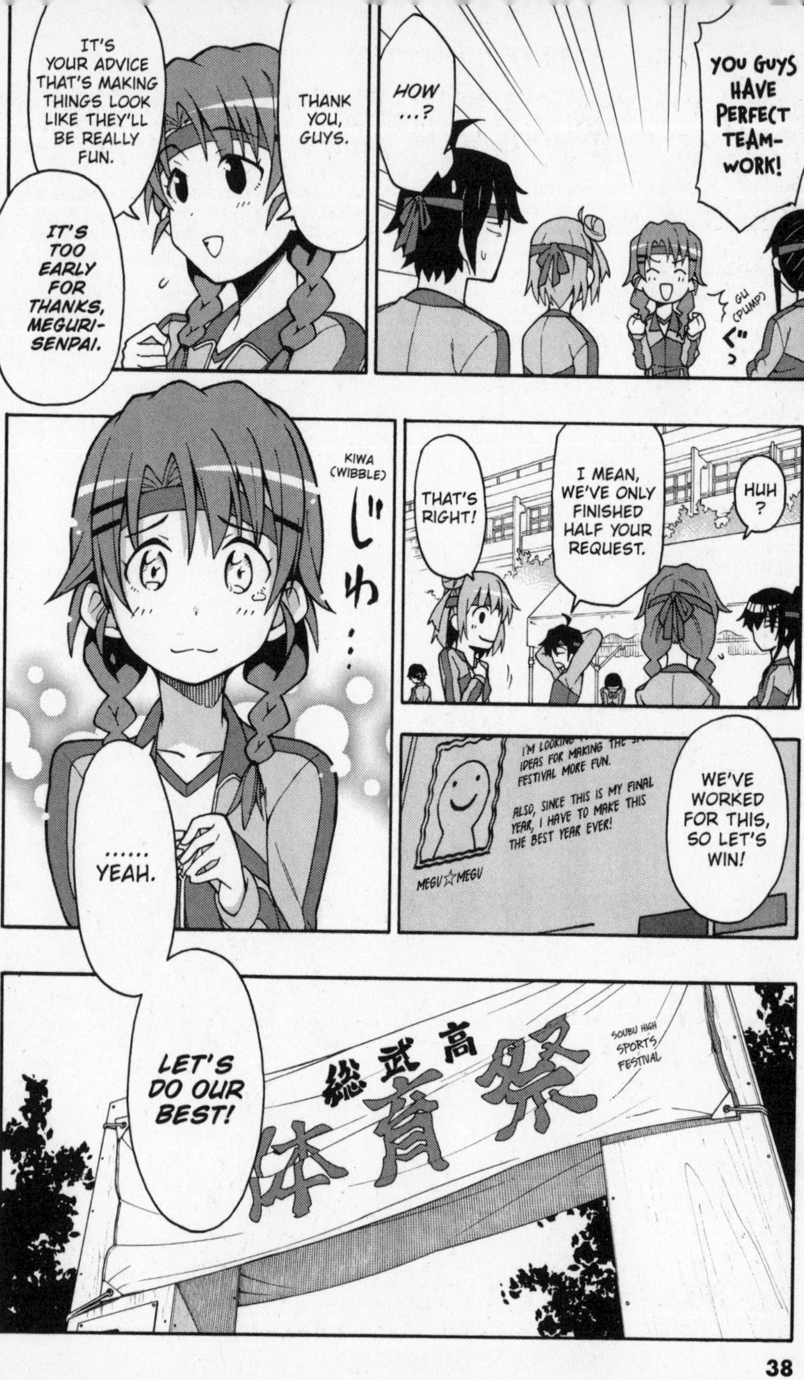

YOU GUYS HAVE PERFECT TEAM-WORK!
......
GU (PLUMP)
ぐっ
HOW ...?
THANK YOU, GUYS.
IT'S YOUR ADVICE THAT'S MAKING THINGS LOOK LIKE THEY'LL BE REALLY FUN.
IT'S TOO EARLY FOR THANKS, MEGURI-SENPAI.
HUH?
I MEAN, WE'VE ONLY FINISHED HALF YOUR REQUEST.
THAT'S RIGHT!
WE'VE WORKED FOR THIS, SO LET'S WIN!
FESTIVAL MORE FUN.
ALSO, SINCE THIS IS MY FINAL YEAR, I HAVE TO MAKE THIS THE BEST YEAR EVER!
MEGU☆MEGU
KIWA (WIBBLE)
じわ…
...... YEAH.
SOUBU HIGH SPORTS FESTIVAL
総武高 体育祭
LET'S DO OUR BEST!

CHAPTER 49 ··· THAT'S WHY THEIR FESTIVAL WON'T END.

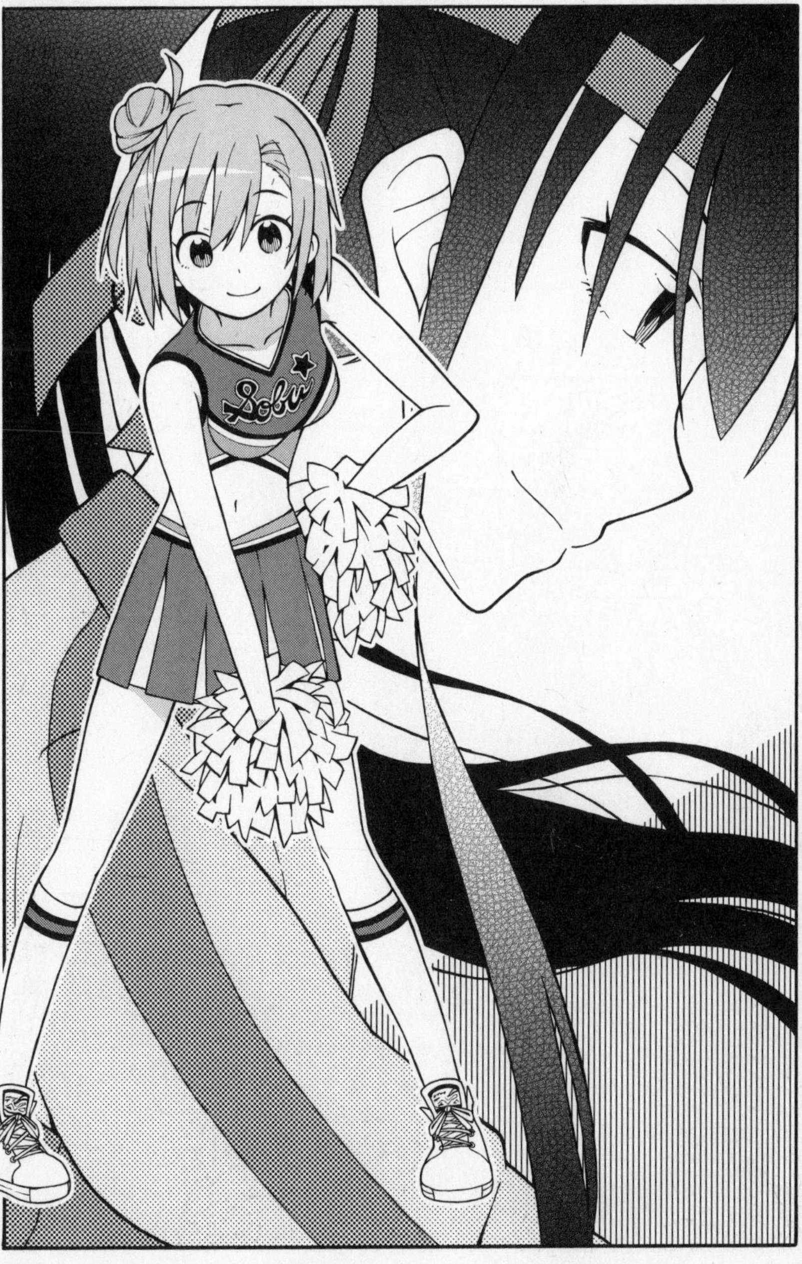
Sobu

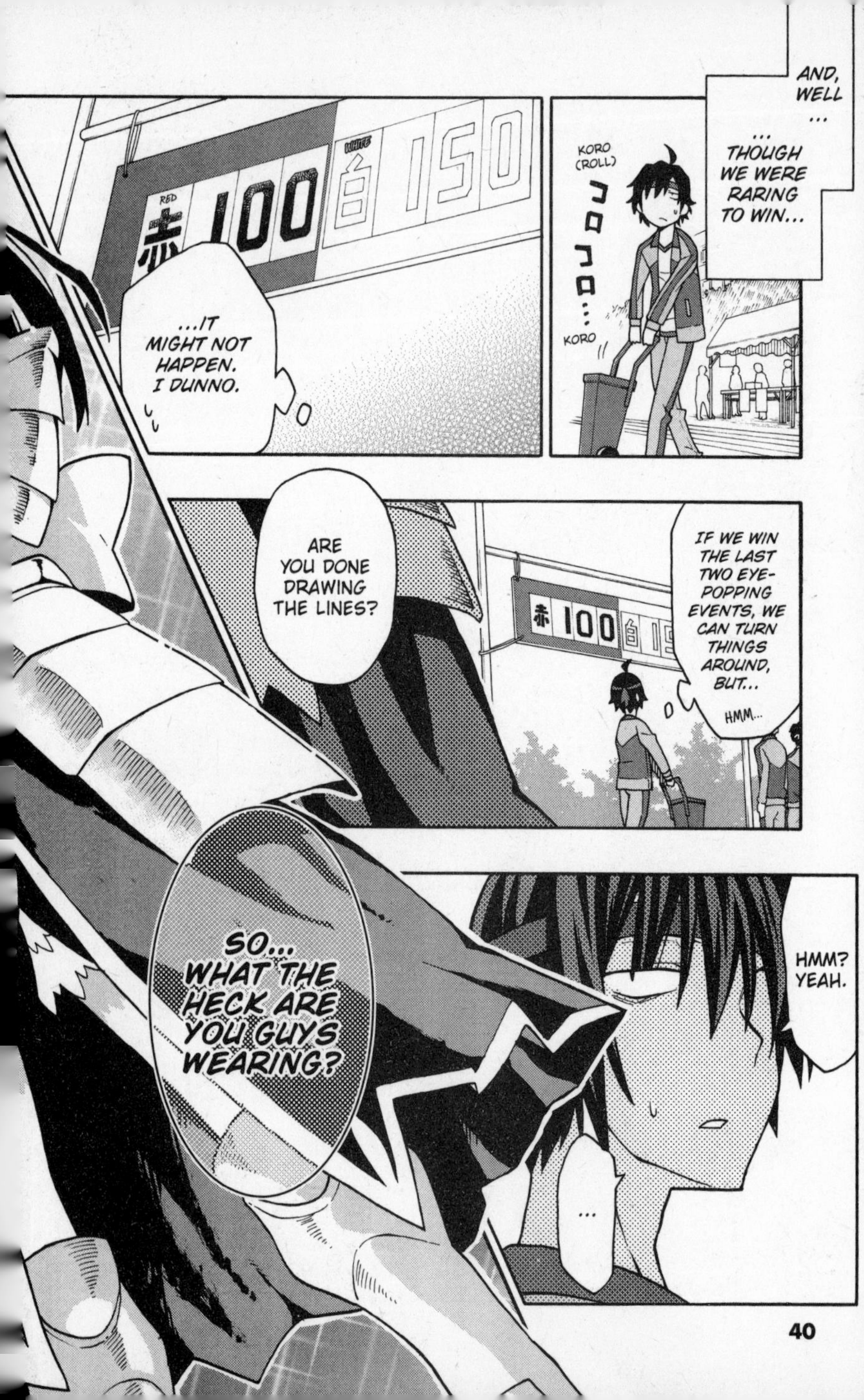
AND, WELL ...
... THOUGH WE WERE RARING TO WIN...
KORO (ROLL)
コロコロ...
KORO
RED
赤 100
WHITE
白 150
...IT MIGHT NOT HAPPEN. I DUNNO.
IF WE WIN THE LAST TWO EYE-POPPING EVENTS, WE CAN TURN THINGS AROUND, BUT...
HMM...
ARE YOU DONE DRAWING THE LINES?
HMM? YEAH.
...
SO... WHAT THE HECK ARE YOU GUYS WEARING?

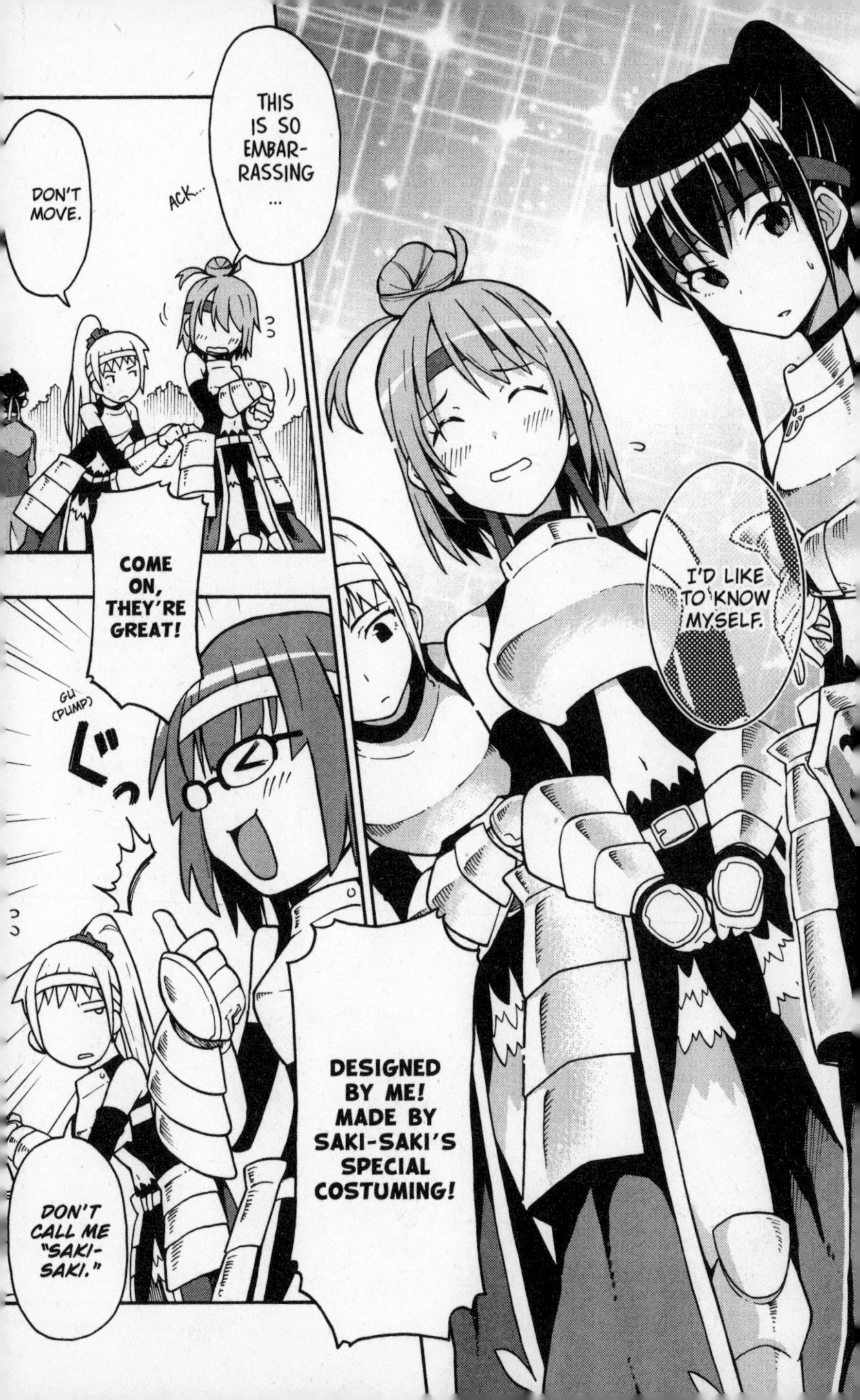
I'D LIKE TO KNOW MYSELF.
THIS IS SO EMBARRASSING...
ACK...
DON'T MOVE.
COME ON, THEY'RE GREAT!
ぐっ
GU (PUMP)
DESIGNED BY ME! MADE BY SAKI-SAKI'S SPECIAL COSTUMING!
DON'T CALL ME "SAKI-SAKI."

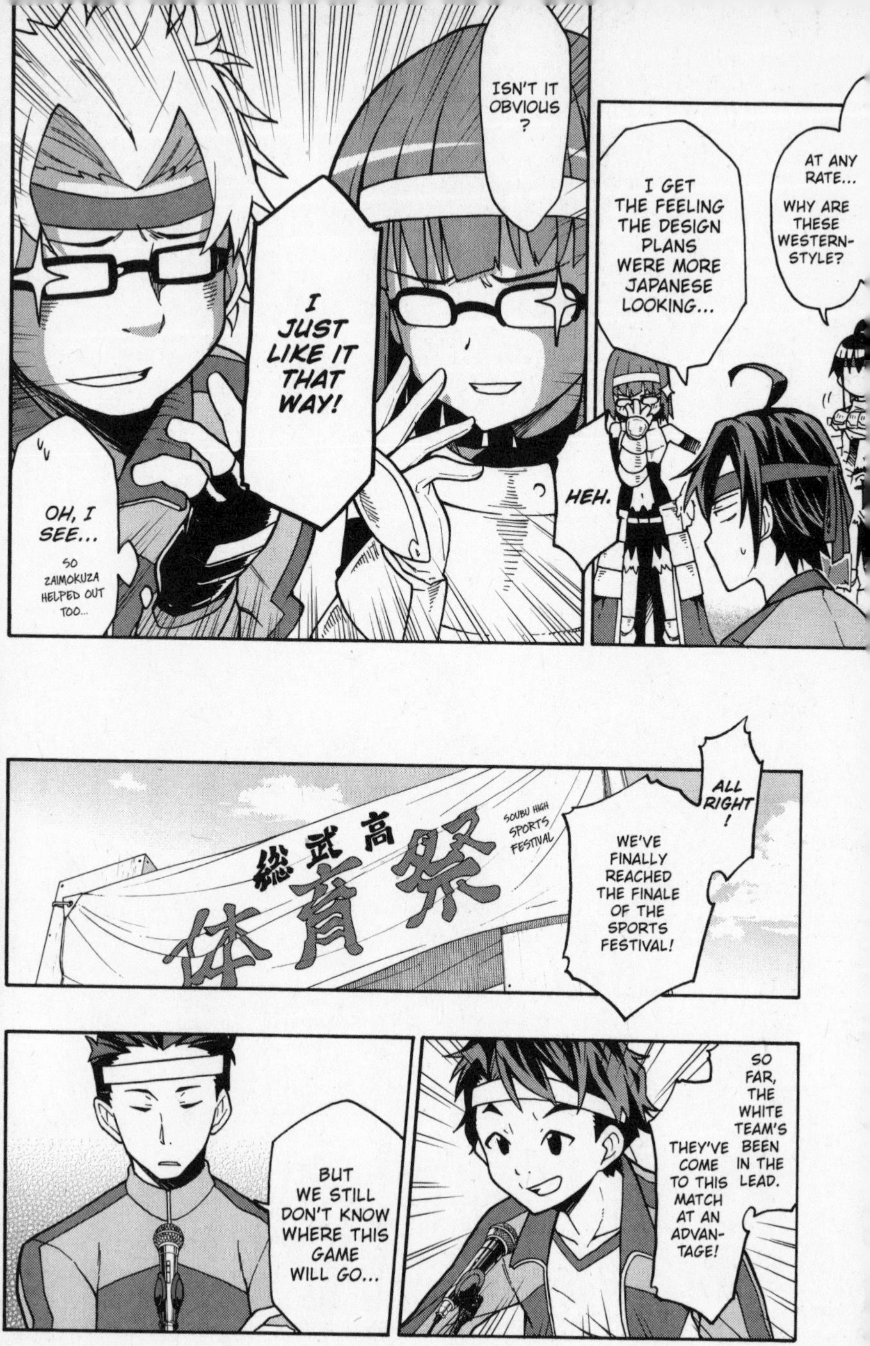
AT ANY RATE... WHY ARE THESE WESTERN-STYLE?
I GET THE FEELING THE DESIGN PLANS WERE MORE JAPANESE LOOKING...
ISN'T IT OBVIOUS?
HEH.
I JUST LIKE IT THAT WAY!
OH, I SEE...
SO ZAIMOKUZA HELPED OUT TOO...
ALL RIGHT!
WE'VE FINALLY REACHED THE FINALE OF THE SPORTS FESTIVAL!
総武高
体育祭
SOUBU HIGH SPORTS FESTIVAL
SO FAR, THE WHITE TEAM'S BEEN IN THE LEAD.
THEY'VE COME TO THIS MATCH AT AN ADVANTAGE!
BUT WE STILL DON'T KNOW WHERE THIS GAME WILL GO...

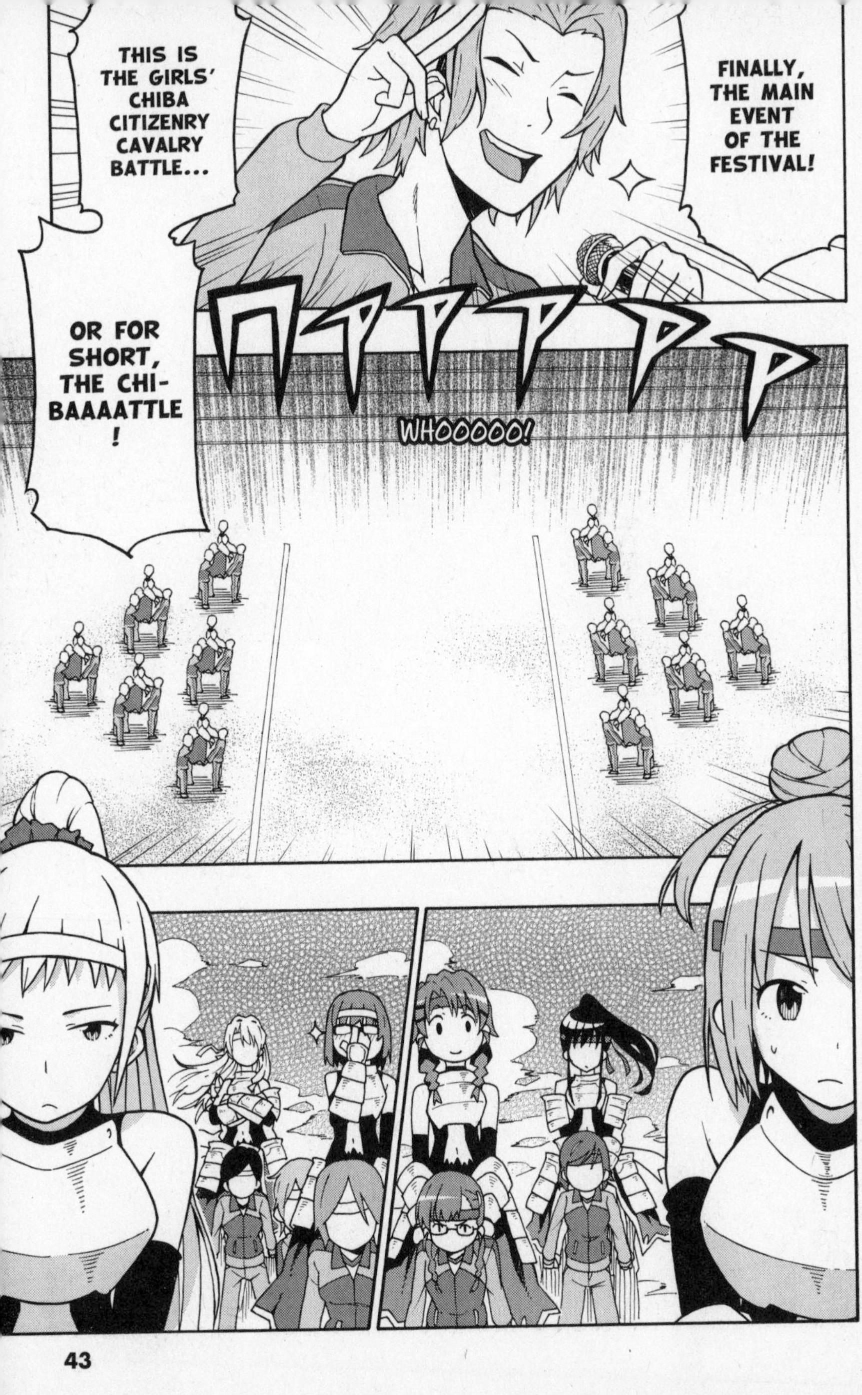
FINALLY, THE MAIN EVENT OF THE FESTIVAL!
THIS IS THE GIRLS' CHIBA CITIZENRY CAVALRY BATTLE...
OR FOR SHORT, THE CHI-BAAAATTLE!
WHOOOOO!

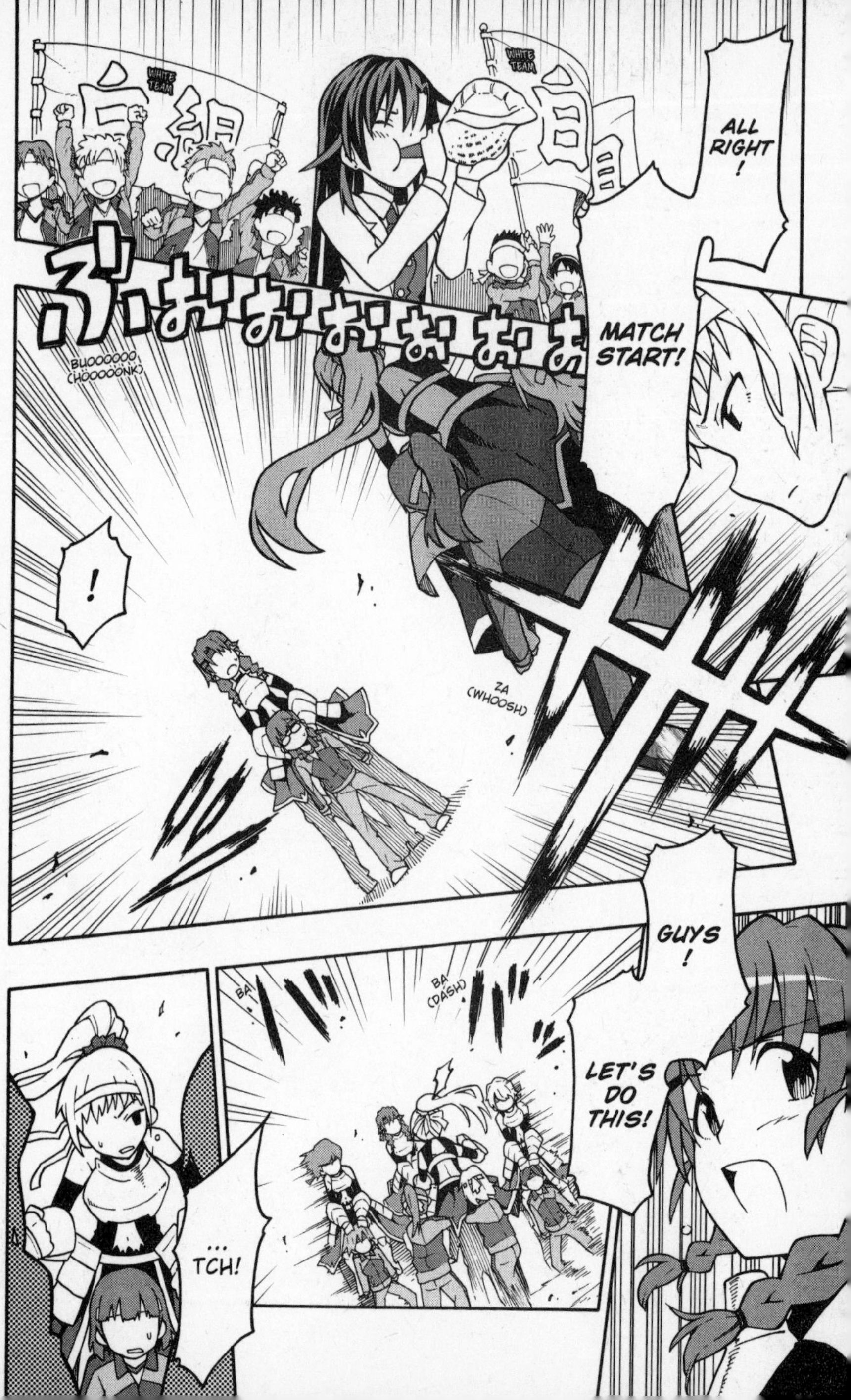
ALL RIGHT!
WHITE TEAM
WHITE TEAM
MATCH START!
BUOOOOOO (HOOOOONK)
!
ZA (WHOOSH)
GUYS! LET'S DO THIS!
BA (DASH)
BA
... TCH!

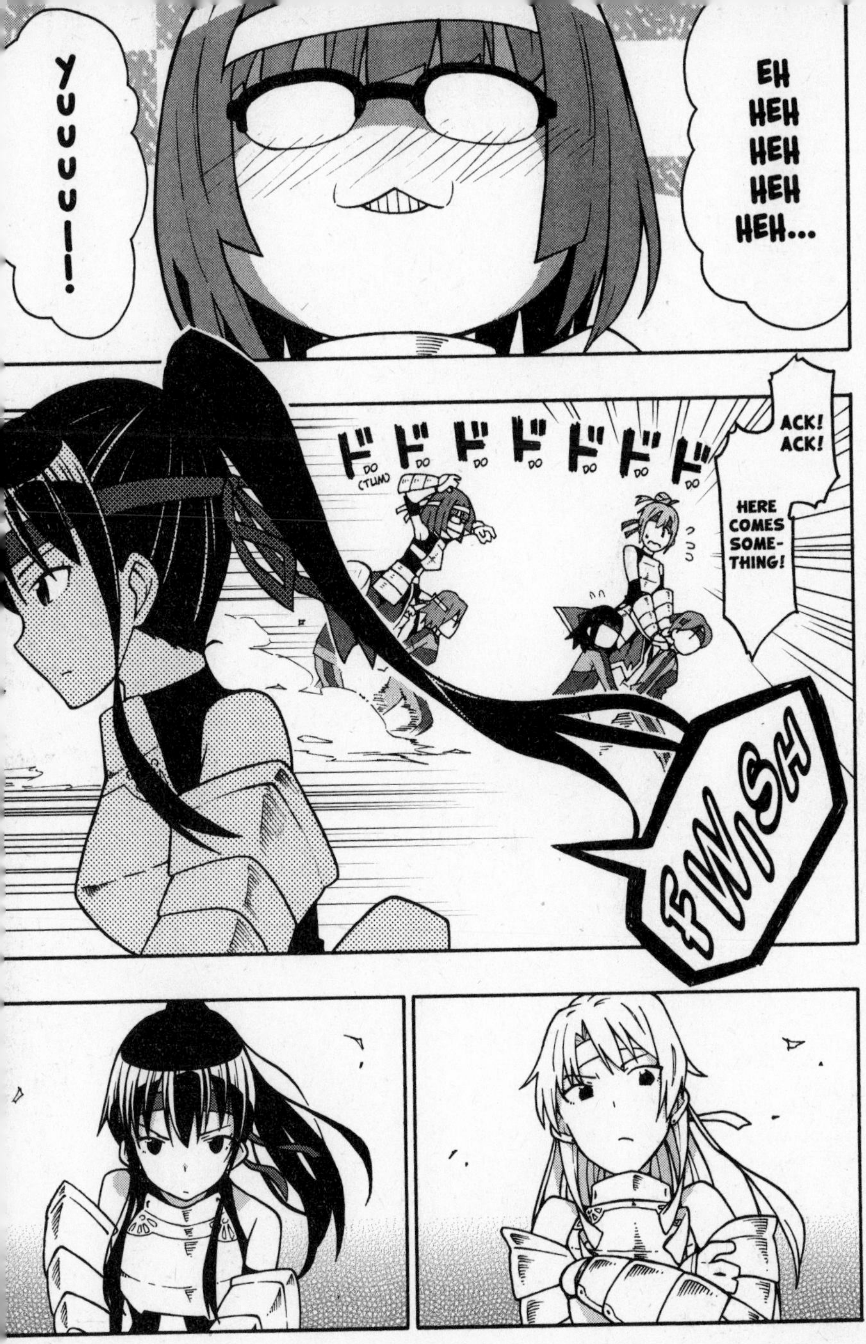
EH HEH HEH HEH HEH...
YUUUUI!
ACK! ACK!
HERE COMES SOME-THING!
ドドドドドドド
DO (TUM) DO DO DO DO DO DO
FWISH

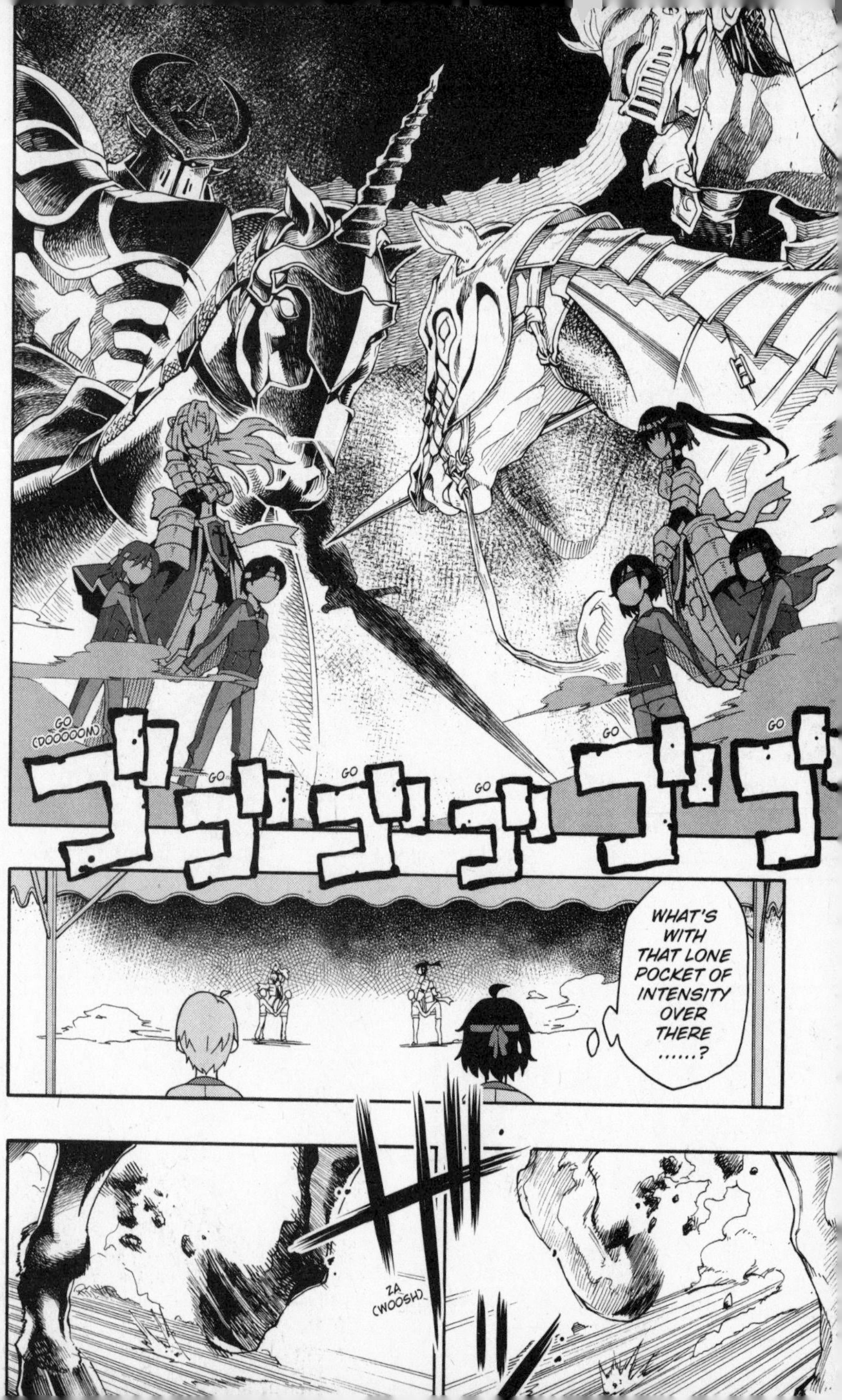
GO
GO
GO
GO
GO
GO (DOOOOOM)
WHAT'S WITH THAT LONE POCKET OF INTENSITY OVER THERE ......?
ZA (WOOSH)

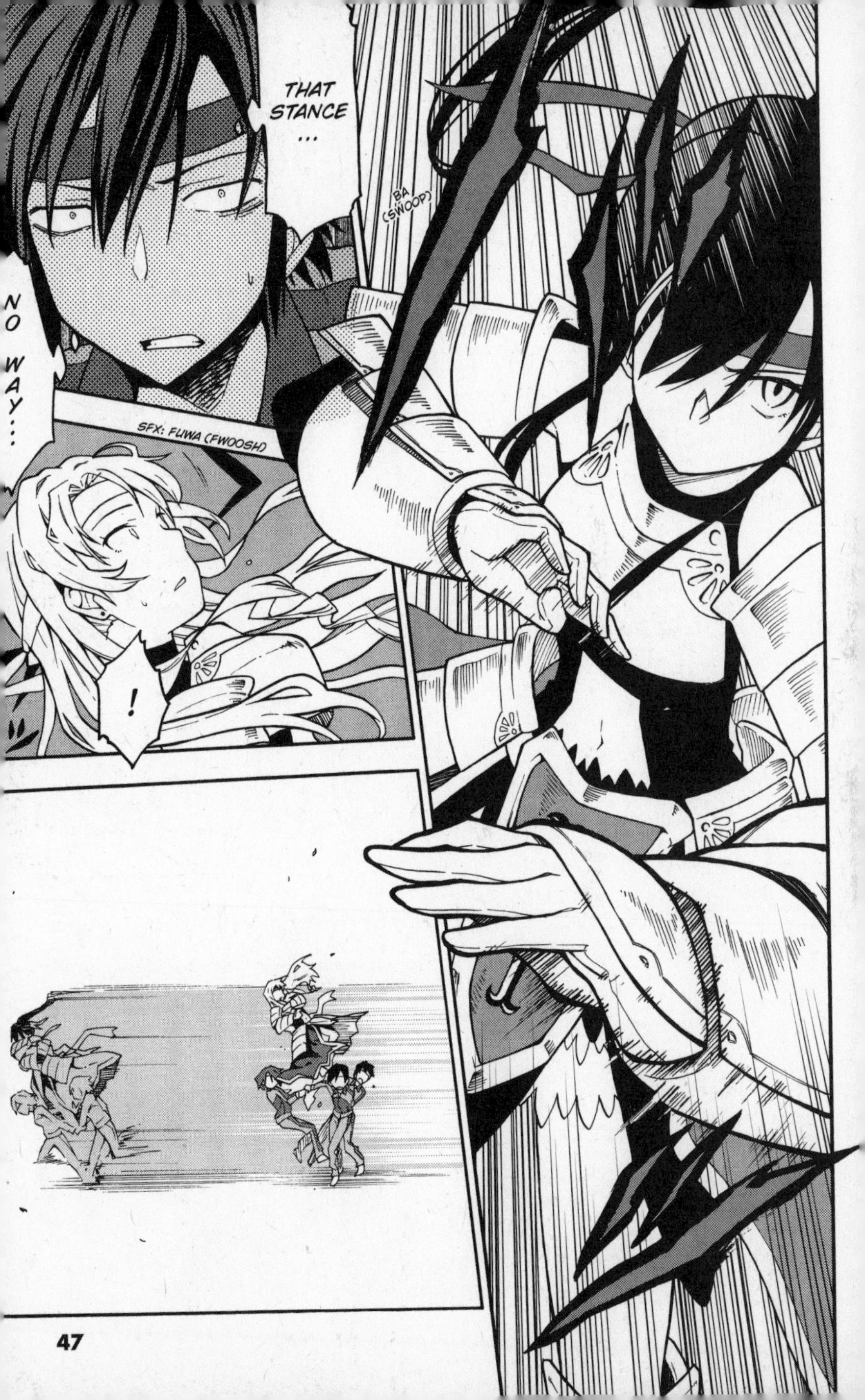
BA (SWOOP)
THAT STANCE...
NO WAY...
SFX: FUWA (FWOOSH)
!

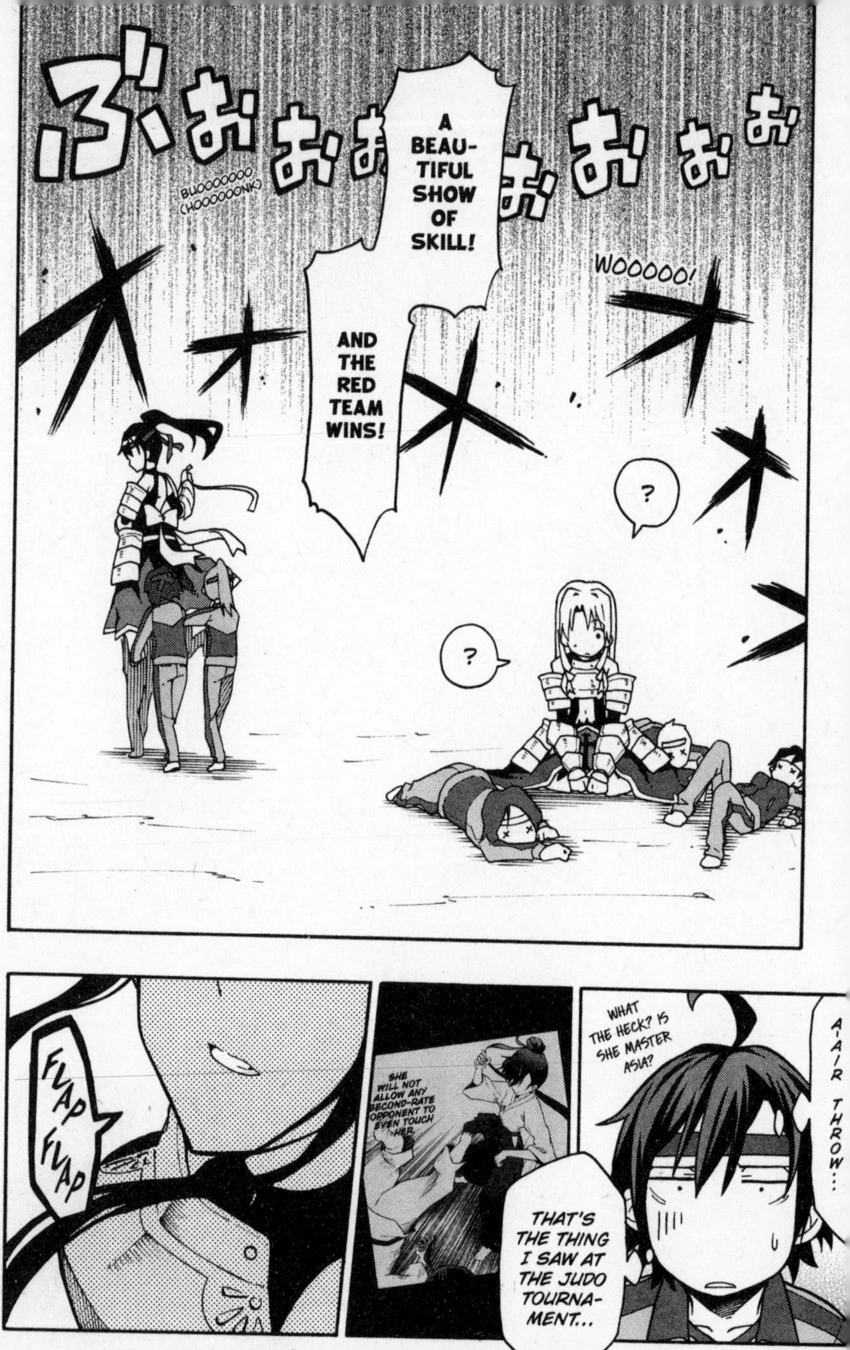

ぶおおおおおおおお
BUOOOOOOOO (HOOOOOONK)
A BEAU-TIFUL SHOW OF SKILL!
AND THE RED TEAM WINS!
WOOOOO!
?
?
A-AIR THROW...
WHAT THE HECK? IS SHE MASTER ASIA?
THAT'S THE THING I SAW AT THE JUDO TOURNA-MENT...
SHE WILL NOT ALLOW ANY SECOND-RATE OPPONENT TO EVEN TOUCH HER.
FLAP FLAP

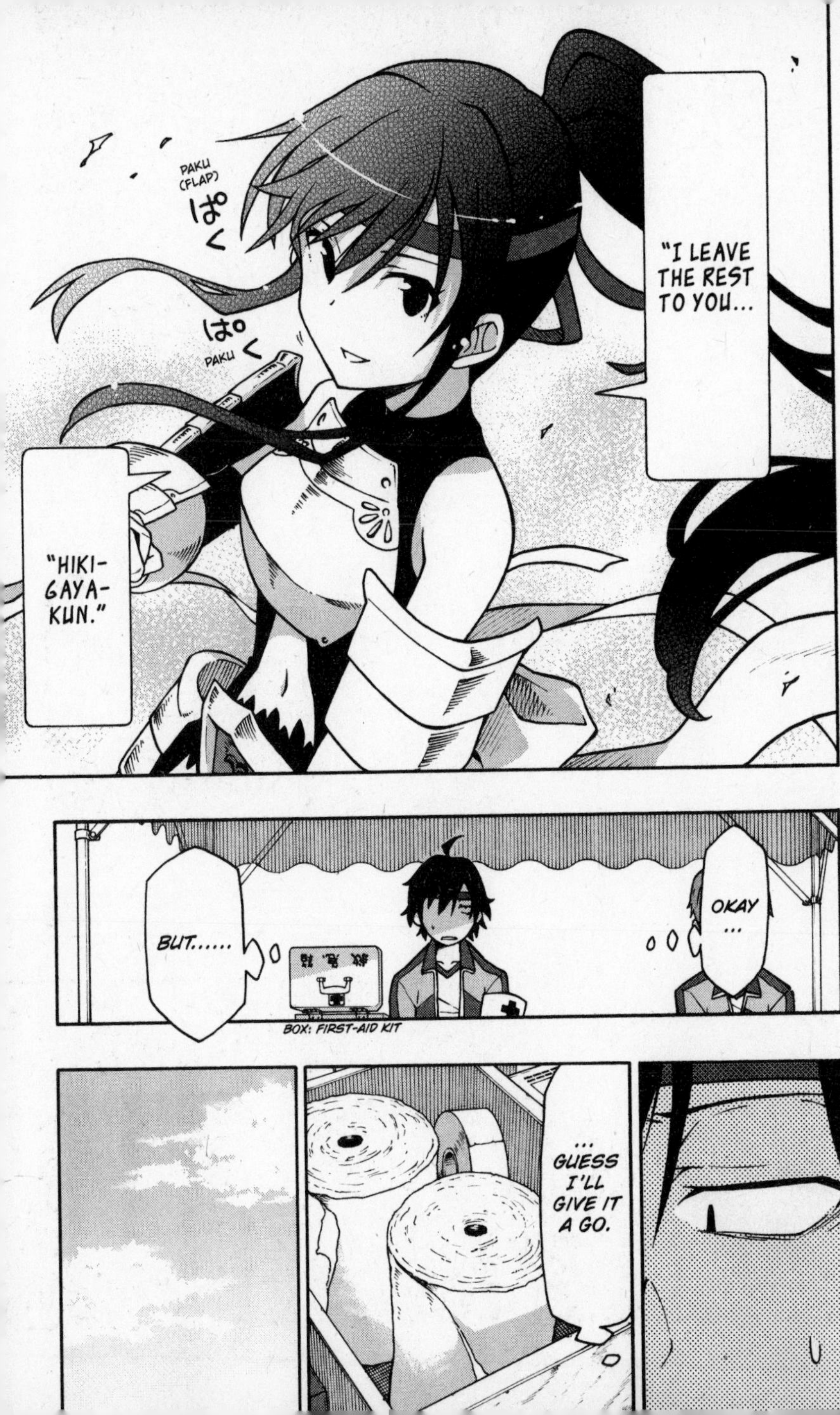
"I LEAVE THE REST TO YOU...
ぱく
PAKU (FLAP)
ぱく
PAKU
"HIKI-GAYA-KUN."
OKAY...
BUT......
BOX: FIRST-AID KIT
...GUESS I'LL GIVE IT A GO.

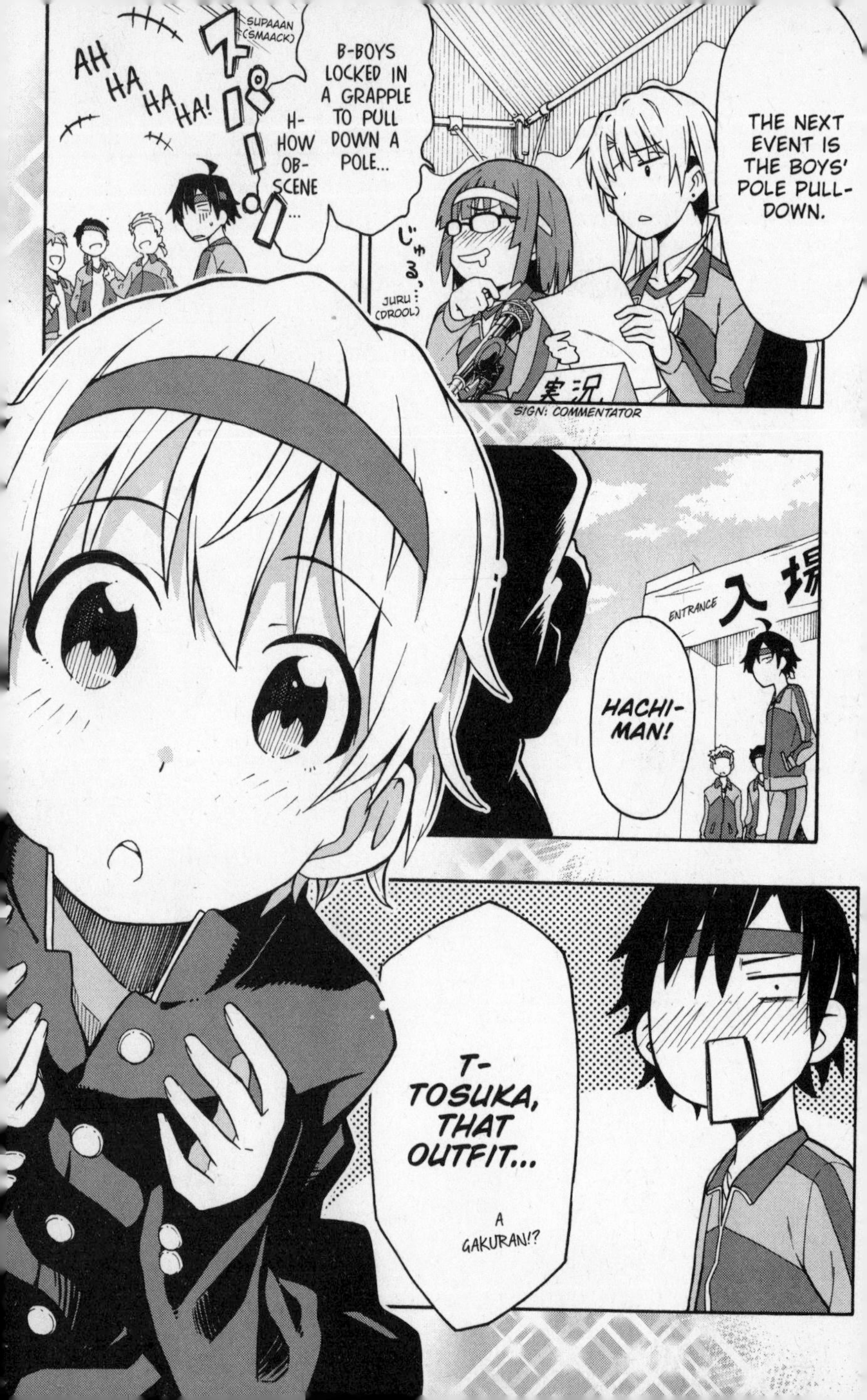
THE NEXT EVENT IS THE BOYS' POLE PULL-DOWN.
実況
SIGN: COMMENTATOR
じゅるっ
JURU (DROOL)
B-BOYS LOCKED IN A GRAPPLE TO PULL DOWN A POLE...
H-HOW OB-SCENE...
SUPAAAN (SMAACK)
AH HA HA HA!
入場
ENTRANCE
HACHI-MAN!
T-TOSUKA, THAT OUTFIT...
A GAKURAN!?

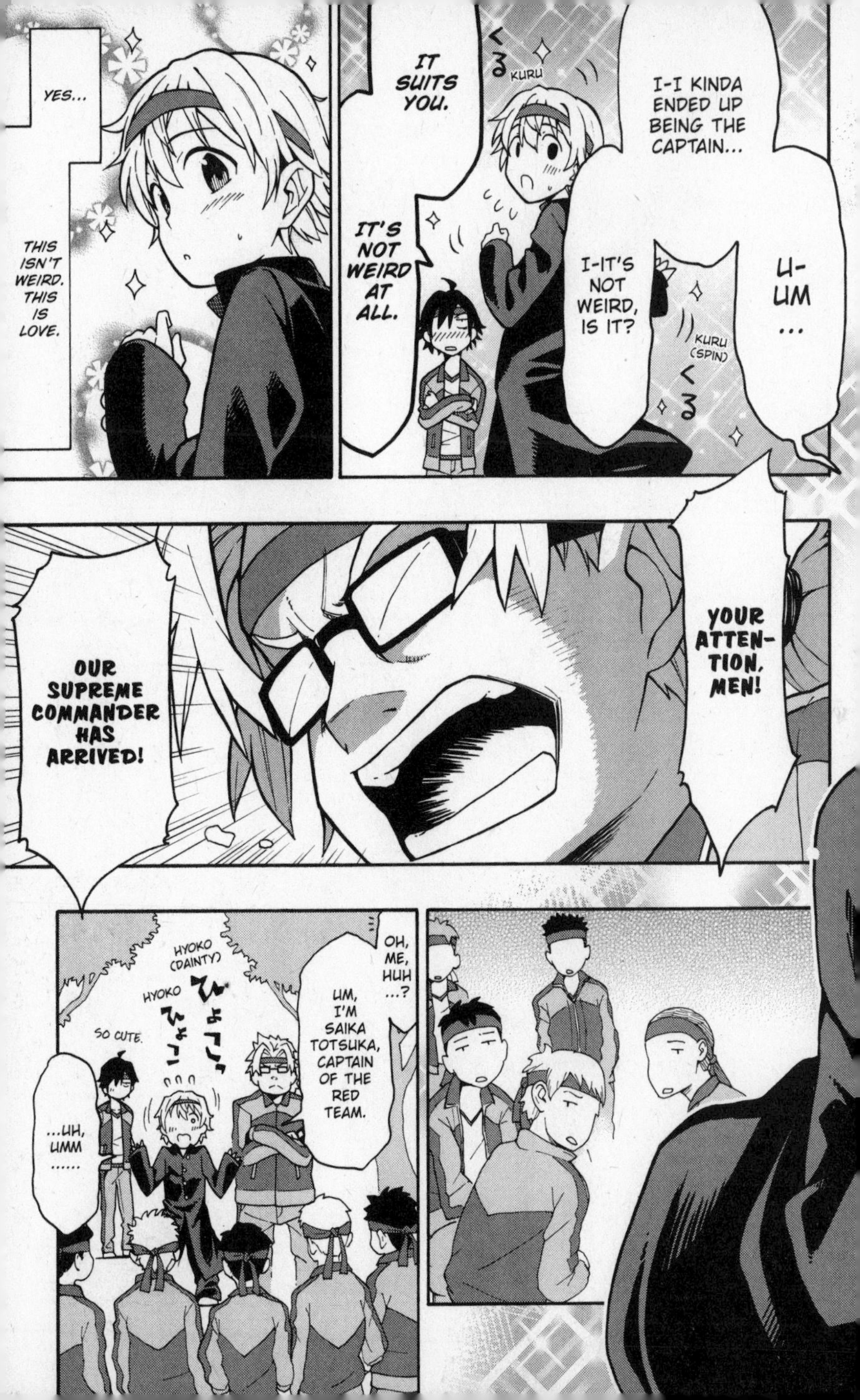
U-UM...
I-I KINDA ENDED UP BEING THE CAPTAIN...
くる KURU
I-IT'S NOT WEIRD, IS IT?
KURU (SPIN) くる
IT SUITS YOU.
IT'S NOT WEIRD AT ALL.
YES...
THIS ISN'T WEIRD. THIS IS LOVE.
YOUR ATTEN-TION, MEN!
OUR SUPREME COMMANDER HAS ARRIVED!
OH, ME, HUH...?
UM, I'M SAIKA TOTSUKA, CAPTAIN OF THE RED TEAM.
HYOKO (DAINTY) ひょこ
HYOKO ひょこ
SO CUTE.
...UH, UMM ......

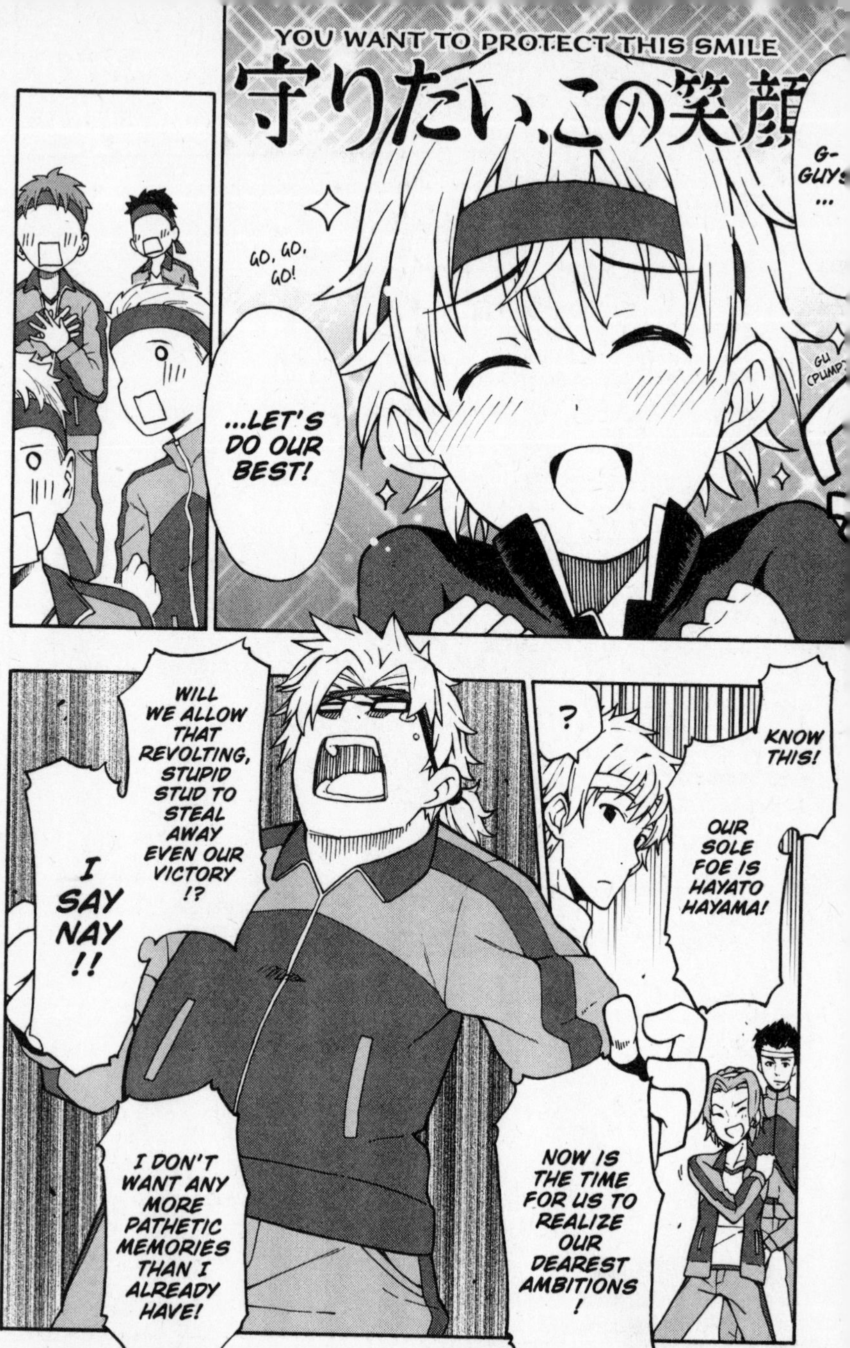
YOU WANT TO PROTECT THIS SMILE
守りたいこの笑顔
G-GUYS...
GU (PUMP
GO, GO, GO!
...LET'S DO OUR BEST!
?
KNOW THIS!
OUR SOLE FOE IS HAYATO HAYAMA!
NOW IS THE TIME FOR US TO REALIZE OUR DEAREST AMBITIONS!
WILL WE ALLOW THAT REVOLTING, STUPID STUD TO STEAL AWAY EVEN OUR VICTORY!?
I SAY NAY!!
I DON'T WANT ANY MORE PATHETIC MEMORIES THAN I ALREADY HAVE!

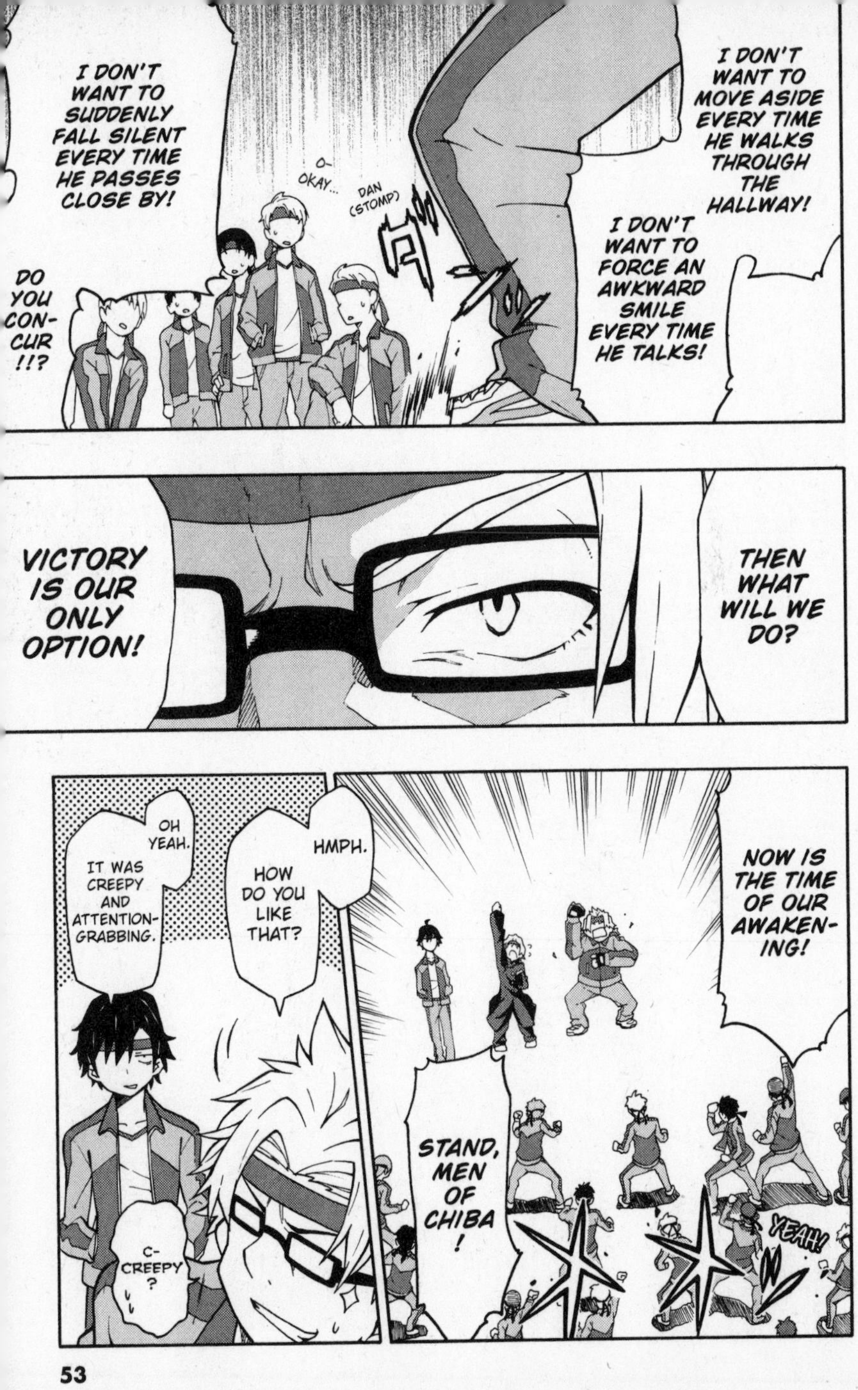
I DON'T WANT TO MOVE ASIDE EVERY TIME HE WALKS THROUGH THE HALLWAY!
I DON'T WANT TO FORCE AN AWKWARD SMILE EVERY TIME HE TALKS!
DAN (STOMP)
O-OKAY...
I DON'T WANT TO SUDDENLY FALL SILENT EVERY TIME HE PASSES CLOSE BY!
DO YOU CONCUR!!?
THEN WHAT WILL WE DO?
VICTORY IS OUR ONLY OPTION!
NOW IS THE TIME OF OUR AWAKENING!
STAND, MEN OF CHIBA!
YEAH!
HMPH.
HOW DO YOU LIKE THAT?
OH YEAH.
IT WAS CREEPY AND ATTENTION-GRABBING.
C-CREEPY?

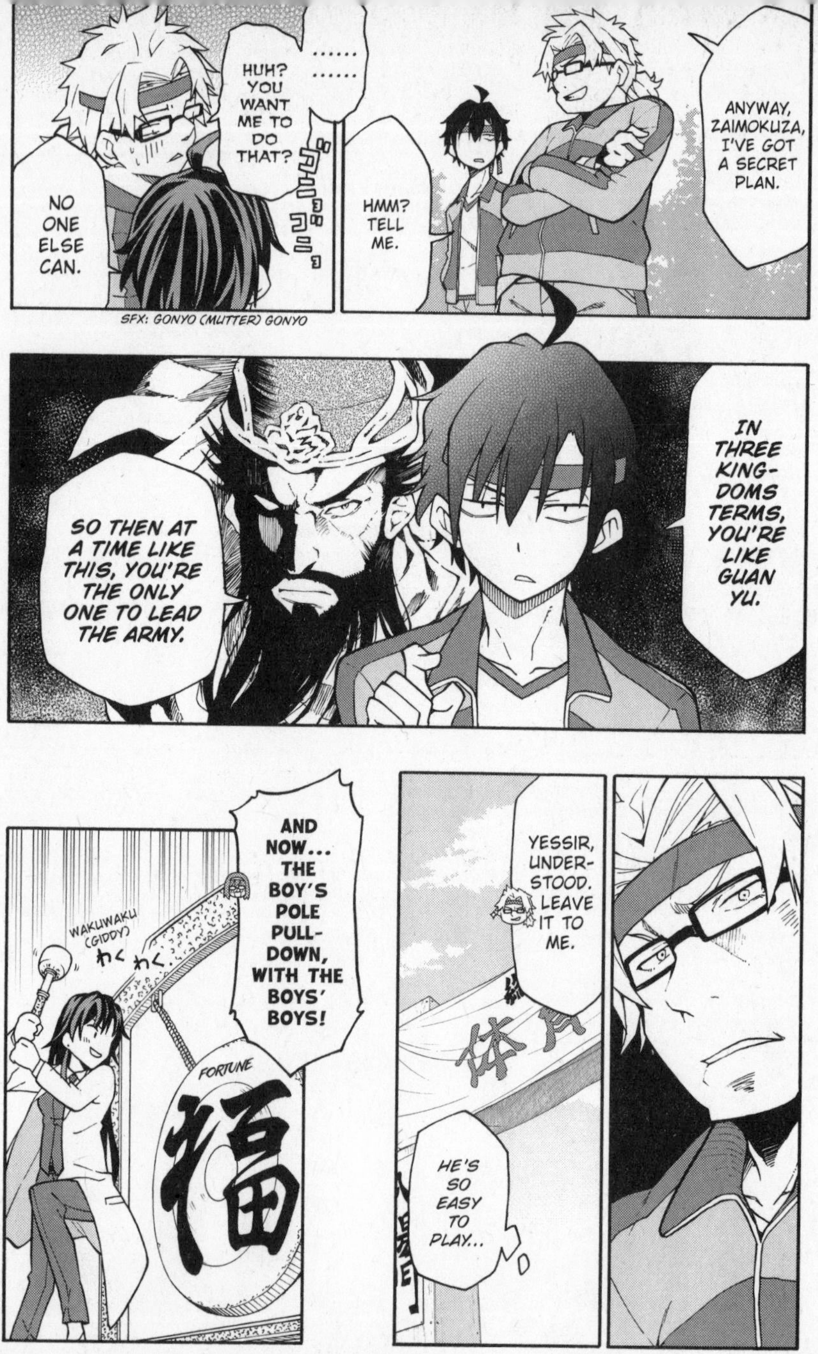
ANYWAY, ZAIMOKUZA, I'VE GOT A SECRET PLAN.
HMM? TELL ME.
......
......
HUH? YOU WANT ME TO DO THAT?
ゴニョゴニョ
NO ONE ELSE CAN.
SFX: GONYO (MUTTER) GONYO
IN THREE KING-DOMS TERMS, YOU'RE LIKE GUAN YU.
SO THEN AT A TIME LIKE THIS, YOU'RE THE ONLY ONE TO LEAD THE ARMY.
YESSIR, UNDER-STOOD. LEAVE IT TO ME.
HE'S SO EASY TO PLAY...
AND NOW... THE BOY'S POLE PULL-DOWN, WITH THE BOYS' BOYS!
WAKUWAKU (GIDDY)
わくわく
FORTUNE
福

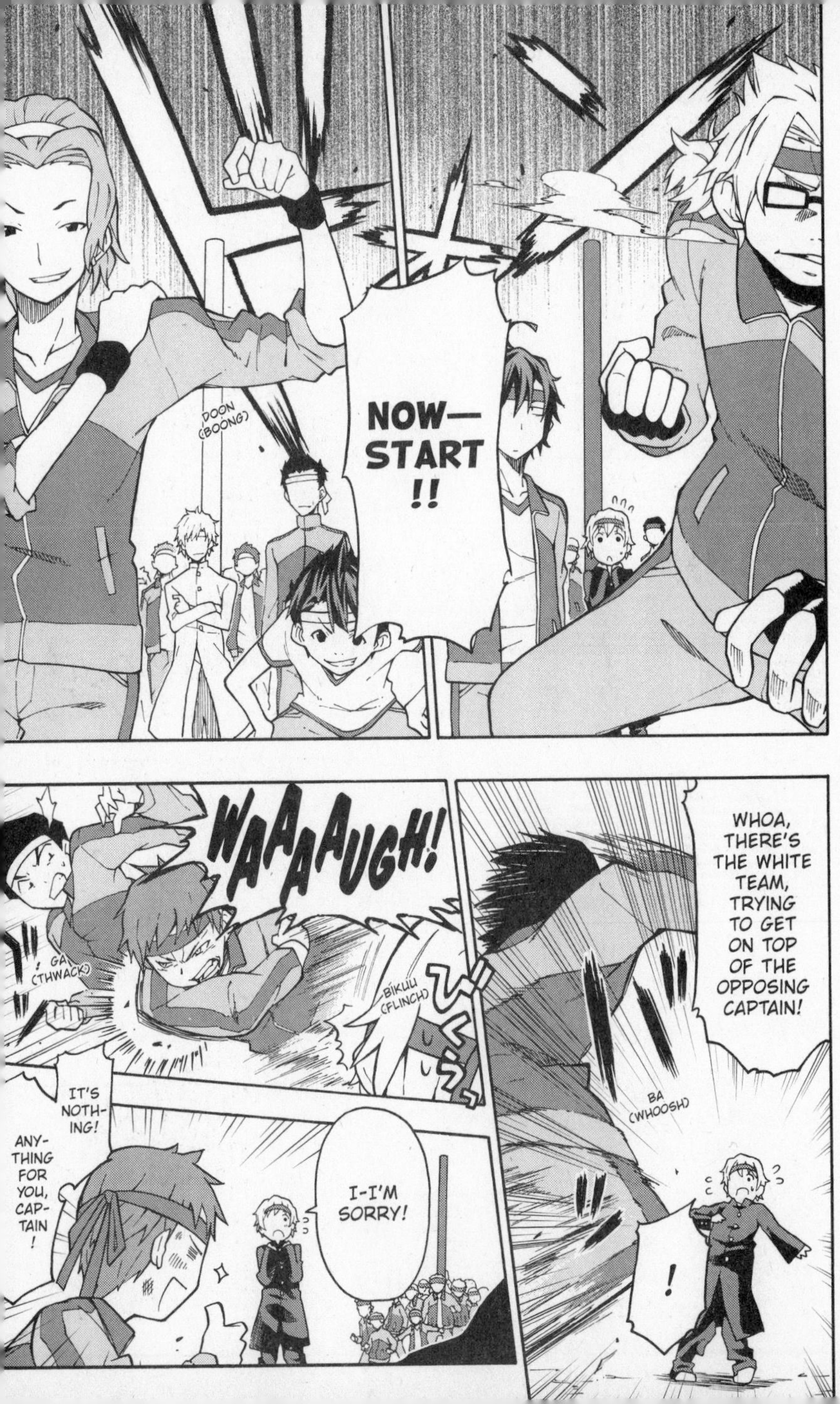
DOON (BOONG)
NOW— START !!
WHOA, THERE'S THE WHITE TEAM, TRYING TO GET ON TOP OF THE OPPOSING CAPTAIN!
BA (WHOOSH)
!
WAAAAUGH!
GA (THWACK)
BIKUU (FLINCH)
I-I'M SORRY!
IT'S NOTHING!
ANYTHING FOR YOU, CAPTAIN!

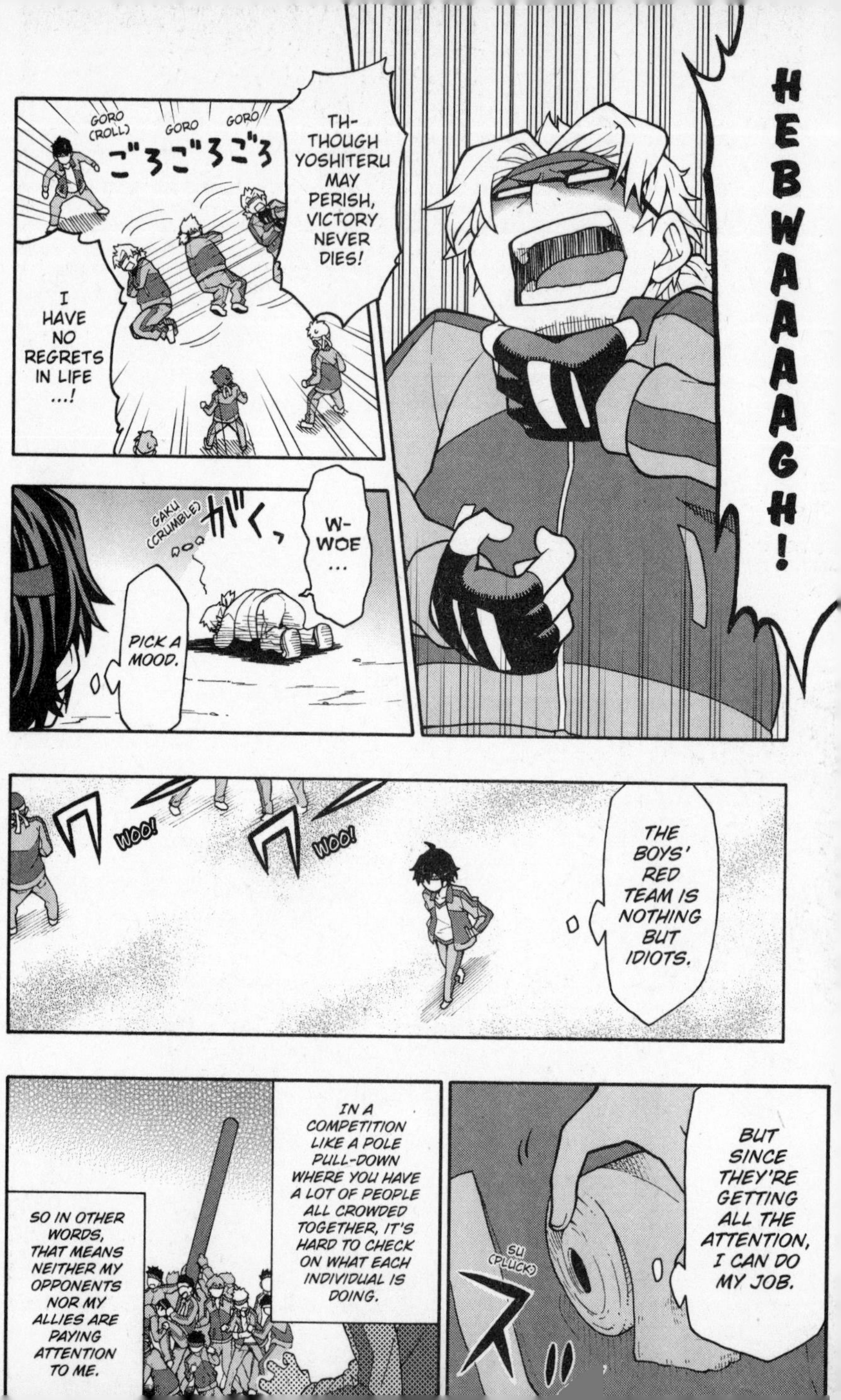
HEBWAAAAAGH!
TH-THOUGH YOSHITERU MAY PERISH, VICTORY NEVER DIES!
I HAVE NO REGRETS IN LIFE ...!
GORO (ROLL) GORO GORO
ごろごろごろ
W-WOE ...
GAKU (CRUMBLE)
がくっ
PICK A MOOD.
THE BOYS' RED TEAM IS NOTHING BUT IDIOTS.
WOO!
WOO!
BUT SINCE THEY'RE GETTING ALL THE ATTENTION, I CAN DO MY JOB.
SU (PLUCK)
IN A COMPETITION LIKE A POLE PULL-DOWN WHERE YOU HAVE A LOT OF PEOPLE ALL CROWDED TOGETHER, IT'S HARD TO CHECK ON WHAT EACH INDIVIDUAL IS DOING.
SO IN OTHER WORDS, THAT MEANS NEITHER MY OPPONENTS NOR MY ALLIES ARE PAYING ATTENTION TO ME.

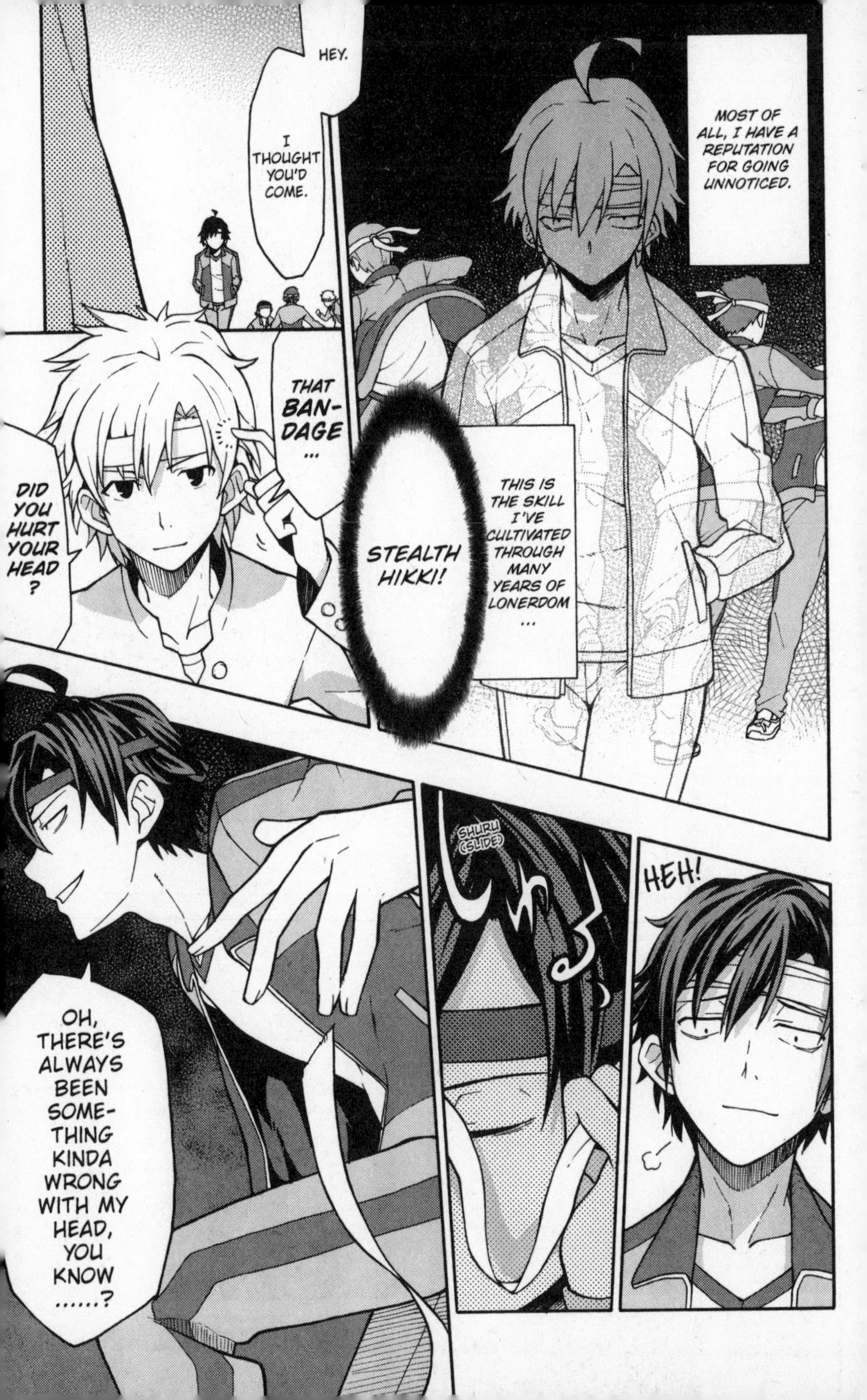
MOST OF ALL, I HAVE A REPUTATION FOR GOING UNNOTICED.
THIS IS THE SKILL I'VE CULTIVATED THROUGH MANY YEARS OF LONERDOM...
STEALTH HIKKI!
HEY.
I THOUGHT YOU'D COME.
THAT BAN-DAGE...
DID YOU HURT YOUR HEAD?
HEH!
SHURU (SLIDE)
OH, THERE'S ALWAYS BEEN SOME-THING KINDA WRONG WITH MY HEAD, YOU KNOW......?

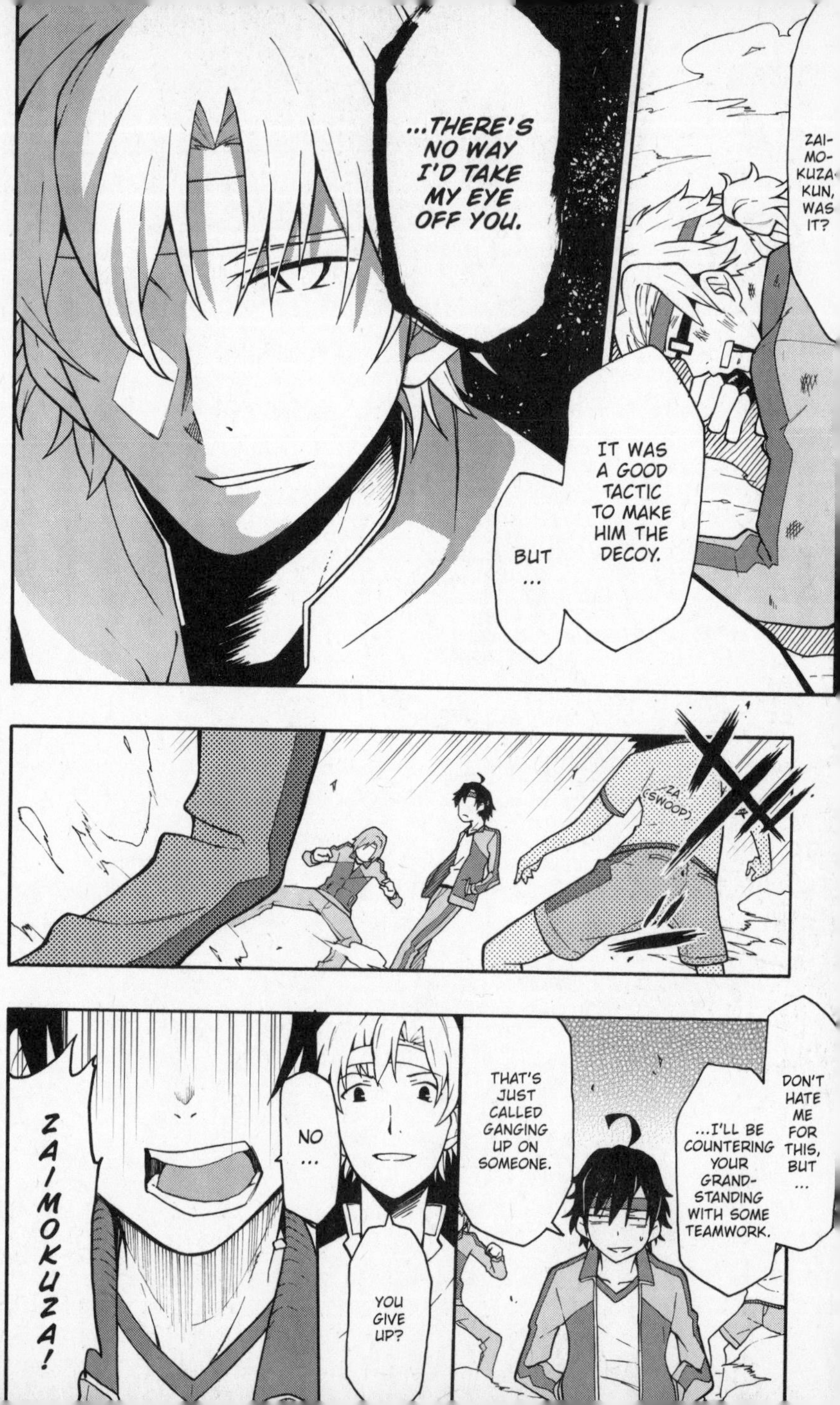
ZAI-MOKUZA-KUN, WAS IT?
IT WAS A GOOD TACTIC TO MAKE HIM THE DECOY.
BUT ...
...THERE'S NO WAY I'D TAKE MY EYE OFF YOU.
ZA (SWOOP)
DON'T HATE ME FOR THIS, BUT ...
...I'LL BE COUNTERING YOUR GRAND-STANDING WITH SOME TEAMWORK.
THAT'S JUST CALLED GANGING UP ON SOMEONE.
NO ...
YOU GIVE UP?
ZAIMOKUZA!

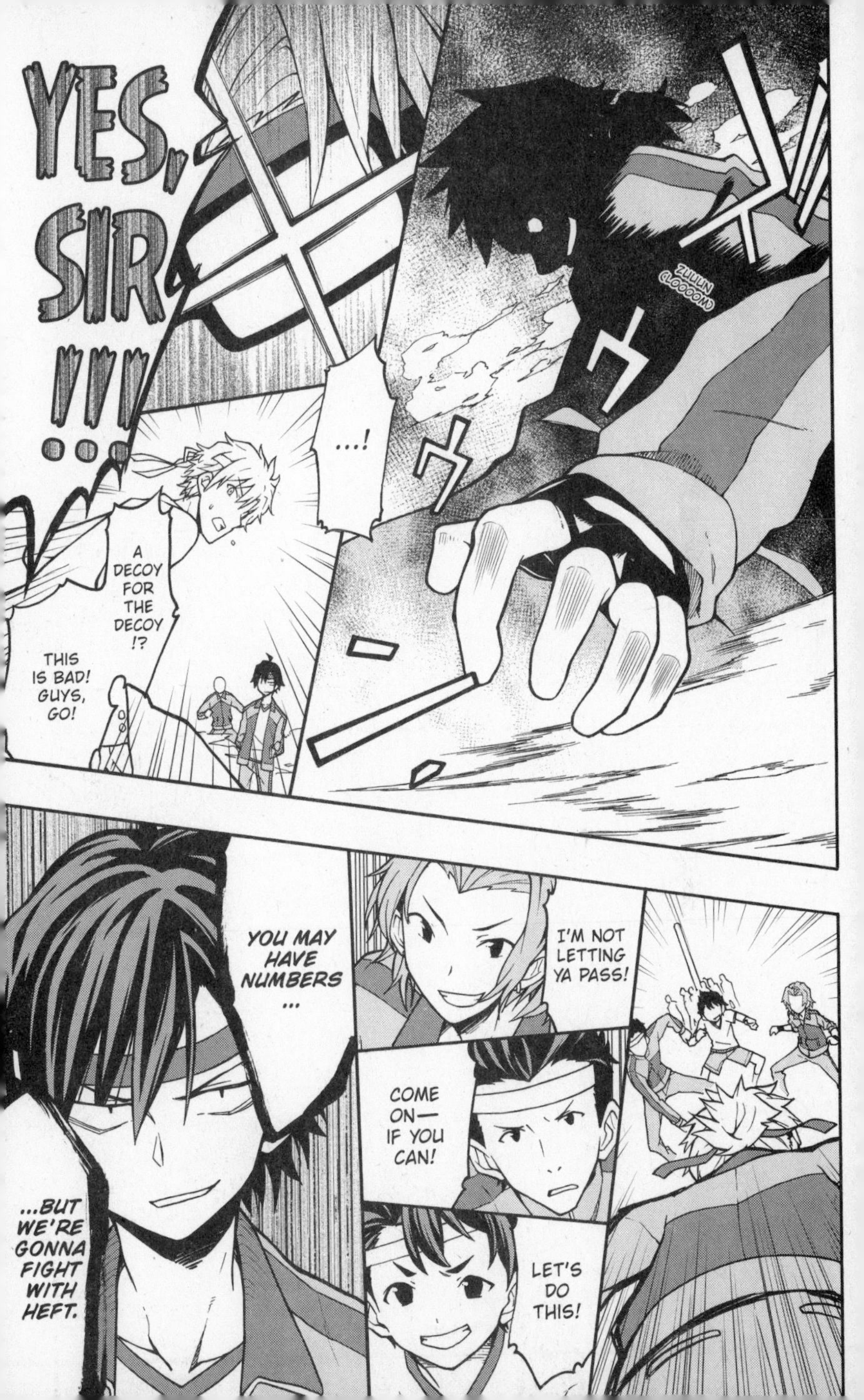
ZUUUN
(WOOOOM)
YES, SIR!!!
...!
A DECOY FOR THE DECOY!?
THIS IS BAD! GUYS, GO!
I'M NOT LETTING YA PASS!
YOU MAY HAVE NUMBERS...
COME ON— IF YOU CAN!
LET'S DO THIS!
...BUT WE'RE GONNA FIGHT WITH HEFT.

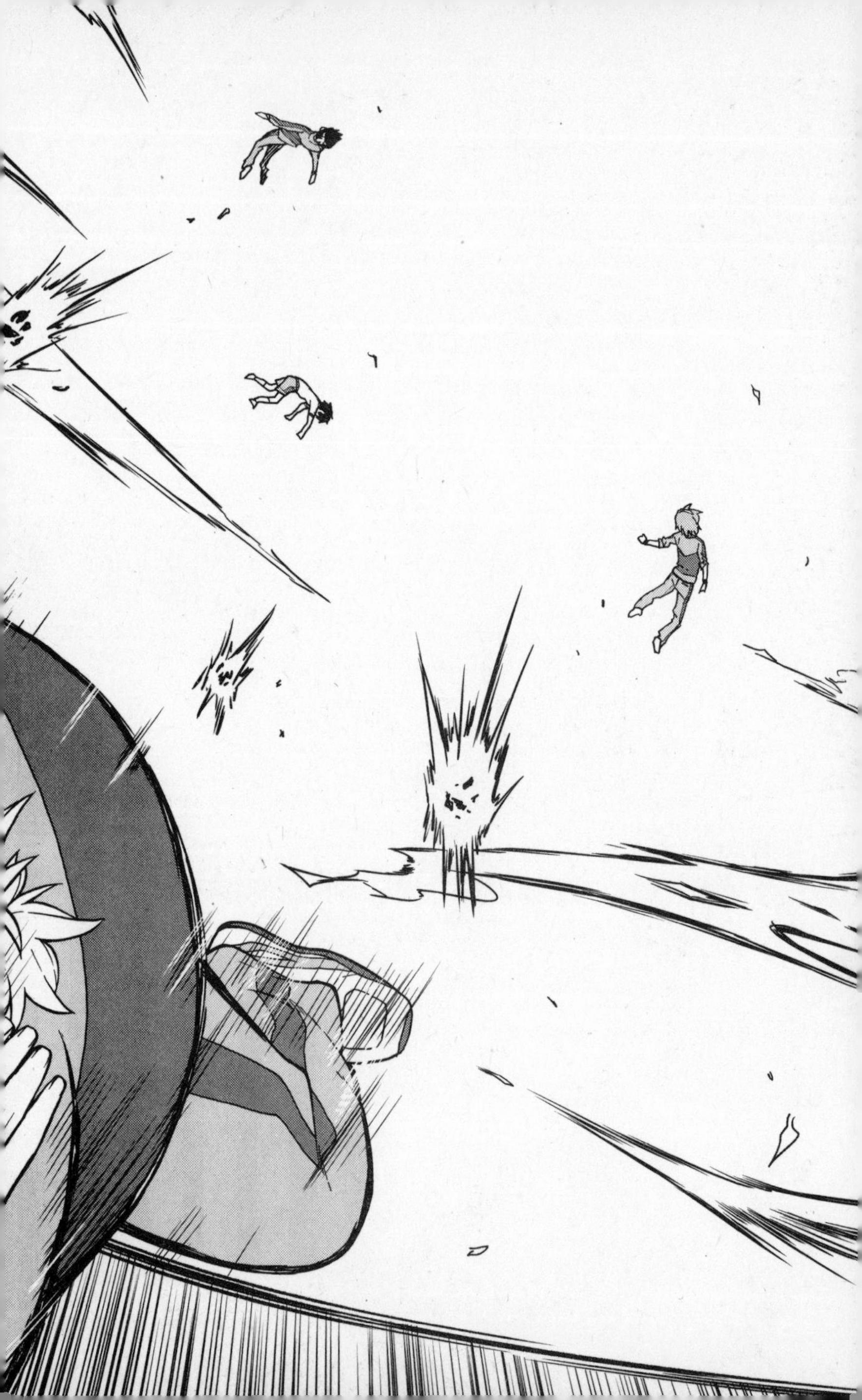

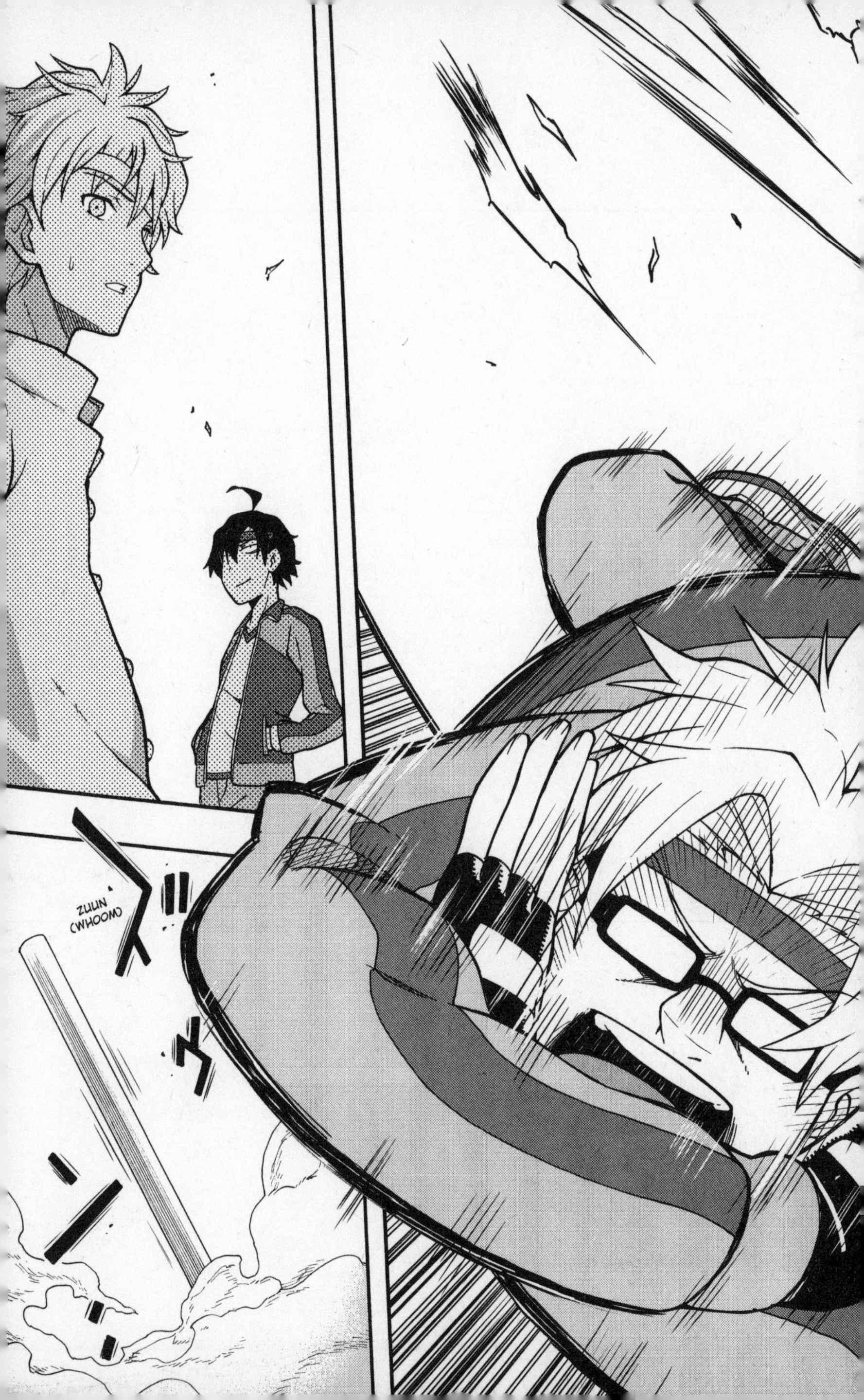
ZUUN
(WHOOM)

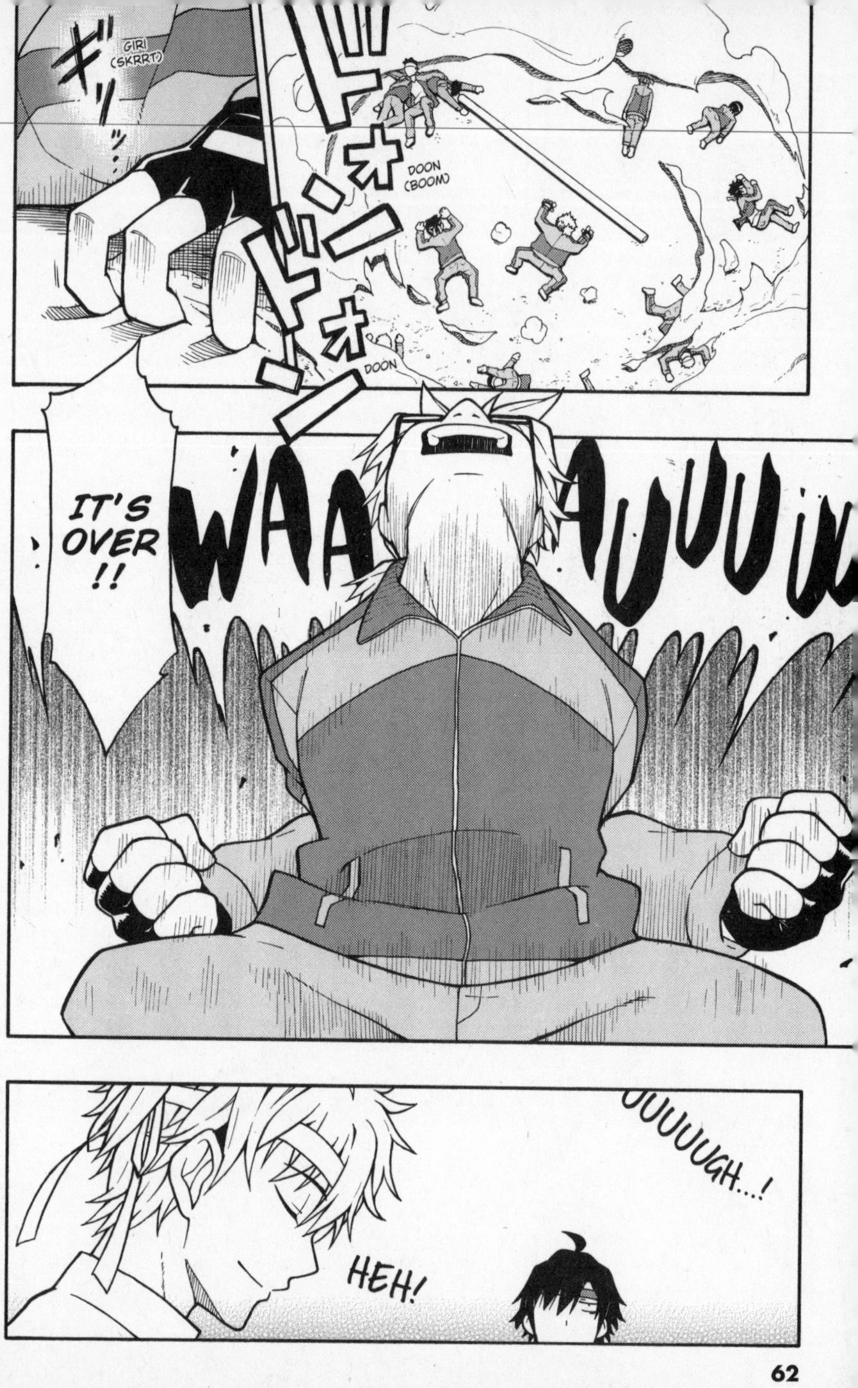

ドォーン
DOON (BOOM)
ドォーン
DOON
ギリッ
GIRI (SKRRT)
WAAAUUUU
IT'S OVER!!
UUUUUUGH...!
HEH!

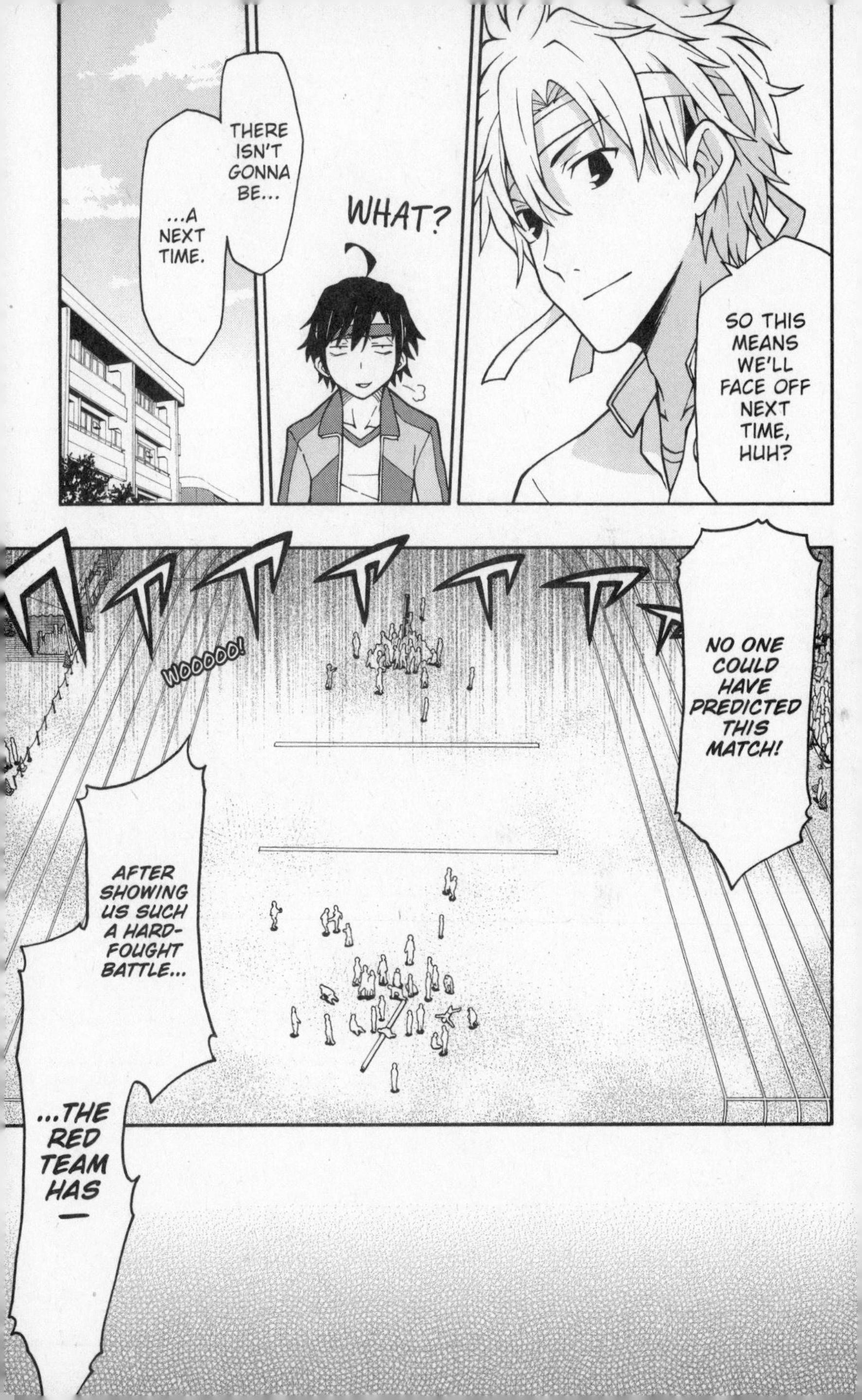
SO THIS MEANS WE'LL FACE OFF NEXT TIME, HUH?
WHAT?
THERE ISN'T GONNA BE...
...A NEXT TIME.
NO ONE COULD HAVE PREDICTED THIS MATCH!
WOOOOOO!
AFTER SHOWING US SUCH A HARD-FOUGHT BATTLE...
...THE RED TEAM HAS —

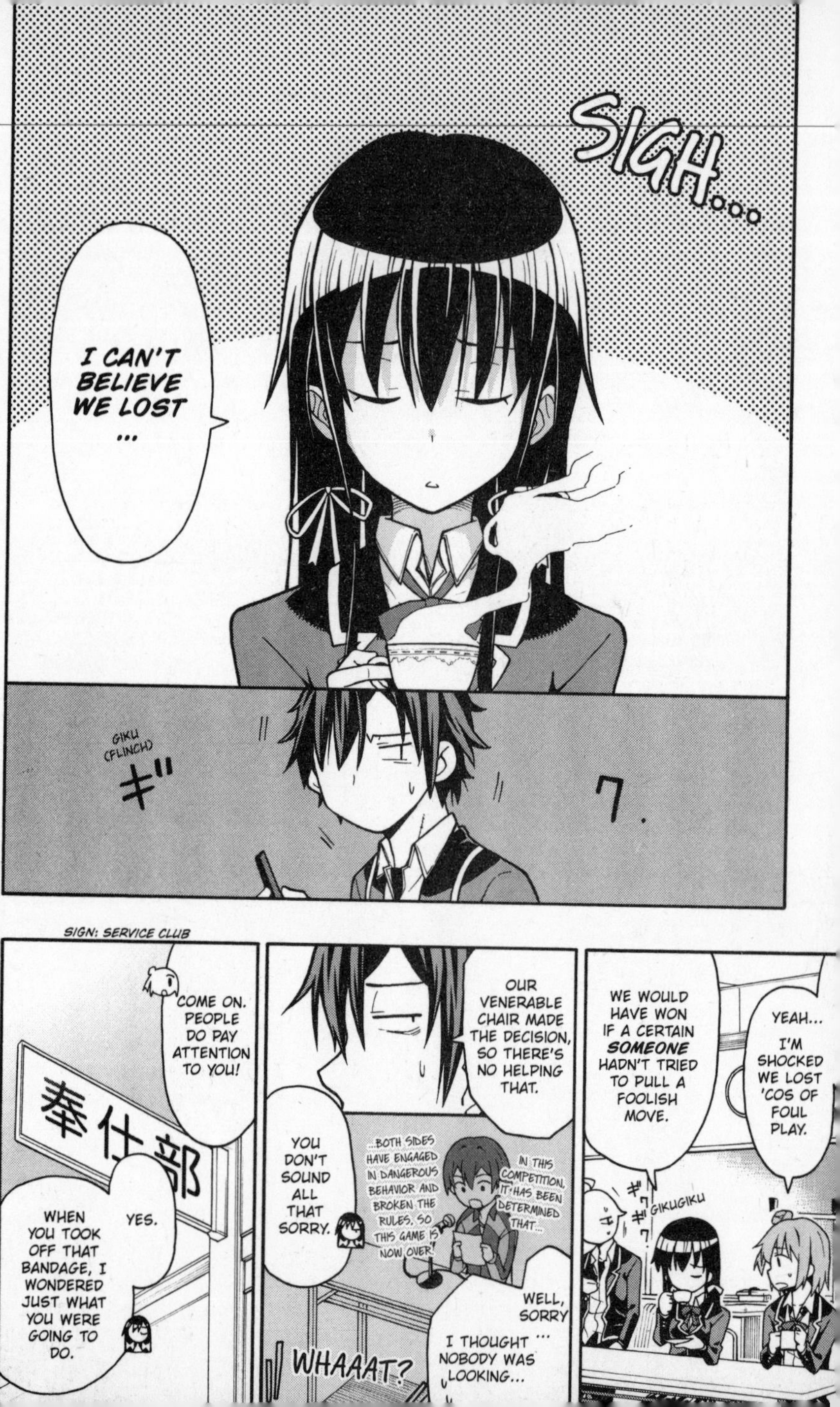
SIGH...
I CAN'T BELIEVE WE LOST...
GIKU (FLINCH)
ギク.
SIGN: SERVICE CLUB
YEAH... I'M SHOCKED WE LOST 'COS OF FOUL PLAY.
WE WOULD HAVE WON IF A CERTAIN *SOMEONE* HADN'T TRIED TO PULL A FOOLISH MOVE.
ギクギク
GIKUGIKU
OUR VENERABLE CHAIR MADE THE DECISION, SO THERE'S NO HELPING THAT.
IN THIS COMPETITION, IT HAS BEEN DETERMINED THAT...
...BOTH SIDES HAVE ENGAGED IN DANGEROUS BEHAVIOR AND BROKEN THE RULES, SO THIS GAME IS NOW OVER!
YOU DON'T SOUND ALL THAT SORRY.
WELL, SORRY...
I THOUGHT NOBODY WAS LOOKING...
WHAAAT?
COME ON. PEOPLE DO PAY ATTENTION TO YOU!
奉仕部
YES.
WHEN YOU TOOK OFF THAT BANDAGE, I WONDERED JUST WHAT YOU WERE GOING TO DO.

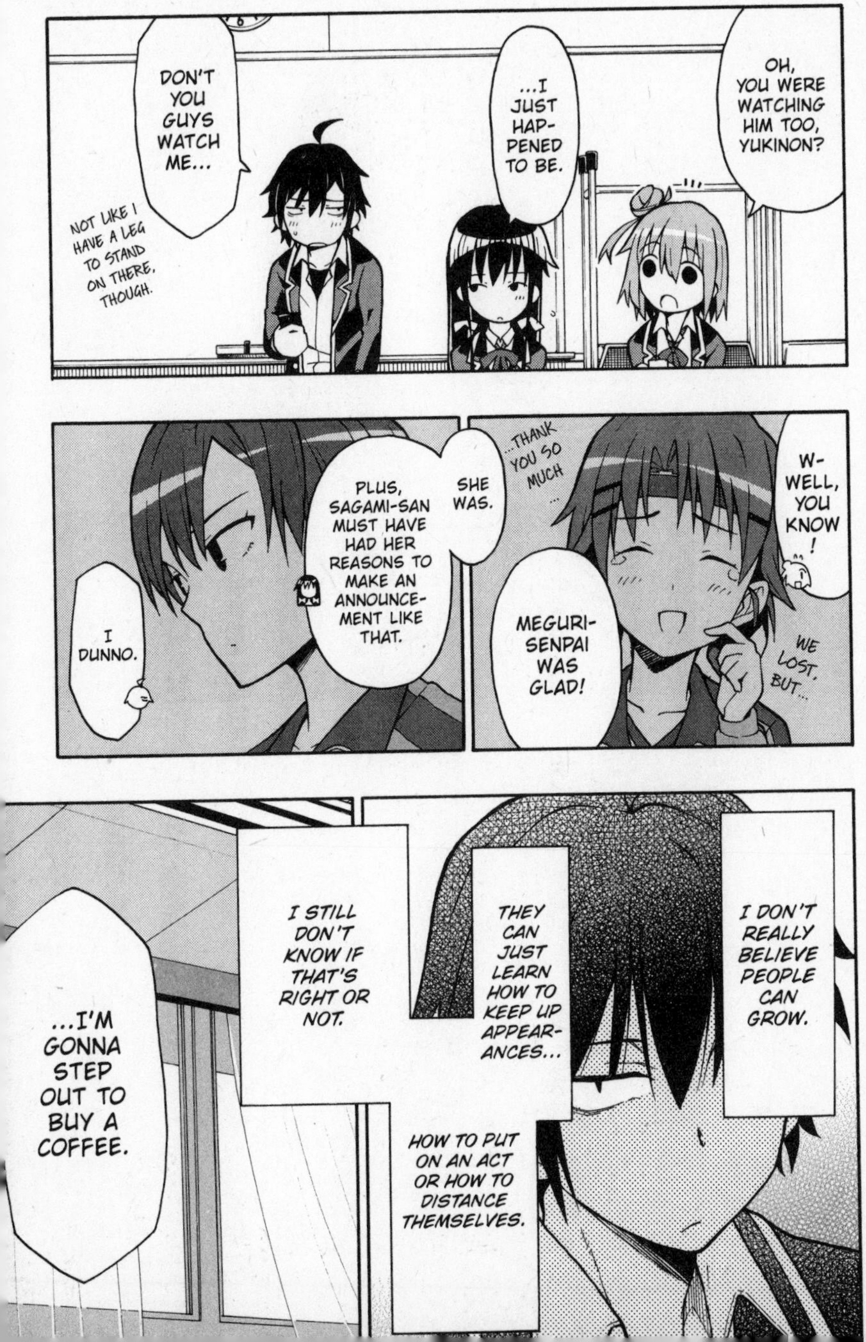
OH, YOU WERE WATCHING HIM TOO, YUKINON?
...I JUST HAP-PENED TO BE.
DON'T YOU GUYS WATCH ME...
NOT LIKE I HAVE A LEG TO STAND ON THERE, THOUGH.
W-WELL, YOU KNOW!
WE LOST, BUT...
MEGURI-SENPAI WAS GLAD!
...THANK YOU SO MUCH...
SHE WAS.
PLUS, SAGAMI-SAN MUST HAVE HAD HER REASONS TO MAKE AN ANNOUNCE-MENT LIKE THAT.
I DUNNO.
I DON'T REALLY BELIEVE PEOPLE CAN GROW.
THEY CAN JUST LEARN HOW TO KEEP UP APPEAR-ANCES...
HOW TO PUT ON AN ACT OR HOW TO DISTANCE THEMSELVES.
I STILL DON'T KNOW IF THAT'S RIGHT OR NOT.
...I'M GONNA STEP OUT TO BUY A COFFEE.

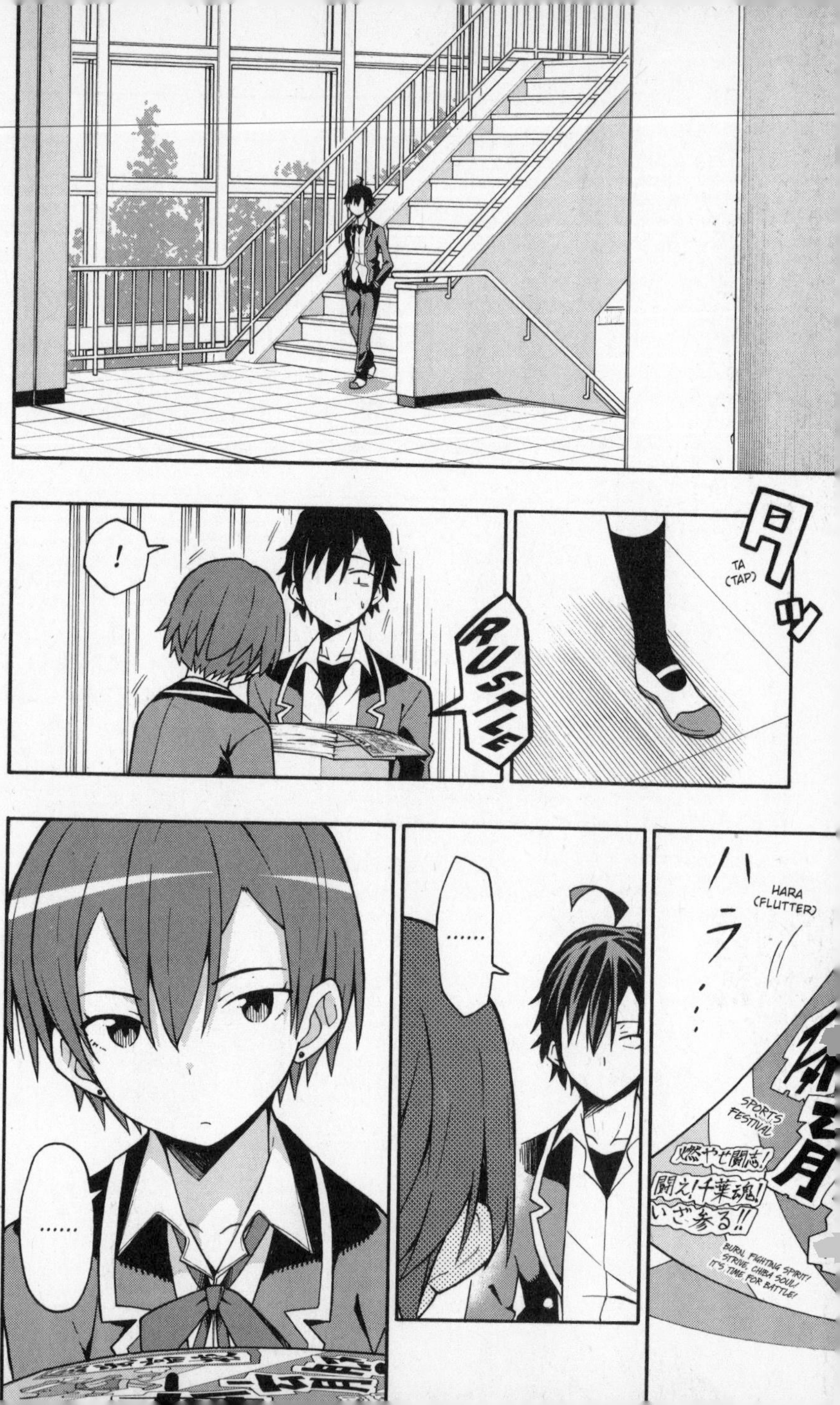

タッ
TA (TAP)
!
RUSTLE
ハラ…
HARA (FLUTTER)
SPORTS FESTIVAL
燃やせ闘志!
闘え!千葉魂!
いざ参る!!
BURN, FIGHTING SPIRIT! STRIVE, CHIBA SOUL! IT'S TIME FOR BATTLE!
……
……

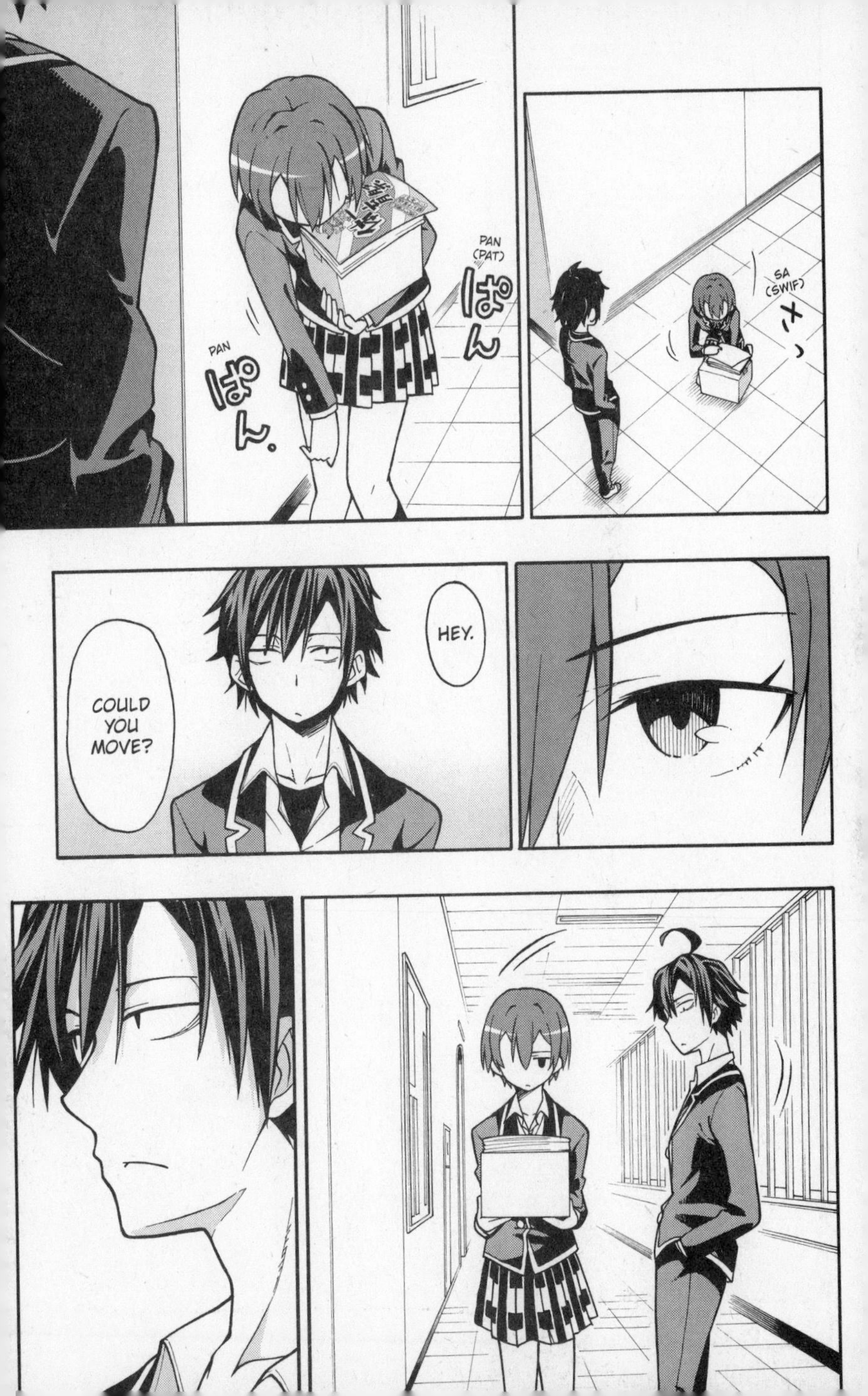
SA
(SWIF)
さっ
PAN
(PAT)
ぱん
PAN
ぱん。
HEY.
COULD YOU MOVE?

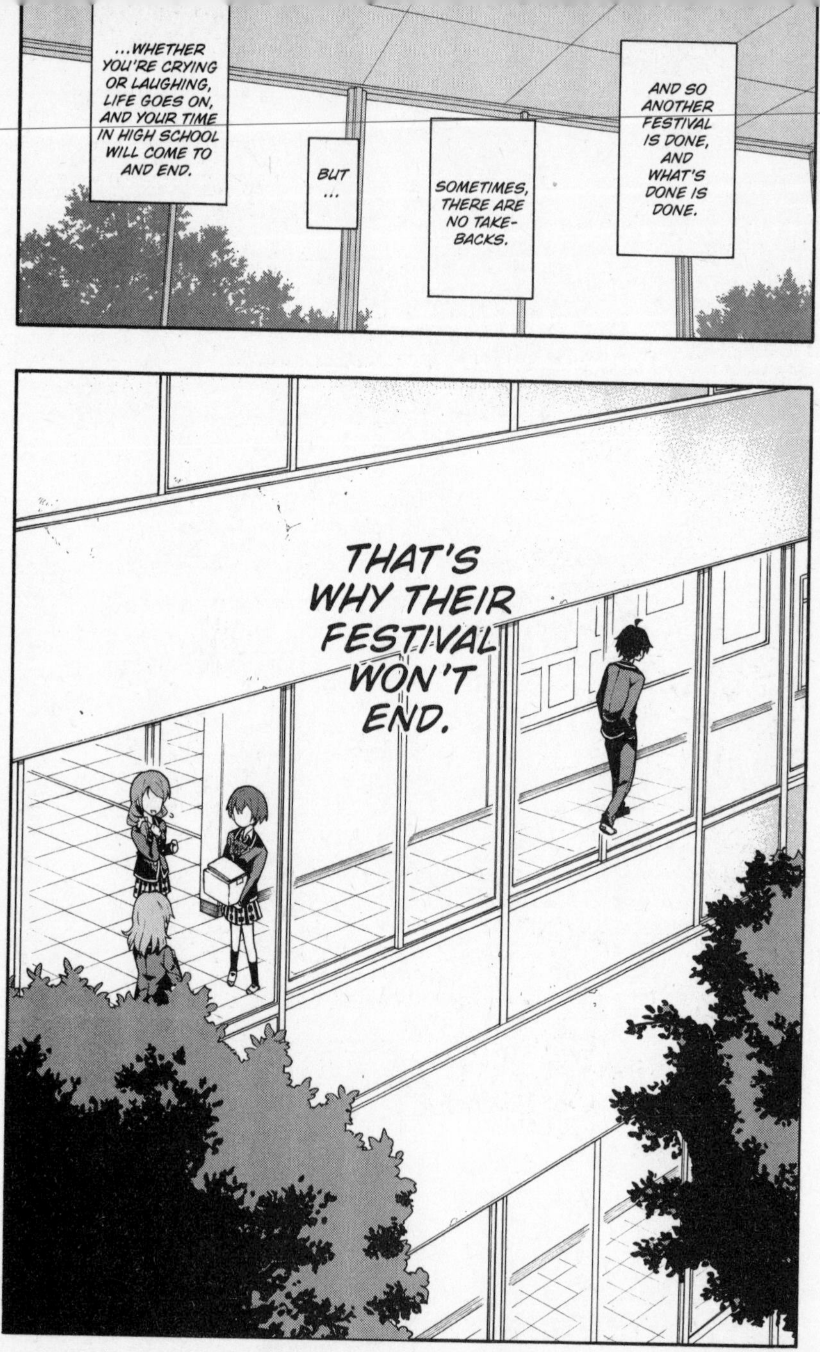
AND SO ANOTHER FESTIVAL IS DONE, AND WHAT'S DONE IS DONE.
SOMETIMES, THERE ARE NO TAKE-BACKS.
BUT ...
...WHETHER YOU'RE CRYING OR LAUGHING, LIFE GOES ON, AND YOUR TIME IN HIGH SCHOOL WILL COME TO AND END.
THAT'S WHY THEIR FESTIVAL WON'T END.

CHAPTER 50 ... KAKERU TOBE IS JUST HOPELESSLY SHALLOW.

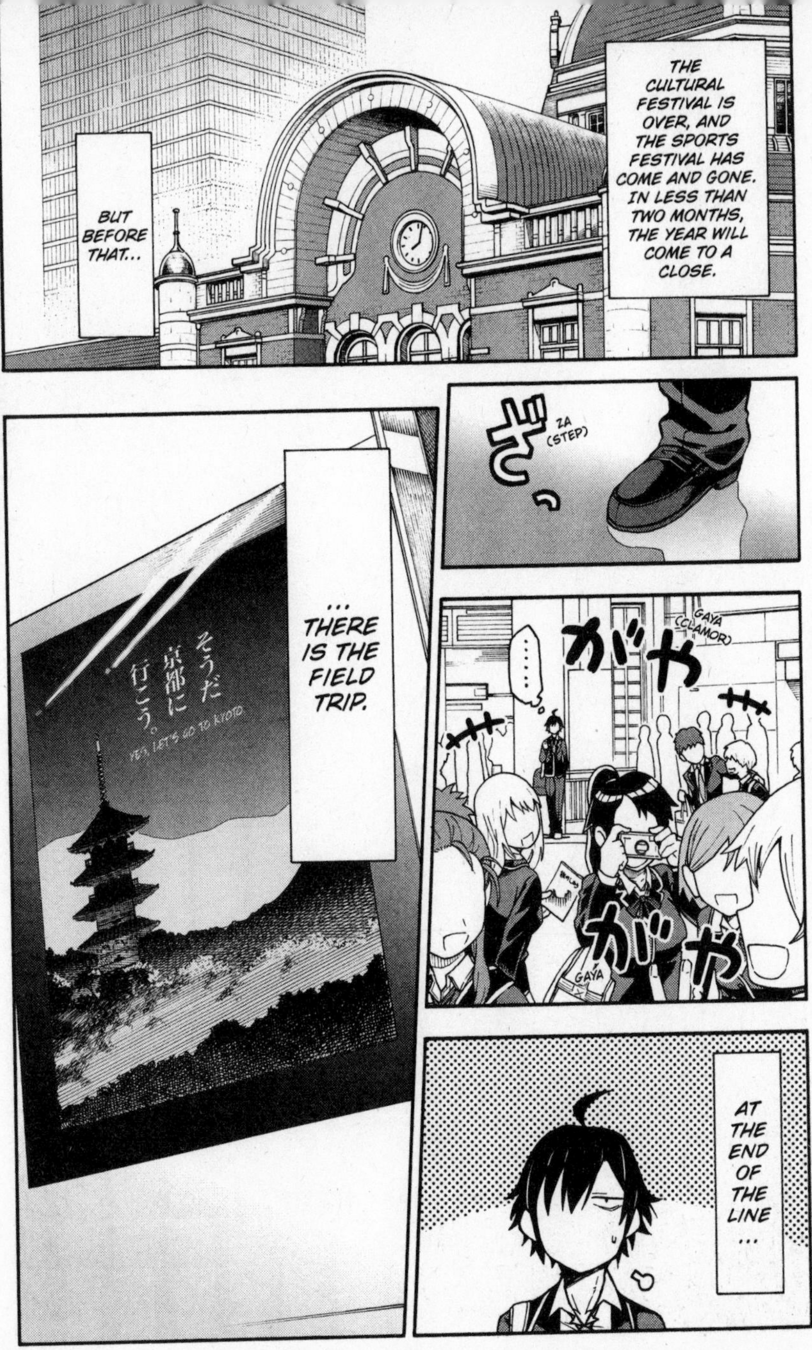
THE CULTURAL FESTIVAL IS OVER, AND THE SPORTS FESTIVAL HAS COME AND GONE. IN LESS THAN TWO MONTHS, THE YEAR WILL COME TO A CLOSE.
BUT BEFORE THAT...
ざっ
ZA (STEP)
......
がや
GAYA (CLAMOR)
がや
GAYA
AT THE END OF THE LINE...
...THERE IS THE FIELD TRIP.
そうだ京都に行こう。
YES, LET'S GO TO KYOTO

CHAPTER 50 ··· KAKERU TOBE IS JUST HOPELESSLY SHALLOW.

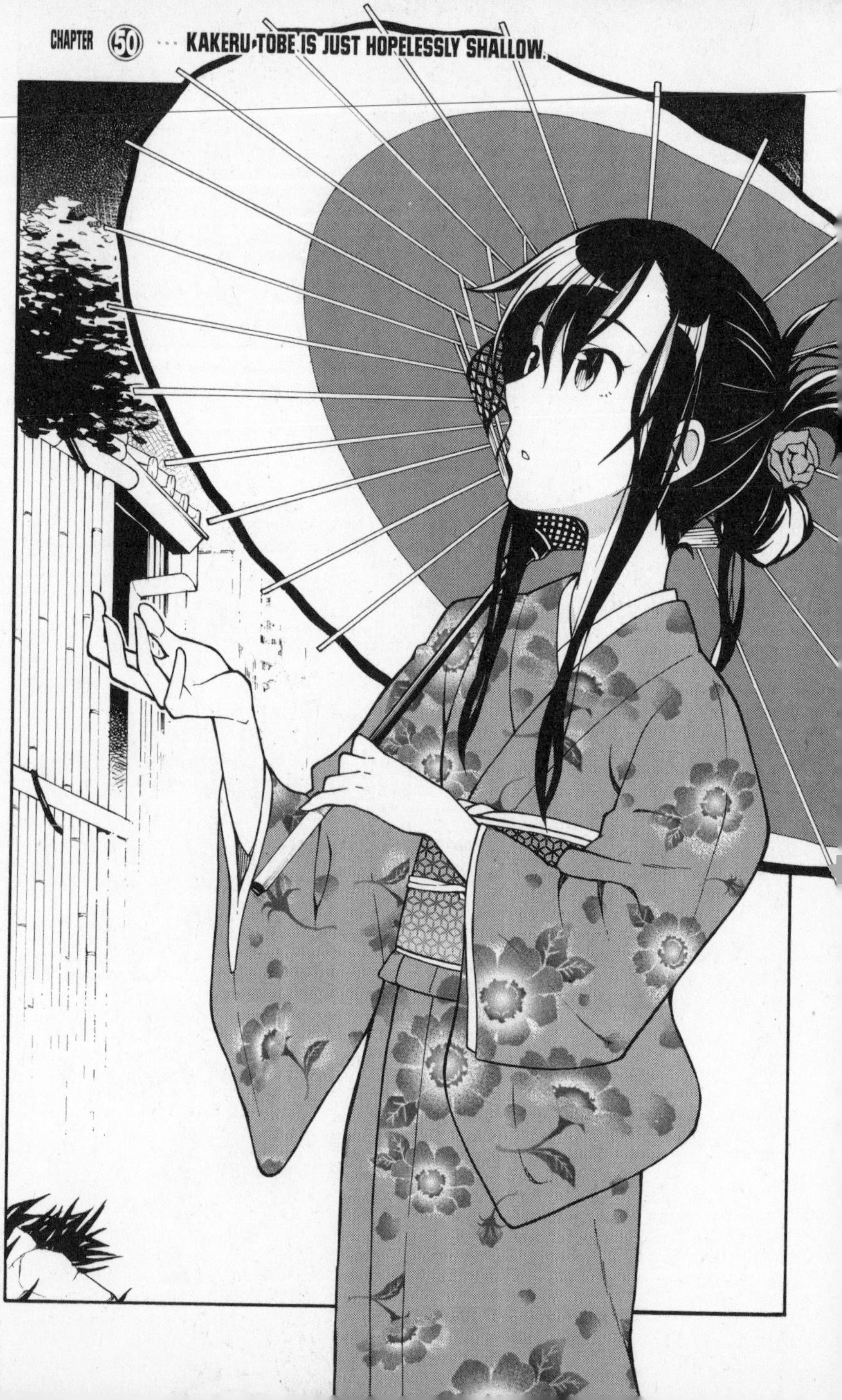

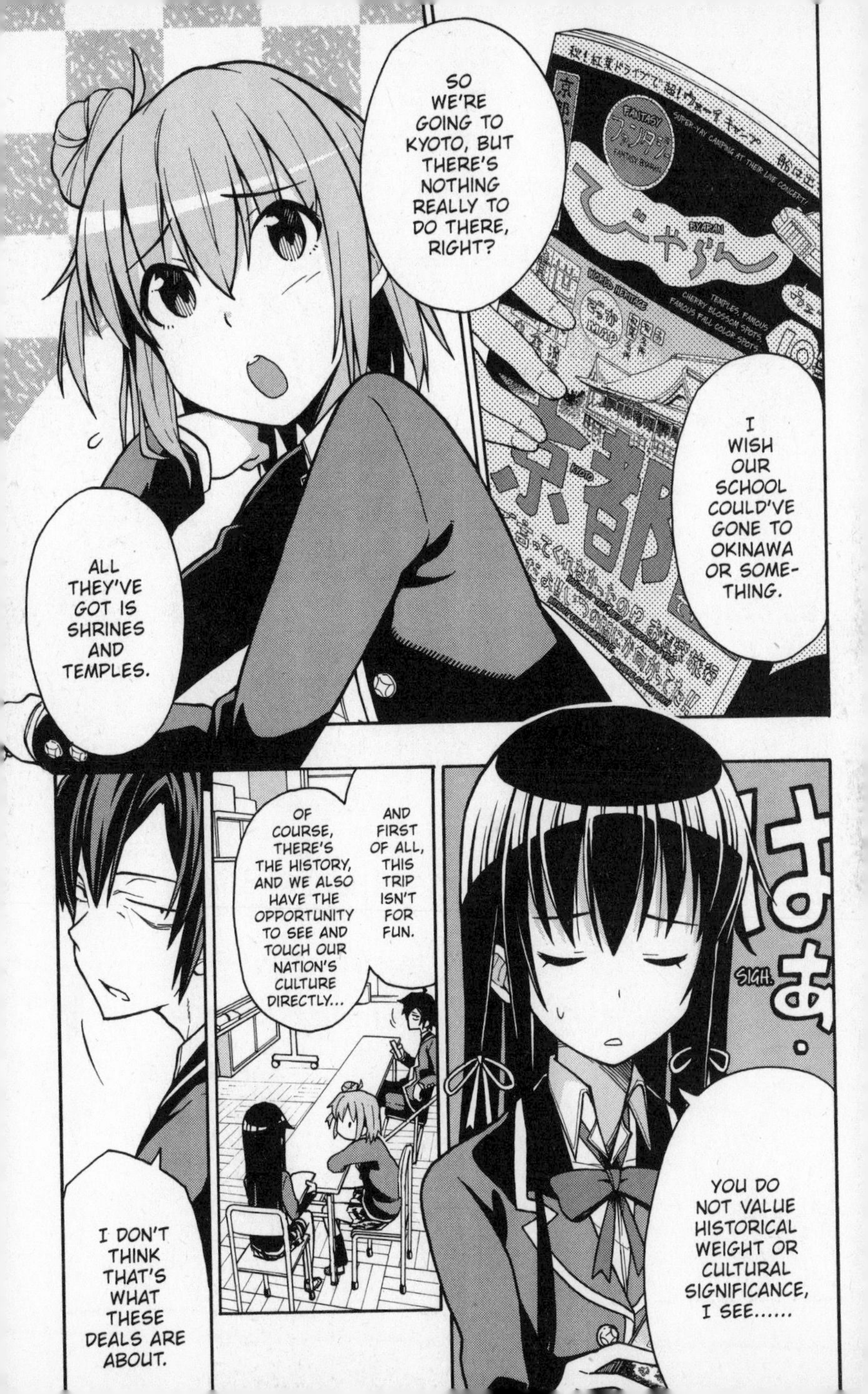
SO WE'RE GOING TO KYOTO, BUT THERE'S NOTHING REALLY TO DO THERE, RIGHT?
FANTASY
SUPER-YAY CAMPING AT THEIR LIVE CONCERT!
BYARAN
WORLD HERITAGE
TEMPLES, FAMOUS CHERRY BLOSSOM SPOTS, FAMOUS FALL COLOR SPOTS
KYOTO
I WISH OUR SCHOOL COULD'VE GONE TO OKINAWA OR SOME-THING.
ALL THEY'VE GOT IS SHRINES AND TEMPLES.
はぁ。
SIGH.
YOU DO NOT VALUE HISTORICAL WEIGHT OR CULTURAL SIGNIFICANCE, I SEE......
AND FIRST OF ALL, THIS TRIP ISN'T FOR FUN.
OF COURSE, THERE'S THE HISTORY, AND WE ALSO HAVE THE OPPORTUNITY TO SEE AND TOUCH OUR NATION'S CULTURE DIRECTLY...
I DON'T THINK THAT'S WHAT THESE DEALS ARE ABOUT.

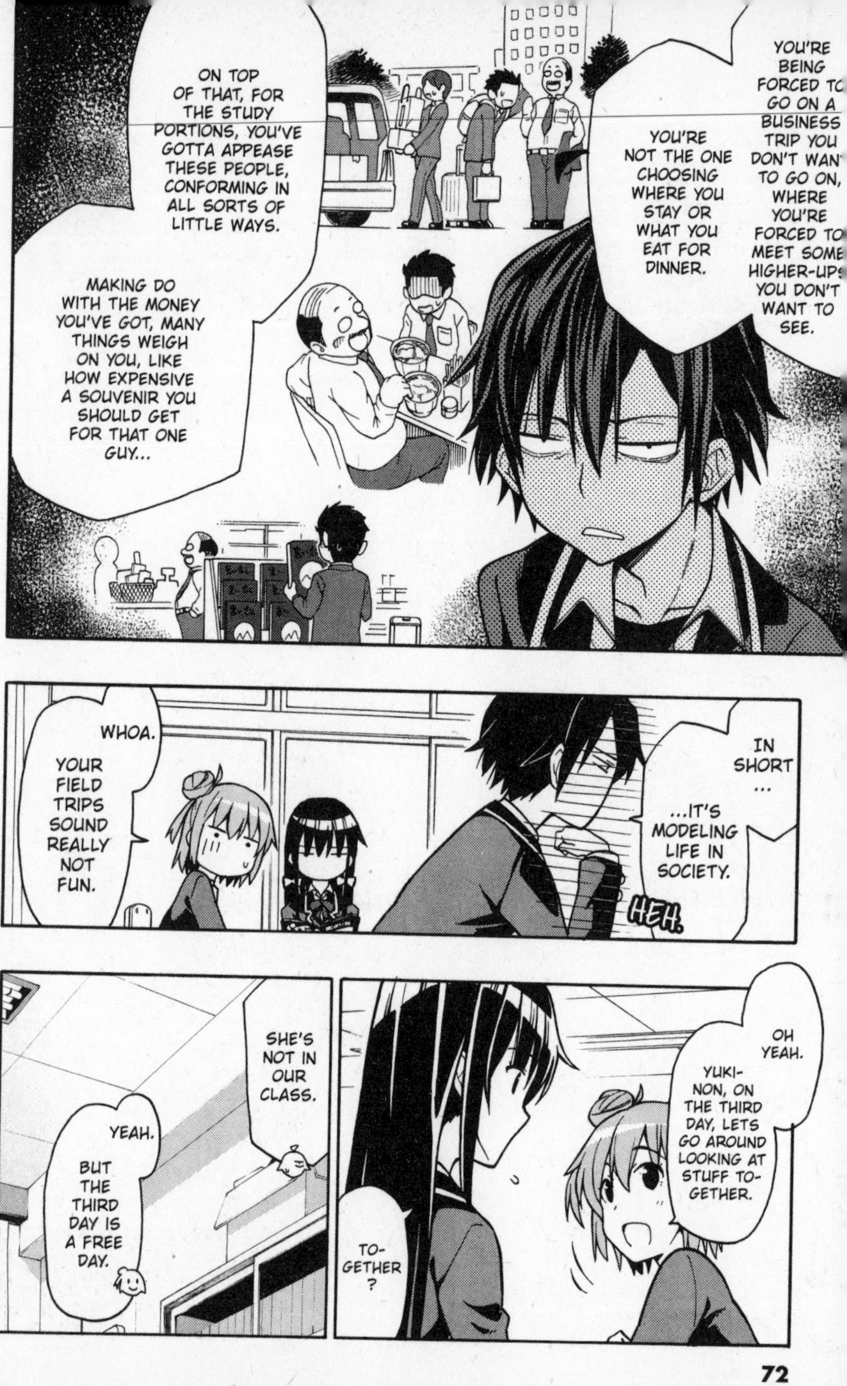
YOU'RE BEING FORCED TO GO ON A BUSINESS TRIP YOU DON'T WANT TO GO ON, WHERE YOU'RE FORCED TO MEET SOME HIGHER-UPS YOU DON'T WANT TO SEE.
YOU'RE NOT THE ONE CHOOSING WHERE YOU STAY OR WHAT YOU EAT FOR DINNER.
ON TOP OF THAT, FOR THE STUDY PORTIONS, YOU'VE GOTTA APPEASE THESE PEOPLE, CONFORMING IN ALL SORTS OF LITTLE WAYS.
MAKING DO WITH THE MONEY YOU'VE GOT, MANY THINGS WEIGH ON YOU, LIKE HOW EXPENSIVE A SOUVENIR YOU SHOULD GET FOR THAT ONE GUY...
IN SHORT...
...IT'S MODELING LIFE IN SOCIETY.
HEH.
WHOA.
YOUR FIELD TRIPS SOUND REALLY NOT FUN.
OH YEAH.
YUKI-NON, ON THE THIRD DAY, LETS GO AROUND LOOKING AT STUFF TO-GETHER.
TO-GETHER?
SHE'S NOT IN OUR CLASS.
YEAH.
BUT THE THIRD DAY IS A FREE DAY.

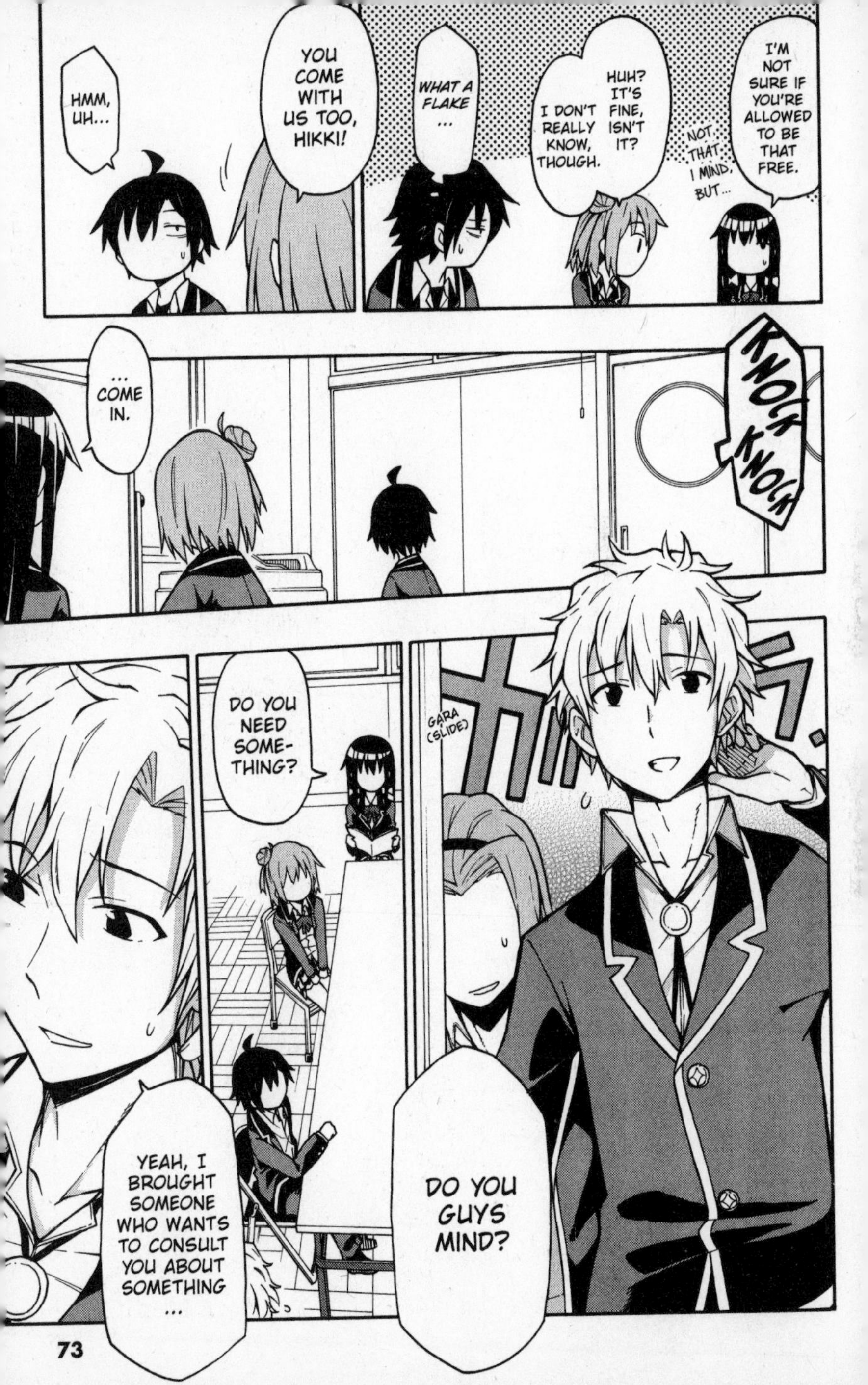
I'M NOT SURE IF YOU'RE ALLOWED TO BE THAT FREE.
NOT THAT I MIND, BUT...
HUH? IT'S FINE, ISN'T IT?
I DON'T REALLY KNOW, THOUGH.
WHAT A FLAKE...
YOU COME WITH US TOO, HIKKI!
HMM, UH...
KNOCK KNOCK
...COME IN.
GARA (SLIDE)
DO YOU GUYS MIND?
DO YOU NEED SOMETHING?
YEAH, I BROUGHT SOMEONE WHO WANTS TO CONSULT YOU ABOUT SOMETHING...

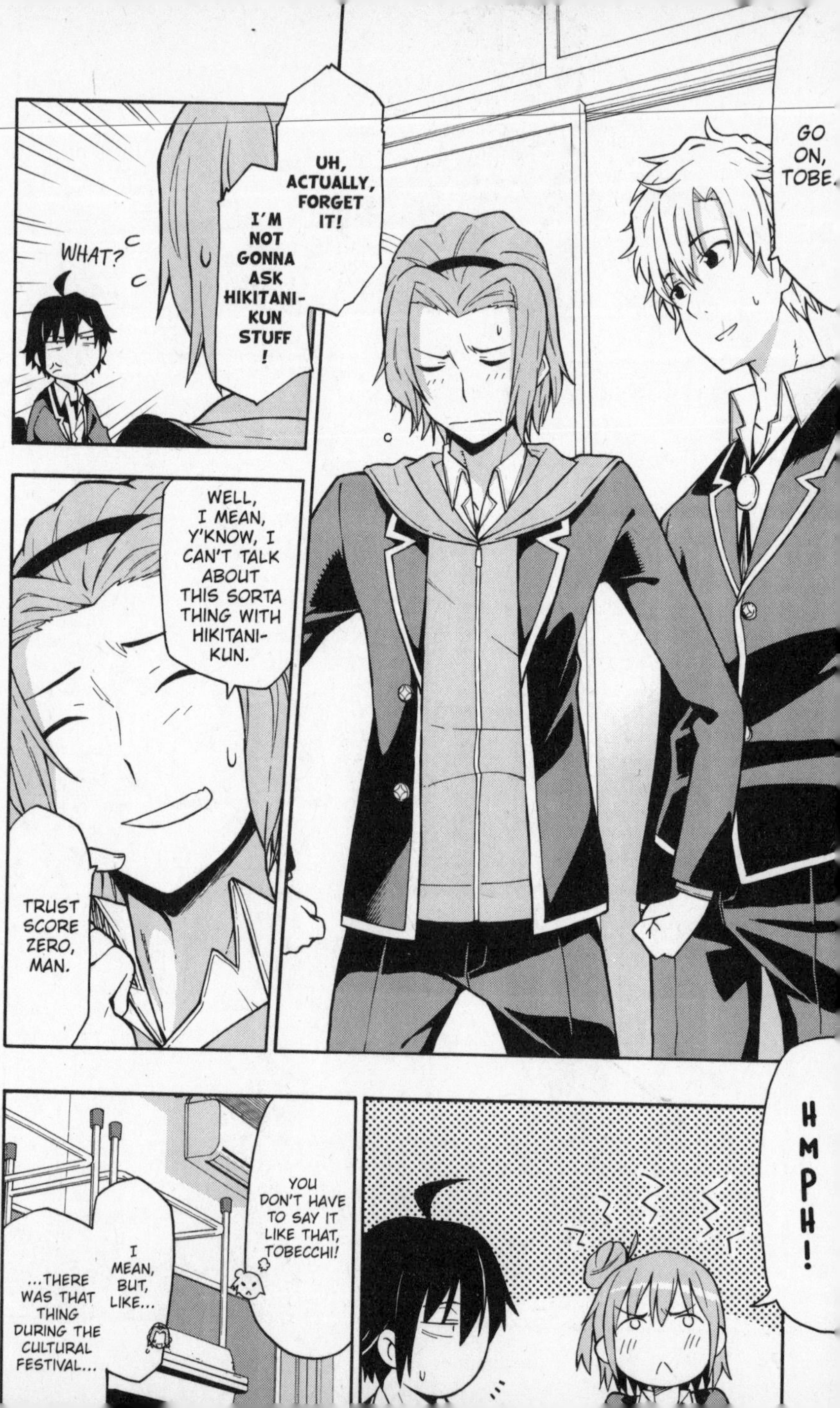
GO ON, TOBE.
UH, ACTUALLY, FORGET IT!
I'M NOT GONNA ASK HIKITANI-KUN STUFF!
WHAT?
WELL, I MEAN, Y'KNOW, I CAN'T TALK ABOUT THIS SORTA THING WITH HIKITANI-KUN.
TRUST SCORE ZERO, MAN.
HMPH!
YOU DON'T HAVE TO SAY IT LIKE THAT, TOBECCHI!
I MEAN, BUT, LIKE...
...THERE WAS THAT THING DURING THE CULTURAL FESTIVAL...

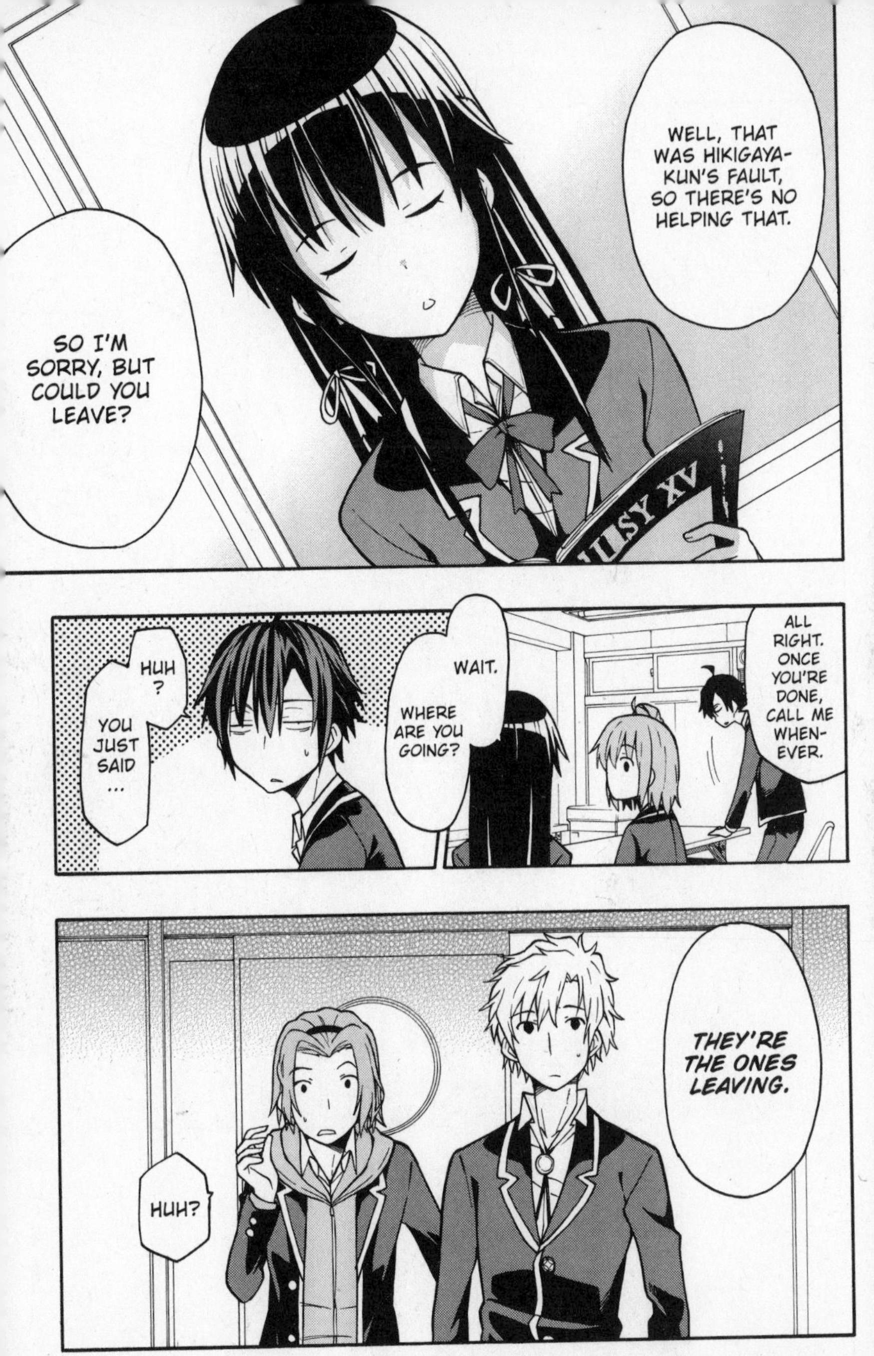
WELL, THAT WAS HIKIGAYA-KUN'S FAULT, SO THERE'S NO HELPING THAT.
SO I'M SORRY, BUT COULD YOU LEAVE?
ALL RIGHT. ONCE YOU'RE DONE, CALL ME WHEN-EVER.
WAIT.
WHERE ARE YOU GOING?
HUH?
YOU JUST SAID...
THEY'RE THE ONES LEAVING.
HUH?

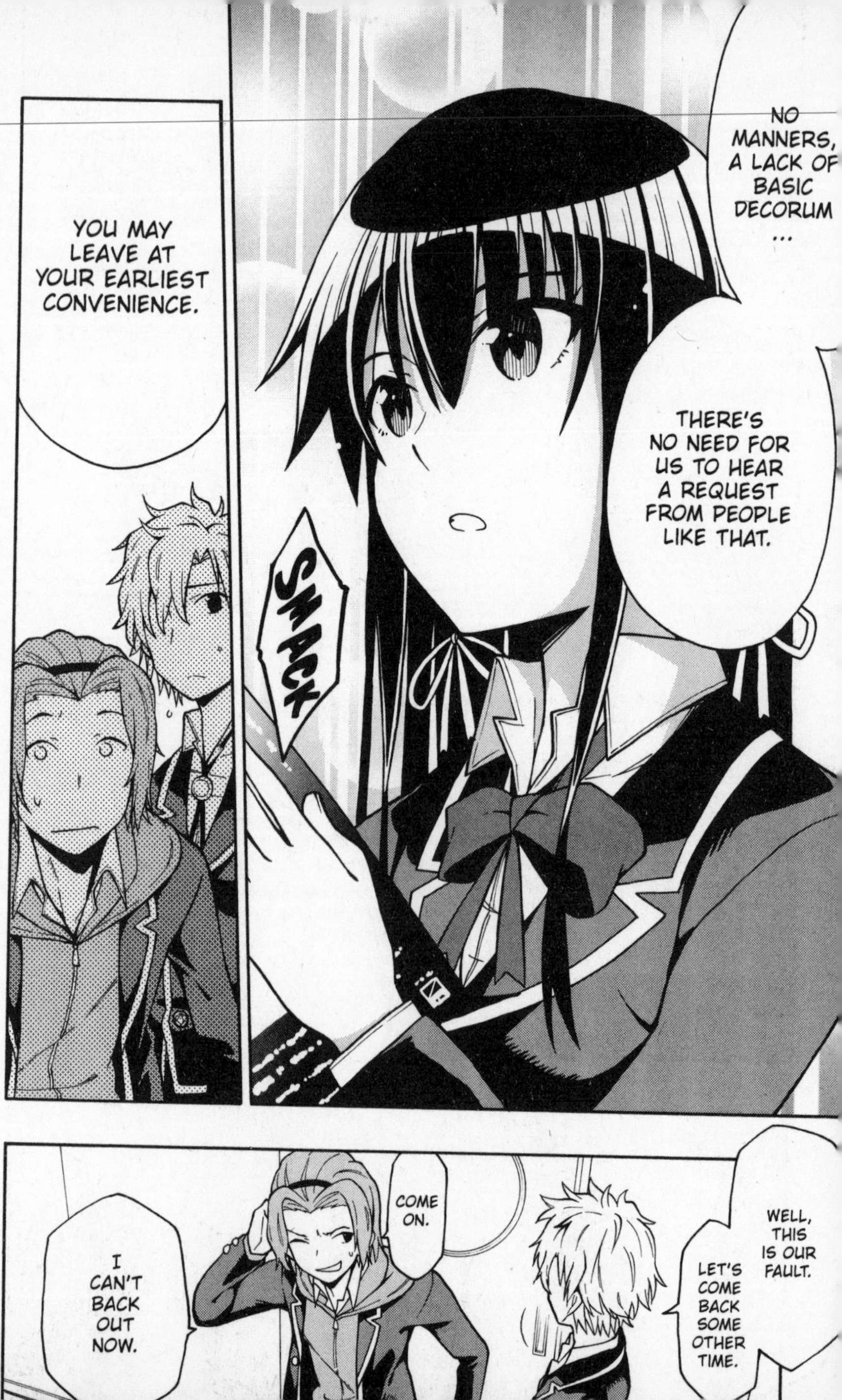
NO MANNERS, A LACK OF BASIC DECORUM ...
THERE'S NO NEED FOR US TO HEAR A REQUEST FROM PEOPLE LIKE THAT.
SMACK
YOU MAY LEAVE AT YOUR EARLIEST CONVENIENCE.
WELL, THIS IS OUR FAULT.
LET'S COME BACK SOME OTHER TIME.
COME ON.
I CAN'T BACK OUT NOW.

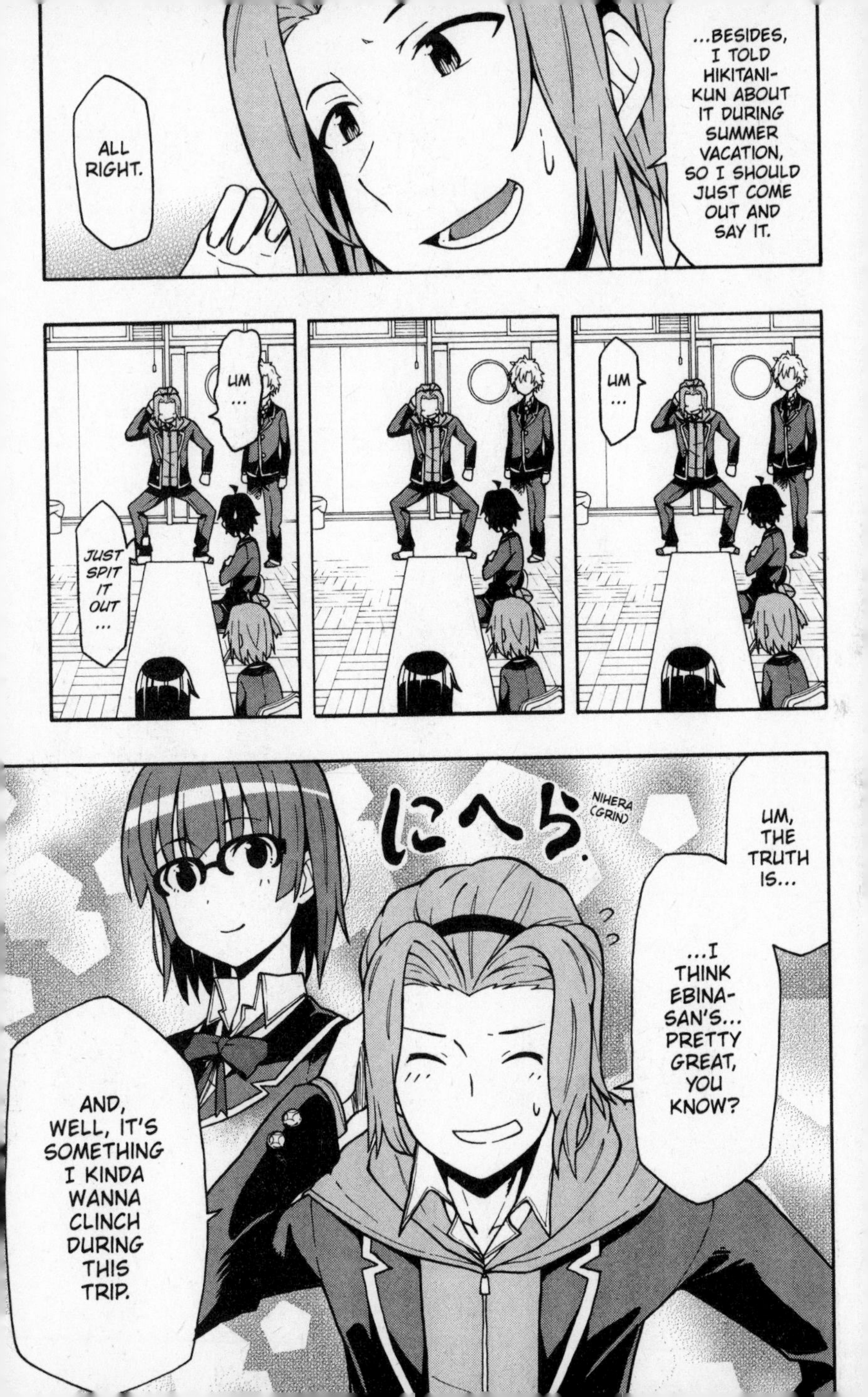
...BESIDES, I TOLD HIKITANI-KUN ABOUT IT DURING SUMMER VACATION, SO I SHOULD JUST COME OUT AND SAY IT.
ALL RIGHT.
UM ...
UM ...
JUST SPIT IT OUT ...
UM, THE TRUTH IS...
にへら
NIHERA (GRIN)
...I THINK EBINA-SAN'S... PRETTY GREAT, YOU KNOW?
AND, WELL, IT'S SOMETHING I KINDA WANNA CLINCH DURING THIS TRIP.

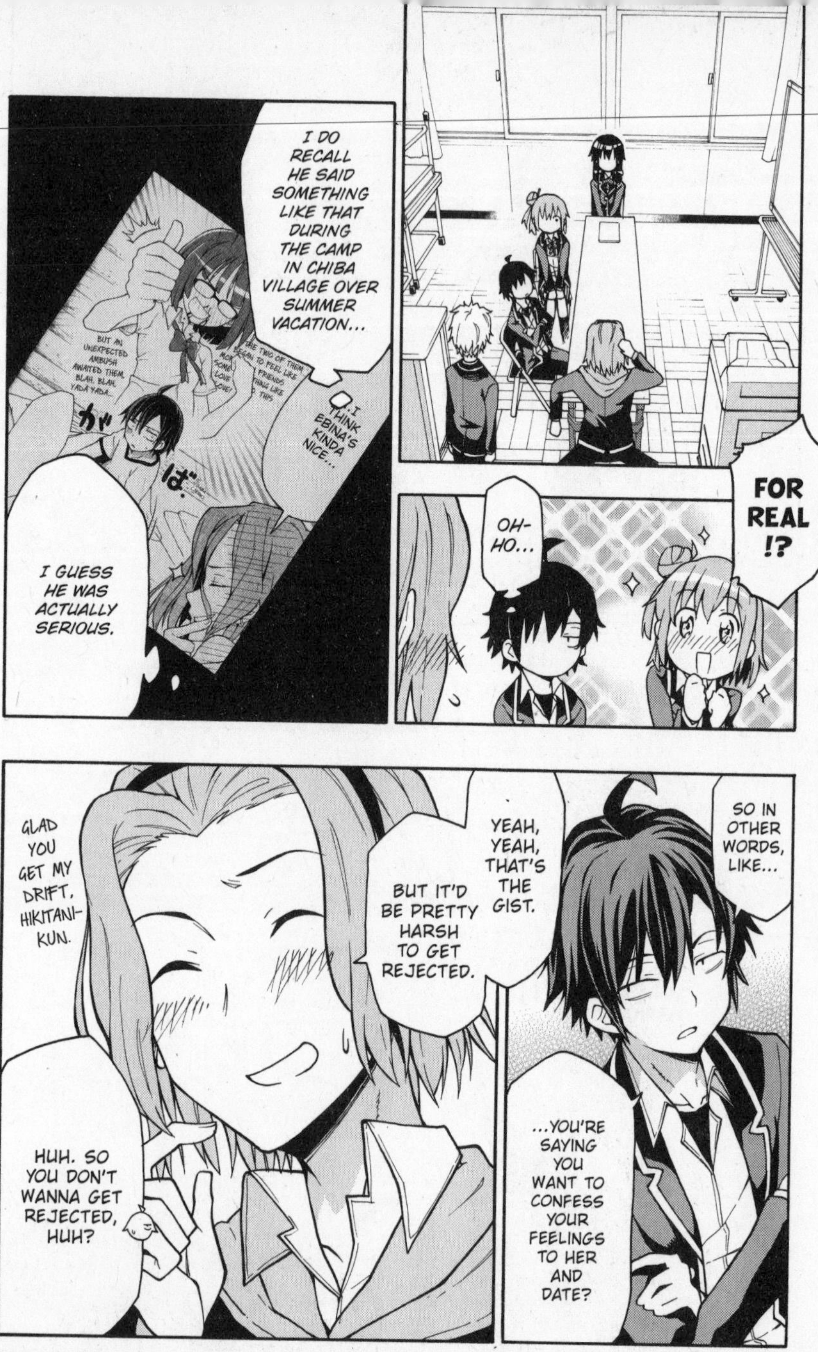
FOR REAL!?
OH-HO...
I DO RECALL HE SAID SOMETHING LIKE THAT DURING THE CAMP IN CHIBA VILLAGE OVER SUMMER VACATION...
...I THINK EBINA'S KINDA NICE...
THE TWO OF THEM BEGAN TO FEEL LIKE
SOME LOVE LOVE!
BUT AN UNEXPECTED AMBUSH AWAITED THEM. BLAH, BLAH, YADA YADA...
がば
I GUESS HE WAS ACTUALLY SERIOUS.
SO IN OTHER WORDS, LIKE...
...YOU'RE SAYING YOU WANT TO CONFESS YOUR FEELINGS TO HER AND DATE?
YEAH, YEAH, THAT'S THE GIST.
BUT IT'D BE PRETTY HARSH TO GET REJECTED.
GLAD YOU GET MY DRIFT, HIKITANI-KUN.
HUH. SO YOU DON'T WANNA GET REJECTED, HUH?

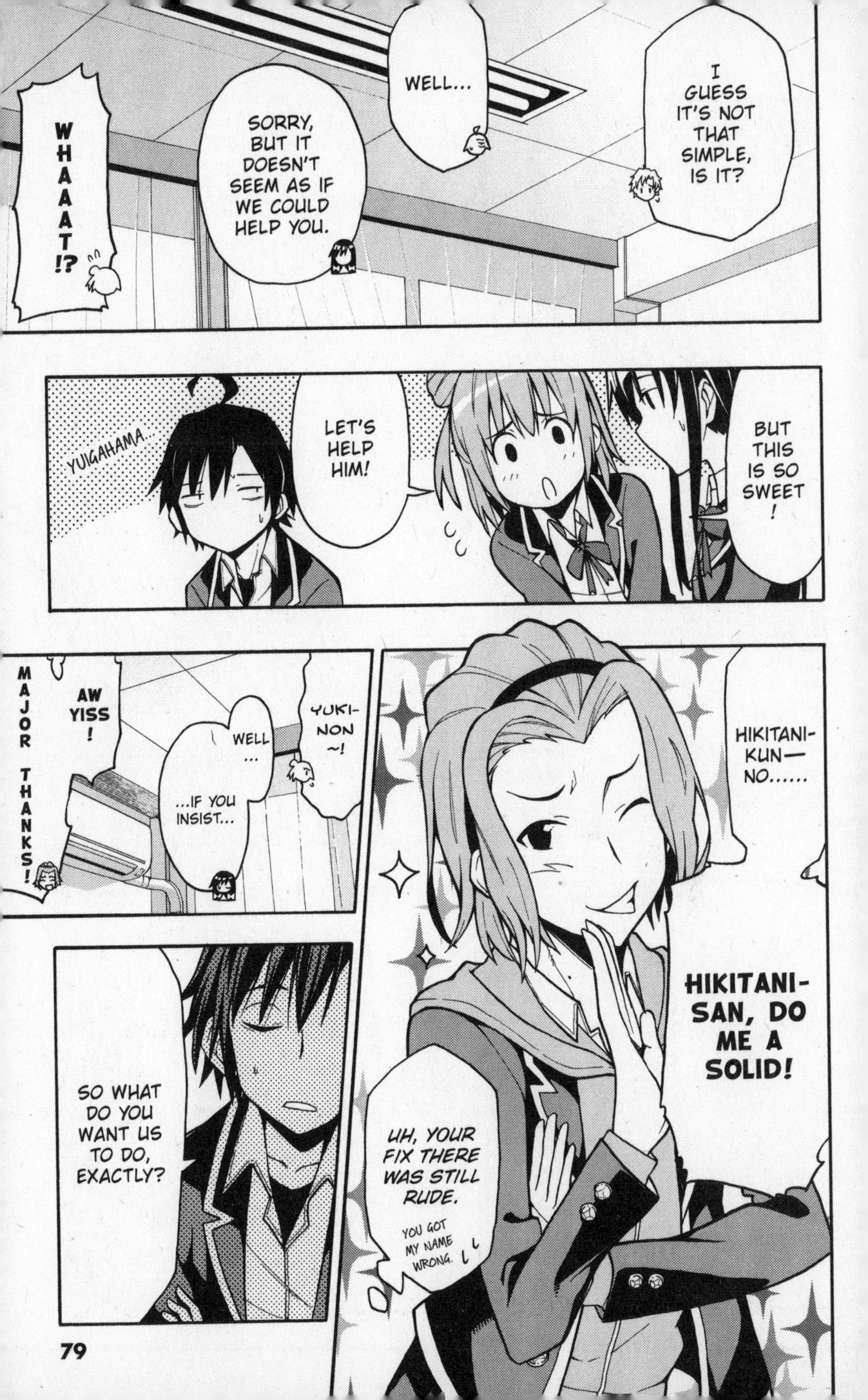
I GUESS IT'S NOT THAT SIMPLE, IS IT?
WELL...
SORRY, BUT IT DOESN'T SEEM AS IF WE COULD HELP YOU.
WHAAAAT!?
BUT THIS IS SO SWEET!
LET'S HELP HIM!
YUIGAHAMA...
HIKITANI-KUN—NO......
HIKITANI-SAN, DO ME A SOLID!
UH, YOUR FIX THERE WAS STILL RUDE.
YOU GOT MY NAME WRONG.
YUKI-NON~!
WELL...
...IF YOU INSIST...
AW YISS!
MAJOR THANKS!
SO WHAT DO YOU WANT US TO DO, EXACTLY?

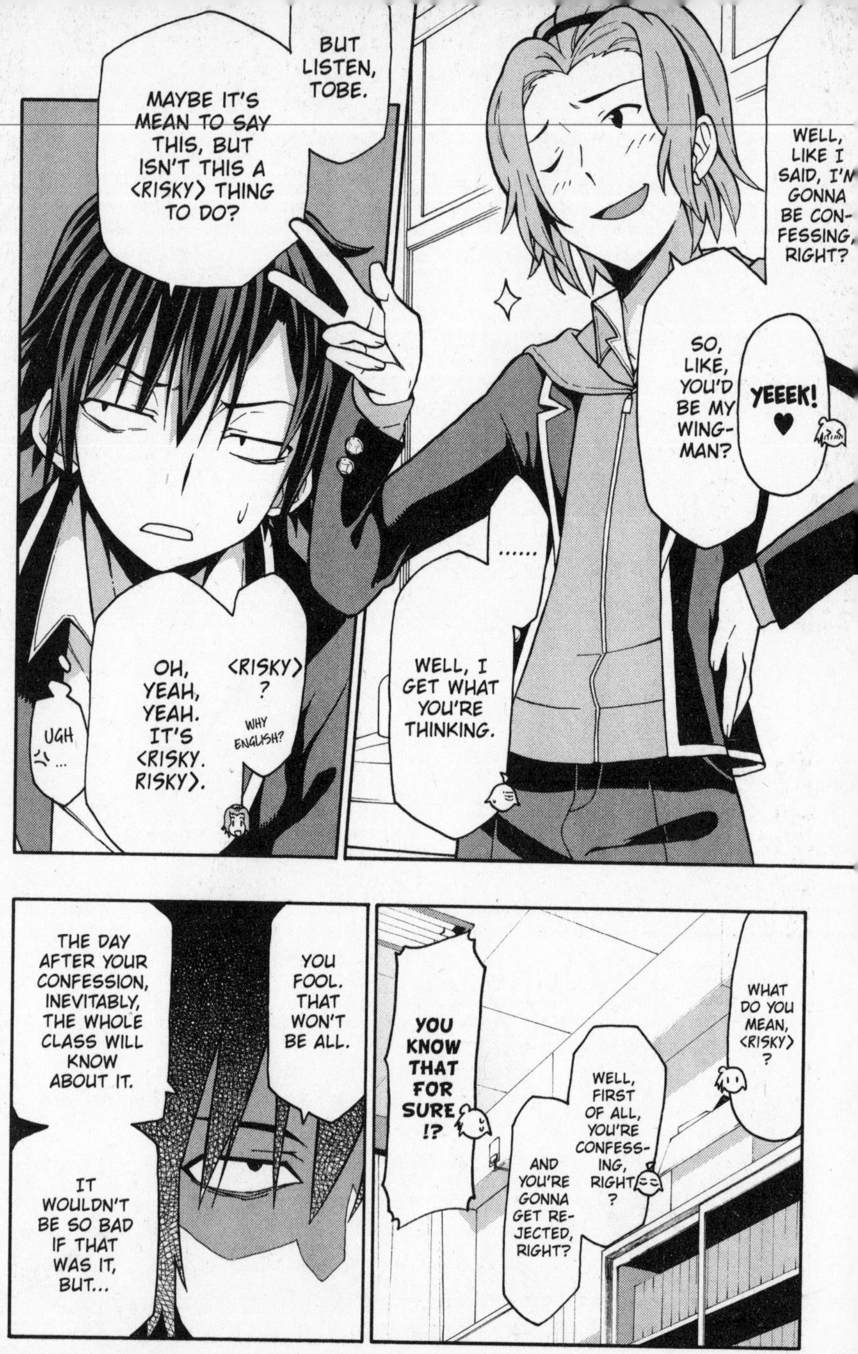
WELL, LIKE I SAID, I'M GONNA BE CONFESSING, RIGHT?
SO, LIKE, YOU'D BE MY WINGMAN?
YEEEK! ♥
BUT LISTEN, TOBE.
MAYBE IT'S MEAN TO SAY THIS, BUT ISN'T THIS A <RISKY> THING TO DO?
......
WELL, I GET WHAT YOU'RE THINKING.
<RISKY>?
WHY ENGLISH?
OH, YEAH, YEAH. IT'S <RISKY. RISKY>.
UGH ...
WHAT DO YOU MEAN, <RISKY>?
WELL, FIRST OF ALL, YOU'RE CONFESSING, RIGHT?
AND YOU'RE GONNA GET REJECTED, RIGHT?
YOU KNOW THAT FOR SURE!?
YOU FOOL. THAT WON'T BE ALL.
THE DAY AFTER YOUR CONFESSION, INEVITABLY, THE WHOLE CLASS WILL KNOW ABOUT IT.
IT WOULDN'T BE SO BAD IF THAT WAS IT, BUT...

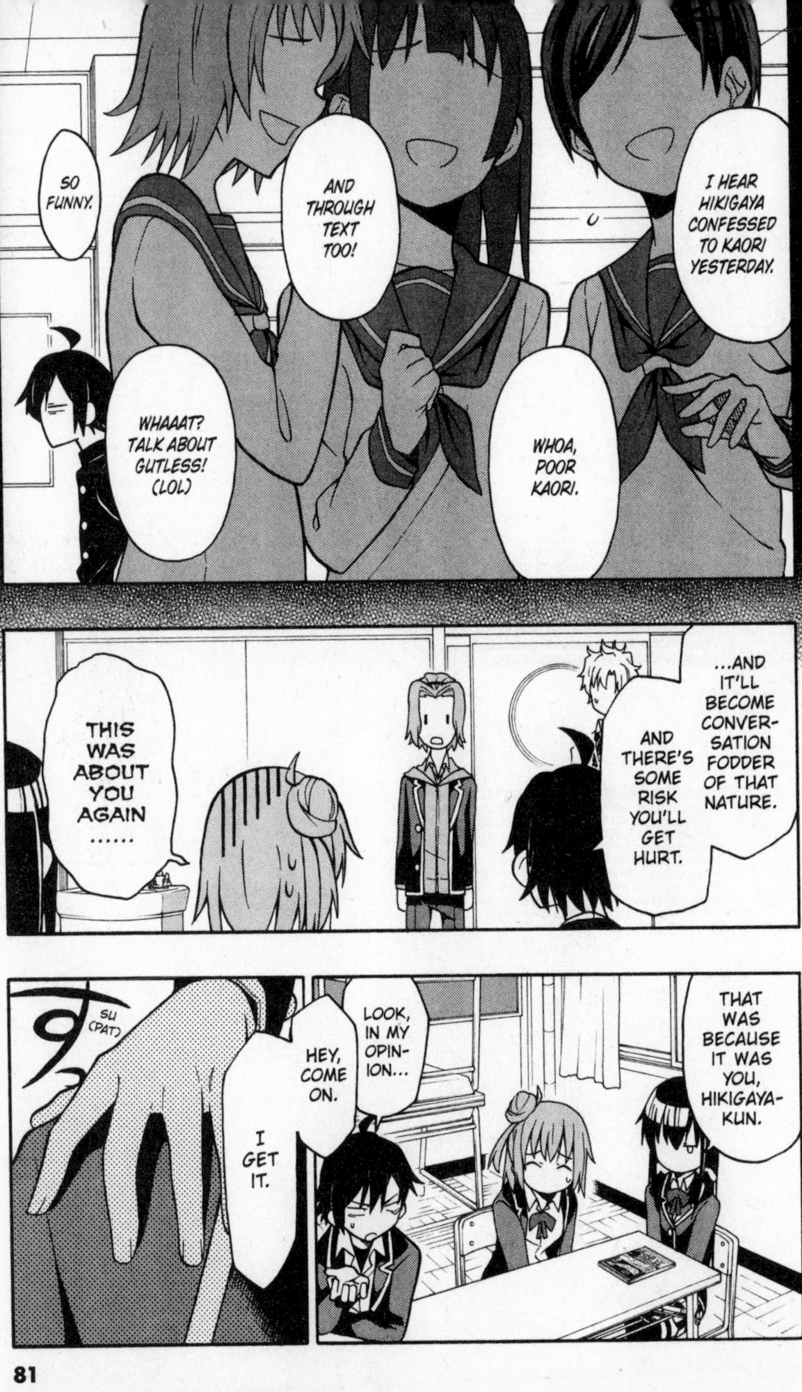
I HEAR HIKIGAYA CONFESSED TO KAORI YESTERDAY.
WHOA, POOR KAORI.
AND THROUGH TEXT TOO!
WHAAAT? TALK ABOUT GUTLESS! (LOL)
SO FUNNY.
...AND IT'LL BECOME CONVERSATION FODDER OF THAT NATURE.
AND THERE'S SOME RISK YOU'LL GET HURT.
THIS WAS ABOUT YOU AGAIN......
THAT WAS BECAUSE IT WAS YOU, HIKIGAYA-KUN.
LOOK, IN MY OPINION...
HEY, COME ON.
I GET IT.
SU (PAT)

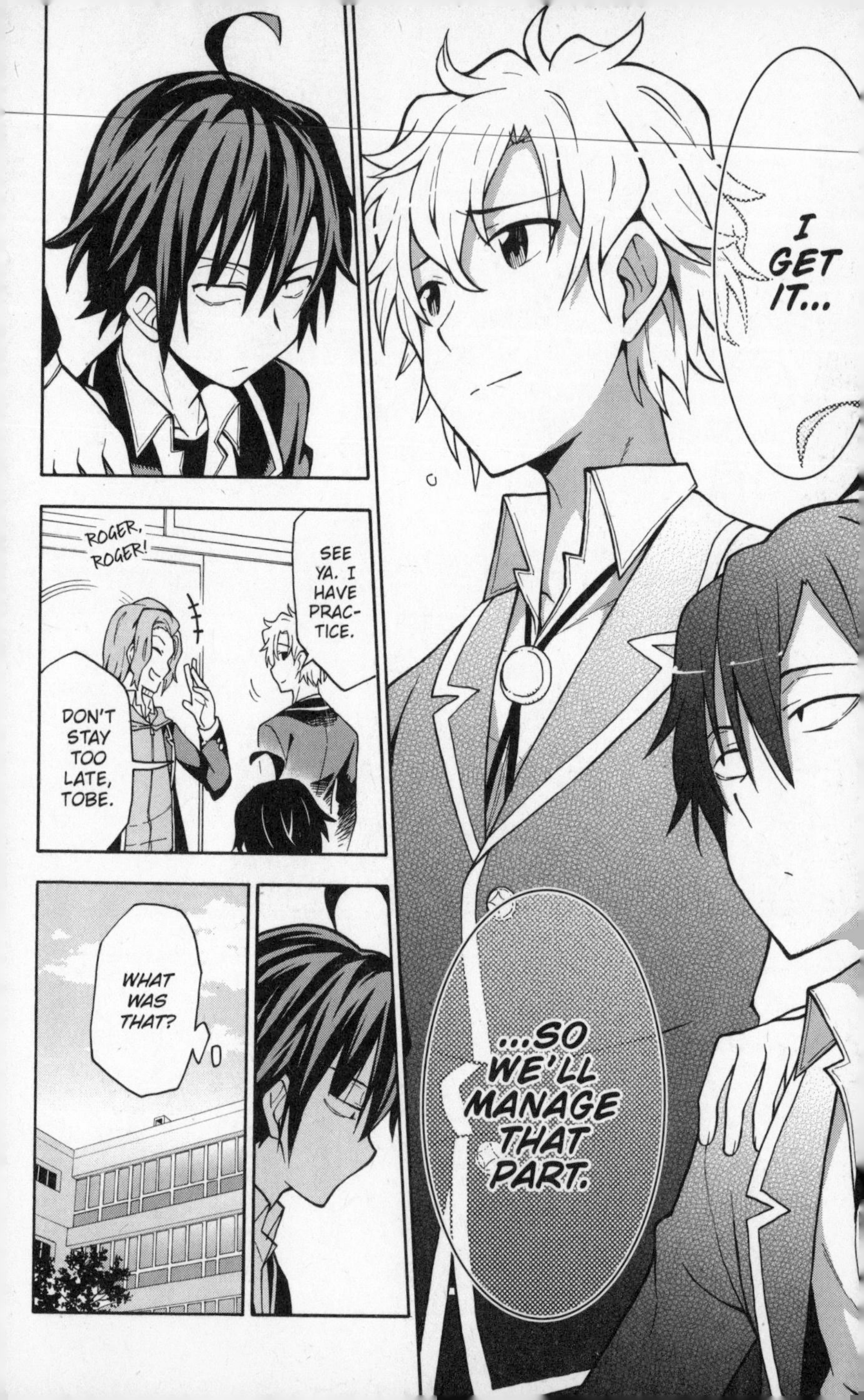
I GET IT...
...SO WE'LL MANAGE THAT PART.
SEE YA. I HAVE PRAC-TICE.
ROGER, ROGER!
DON'T STAY TOO LATE, TOBE.
WHAT WAS THAT?

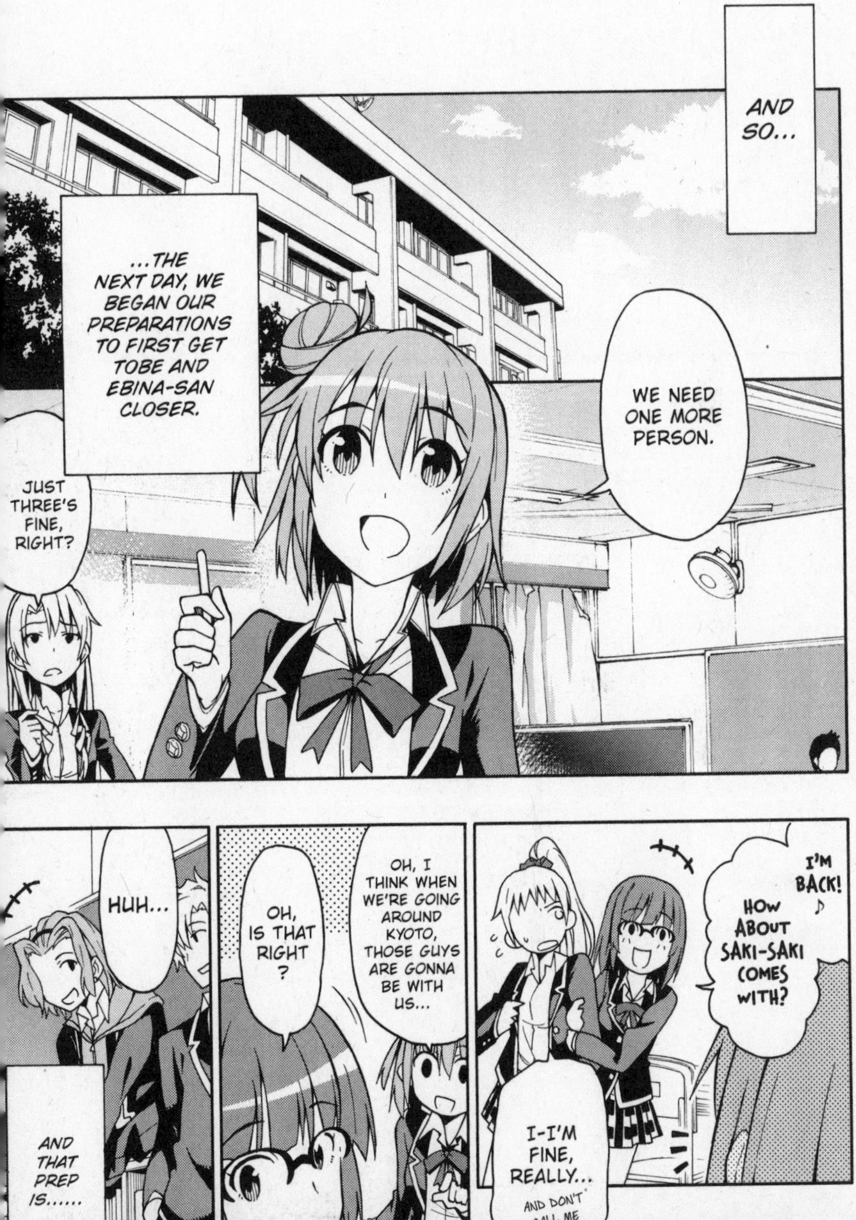
AND SO...
...THE NEXT DAY, WE BEGAN OUR PREPARATIONS TO FIRST GET TOBE AND EBINA-SAN CLOSER.
WE NEED ONE MORE PERSON.
JUST THREE'S FINE, RIGHT?
I'M BACK! ♪
HOW ABOUT SAKI-SAKI COMES WITH?
I-I'M FINE, REALLY...
AND DON'T CALL ME "SAKI-SAKI."
OH, I THINK WHEN WE'RE GOING AROUND KYOTO, THOSE GUYS ARE GONNA BE WITH US...
OH, IS THAT RIGHT?
HUH...
AND THAT PREP IS......

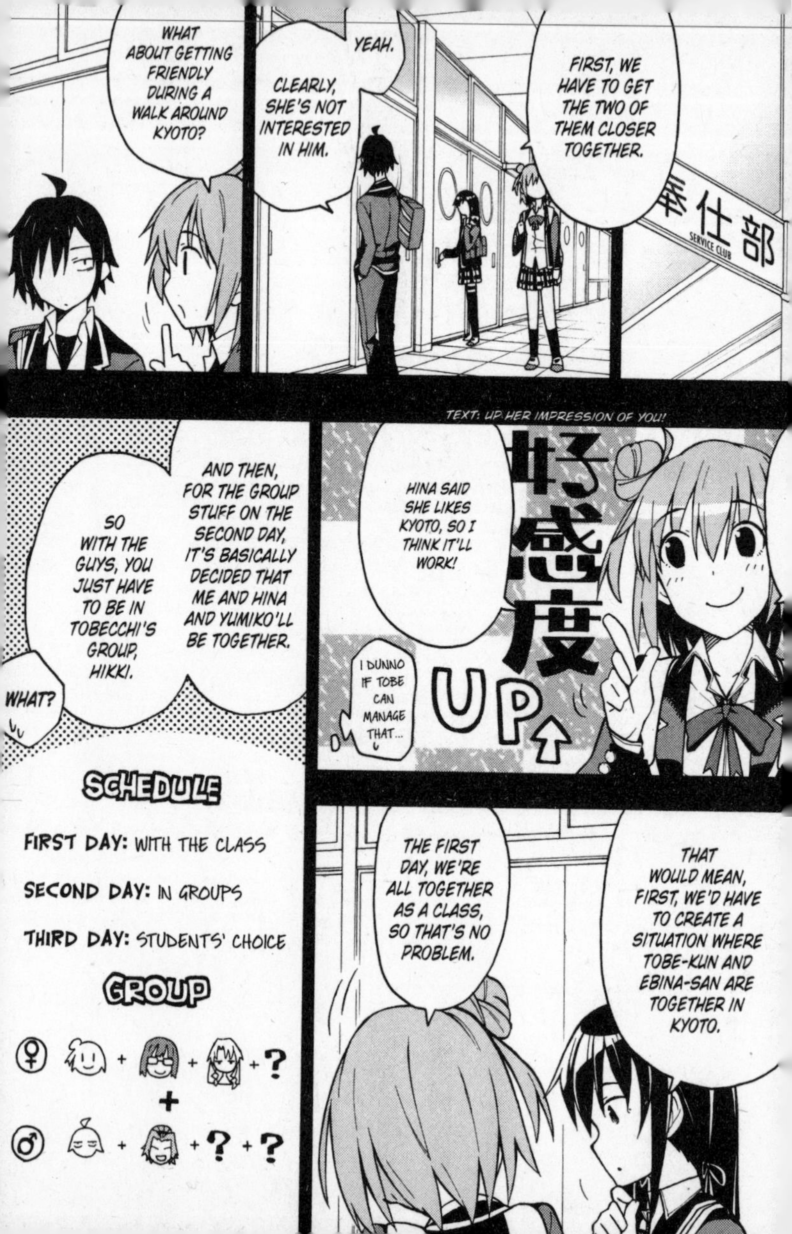
FIRST, WE HAVE TO GET THE TWO OF THEM CLOSER TOGETHER.
奉仕部
SERVICE CLUB
YEAH.
CLEARLY, SHE'S NOT INTERESTED IN HIM.
WHAT ABOUT GETTING FRIENDLY DURING A WALK AROUND KYOTO?
TEXT: UP HER IMPRESSION OF YOU!
好感度 UP
HINA SAID SHE LIKES KYOTO, SO I THINK IT'LL WORK!
I DUNNO IF TOBE CAN MANAGE THAT...
AND THEN, FOR THE GROUP STUFF ON THE SECOND DAY, IT'S BASICALLY DECIDED THAT ME AND HINA AND YUMIKO'LL BE TOGETHER.
SO WITH THE GUYS, YOU JUST HAVE TO BE IN TOBECCHI'S GROUP, HIKKI.
WHAT?
THAT WOULD MEAN, FIRST, WE'D HAVE TO CREATE A SITUATION WHERE TOBE-KUN AND EBINA-SAN ARE TOGETHER IN KYOTO.
THE FIRST DAY, WE'RE ALL TOGETHER AS A CLASS, SO THAT'S NO PROBLEM.
SCHEDULE
FIRST DAY: WITH THE CLASS
SECOND DAY: IN GROUPS
THIRD DAY: STUDENTS' CHOICE
GROUP
♀ + + + ?
+
♂ + + ? + ?

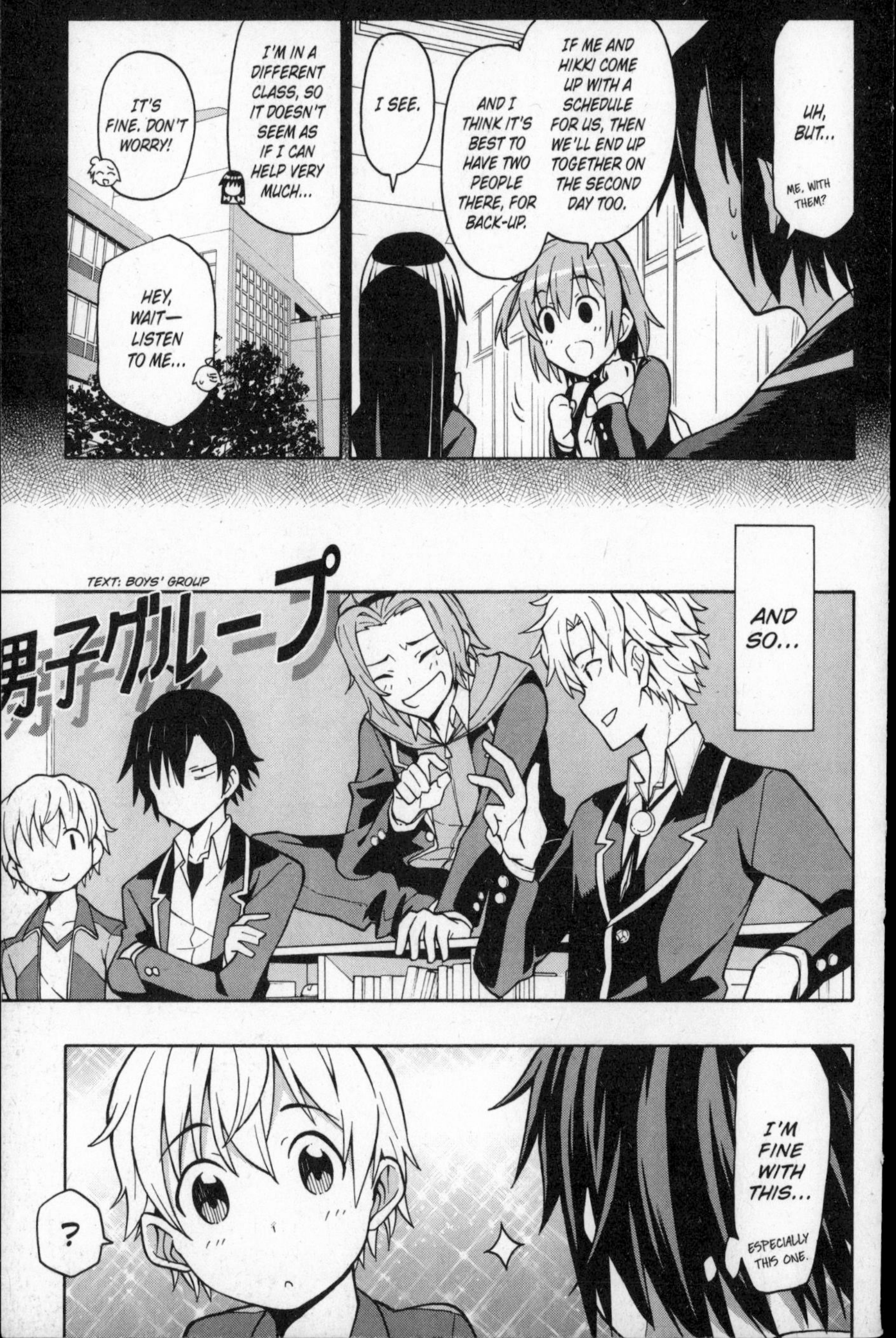
UH, BUT...
ME, WITH THEM?
IF ME AND HIKKI COME UP WITH A SCHEDULE FOR US, THEN WE'LL END UP TOGETHER ON THE SECOND DAY TOO.
AND I THINK IT'S BEST TO HAVE TWO PEOPLE THERE, FOR BACK-UP.
I SEE.
I'M IN A DIFFERENT CLASS, SO IT DOESN'T SEEM AS IF I CAN HELP VERY MUCH...
IT'S FINE. DON'T WORRY!
HEY, WAIT— LISTEN TO ME...
AND SO...
男子グループ
TEXT: BOYS' GROUP
I'M FINE WITH THIS...
ESPECIALLY THIS ONE.
?

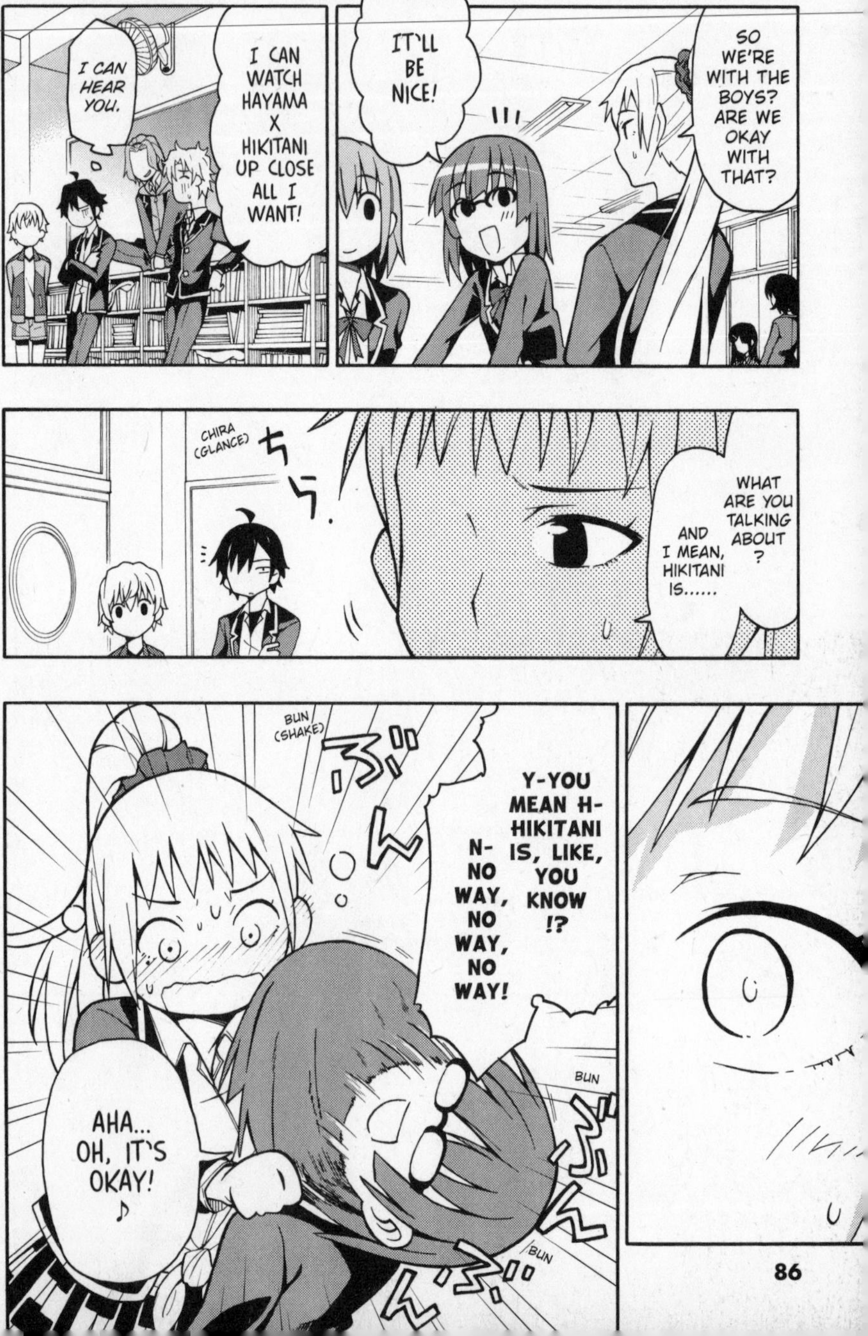
SO WE'RE WITH THE BOYS? ARE WE OKAY WITH THAT?
IT'LL BE NICE!
I CAN WATCH HAYAMA X HIKITANI UP CLOSE ALL I WANT!
I CAN HEAR YOU.
WHAT ARE YOU TALKING ABOUT?
AND I MEAN, HIKITANI IS......
CHIRA (GLANCE)
Y-YOU MEAN H-HIKITANI IS, LIKE, YOU KNOW!?
N-NO WAY, NO WAY, NO WAY!
BUN (SHAKE)
BUN
BUN
AHA... OH, IT'S OKAY! ♪

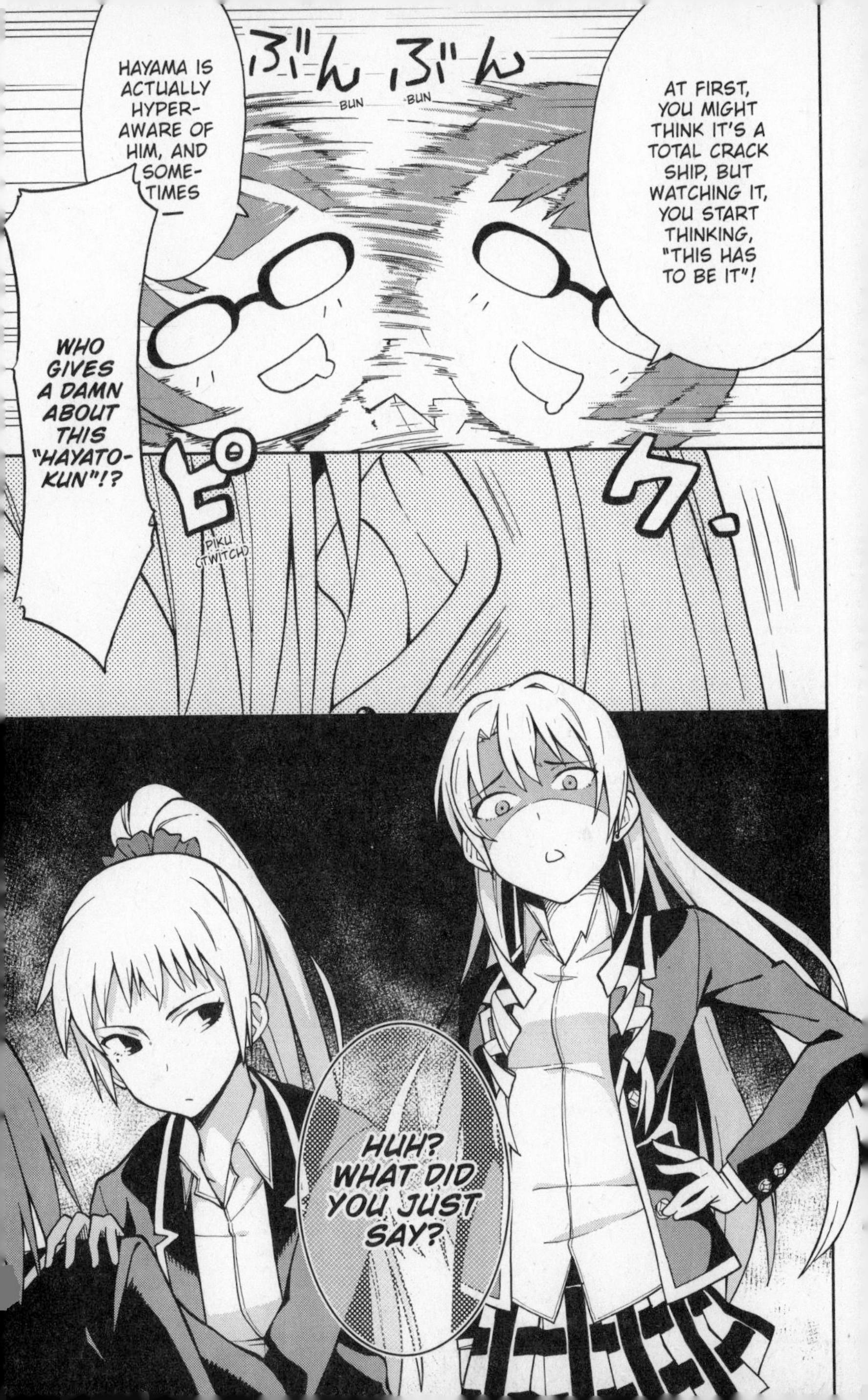
AT FIRST, YOU MIGHT THINK IT'S A TOTAL CRACK SHIP, BUT WATCHING IT, YOU START THINKING, "THIS HAS TO BE IT"!
ぶんぶん
BUN BUN
HAYAMA IS ACTUALLY HYPER-AWARE OF HIM, AND SOME-TIMES—
ピク
PIKU (TWITCH)
WHO GIVES A DAMN ABOUT THIS "HAYATO-KUN"!?
HUH? WHAT DID YOU JUST SAY?

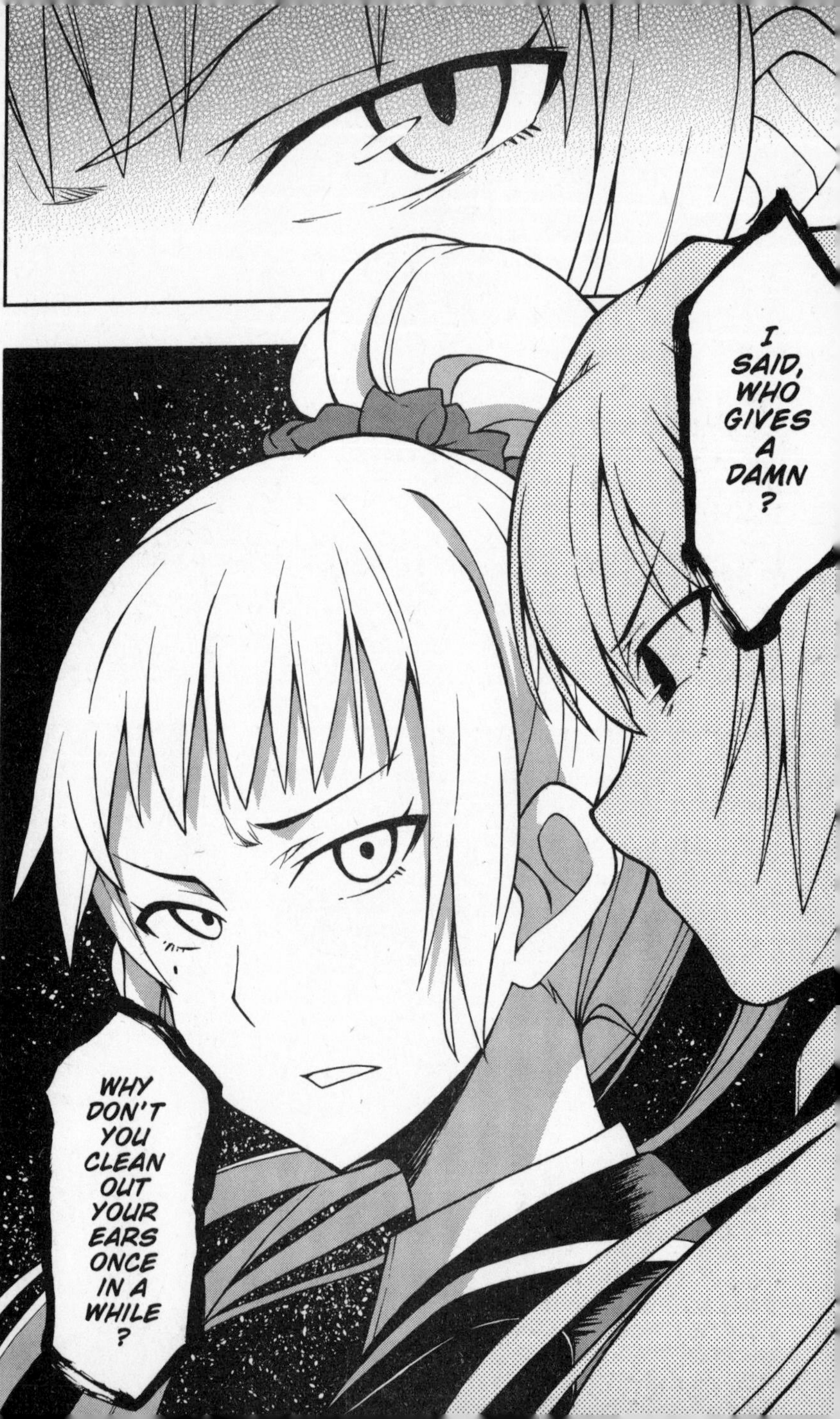
I SAID, WHO GIVES A DAMN ?
WHY DON'T YOU CLEAN OUT YOUR EARS ONCE IN A WHILE ?

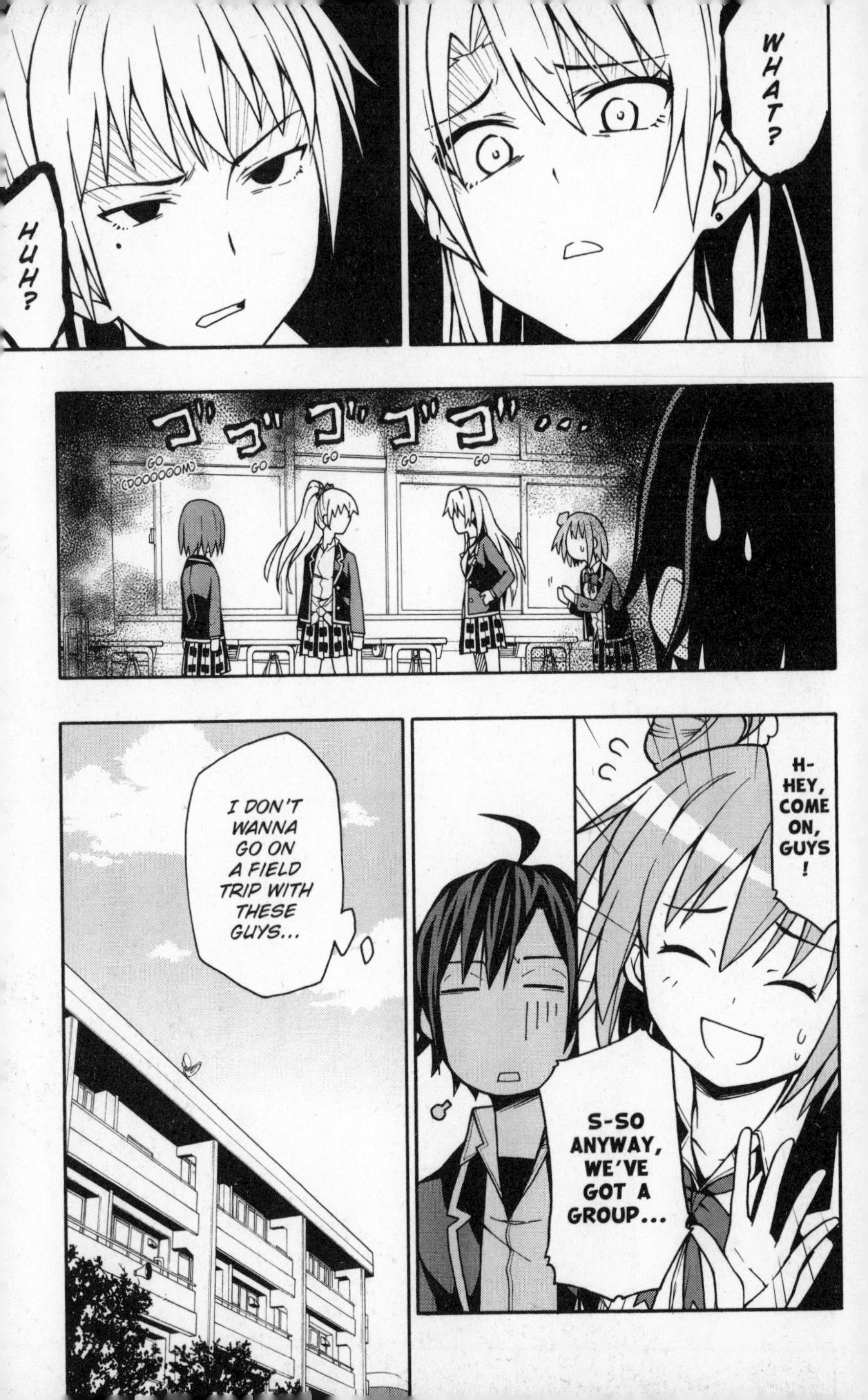
WHAT?
HUH?
ゴゴゴゴゴ...
GO GO GO GO GO (DOOOOOOM)
H-HEY, COME ON, GUYS!
S-SO ANYWAY, WE'VE GOT A GROUP...
I DON'T WANNA GO ON A FIELD TRIP WITH THESE GUYS...

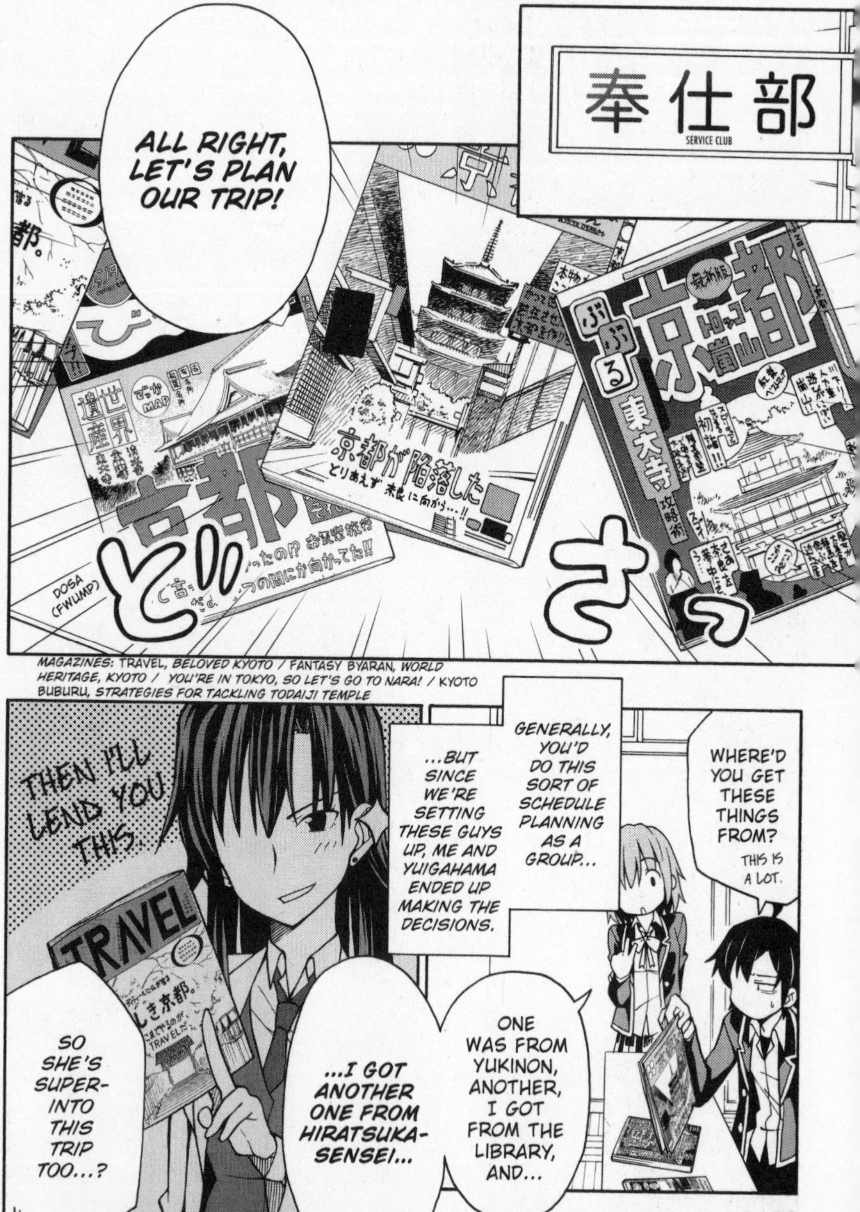
奉仕部
SERVICE CLUB
ALL RIGHT, LET'S PLAN OUR TRIP!
京都が陥落した
とりあえず奈良に向かう…!!
DOSA (FWUMP)
MAGAZINES: TRAVEL, BELOVED KYOTO / FANTASY BYARAN, WORLD HERITAGE, KYOTO / YOU'RE IN TOKYO, SO LET'S GO TO NARA! / KYOTO BUBURU, STRATEGIES FOR TACKLING TODAIJI TEMPLE
WHERE'D YOU GET THESE THINGS FROM?
THIS IS A LOT.
GENERALLY, YOU'D DO THIS SORT OF SCHEDULE PLANNING AS A GROUP...
...BUT SINCE WE'RE SETTING THESE GUYS UP, ME AND YUIGAHAMA ENDED UP MAKING THE DECISIONS.
ONE WAS FROM YUKINON, ANOTHER, I GOT FROM THE LIBRARY, AND...
...I GOT ANOTHER ONE FROM HIRATSUKA-SENSEI...
THEN I'LL LEND YOU THIS.
TRAVEL
SO SHE'S SUPER-INTO THIS TRIP TOO...?

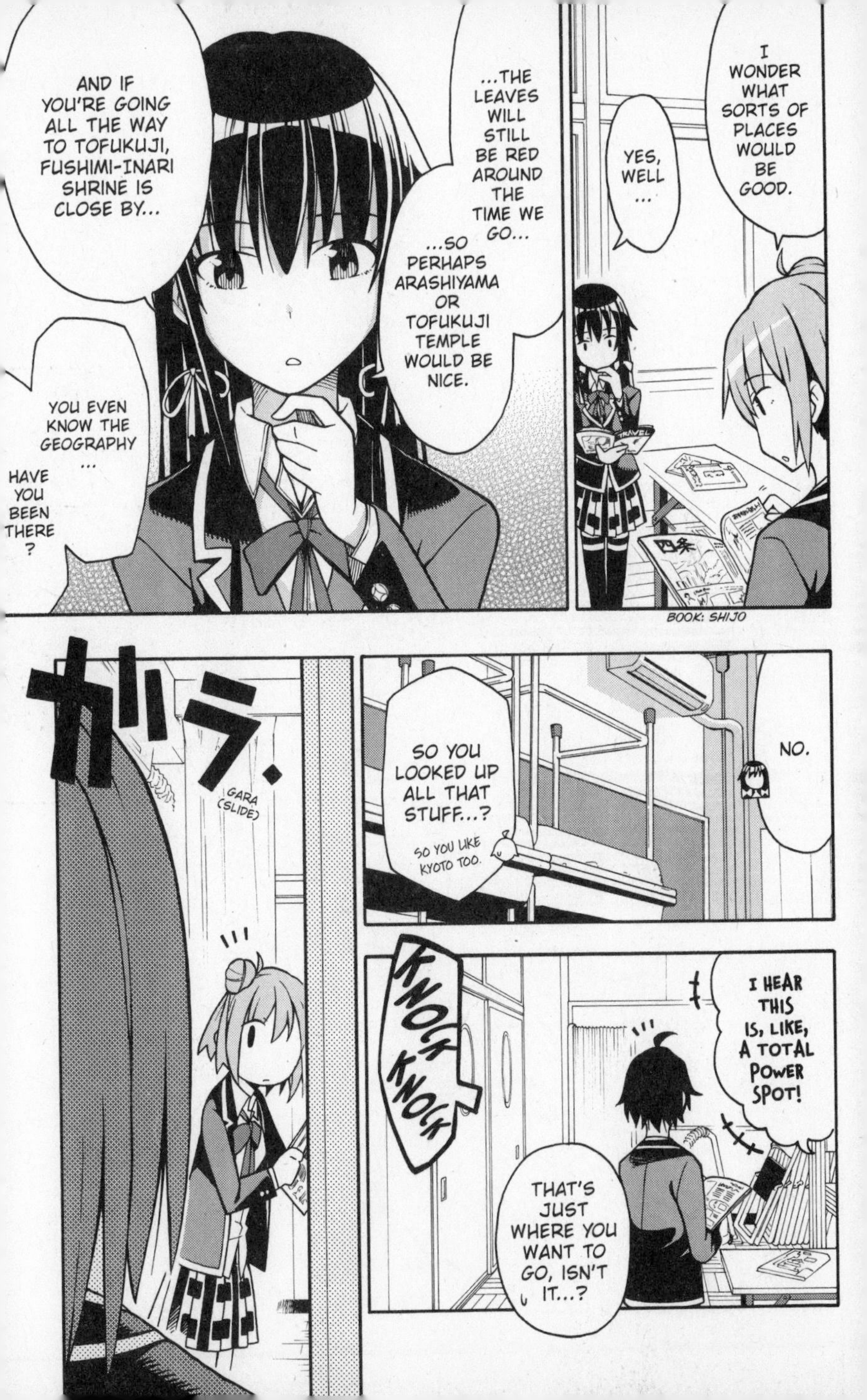
I WONDER WHAT SORTS OF PLACES WOULD BE GOOD.
YES, WELL...
BOOK: SHIJO
...THE LEAVES WILL STILL BE RED AROUND THE TIME WE GO...
...SO PERHAPS ARASHIYAMA OR TOFUKUJI TEMPLE WOULD BE NICE.
AND IF YOU'RE GOING ALL THE WAY TO TOFUKUJI, FUSHIMI-INARI SHRINE IS CLOSE BY...
YOU EVEN KNOW THE GEOGRAPHY...
HAVE YOU BEEN THERE?
NO.
SO YOU LOOKED UP ALL THAT STUFF...?
SO YOU LIKE KYOTO TOO.
I HEAR THIS IS, LIKE, A TOTAL POWER SPOT!
THAT'S JUST WHERE YOU WANT TO GO, ISN'T IT...?
KNOCK KNOCK
ガラ.
GARA (SLIDE)

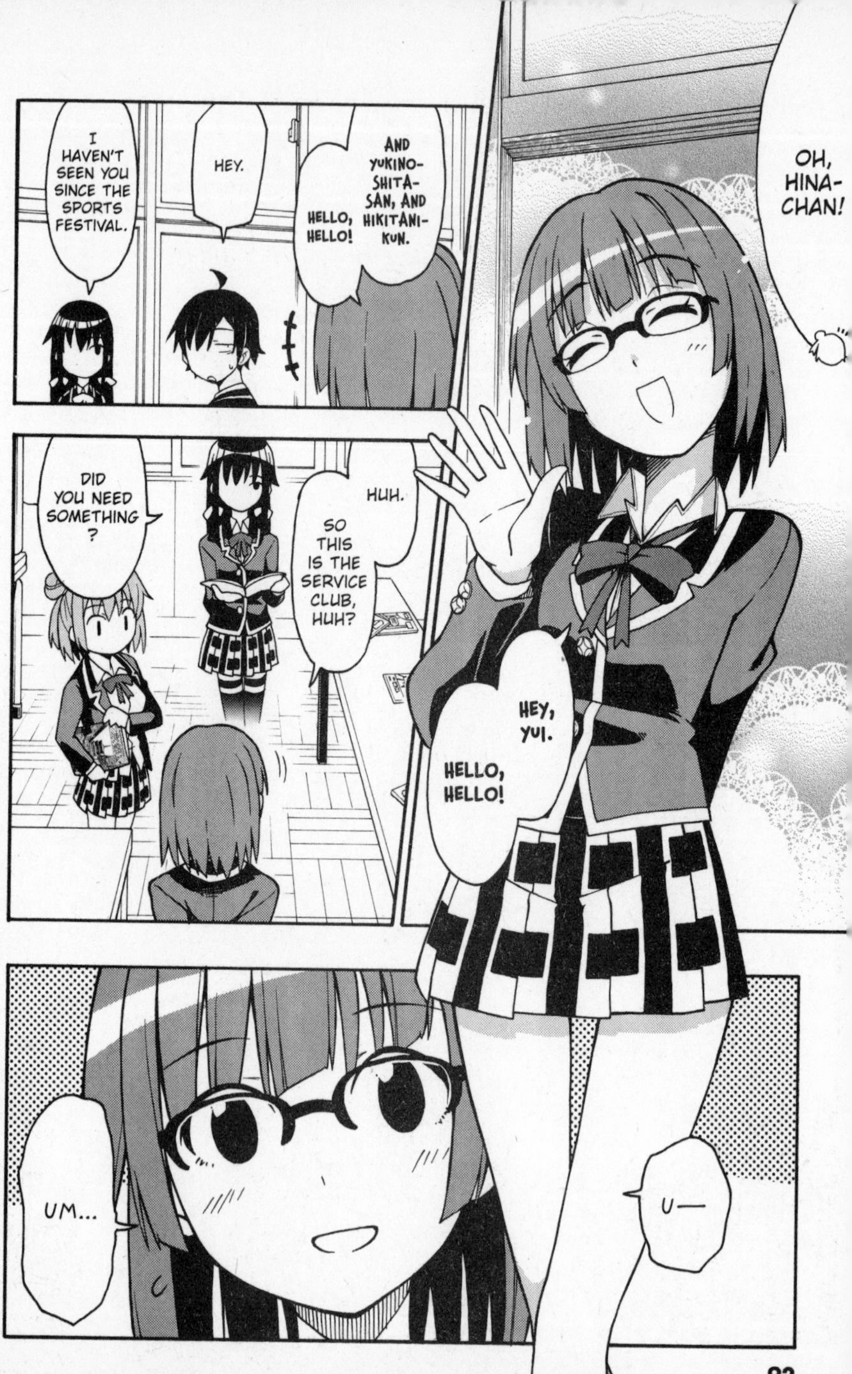
OH, HINA-CHAN!
HEY, YUI.
HELLO, HELLO!
AND YUKINO-SHITA-SAN, AND HIKITANI-KUN.
HELLO, HELLO!
HEY.
I HAVEN'T SEEN YOU SINCE THE SPORTS FESTIVAL.
HUH.
SO THIS IS THE SERVICE CLUB, HUH?
DID YOU NEED SOMETHING?
U—
UM...

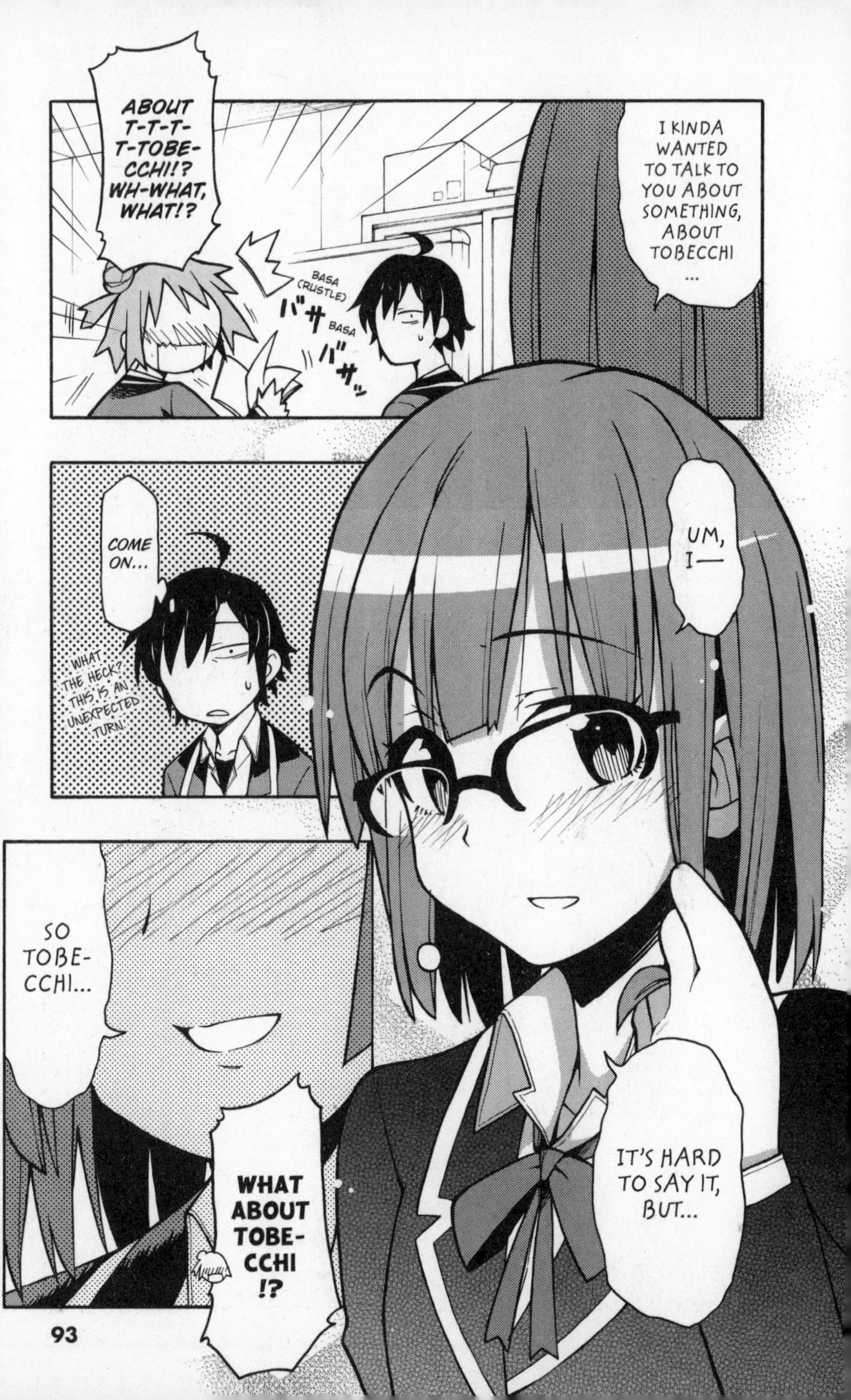
I KINDA WANTED TO TALK TO YOU ABOUT SOMETHING, ABOUT TOBECCHI ...
ABOUT T-T-T-T-TOBE-CCHI!? WH-WHAT, WHAT!?
BASA (RUSTLE)
バサ
BASA
バサッ
UM, I—
IT'S HARD TO SAY IT, BUT...
COME ON...
WHAT THE HECK? THIS IS AN UNEXPECTED TURN.
SO TOBE-CCHI...
WHAT ABOUT TOBE-CCHI !?

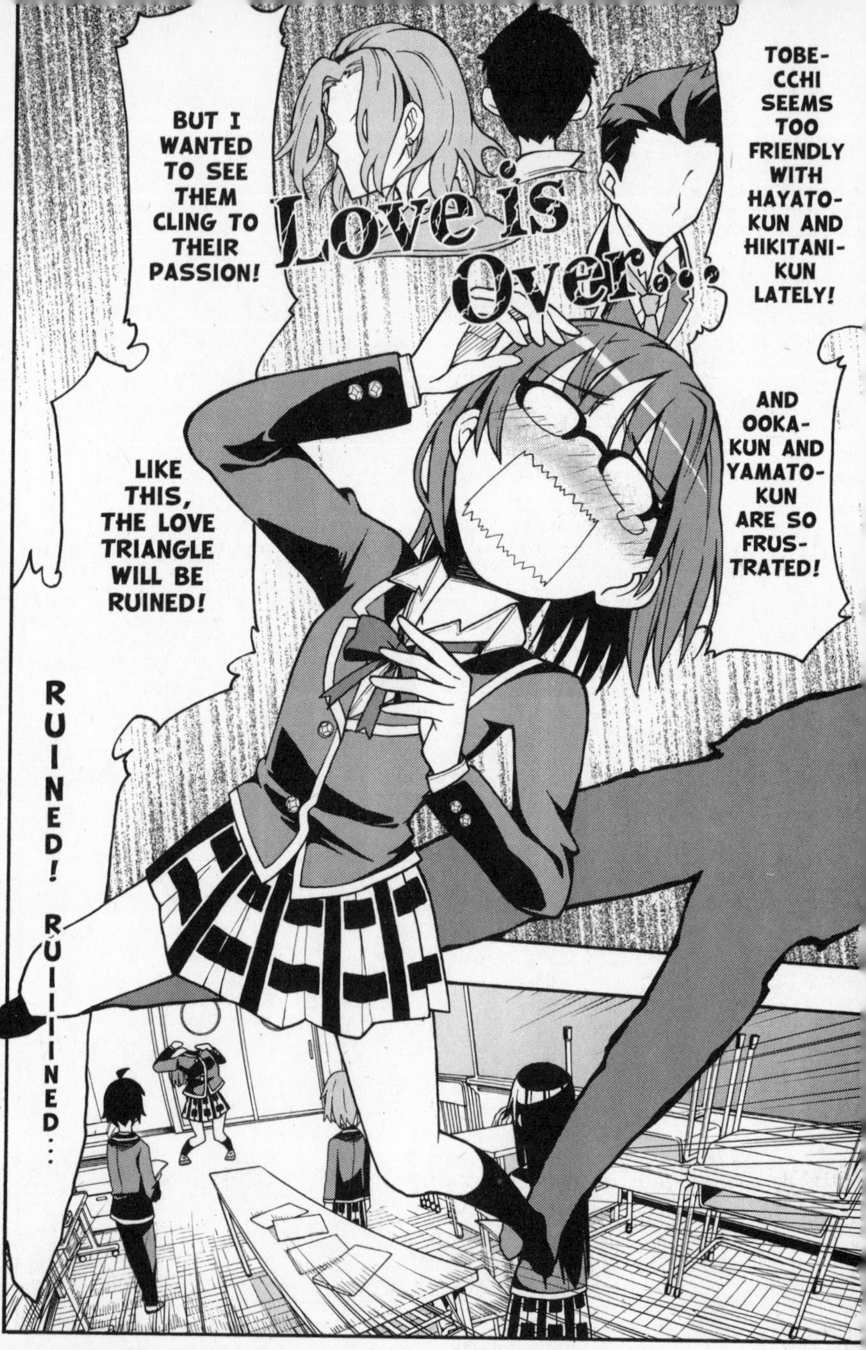
TOBE-CCHI SEEMS TOO FRIENDLY WITH HAYATO-KUN AND HIKITANI-KUN LATELY!
BUT I WANTED TO SEE THEM CLING TO THEIR PASSION!
Love is Over...
AND OOKA-KUN AND YAMATO-KUN ARE SO FRUS-TRATED!
LIKE THIS, THE LOVE TRIANGLE WILL BE RUINED!
RUINED! RUIIIINED...

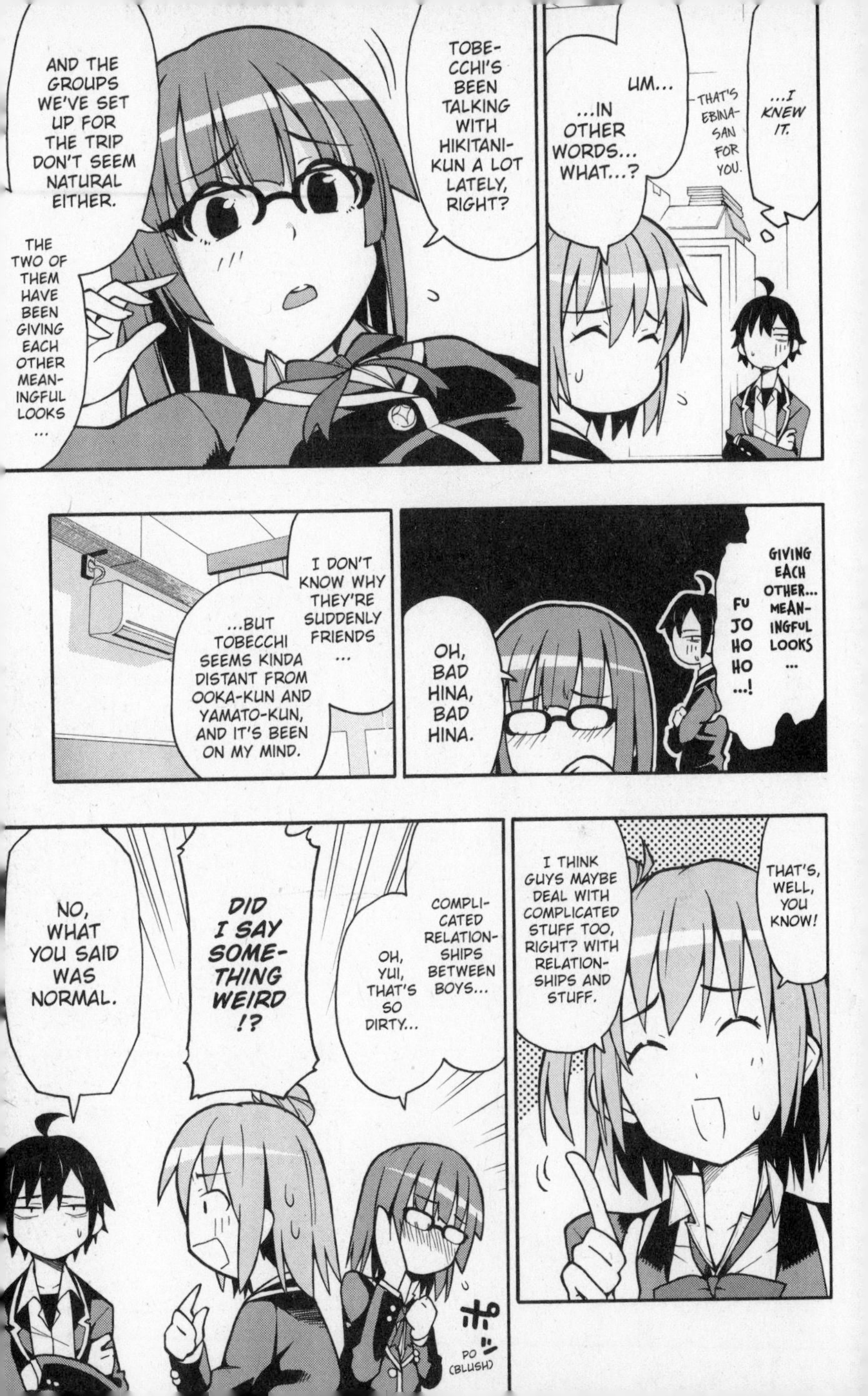
...I KNEW IT.
THAT'S EBINA-SAN FOR YOU.
UM...
...IN OTHER WORDS... WHAT...?
TOBE-CCHI'S BEEN TALKING WITH HIKITANI-KUN A LOT LATELY, RIGHT?
AND THE GROUPS WE'VE SET UP FOR THE TRIP DON'T SEEM NATURAL EITHER.
THE TWO OF THEM HAVE BEEN GIVING EACH OTHER MEAN-INGFUL LOOKS...
GIVING EACH OTHER... MEAN-INGFUL LOOKS...
FU JO HO HO HO...!
OH, BAD HINA, BAD HINA.
I DON'T KNOW WHY THEY'RE SUDDENLY FRIENDS...
...BUT TOBECCHI SEEMS KINDA DISTANT FROM OOKA-KUN AND YAMATO-KUN, AND IT'S BEEN ON MY MIND.
THAT'S, WELL, YOU KNOW!
I THINK GUYS MAYBE DEAL WITH COMPLICATED STUFF TOO, RIGHT? WITH RELATION-SHIPS AND STUFF.
COMPLI-CATED RELATION-SHIPS BETWEEN BOYS...
OH, YUI, THAT'S SO DIRTY...
DID I SAY SOME-THING WEIRD!?
NO, WHAT YOU SAID WAS NORMAL.
PO (BLUSH)

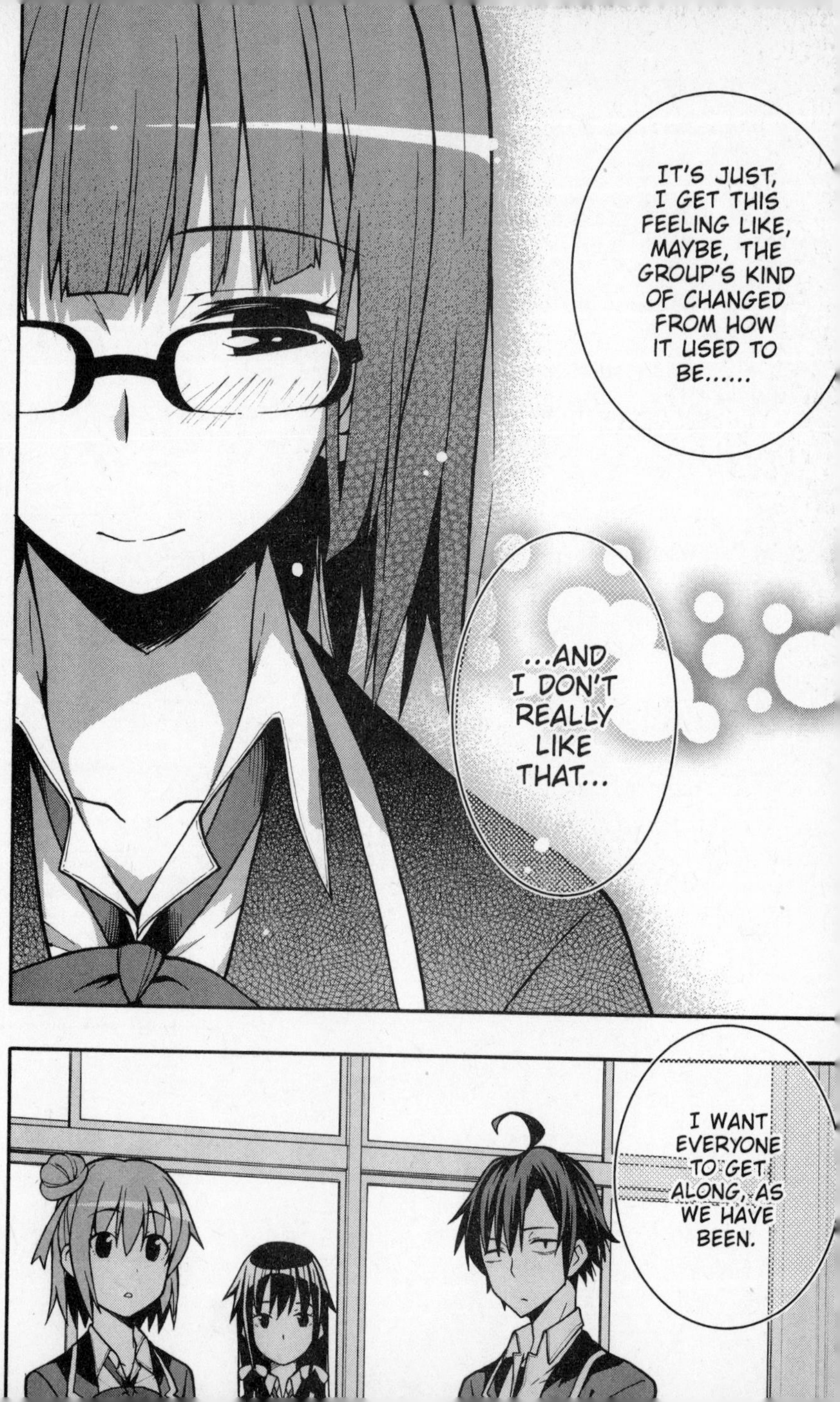
IT'S JUST, I GET THIS FEELING LIKE, MAYBE, THE GROUP'S KIND OF CHANGED FROM HOW IT USED TO BE......
...AND I DON'T REALLY LIKE THAT...
I WANT EVERYONE TO GET ALONG, AS WE HAVE BEEN.

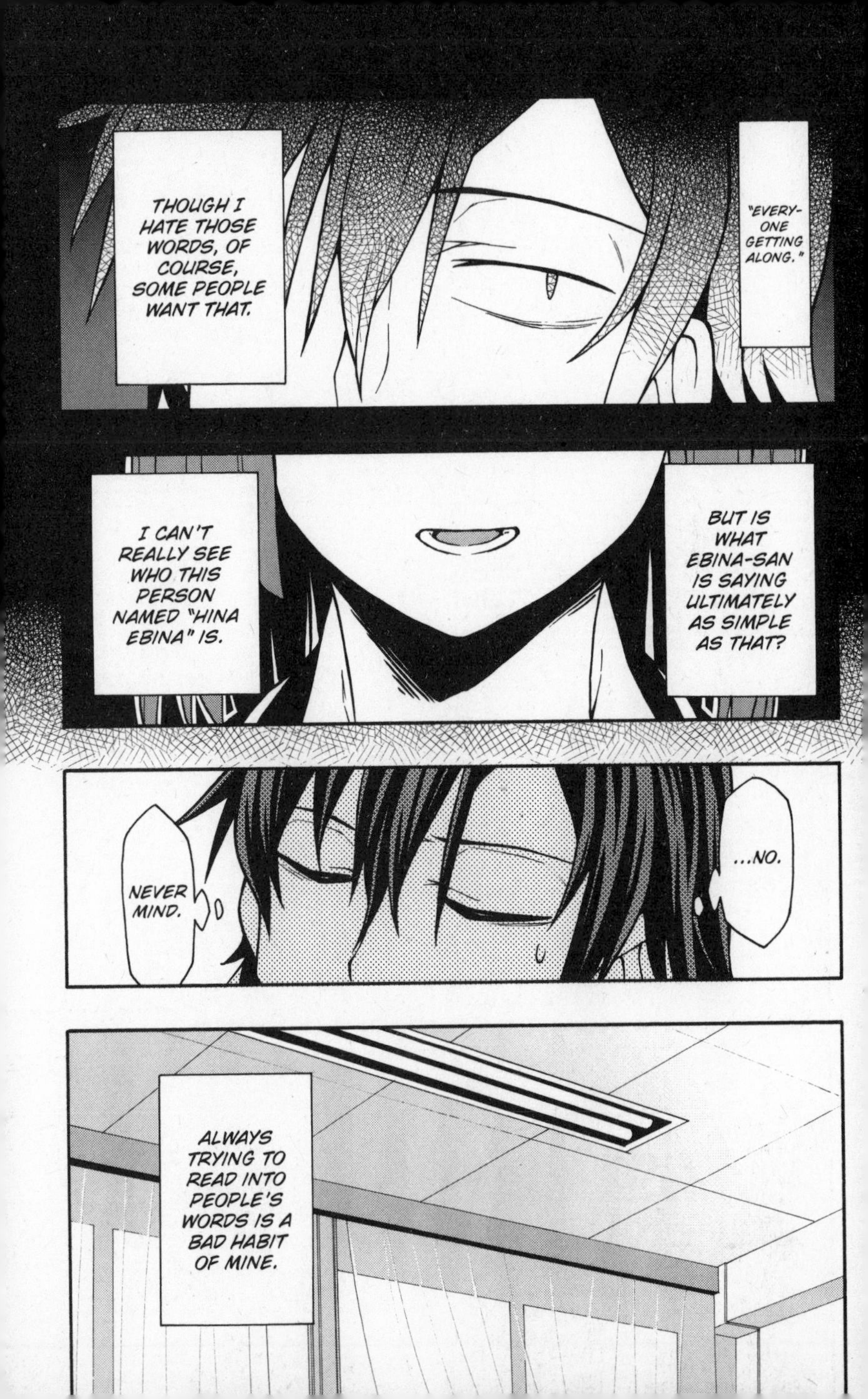
"EVERY-ONE GETTING ALONG."
THOUGH I HATE THOSE WORDS, OF COURSE, SOME PEOPLE WANT THAT.
BUT IS WHAT EBINA-SAN IS SAYING ULTIMATELY AS SIMPLE AS THAT?
I CAN'T REALLY SEE WHO THIS PERSON NAMED "HINA EBINA" IS.
...NO.
NEVER MIND.
ALWAYS TRYING TO READ INTO PEOPLE'S WORDS IS A BAD HABIT OF MINE.

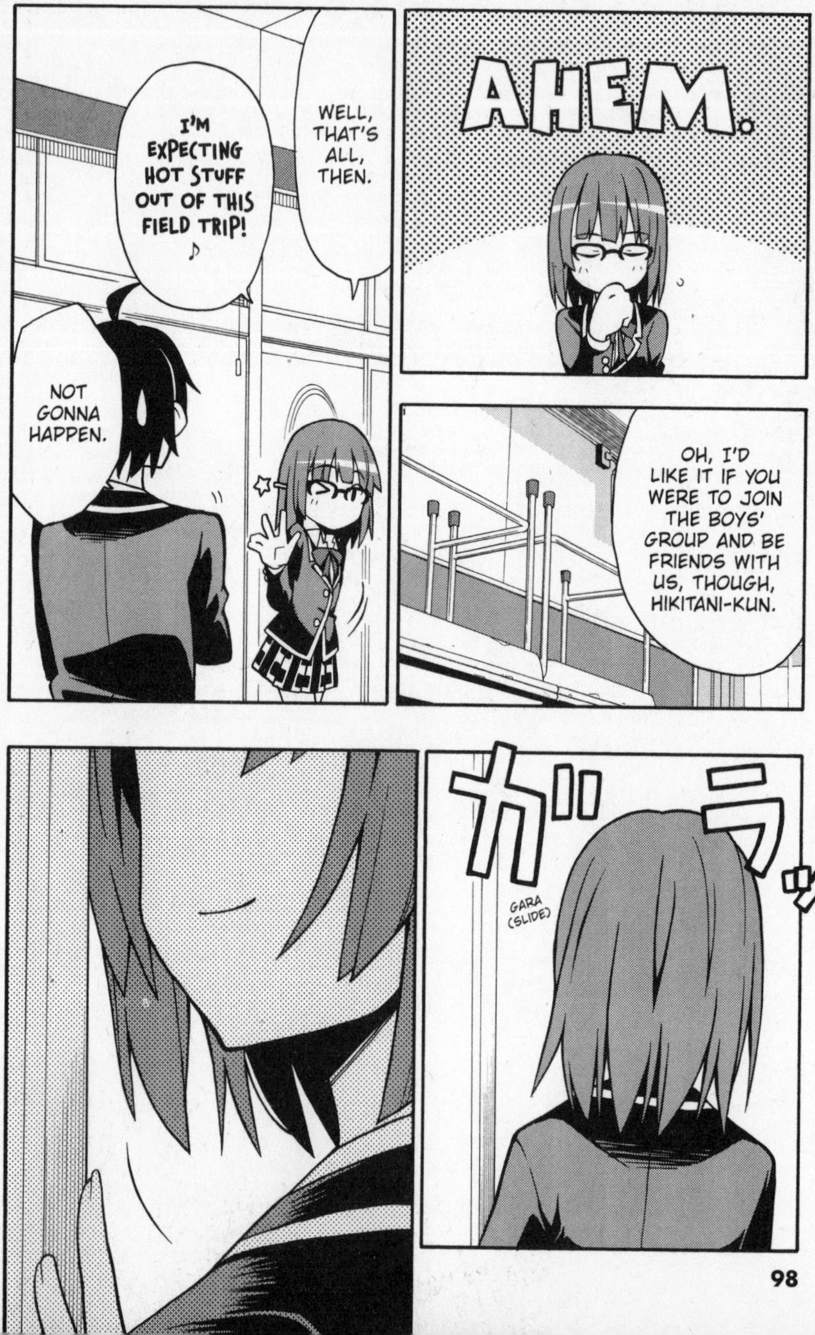
AHEM.
OH, I'D LIKE IT IF YOU WERE TO JOIN THE BOYS' GROUP AND BE FRIENDS WITH US, THOUGH, HIKITANI-KUN.
WELL, THAT'S ALL, THEN.
I'M EXPECTING HOT STUFF OUT OF THIS FIELD TRIP! ♪
NOT GONNA HAPPEN.
ガラッ
GARA (SLIDE)

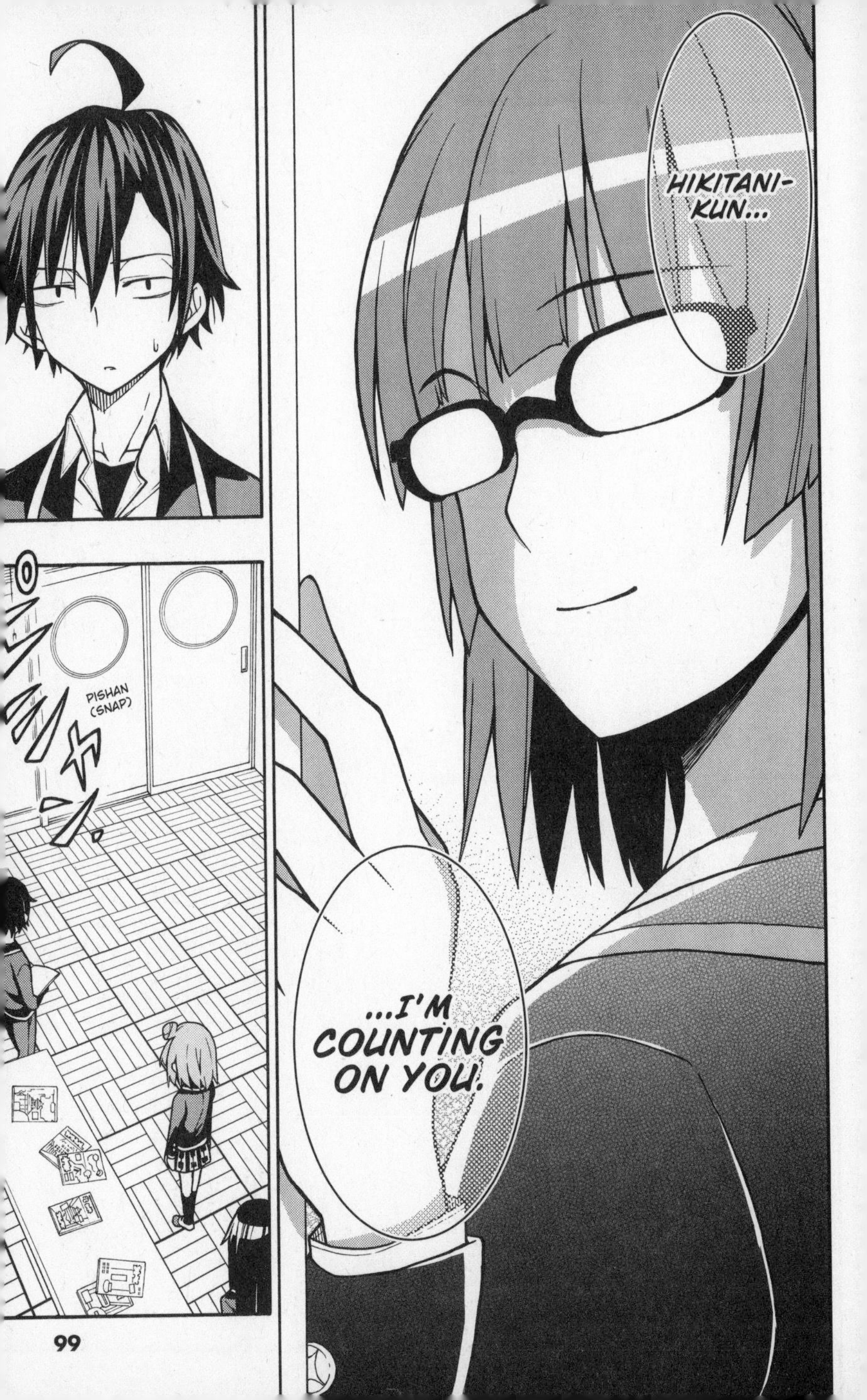
HIKITANI-KUN...
...I'M COUNTING ON YOU.
PISHAN (SNAP)

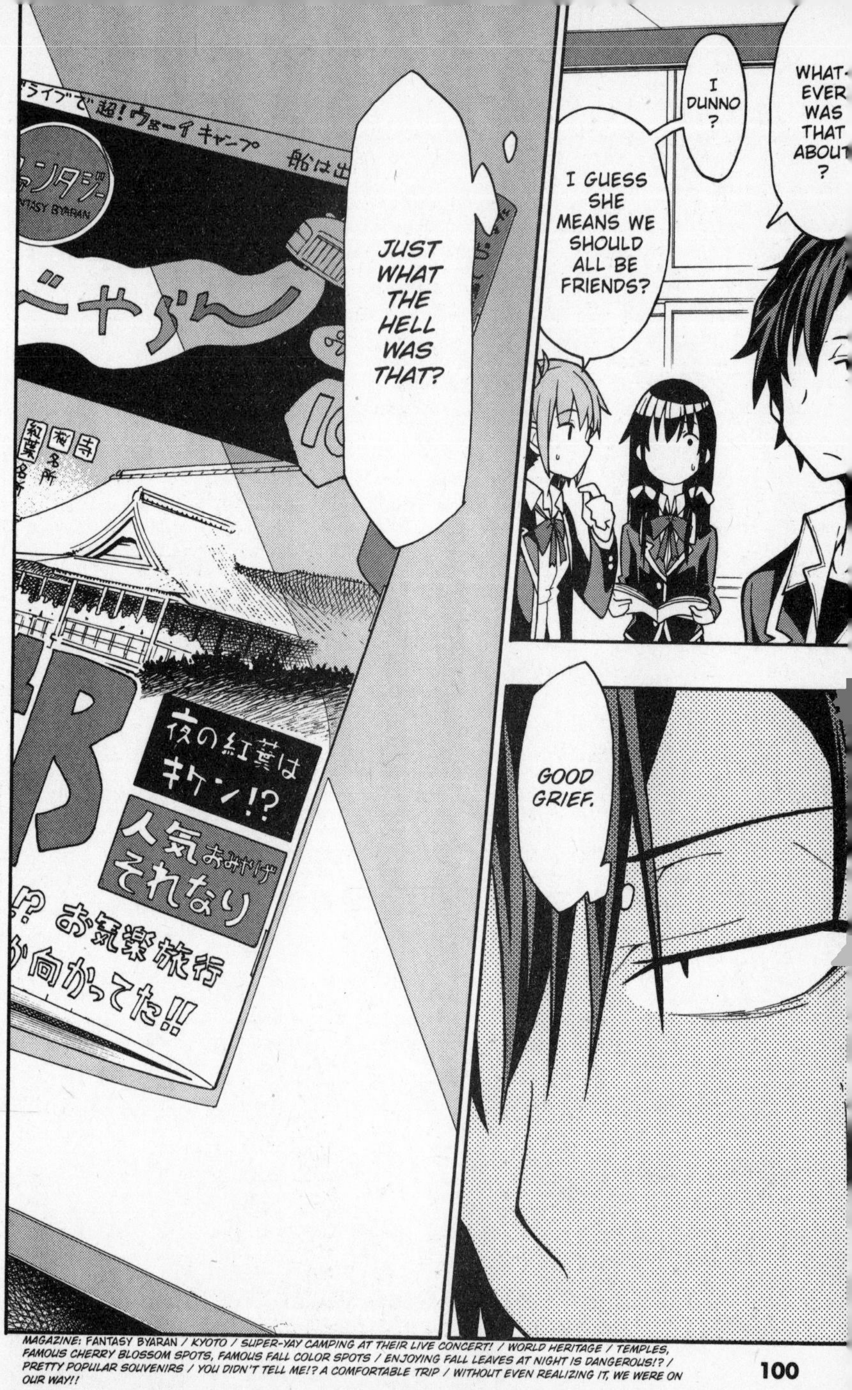
WHAT-EVER WAS THAT ABOUT?
I DUNNO?
I GUESS SHE MEANS WE SHOULD ALL BE FRIENDS?
GOOD GRIEF.
JUST WHAT THE HELL WAS THAT?
FANTASY BYARAN
夜の紅葉はキケン!?
人気おみやげそれなり

MAGAZINE: FANTASY BYARAN / KYOTO / SUPER-YAY CAMPING AT THEIR LIVE CONCERT! / WORLD HERITAGE / TEMPLES, FAMOUS CHERRY BLOSSOM SPOTS, FAMOUS FALL COLOR SPOTS / ENJOYING FALL LEAVES AT NIGHT IS DANGEROUS!? / PRETTY POPULAR SOUVENIRS / YOU DIDN'T TELL ME!? A COMFORTABLE TRIP / WITHOUT EVEN REALIZING IT, WE WERE ON OUR WAY!!

CHAPTER 51 ··· SURREPTITIOUSLY, YUKINO YUKINOSHITA GOES OUT TO TOWN AT NIGHT.

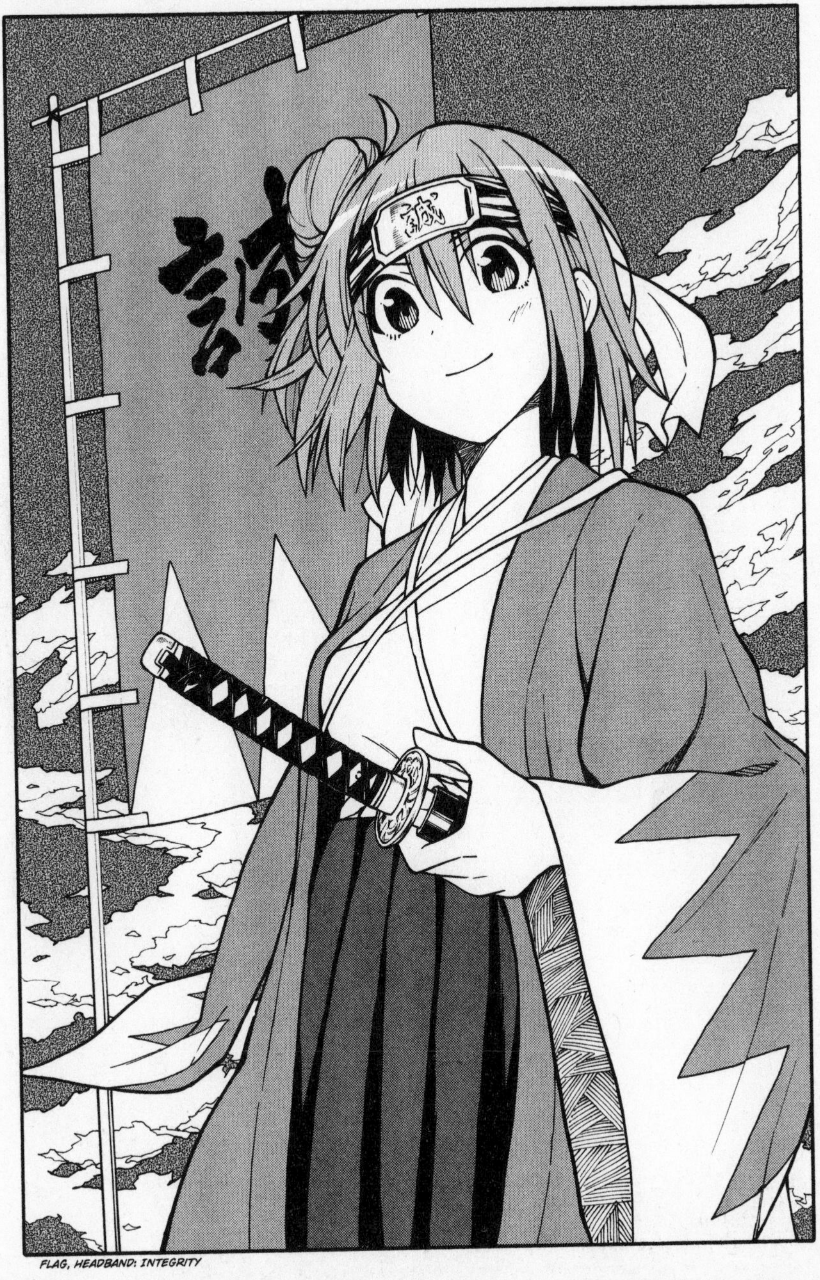

FLAG, HEADBAND: INTEGRITY

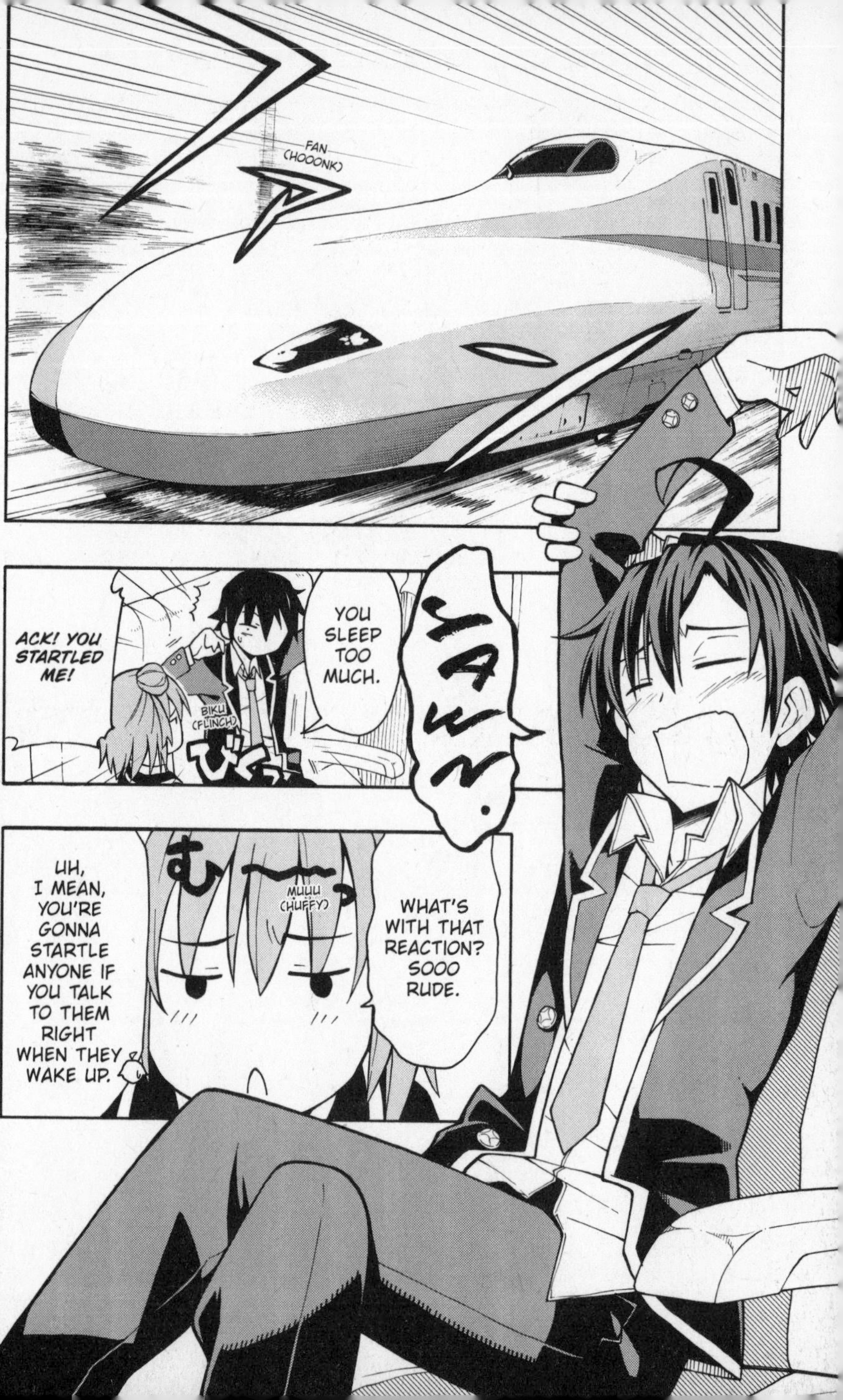
FAN (HOOONK)
YOU SLEEP TOO MUCH.
BIKU (FLINCH)
ACK! YOU STARTLED ME!
WHAT'S WITH THAT REACTION? SOOO RUDE.
MUUU (HUFFY)
UH, I MEAN, YOU'RE GONNA STARTLE ANYONE IF YOU TALK TO THEM RIGHT WHEN THEY WAKE UP.

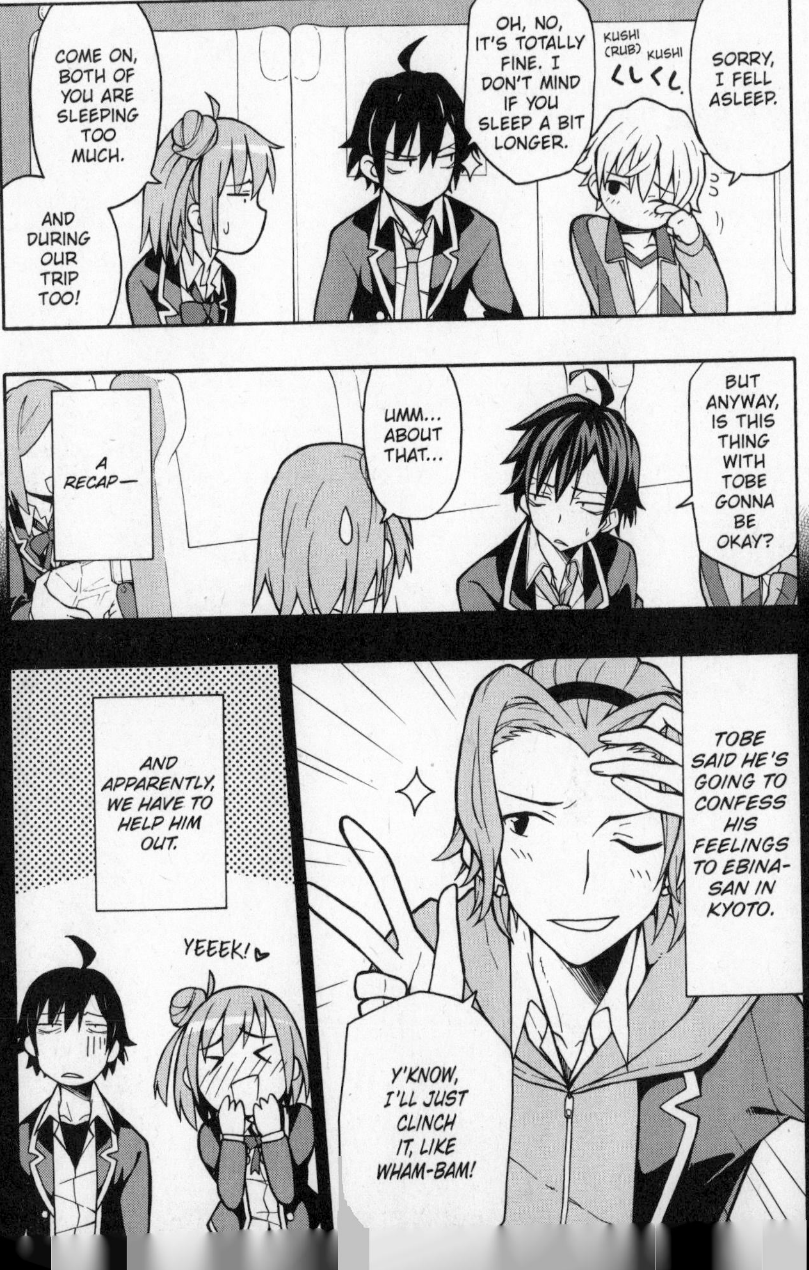
SORRY, I FELL ASLEEP.
KUSHI (RUB) KUSHI
くしくし
OH, NO, IT'S TOTALLY FINE. I DON'T MIND IF YOU SLEEP A BIT LONGER.
COME ON, BOTH OF YOU ARE SLEEPING TOO MUCH.
AND DURING OUR TRIP TOO!
BUT ANYWAY, IS THIS THING WITH TOBE GONNA BE OKAY?
UMM... ABOUT THAT...
A RECAP—
TOBE SAID HE'S GOING TO CONFESS HIS FEELINGS TO EBINA-SAN IN KYOTO.
Y'KNOW, I'LL JUST CLINCH IT, LIKE WHAM-BAM!
AND APPARENTLY, WE HAVE TO HELP HIM OUT.
YEEEK!♥

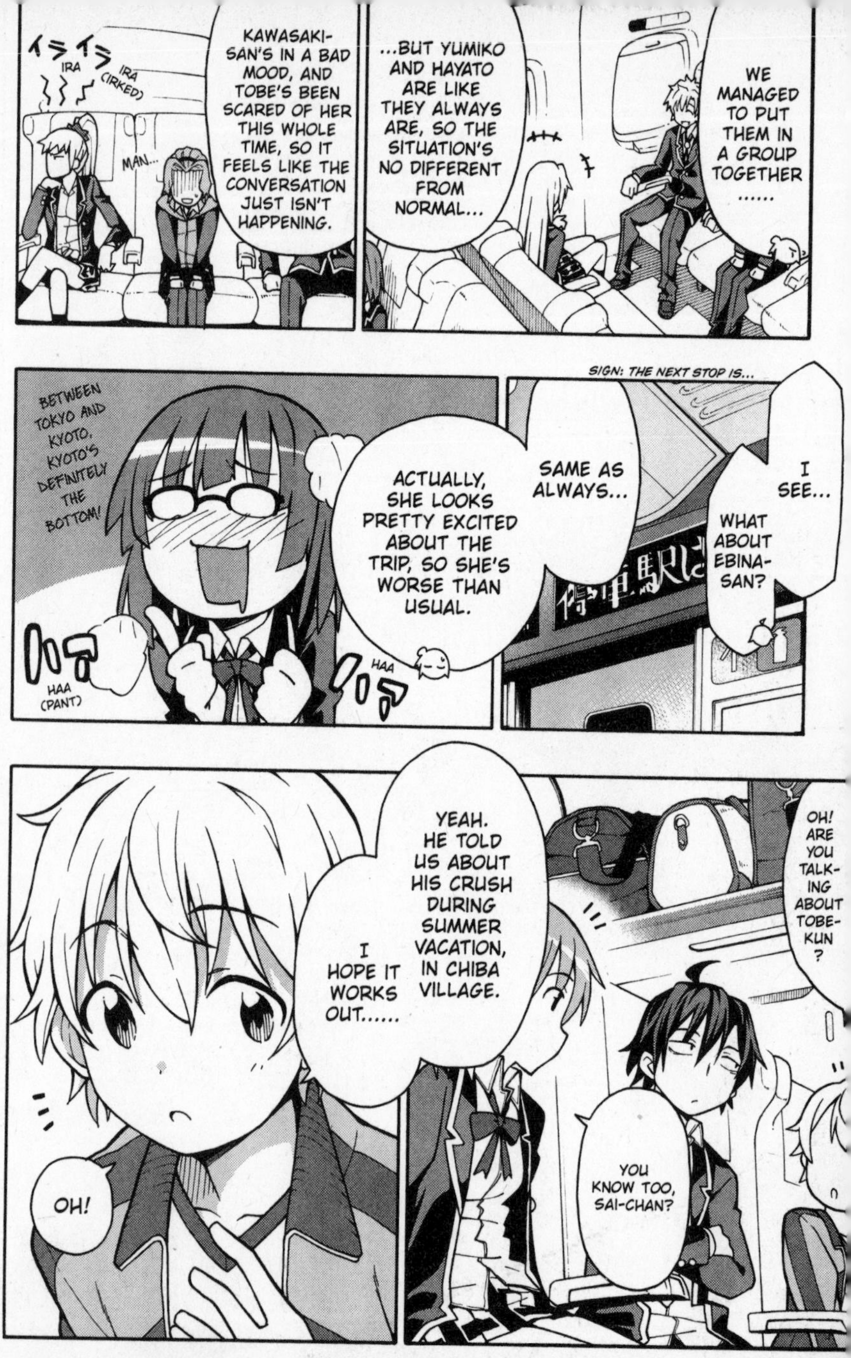
WE MANAGED TO PUT THEM IN A GROUP TOGETHER......
...BUT YUMIKO AND HAYATO ARE LIKE THEY ALWAYS ARE, SO THE SITUATION'S NO DIFFERENT FROM NORMAL...
KAWASAKI-SAN'S IN A BAD MOOD, AND TOBE'S BEEN SCARED OF HER THIS WHOLE TIME, SO IT FEELS LIKE THE CONVERSATION JUST ISN'T HAPPENING.
IRA IRA (IRKED)
MAN...
SIGN: THE NEXT STOP IS...
I SEE...
WHAT ABOUT EBINA-SAN?
SAME AS ALWAYS...
ACTUALLY, SHE LOOKS PRETTY EXCITED ABOUT THE TRIP, SO SHE'S WORSE THAN USUAL.
BETWEEN TOKYO AND KYOTO, KYOTO'S DEFINITELY THE BOTTOM!
HAA
HAA (PANT)
OH! ARE YOU TALKING ABOUT TOBE-KUN?
YOU KNOW TOO, SAI-CHAN?
YEAH. HE TOLD US ABOUT HIS CRUSH DURING SUMMER VACATION, IN CHIBA VILLAGE.
I HOPE IT WORKS OUT......
OH!

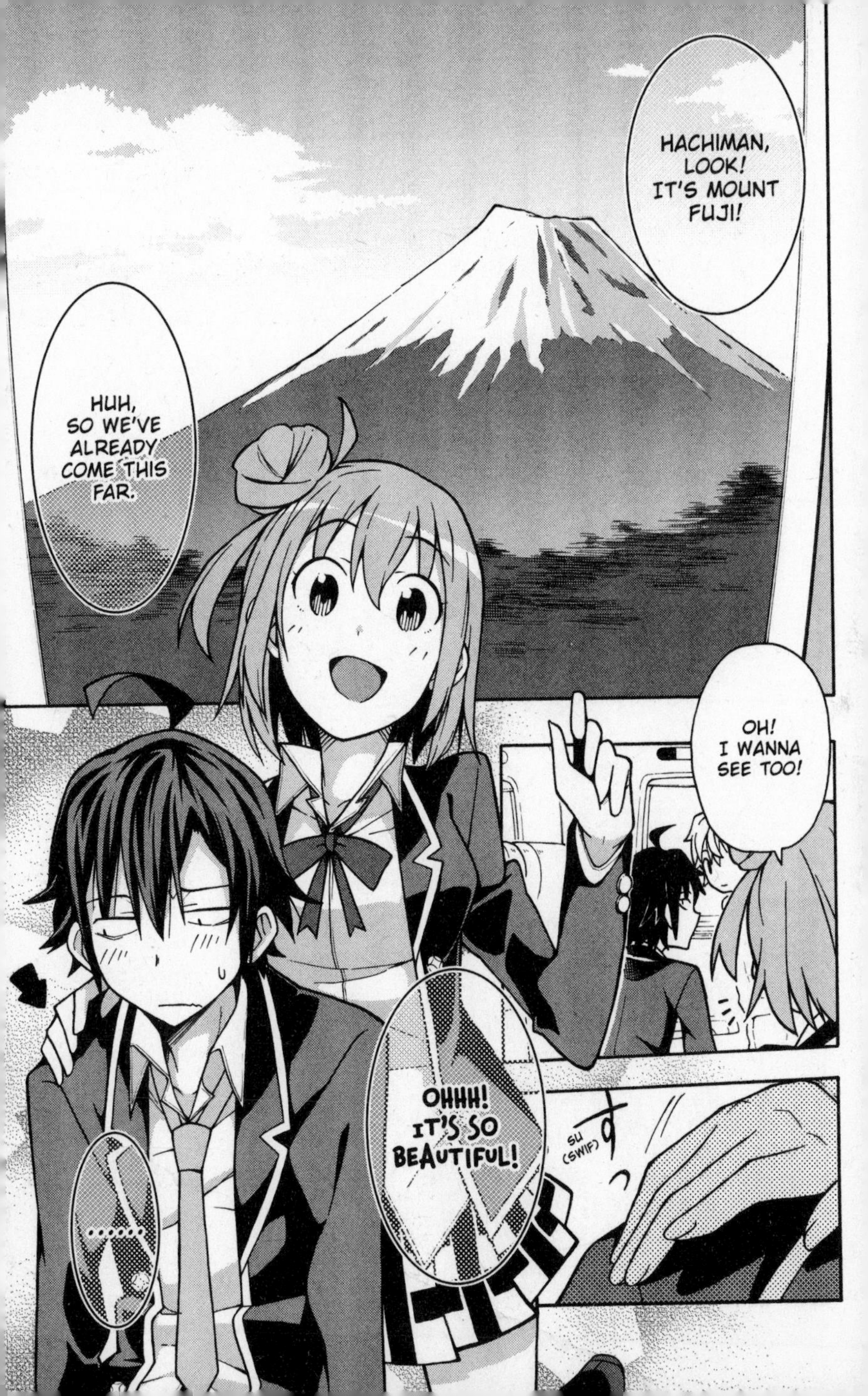
HACHIMAN, LOOK! IT'S MOUNT FUJI!
HUH, SO WE'VE ALREADY COME THIS FAR.
OH! I WANNA SEE TOO!
SU (SWIF)
OHHH! IT'S SO BEAUTIFUL!
......

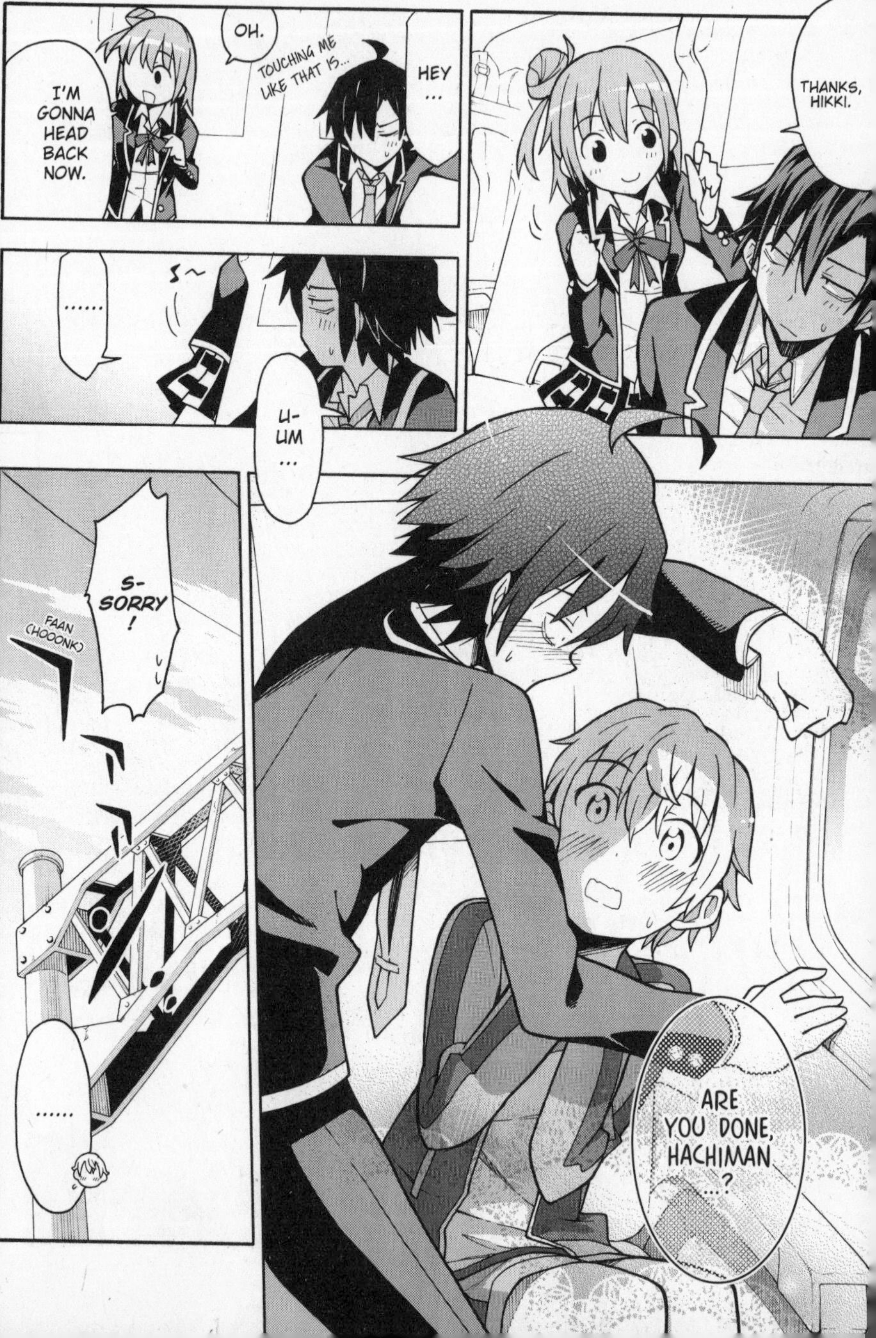
THANKS, HIKKI.
HEY ...
TOUCHING ME LIKE THAT IS...
OH.
I'M GONNA HEAD BACK NOW.
S~
U-UM ...
......
ARE YOU DONE, HACHIMAN ...?
S-SORRY!
FAAN (HOOONK)
......

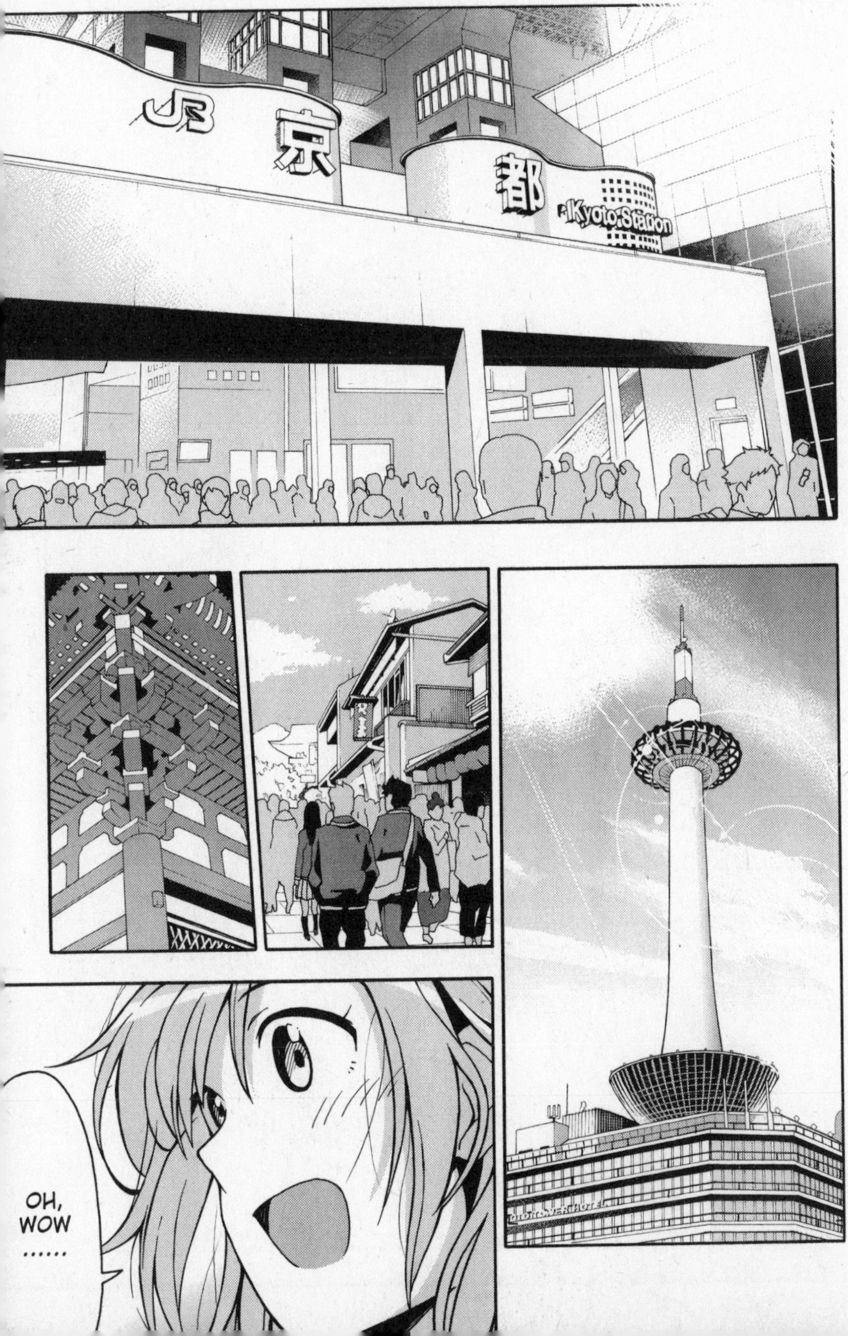
京都
Kyoto Station
OH, WOW ......

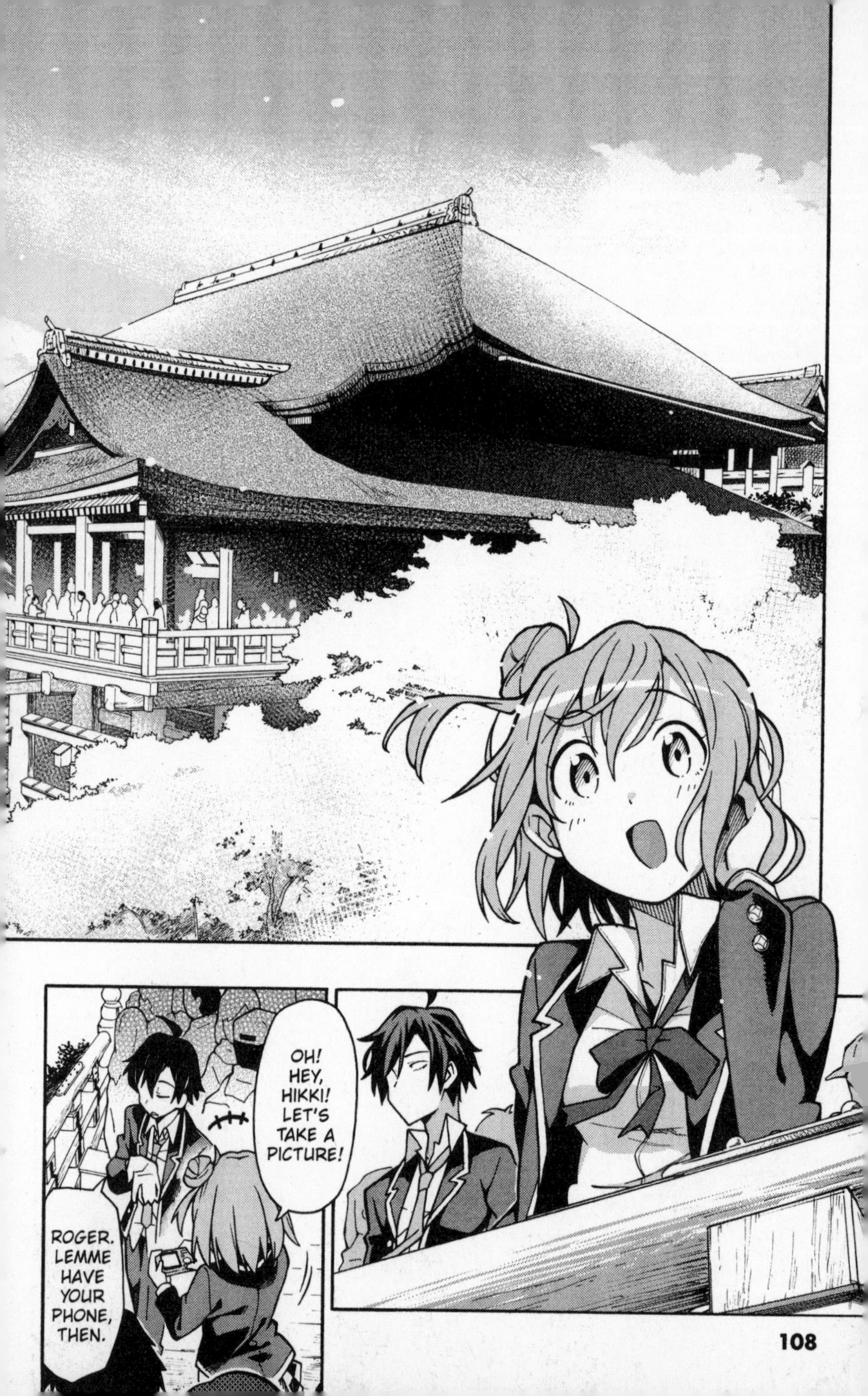
OH! HEY, HIKKI! LET'S TAKE A PICTURE!
ROGER. LEMME HAVE YOUR PHONE, THEN.

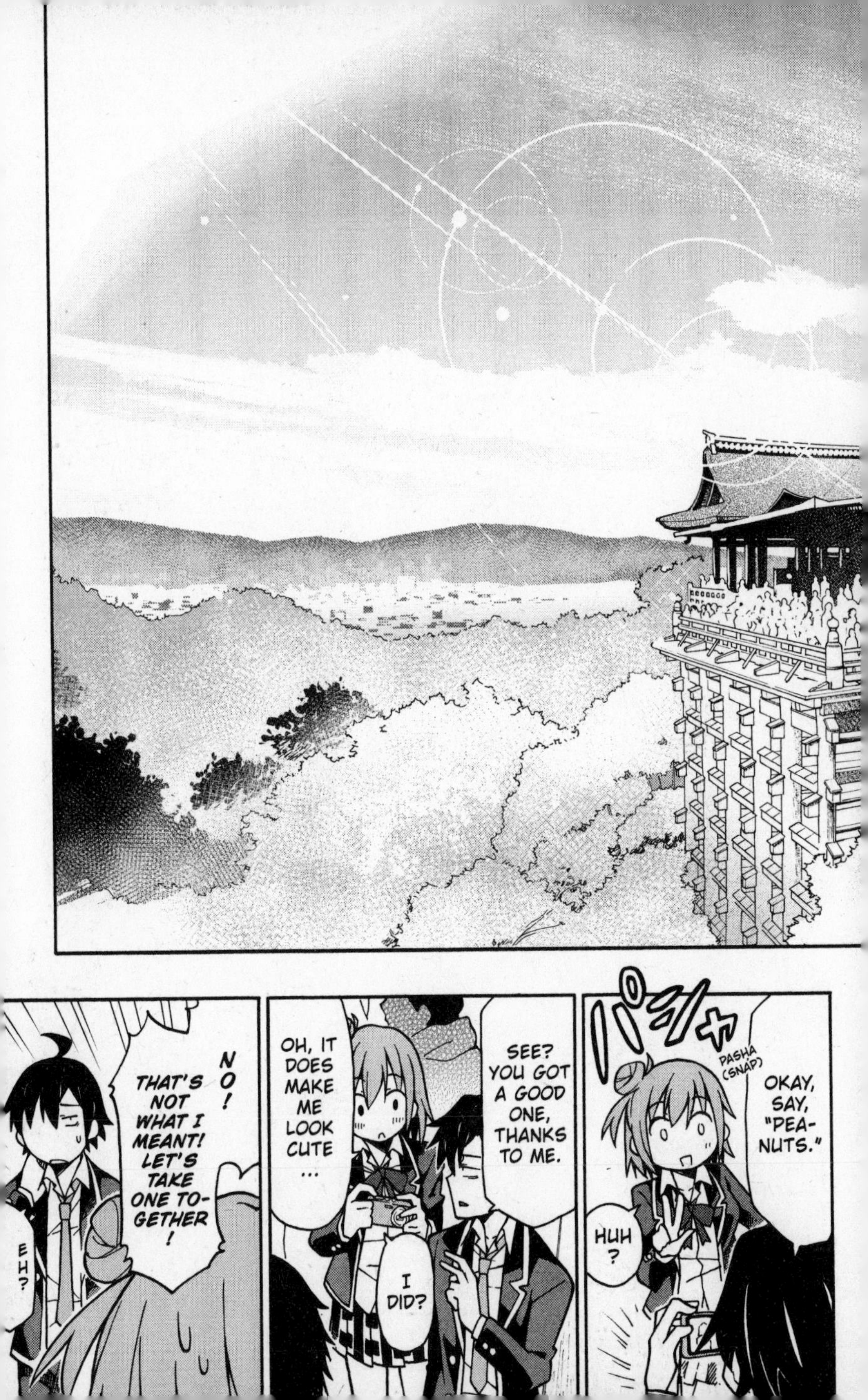
PASHA (SNAP)
OKAY, SAY, "PEA-NUTS."
HUH?
SEE? YOU GOT A GOOD ONE, THANKS TO ME.
OH, IT DOES MAKE ME LOOK CUTE...
I DID?
NO! THAT'S NOT WHAT I MEANT! LET'S TAKE ONE TOGETHER!
EH?

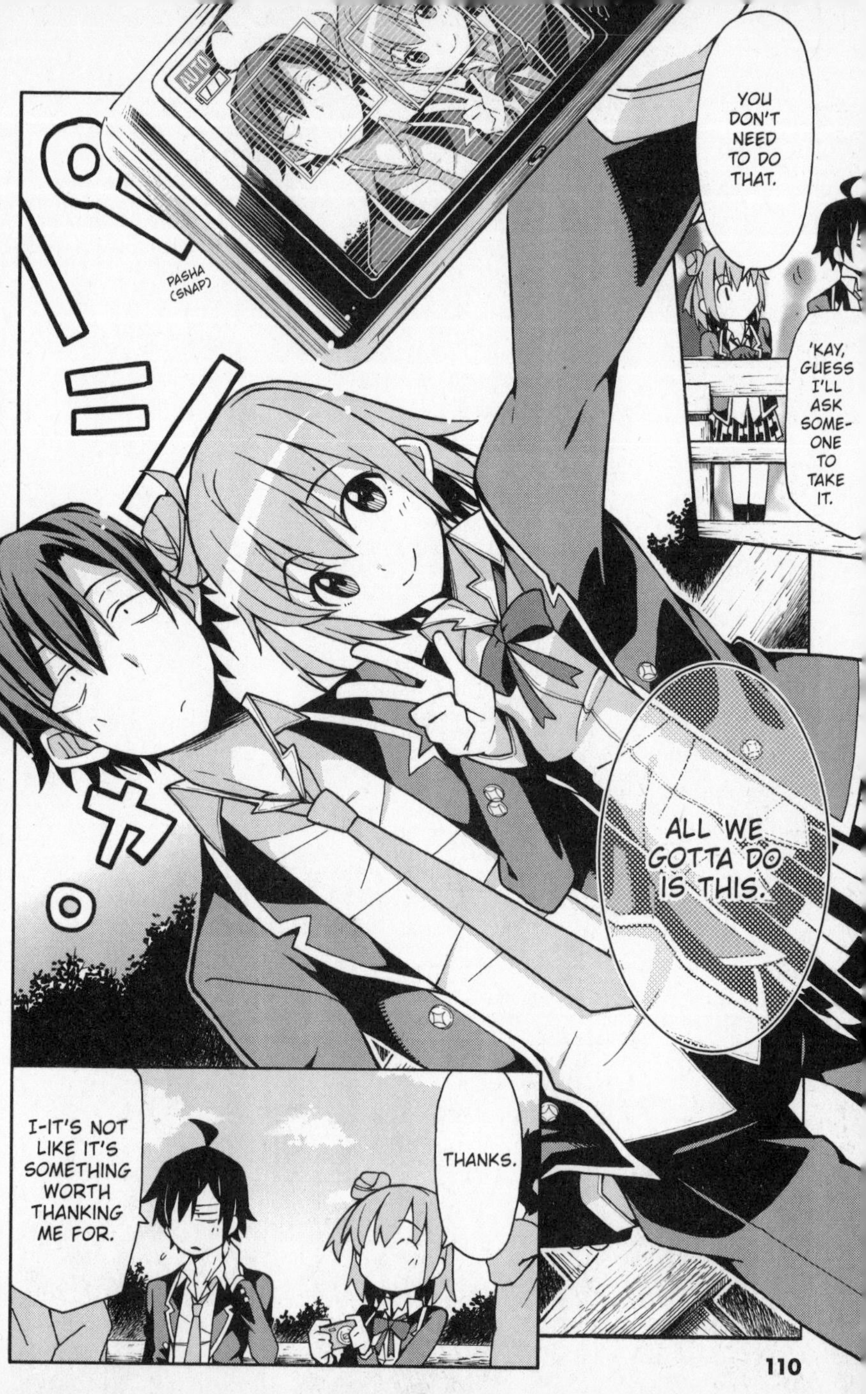
YOU DON'T NEED TO DO THAT.
'KAY, GUESS I'LL ASK SOME-ONE TO TAKE IT.
ALL WE GOTTA DO IS THIS.
PASHA (SNAP)
THANKS.
I-IT'S NOT LIKE IT'S SOMETHING WORTH THANKING ME FOR.

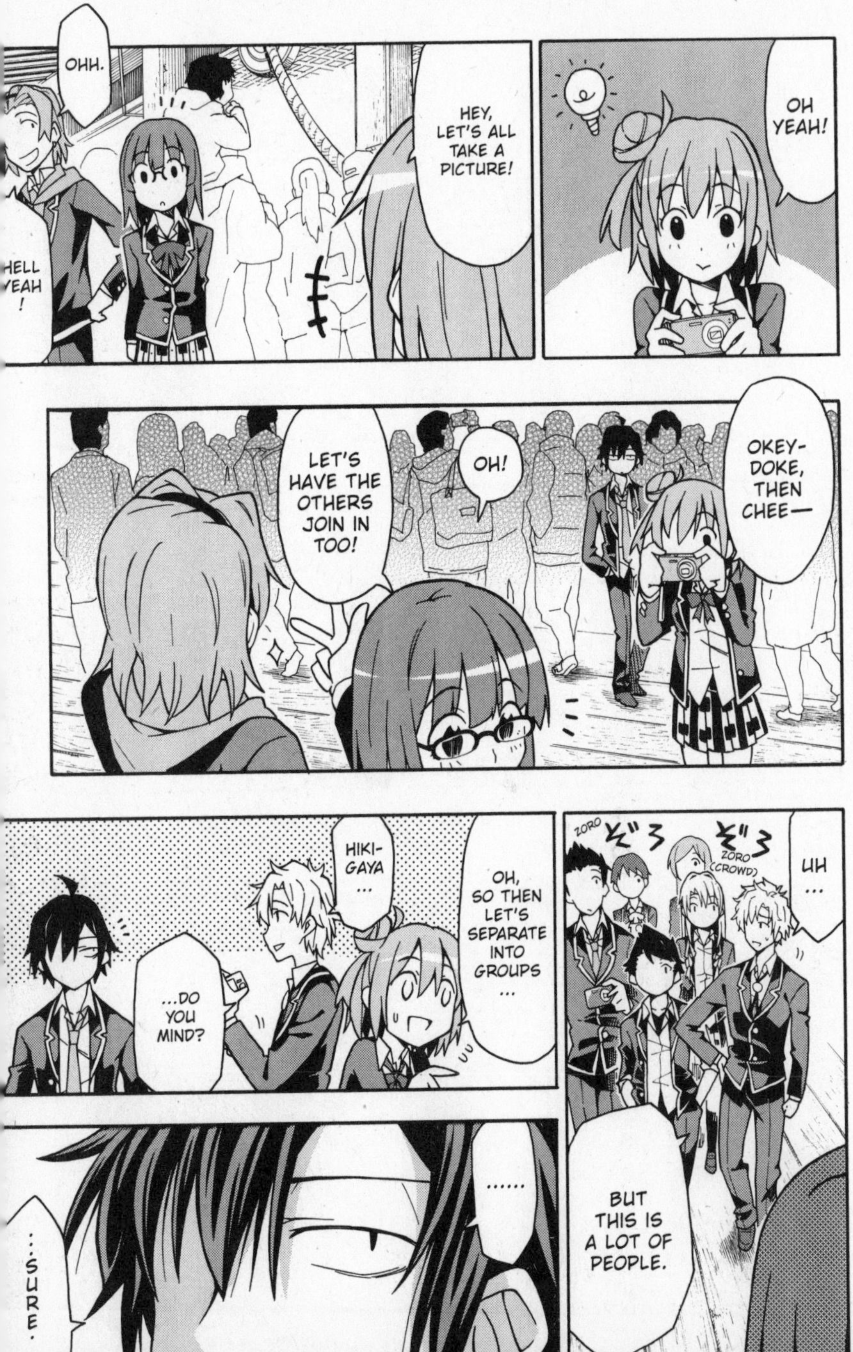
OH YEAH!
HEY, LET'S ALL TAKE A PICTURE!
OHH.
HELL YEAH!
OKEY-DOKE, THEN CHEE—
OH!
LET'S HAVE THE OTHERS JOIN IN TOO!
UH...
ZORO
ZORO (CROWD)
BUT THIS IS A LOT OF PEOPLE.
OH, SO THEN LET'S SEPARATE INTO GROUPS...
HIKI-GAYA...
...DO YOU MIND?
......
...SURE.

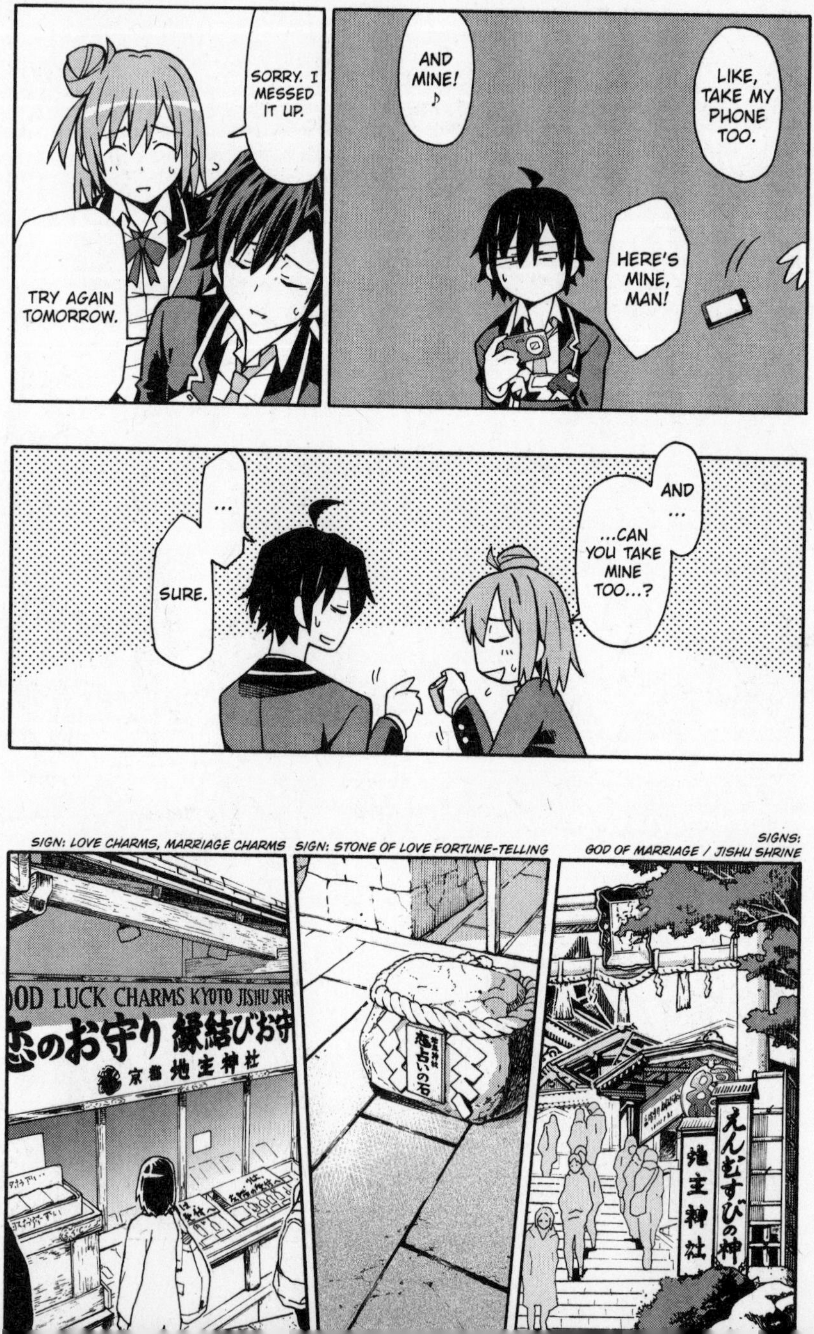
LIKE, TAKE MY PHONE TOO.
AND MINE! ♪
HERE'S MINE, MAN!
SORRY. I MESSED IT UP.
TRY AGAIN TOMORROW.
AND ...
...CAN YOU TAKE MINE TOO...?
...
SURE.
SIGNS: GOD OF MARRIAGE / JISHU SHRINE
えんむすびの神
地主神社
SIGN: STONE OF LOVE FORTUNE-TELLING
恋占いの石
SIGN: LOVE CHARMS, MARRIAGE CHARMS
OOD LUCK CHARMS KYOTO JISHU SHR
恋のお守り 縁結びお守
京都地主神社

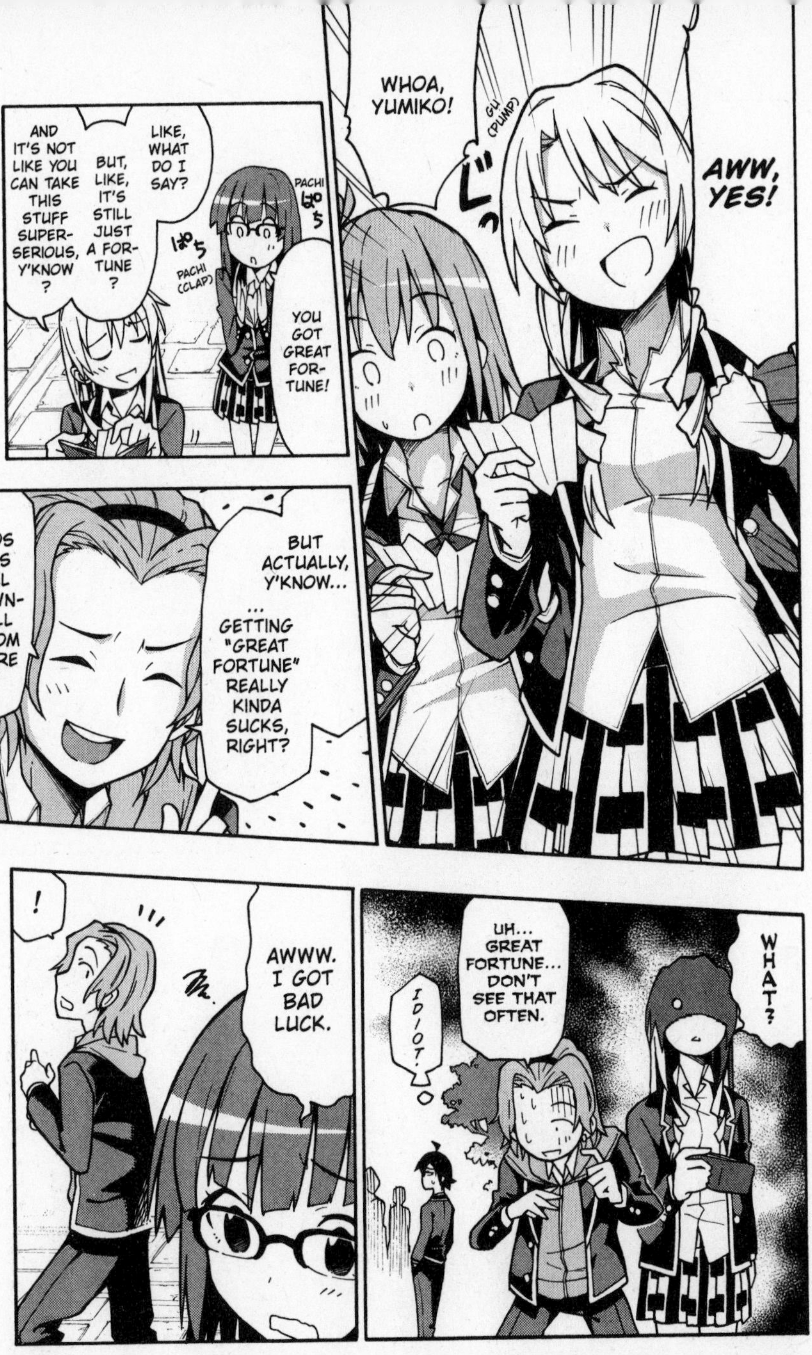
AWW, YES!
じっ GU (PUMP)
WHOA, YUMIKO!
YOU GOT GREAT FORTUNE!
ぱち PACHI ぱち PACHI (CLAP)
LIKE, WHAT DO I SAY?
BUT, LIKE, IT'S STILL JUST A FORTUNE?
AND IT'S NOT LIKE YOU CAN TAKE THIS STUFF SUPER-SERIOUS, Y'KNOW?
BUT ACTUALLY, Y'KNOW...
...GETTING "GREAT FORTUNE" REALLY KINDA SUCKS, RIGHT?
'COS IT'S ALL DOWNHILL FROM HERE!
WHAT?
UH... GREAT FORTUNE... DON'T SEE THAT OFTEN.
IDIOT.
AWWW. I GOT BAD LUCK.
!

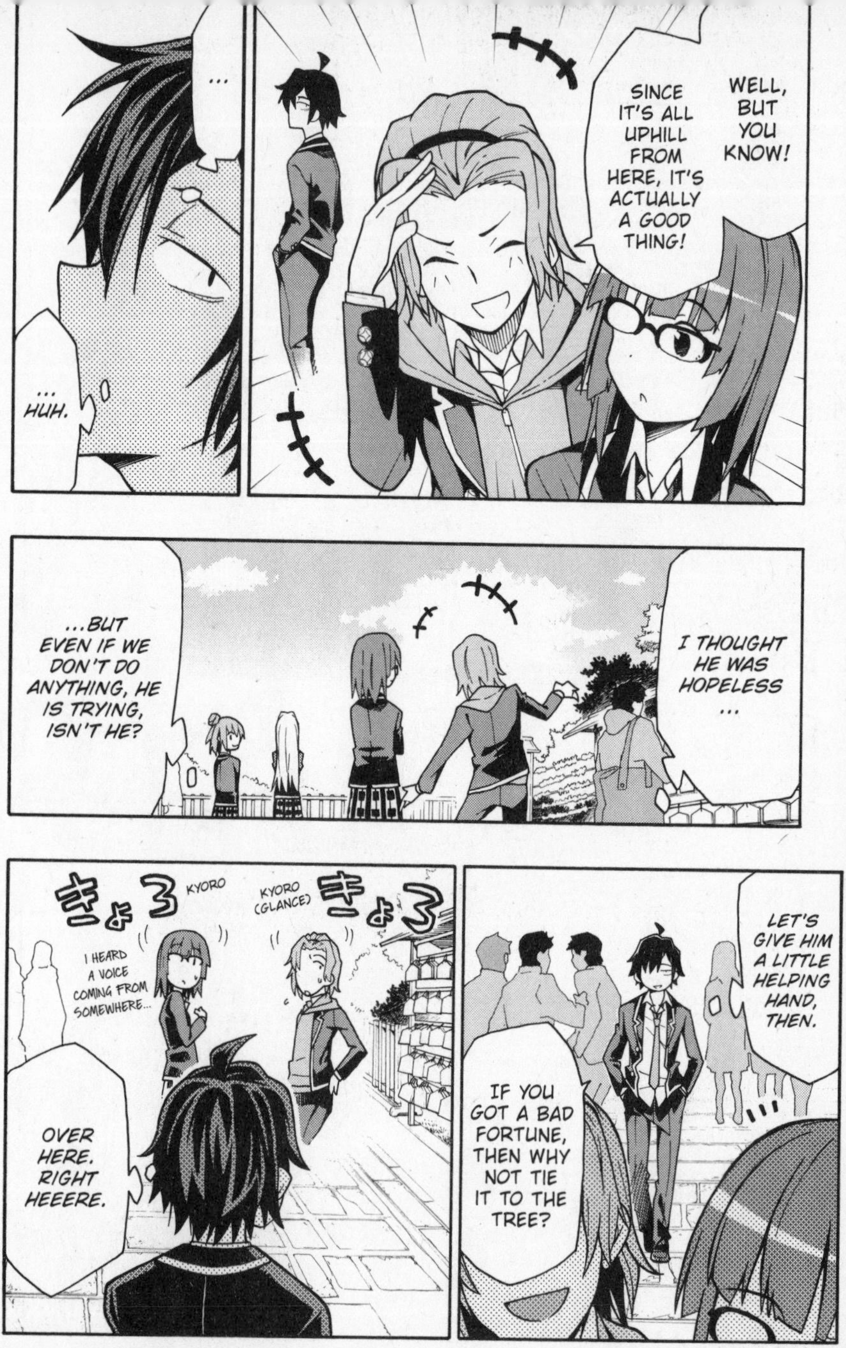
WELL, BUT YOU KNOW!
SINCE IT'S ALL UPHILL FROM HERE, IT'S ACTUALLY A GOOD THING!
...
... HUH.
I THOUGHT HE WAS HOPELESS ...
...BUT EVEN IF WE DON'T DO ANYTHING, HE IS TRYING, ISN'T HE?
LET'S GIVE HIM A LITTLE HELPING HAND, THEN.
IF YOU GOT A BAD FORTUNE, THEN WHY NOT TIE IT TO THE TREE?
きょろ
KYORO (GLANCE)
きょろ
KYORO
I HEARD A VOICE COMING FROM SOMEWHERE...
OVER HERE. RIGHT HEEERE.

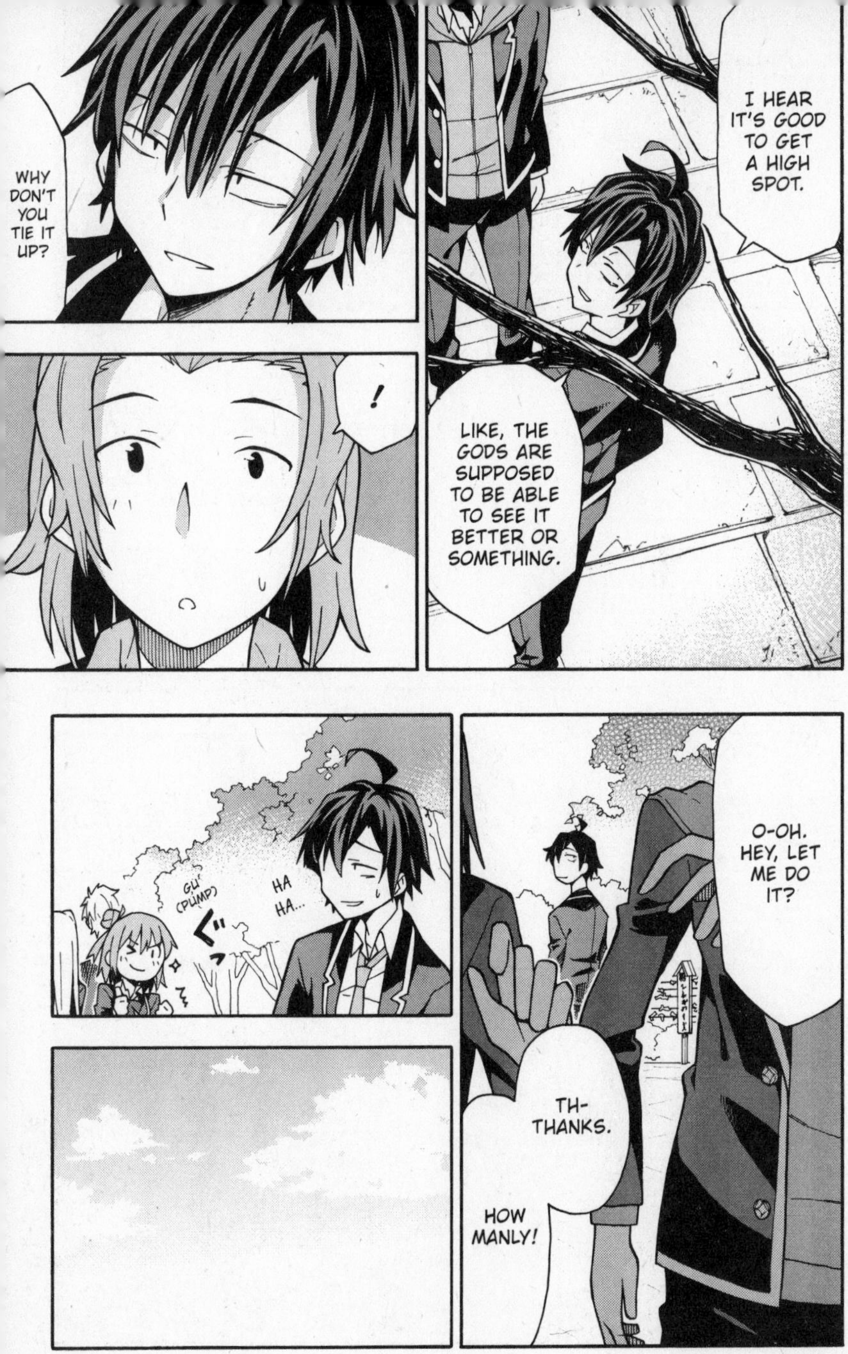
I HEAR IT'S GOOD TO GET A HIGH SPOT.
LIKE, THE GODS ARE SUPPOSED TO BE ABLE TO SEE IT BETTER OR SOMETHING.
WHY DON'T YOU TIE IT UP?
!
O-OH. HEY, LET ME DO IT?
TH- THANKS.
HOW MANLY!
HA HA...
GU (PUMP)

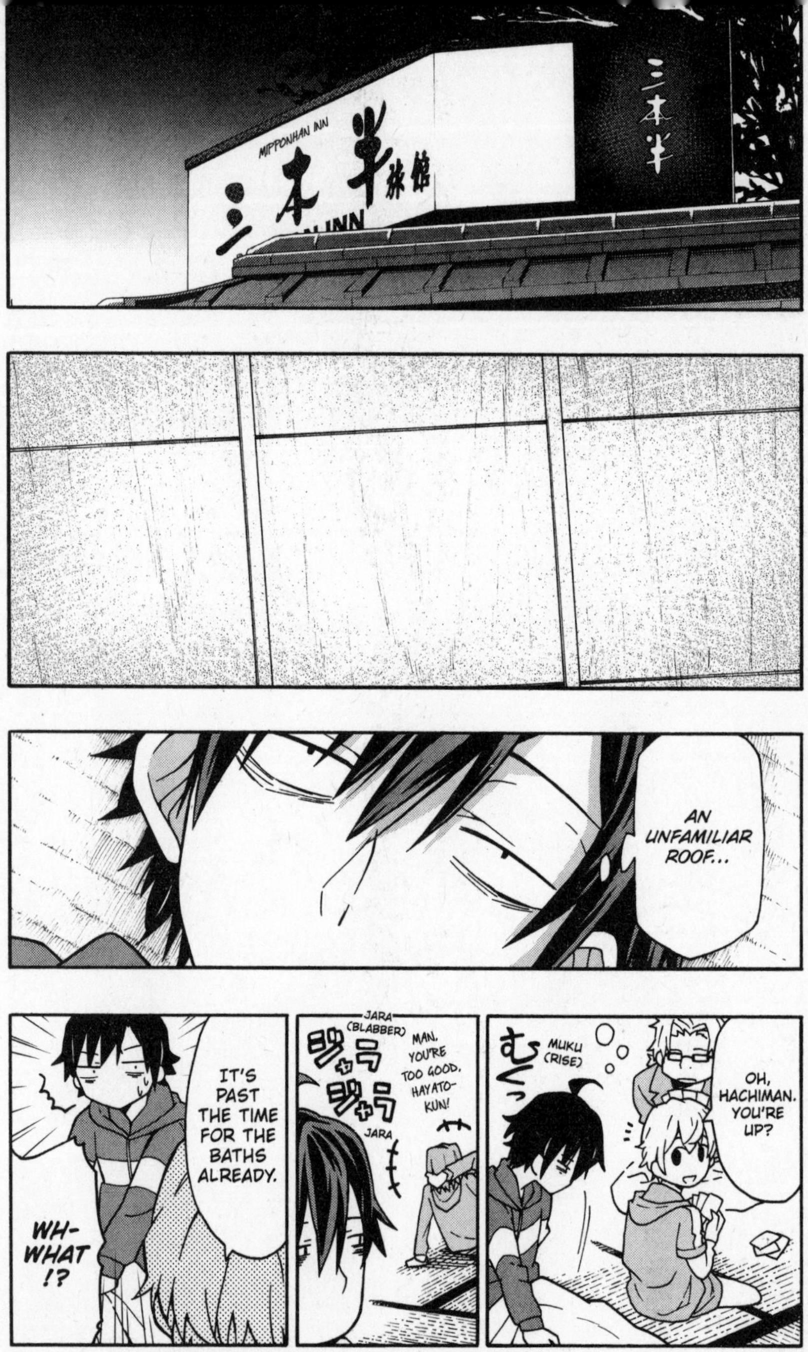
MIPPONHAN INN
三本半旅館
三本半
AN UNFAMILIAR ROOF...
MUKU (RISE)
OH, HACHIMAN. YOU'RE UP?
JARA (BLABBER)
MAN, YOU'RE TOO GOOD, HAYATO-KUN!
JARA
IT'S PAST THE TIME FOR THE BATHS ALREADY.
WH-WHAT!?

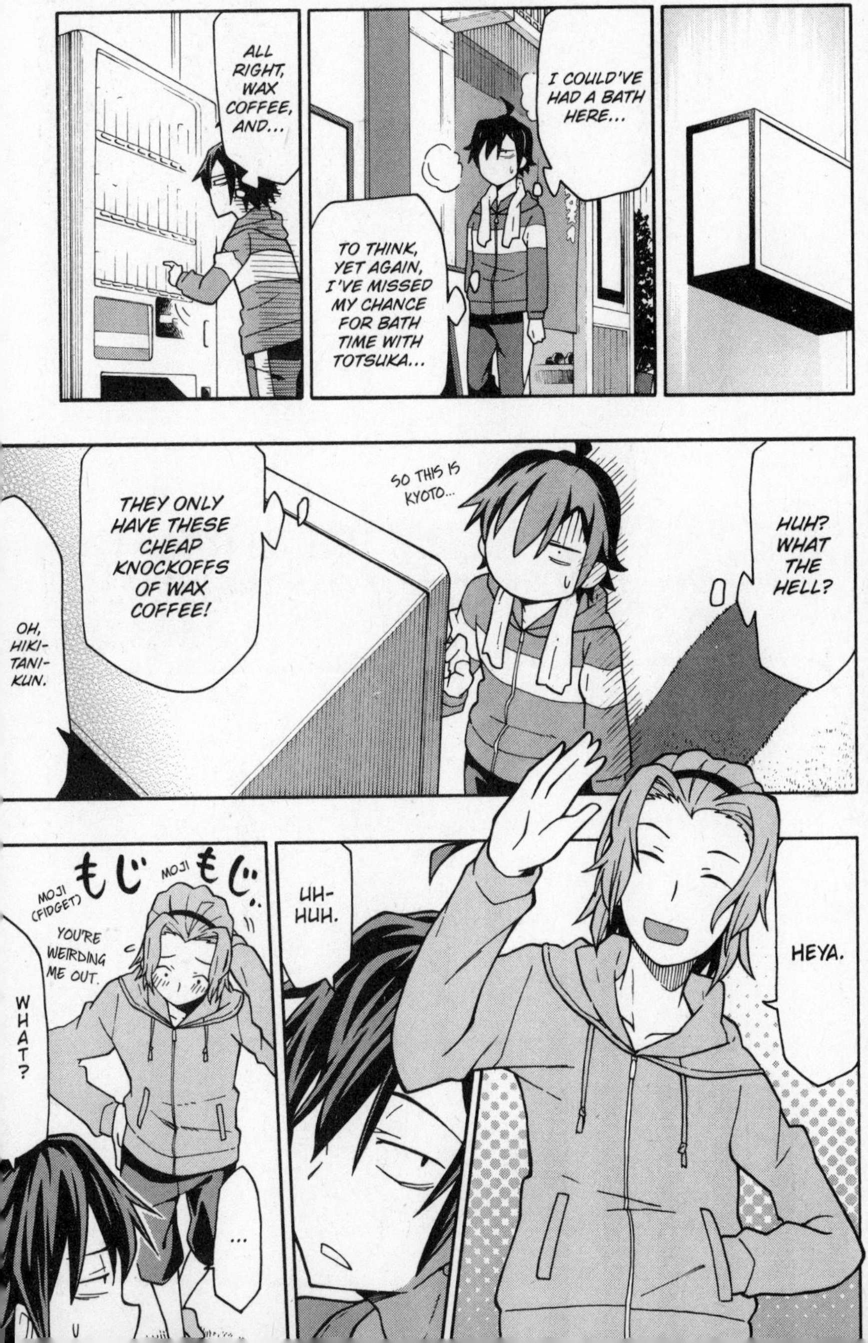
I COULD'VE HAD A BATH HERE...
TO THINK, YET AGAIN, I'VE MISSED MY CHANCE FOR BATH TIME WITH TOTSUKA...
ALL RIGHT, WAX COFFEE, AND...
HUH? WHAT THE HELL?
SO THIS IS KYOTO...
THEY ONLY HAVE THESE CHEAP KNOCKOFFS OF WAX COFFEE!
OH, HIKI-TANI-KUN.
HEYA.
UH-HUH.
MOJI もじ
MOJI (FIDGET) もじ
YOU'RE WEIRDING ME OUT.
WHAT?
...

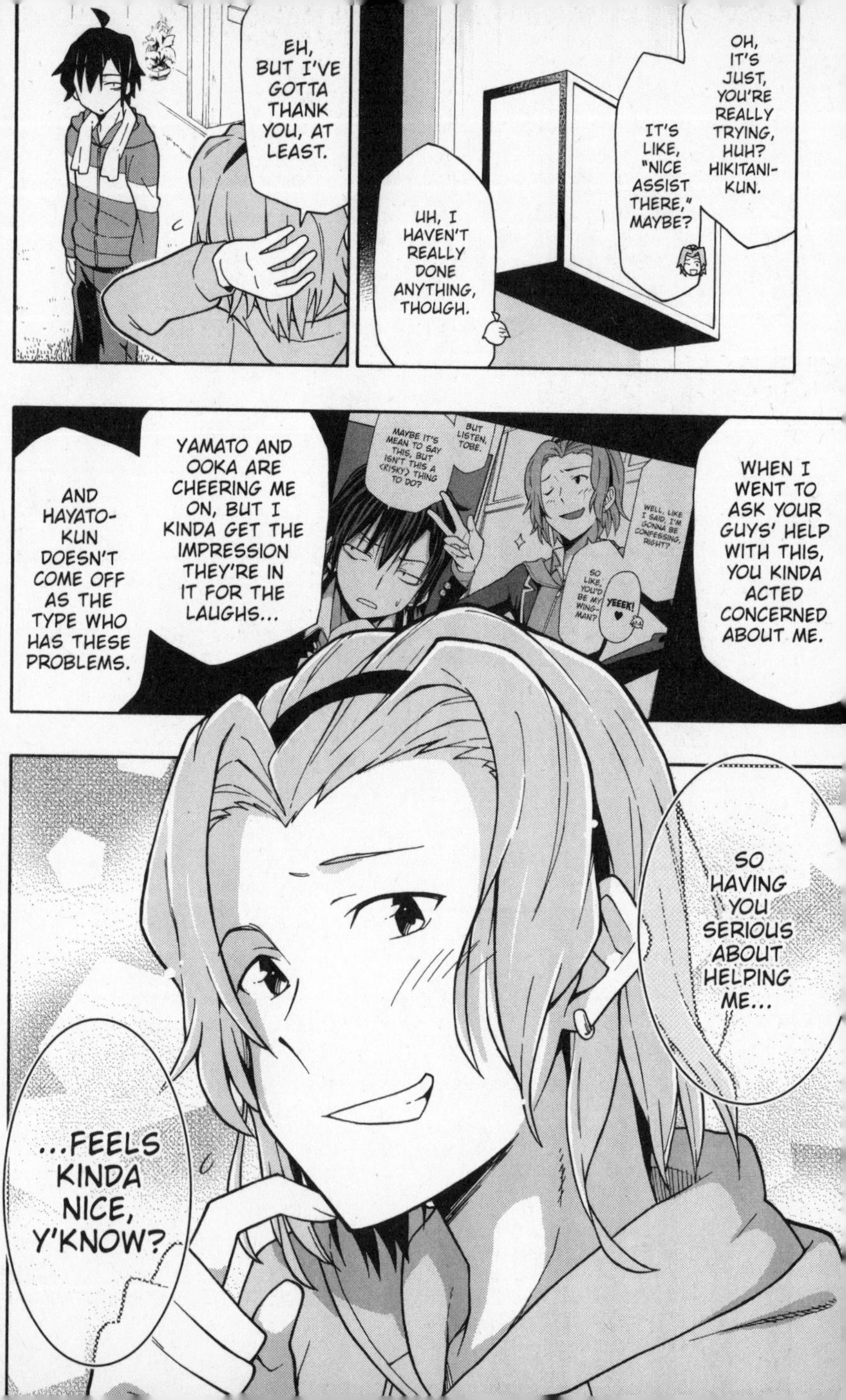
OH, IT'S JUST, YOU'RE REALLY TRYING, HUH? HIKITANI-KUN.
IT'S LIKE, "NICE ASSIST THERE," MAYBE?
UH, I HAVEN'T REALLY DONE ANYTHING, THOUGH.
EH, BUT I'VE GOTTA THANK YOU, AT LEAST.
WHEN I WENT TO ASK YOUR GUYS' HELP WITH THIS, YOU KINDA ACTED CONCERNED ABOUT ME.
BUT LISTEN, TOBE.
MAYBE IT'S MEAN TO SAY THIS, BUT ISN'T THIS A <RISKY> THING TO DO?
WELL, LIKE I SAID, I'M GONNA BE CONFESSING, RIGHT?
SO LIKE, YOU'D BE MY WING-MAN?
YEEEK!
YAMATO AND OOKA ARE CHEERING ME ON, BUT I KINDA GET THE IMPRESSION THEY'RE IN IT FOR THE LAUGHS...
AND HAYATO-KUN DOESN'T COME OFF AS THE TYPE WHO HAS THESE PROBLEMS.
SO HAVING YOU SERIOUS ABOUT HELPING ME...
...FEELS KINDA NICE, Y'KNOW?

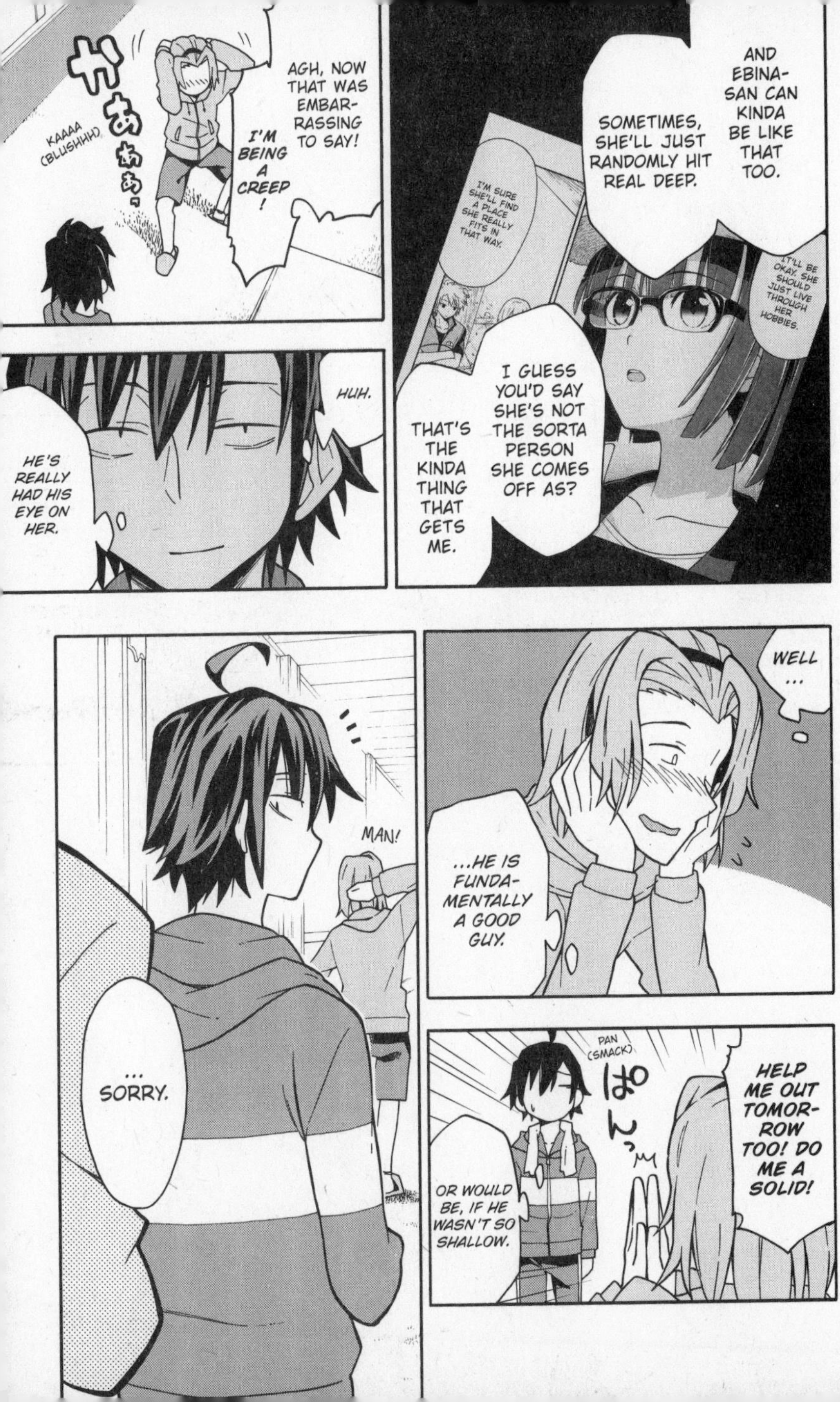
AND EBINA-SAN CAN KINDA BE LIKE THAT TOO.
SOMETIMES, SHE'LL JUST RANDOMLY HIT REAL DEEP.
IT'LL BE OKAY. SHE SHOULD JUST LIVE THROUGH HER HOBBIES.
I'M SURE SHE'LL FIND A PLACE SHE REALLY FITS IN THAT WAY.
I GUESS YOU'D SAY SHE'S NOT THE SORTA PERSON SHE COMES OFF AS?
THAT'S THE KINDA THING THAT GETS ME.
AGH, NOW THAT WAS EMBARRASSING TO SAY!
I'M BEING A CREEP!
かあぁぁ
KAAAA (BLUSHHH)
HUH.
HE'S REALLY HAD HIS EYE ON HER.
WELL...
...HE IS FUNDAMENTALLY A GOOD GUY.
HELP ME OUT TOMORROW TOO! DO ME A SOLID!
ぱんっ
PAN (SMACK)
OR WOULD BE, IF HE WASN'T SO SHALLOW.
MAN!
... SORRY.

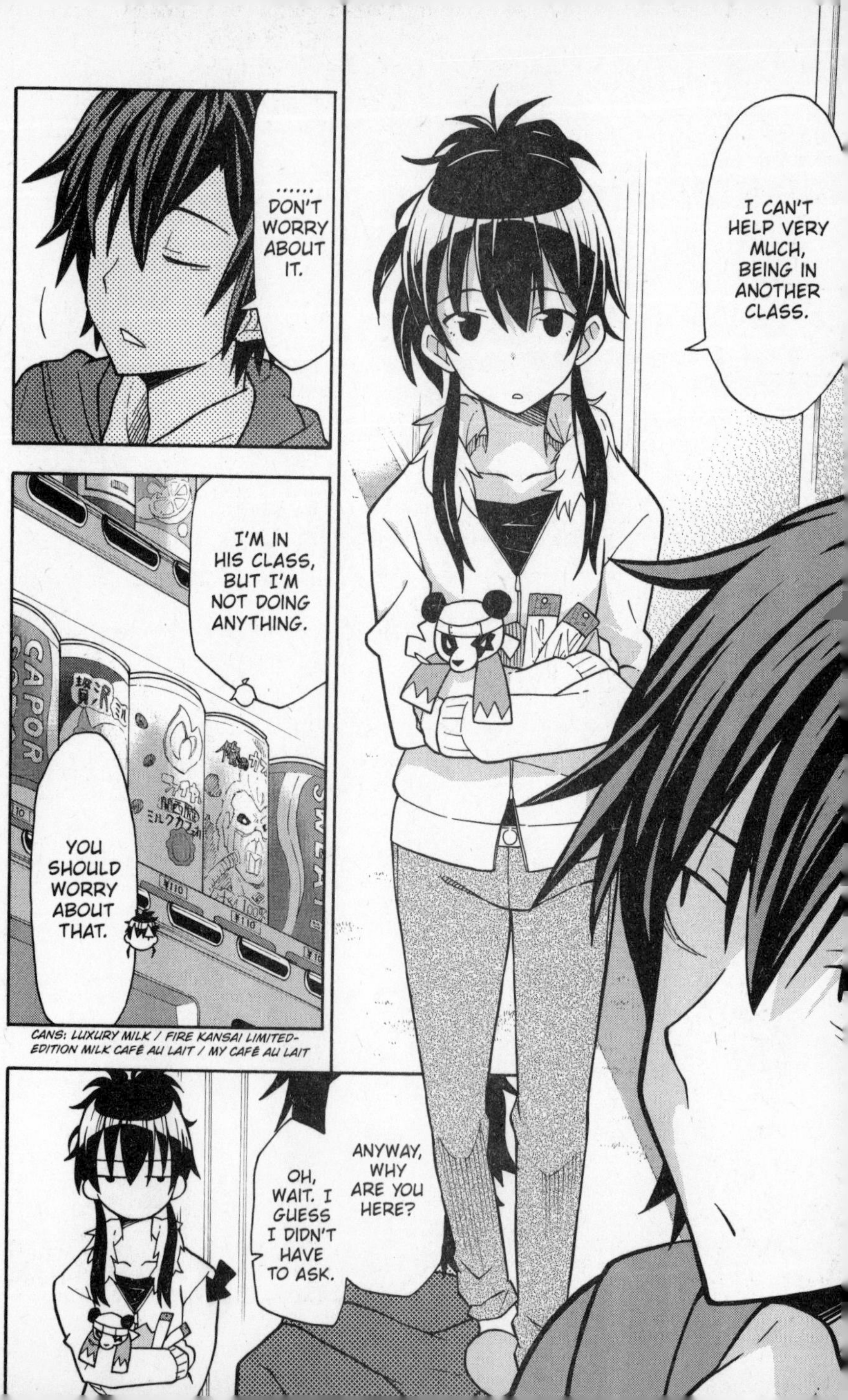
I CAN'T HELP VERY MUCH, BEING IN ANOTHER CLASS.
...... DON'T WORRY ABOUT IT.
I'M IN HIS CLASS, BUT I'M NOT DOING ANYTHING.
YOU SHOULD WORRY ABOUT THAT.
CANS: LUXURY MILK / FIRE KANSAI LIMITED-EDITION MILK CAFÉ AU LAIT / MY CAFÉ AU LAIT
ANYWAY, WHY ARE YOU HERE?
OH, WAIT. I GUESS I DIDN'T HAVE TO ASK.

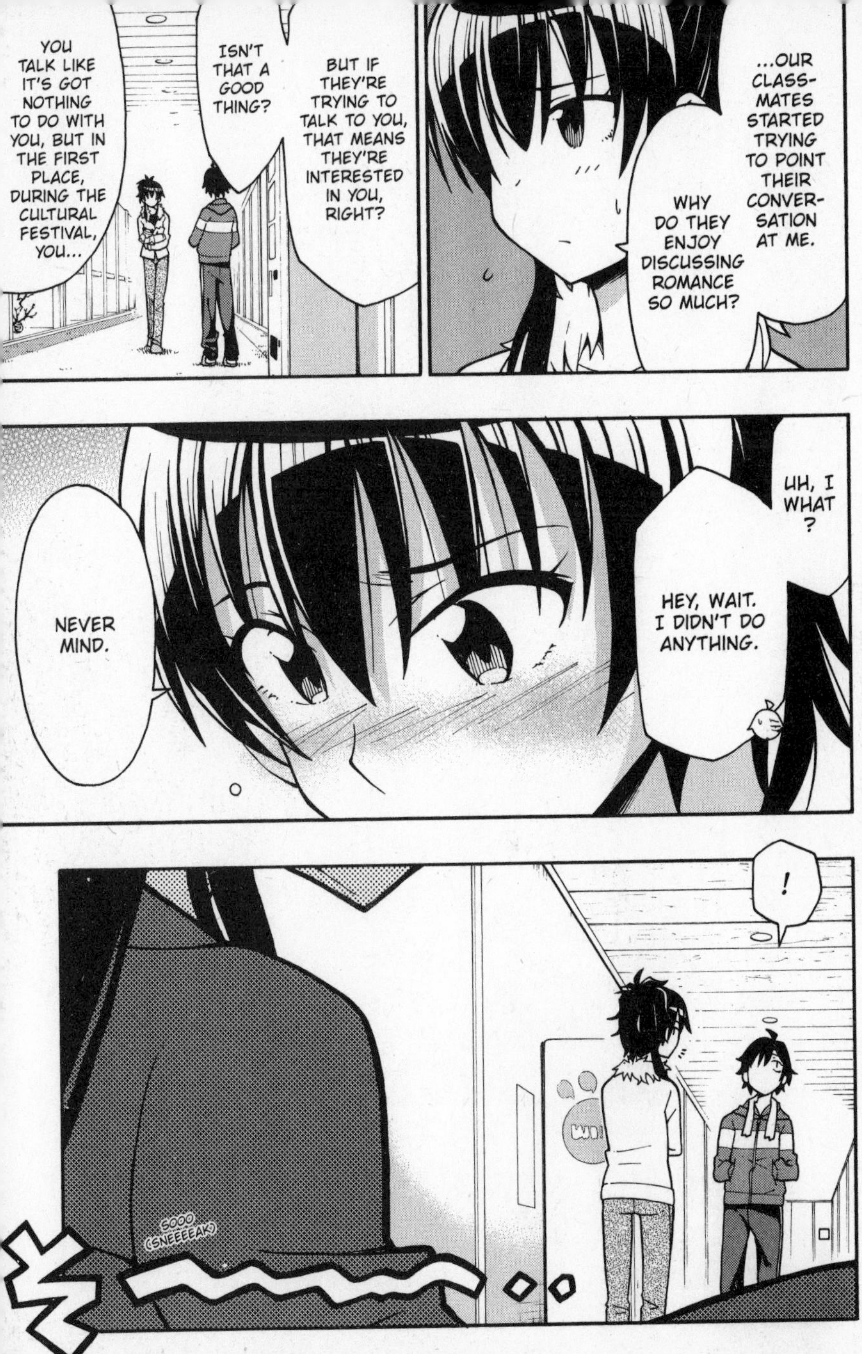
...OUR CLASSMATES STARTED TRYING TO POINT THEIR CONVERSATION AT ME.
WHY DO THEY ENJOY DISCUSSING ROMANCE SO MUCH?
BUT IF THEY'RE TRYING TO TALK TO YOU, THAT MEANS THEY'RE INTERESTED IN YOU, RIGHT?
ISN'T THAT A GOOD THING?
YOU TALK LIKE IT'S GOT NOTHING TO DO WITH YOU, BUT IN THE FIRST PLACE, DURING THE CULTURAL FESTIVAL, YOU...
UH, I WHAT?
HEY, WAIT. I DIDN'T DO ANYTHING.
NEVER MIND.
!
SOOO (SNEEEEAK)

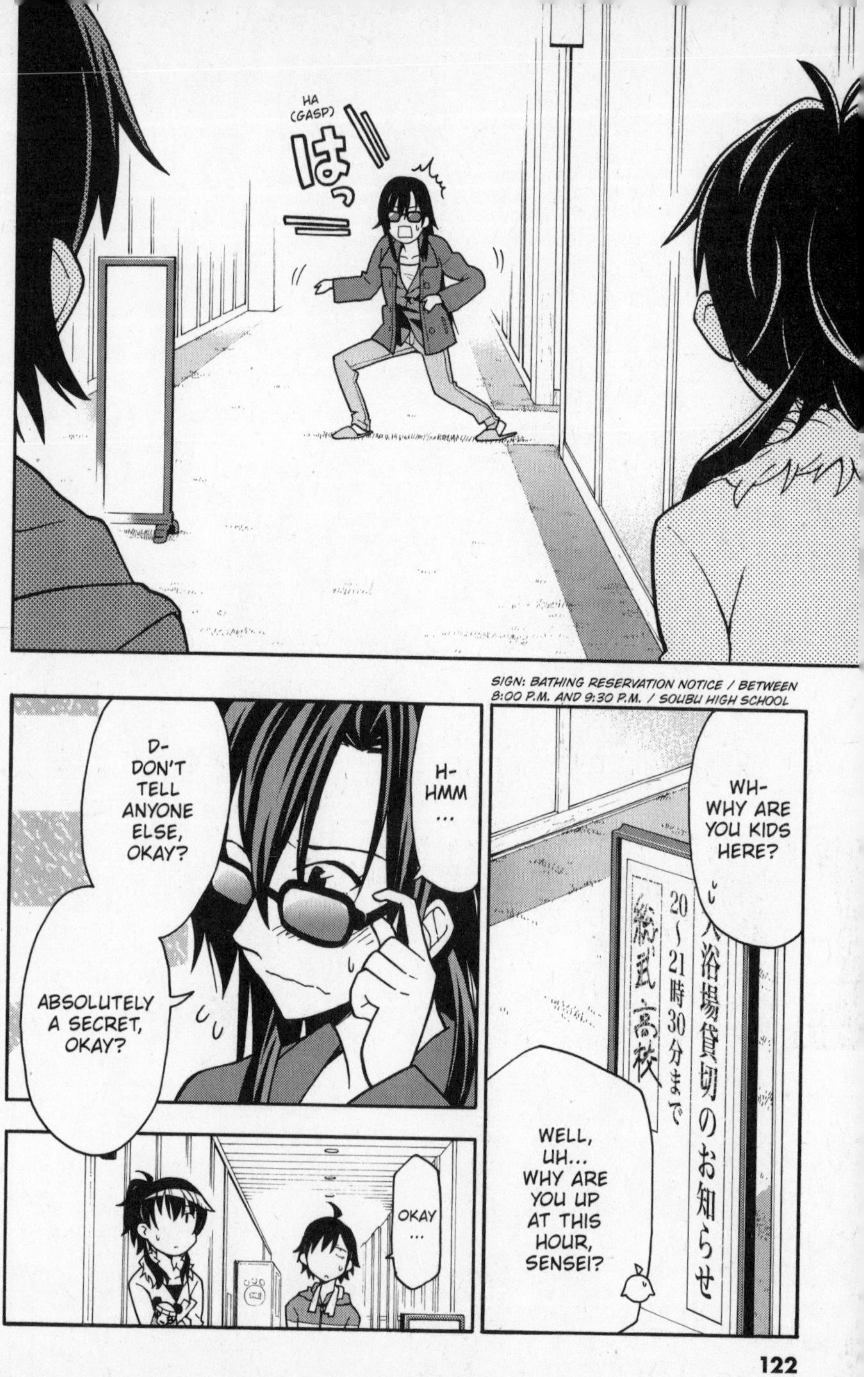
HA (GASP)
はっ
SIGN: BATHING RESERVATION NOTICE / BETWEEN 8:00 P.M. AND 9:30 P.M. / SOUBU HIGH SCHOOL
WH- WHY ARE YOU KIDS HERE?
入浴場貸切のお知らせ
20~21時30分まで
総武高校
WELL, UH... WHY ARE YOU UP AT THIS HOUR, SENSEI?
H- HMM ...
D- DON'T TELL ANYONE ELSE, OKAY?
ABSOLUTELY A SECRET, OKAY?
OKAY ...

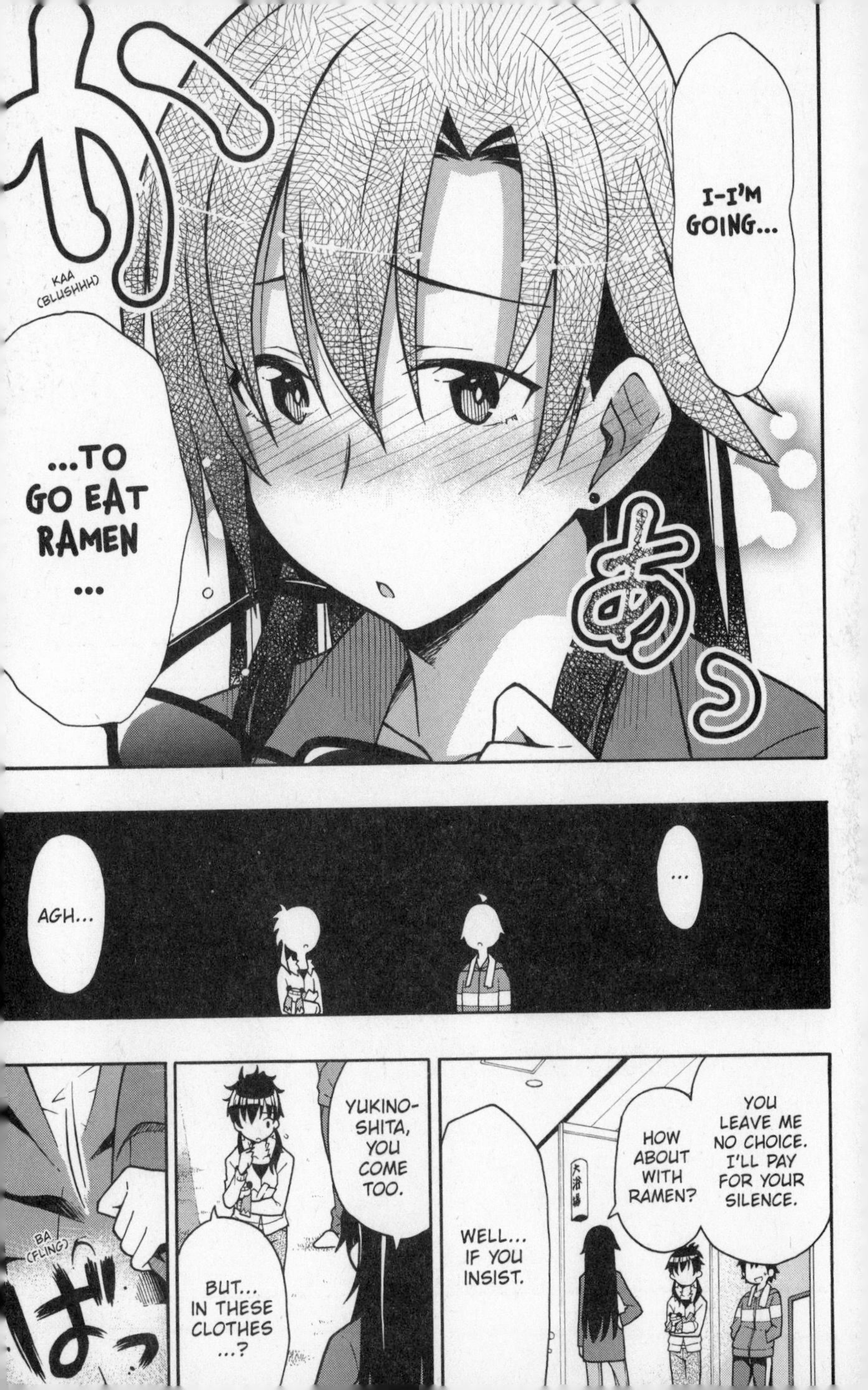
I-I'M GOING...
KAA (BLUSHHH)
...TO GO EAT RAMEN ...
...
AGH...
YOU LEAVE ME NO CHOICE. I'LL PAY FOR YOUR SILENCE.
HOW ABOUT WITH RAMEN?
WELL... IF YOU INSIST.
YUKINO-SHITA, YOU COME TOO.
BUT... IN THESE CLOTHES ...?
BA (FLING)

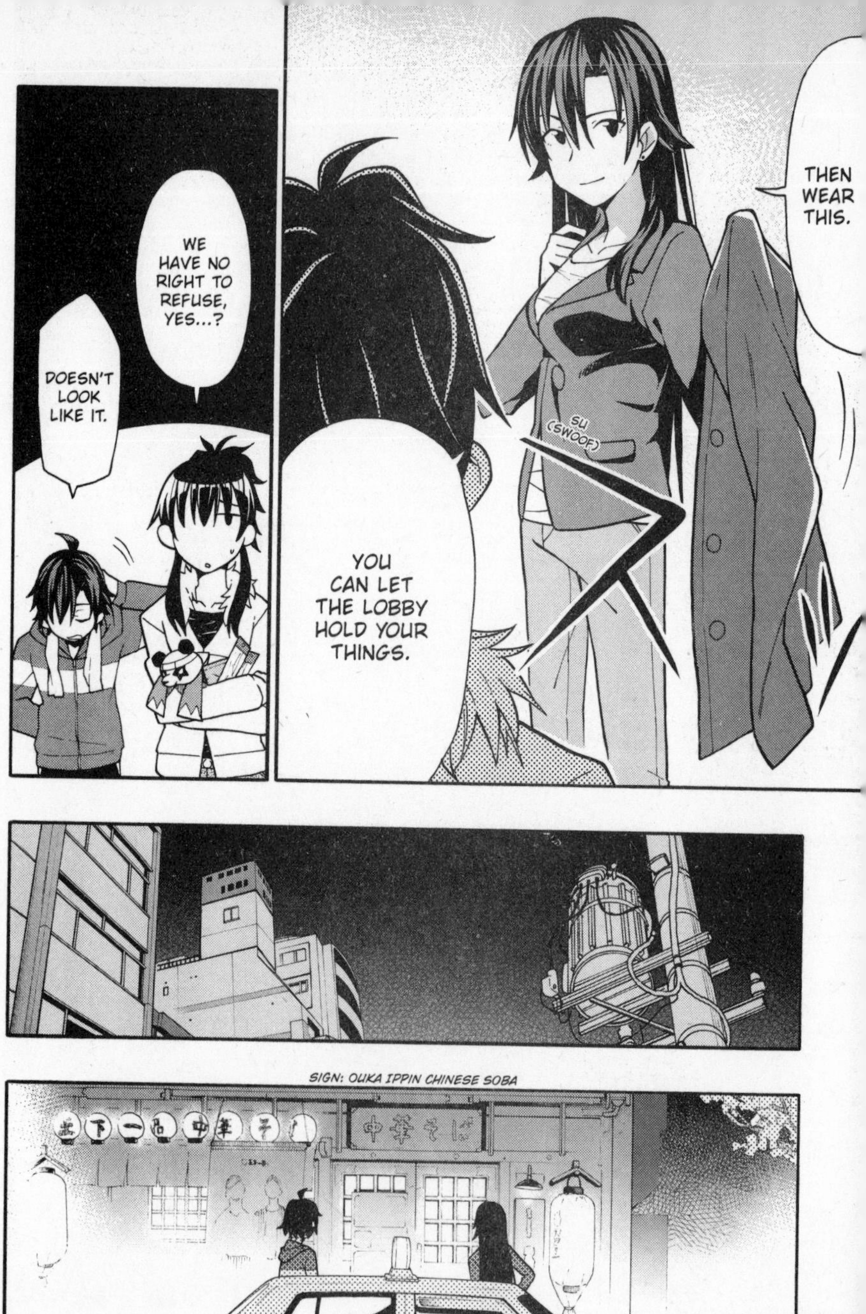
THEN WEAR THIS.
SU (SWOOF)
YOU CAN LET THE LOBBY HOLD YOUR THINGS.
WE HAVE NO RIGHT TO REFUSE, YES...?
DOESN'T LOOK LIKE IT.
SIGN: OUKA IPPIN CHINESE SOBA

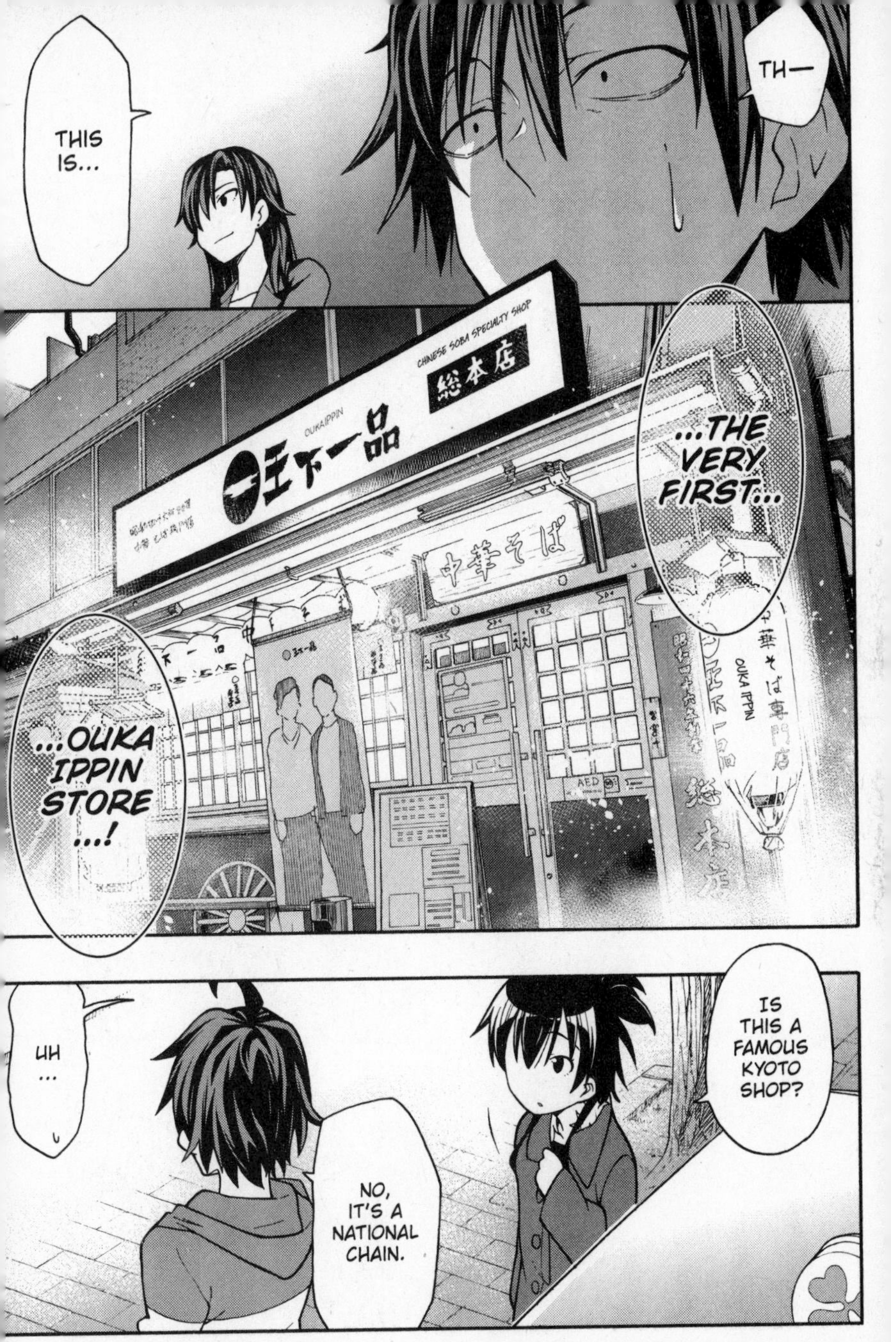
TH—
THIS IS...
CHINESE SOBA SPECIALTY SHOP
総本店
OUKAIPPIN
王下一品
中華そば
OUKA IPPIN
...THE VERY FIRST...
...OUKA IPPIN STORE ...!
IS THIS A FAMOUS KYOTO SHOP?
UH ...
NO, IT'S A NATIONAL CHAIN.

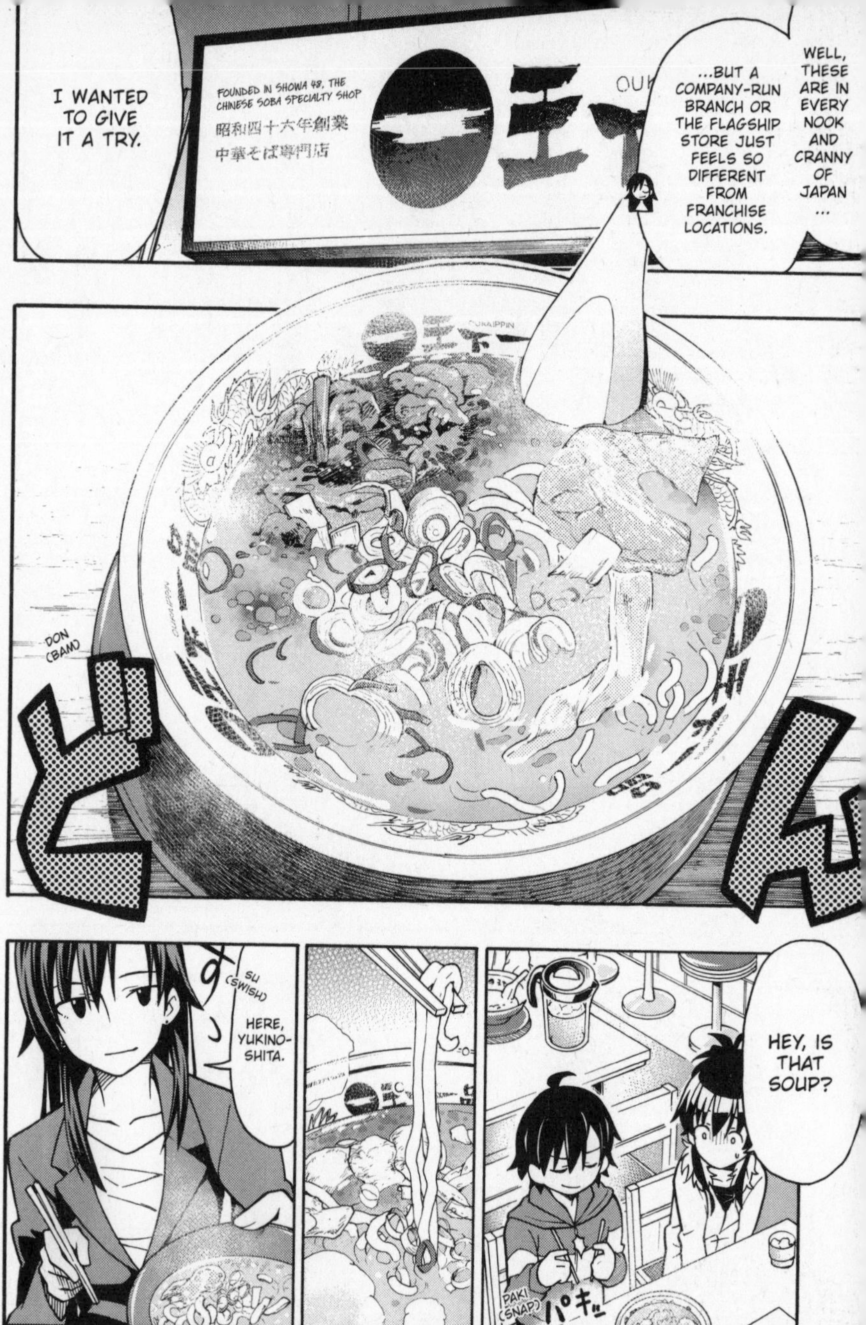
WELL, THESE ARE IN EVERY NOOK AND CRANNY OF JAPAN...
...BUT A COMPANY-RUN BRANCH OR THE FLAGSHIP STORE JUST FEELS SO DIFFERENT FROM FRANCHISE LOCATIONS.
FOUNDED IN SHOWA 48, THE CHINESE SOBA SPECIALTY SHOP
昭和四十六年創業
中華そば専門店
I WANTED TO GIVE IT A TRY.
OUKAIPPIN
DON (BAM)
HEY, IS THAT SOUP?
PAKI (SNAP)
パキッ
す
SU (SWISH)
HERE, YUKINO-SHITA.

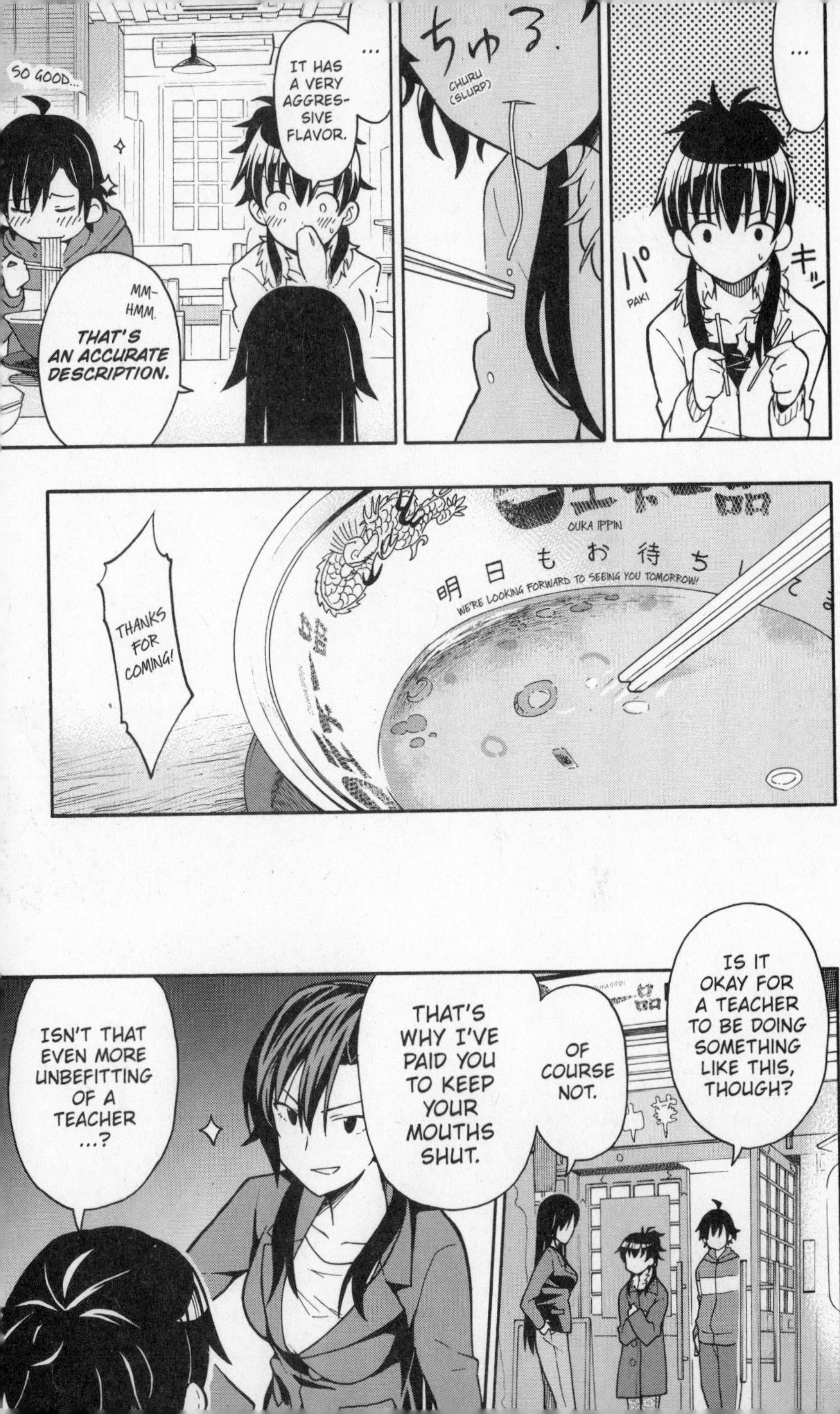
...
パキッ
PAKI
ちゅる
CHURU (SLURP)
...
IT HAS A VERY AGGRES-SIVE FLAVOR.
SO GOOD...
MM-HMM. THAT'S AN ACCURATE DESCRIPTION.
OUKA IPPIN
明日もお待ち
WE'RE LOOKING FORWARD TO SEEING YOU TOMORROW!
THANKS FOR COMING!
IS IT OKAY FOR A TEACHER TO BE DOING SOMETHING LIKE THIS, THOUGH?
OF COURSE NOT.
THAT'S WHY I'VE PAID YOU TO KEEP YOUR MOUTHS SHUT.
ISN'T THAT EVEN MORE UNBEFITTING OF A TEACHER ...?

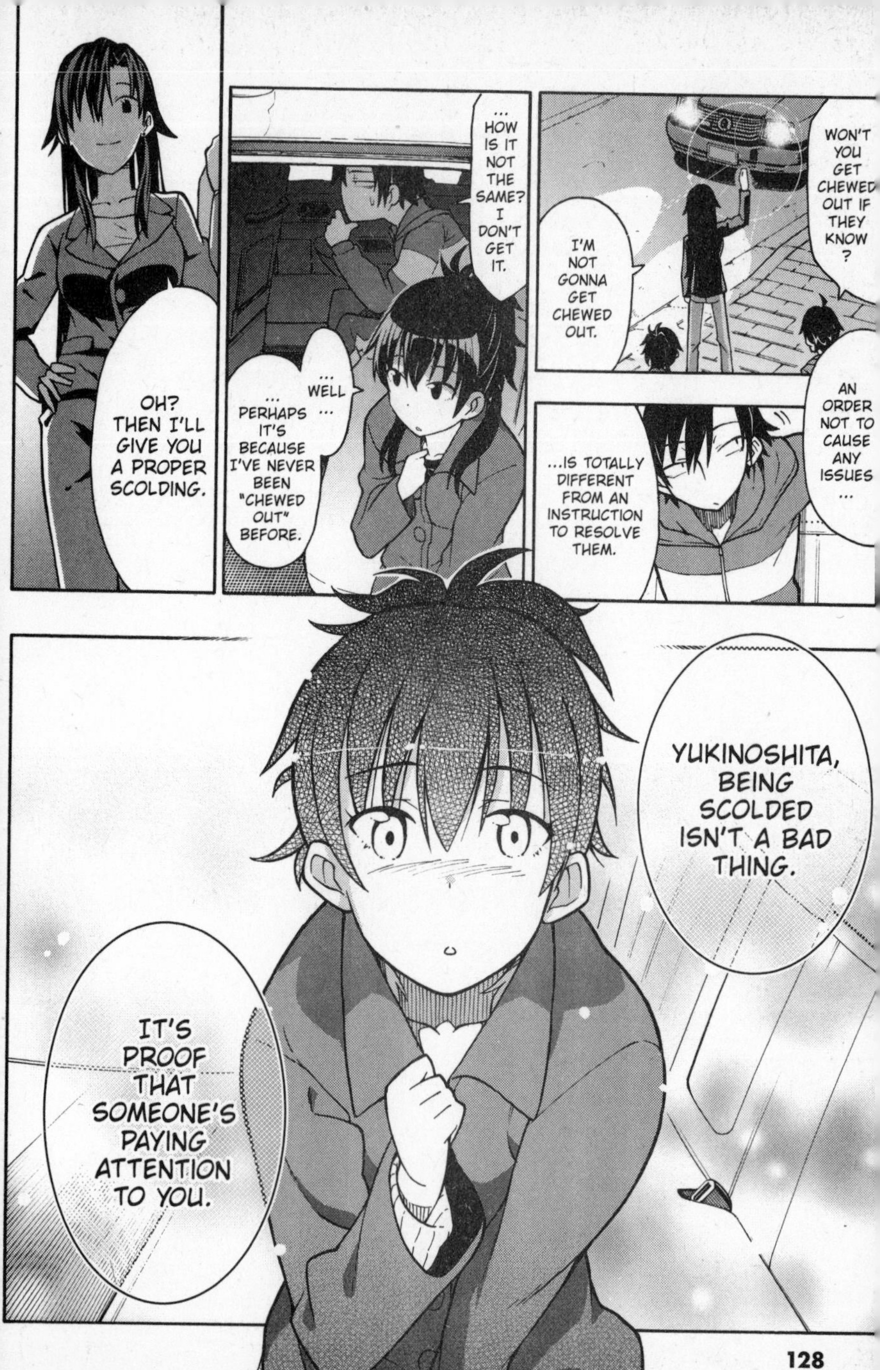
WON'T YOU GET CHEWED OUT IF THEY KNOW?
I'M NOT GONNA GET CHEWED OUT.
AN ORDER NOT TO CAUSE ANY ISSUES...
...IS TOTALLY DIFFERENT FROM AN INSTRUCTION TO RESOLVE THEM.
...HOW IS IT NOT THE SAME? I DON'T GET IT.
...WELL...
...PERHAPS IT'S BECAUSE I'VE NEVER BEEN "CHEWED OUT" BEFORE.
OH? THEN I'LL GIVE YOU A PROPER SCOLDING.
YUKINOSHITA, BEING SCOLDED ISN'T A BAD THING.
IT'S PROOF THAT SOMEONE'S PAYING ATTENTION TO YOU.

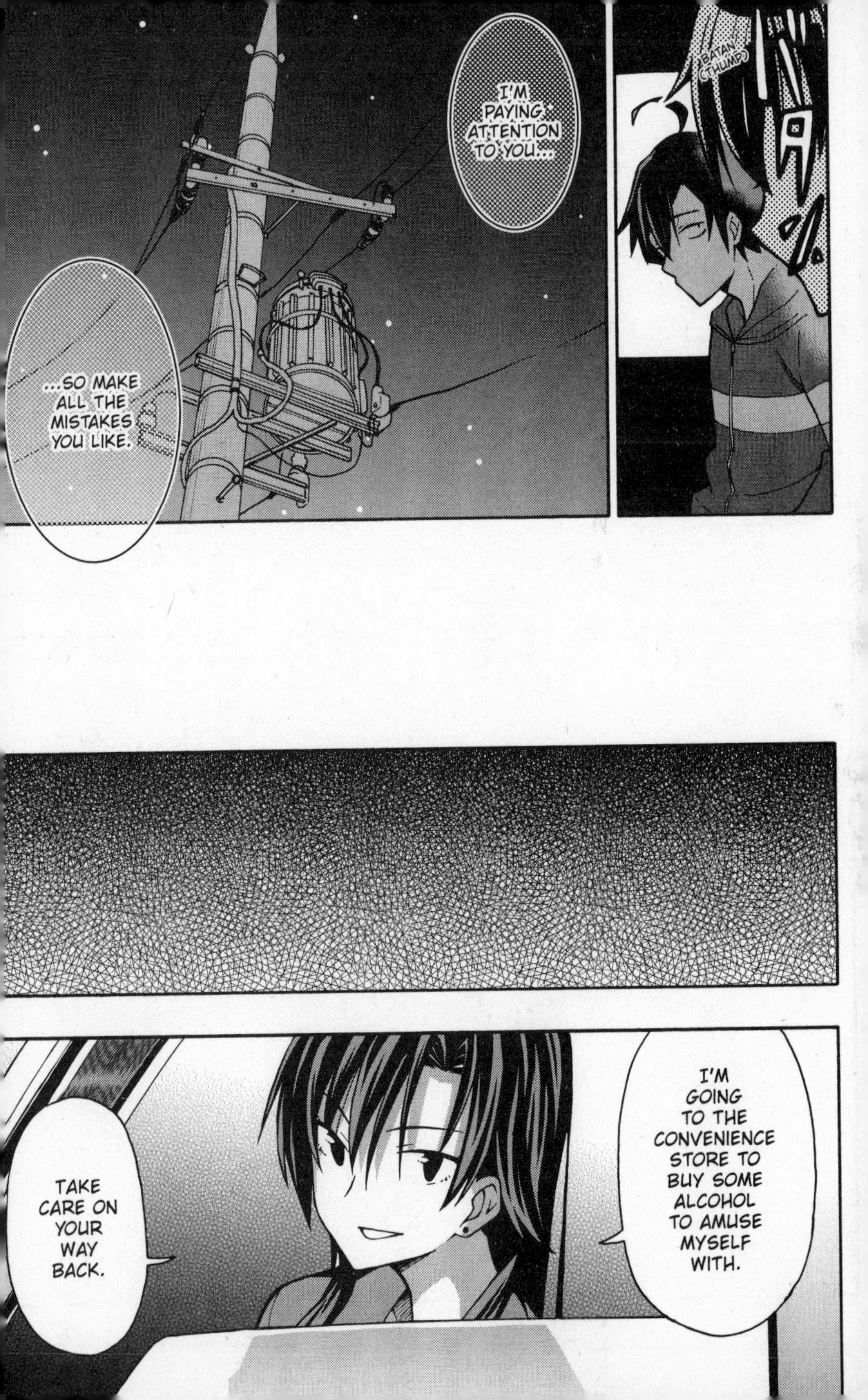
BATAN (THUMP)
I'M PAYING ATTENTION TO YOU...
...SO MAKE ALL THE MISTAKES YOU LIKE.
I'M GOING TO THE CONVENIENCE STORE TO BUY SOME ALCOHOL TO AMUSE MYSELF WITH.
TAKE CARE ON YOUR WAY BACK.

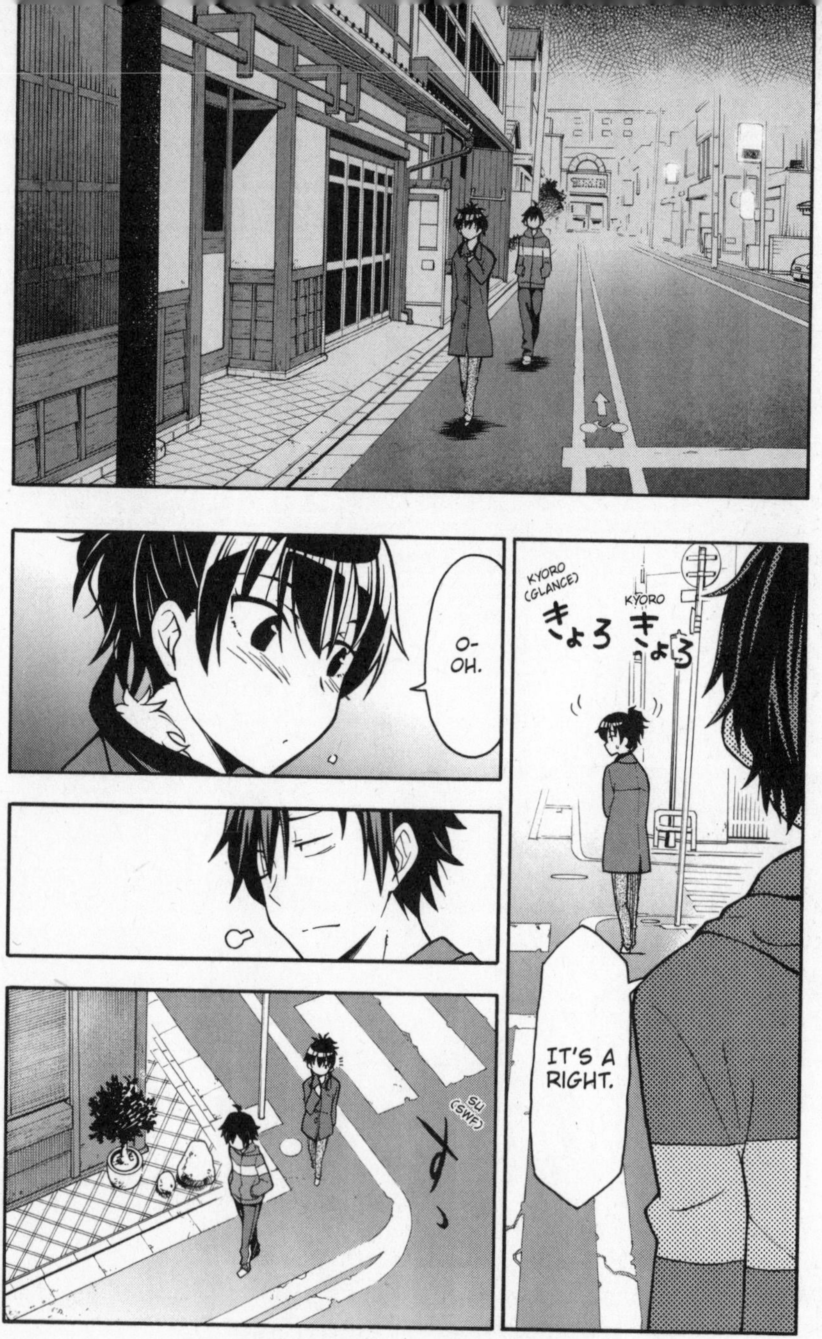
KYORO (GLANCE)
きょろ
KYORO
きょろ
IT'S A RIGHT.
O-OH.
SU (SWF)
す

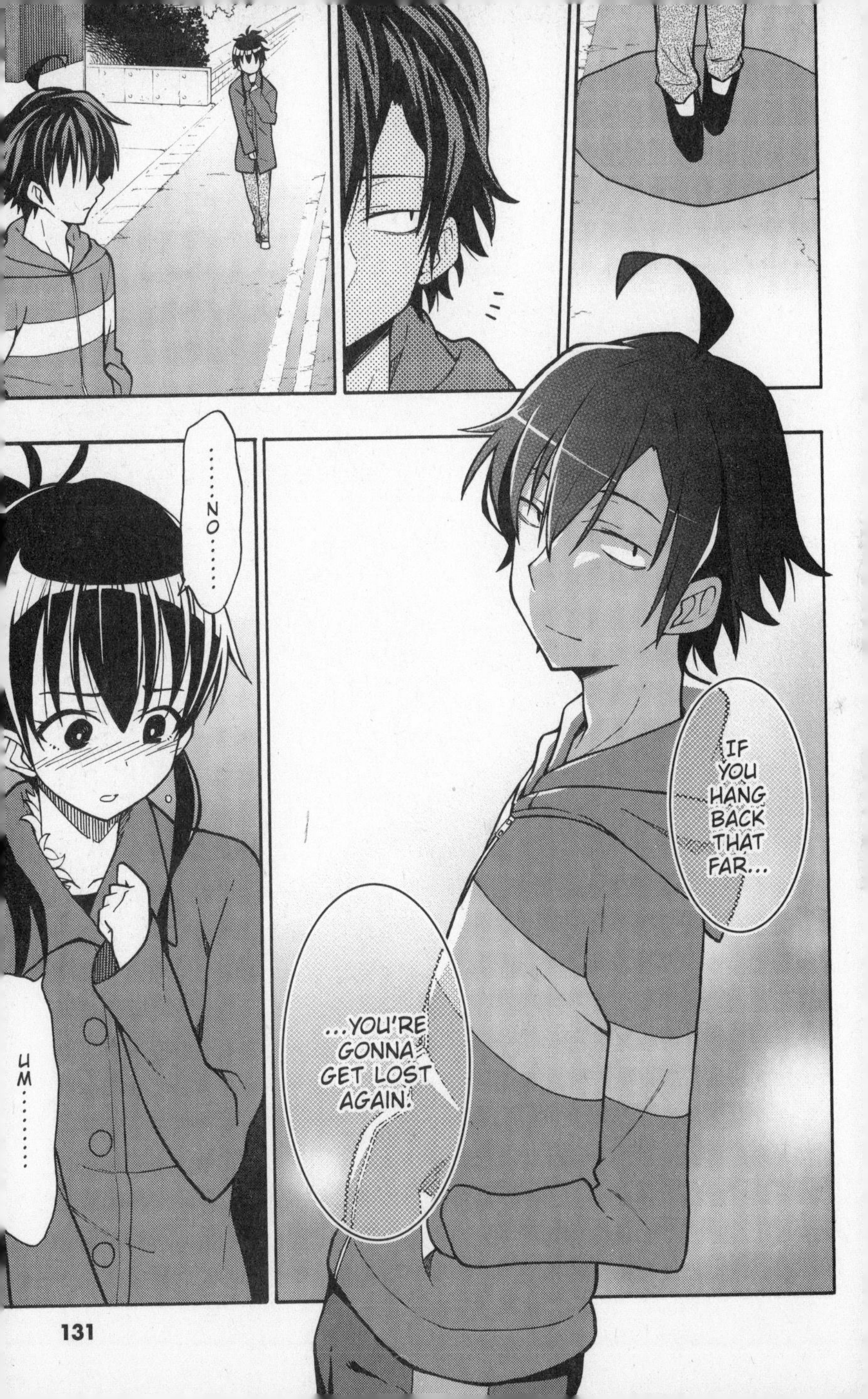
IF YOU HANG BACK THAT FAR...
...YOU'RE GONNA GET LOST AGAIN.
......NO......
UM......

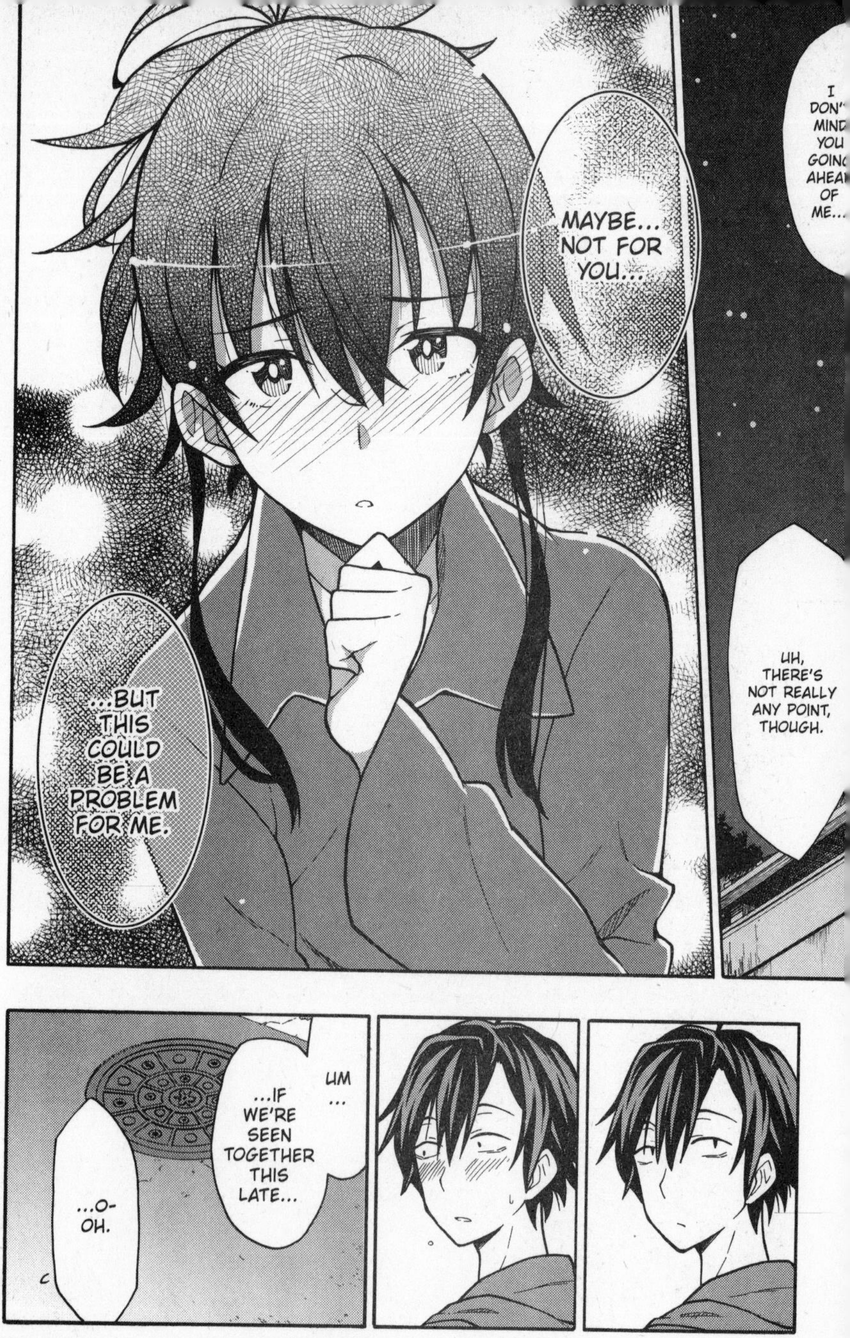
I DON' MIND YOU GOIN AHEA OF ME...
UH, THERE'S NOT REALLY ANY POINT, THOUGH.
MAYBE... NOT FOR YOU...
...BUT THIS COULD BE A PROBLEM FOR ME.
UM ...
...IF WE'RE SEEN TOGETHER THIS LATE...
...O-OH.

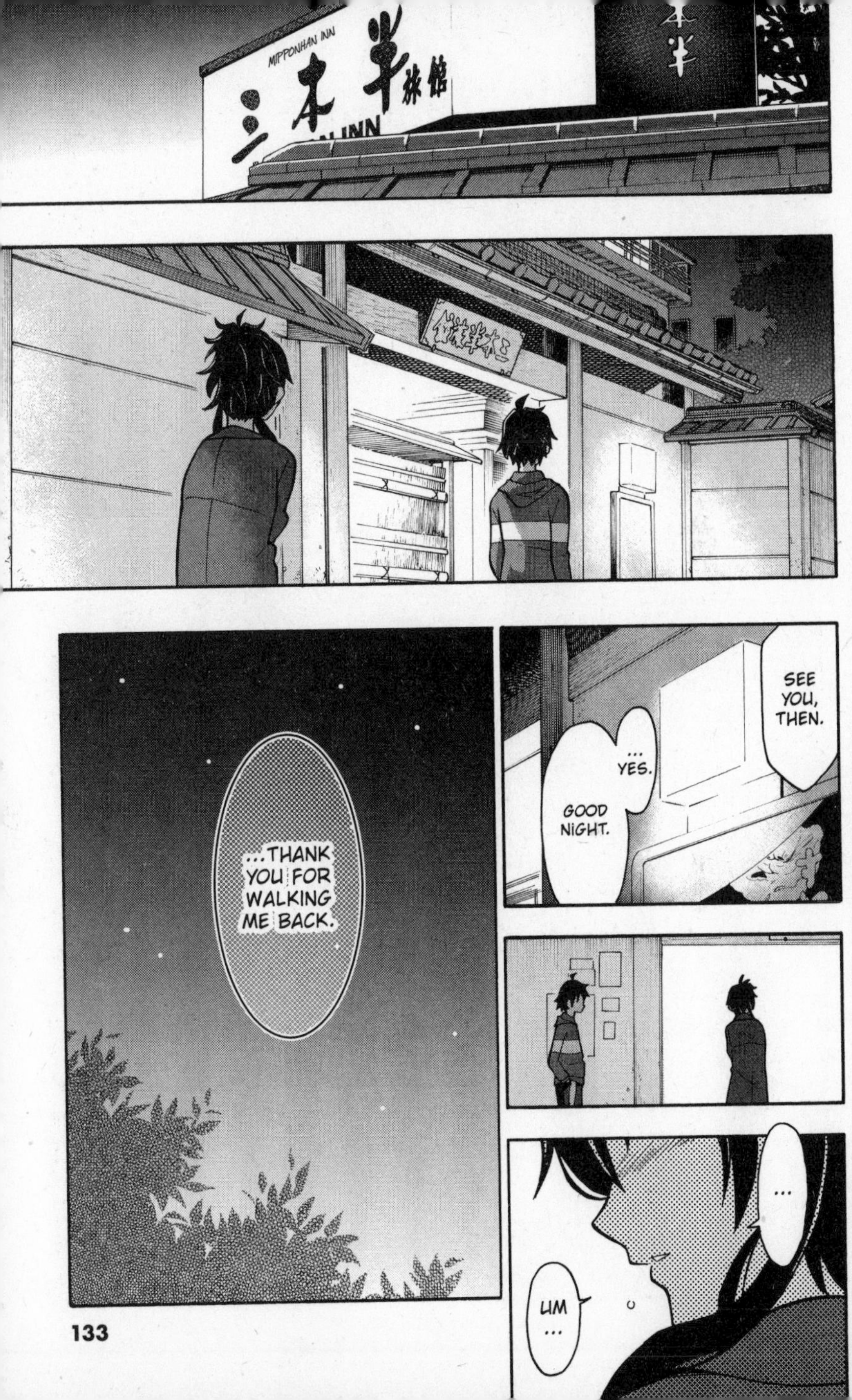
MIPPONHAN INN
三本半旅館
SEE YOU, THEN.
... YES.
GOOD NIGHT.
...
UM ...
...THANK YOU FOR WALKING ME BACK.

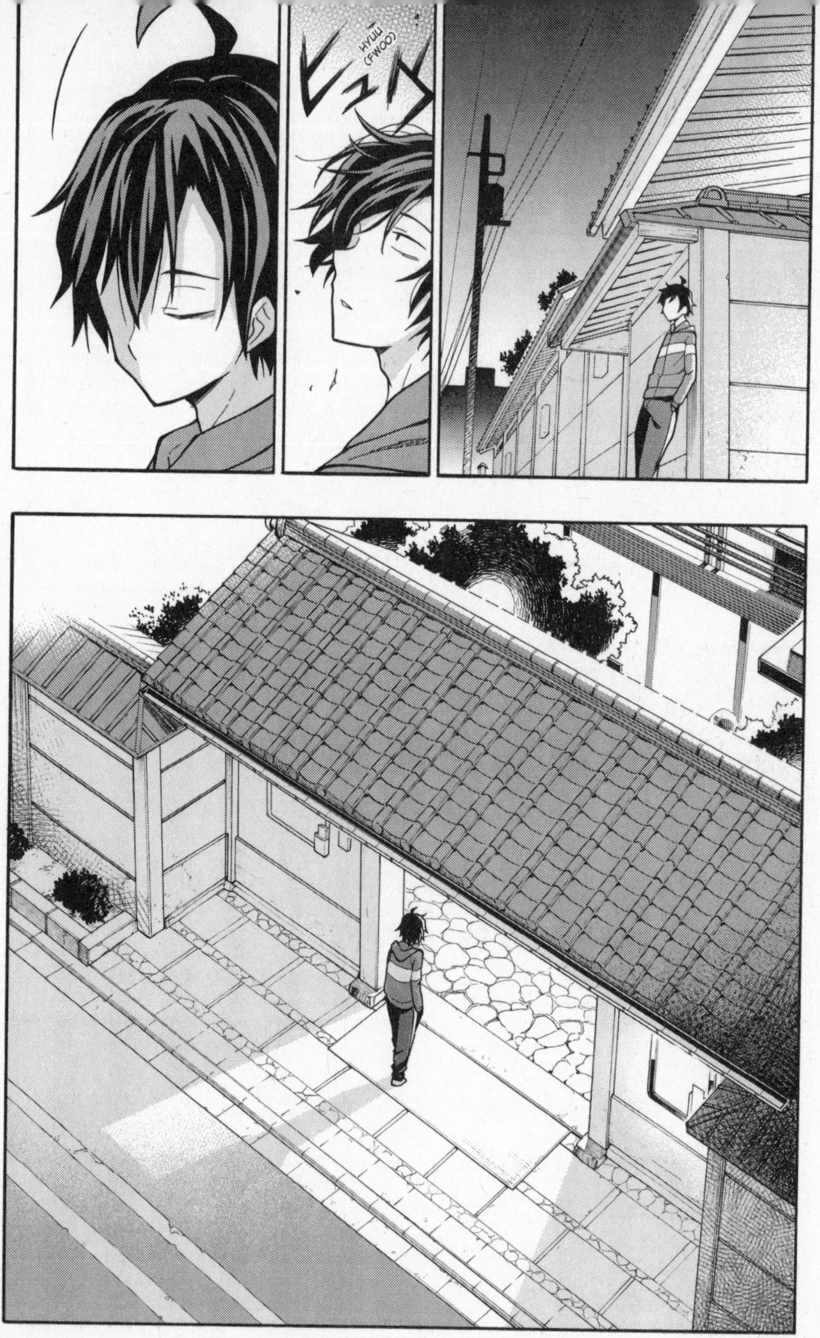
ヒュウ
HYUU
(FWOO)

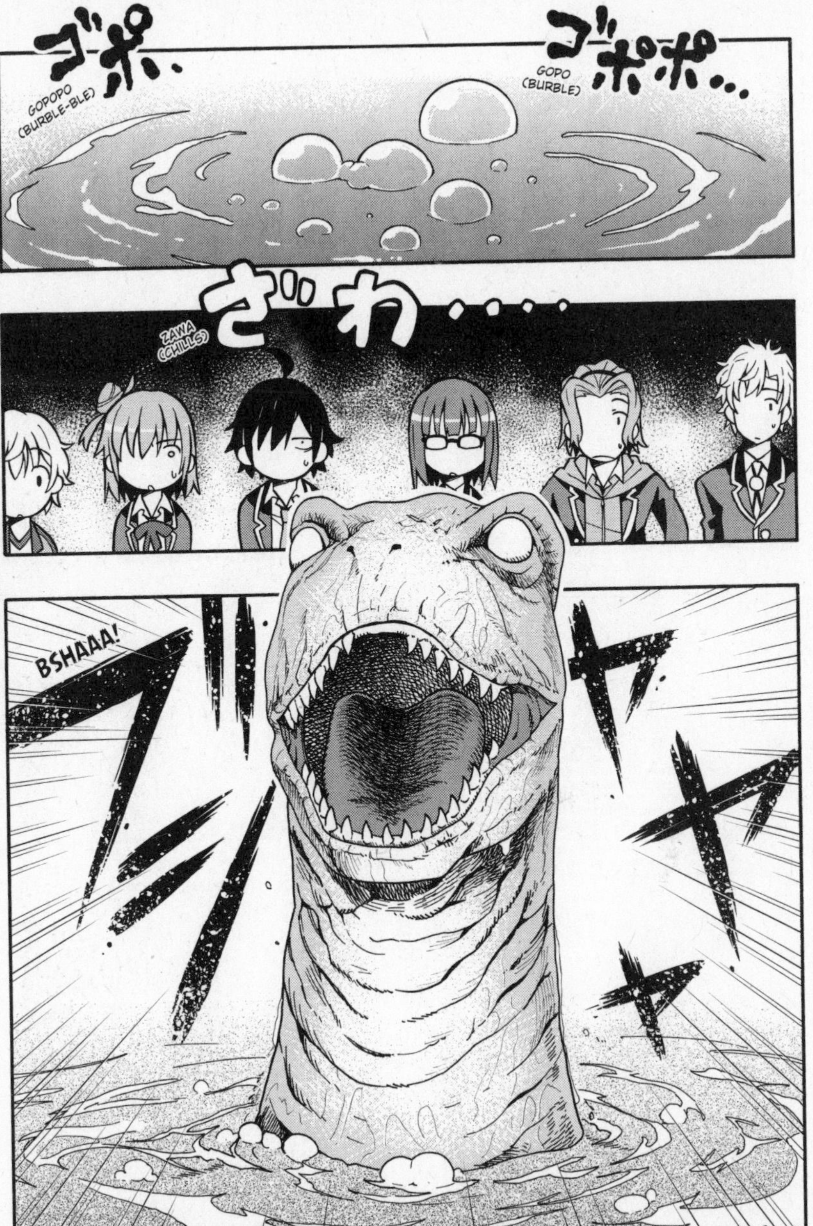
ゴポポ…
GOPO (BURBLE)
ゴポ、
GOPOPO (BURBLE-BLE)
ざわ……
ZAWA (CHILLS)
BSHAAA!

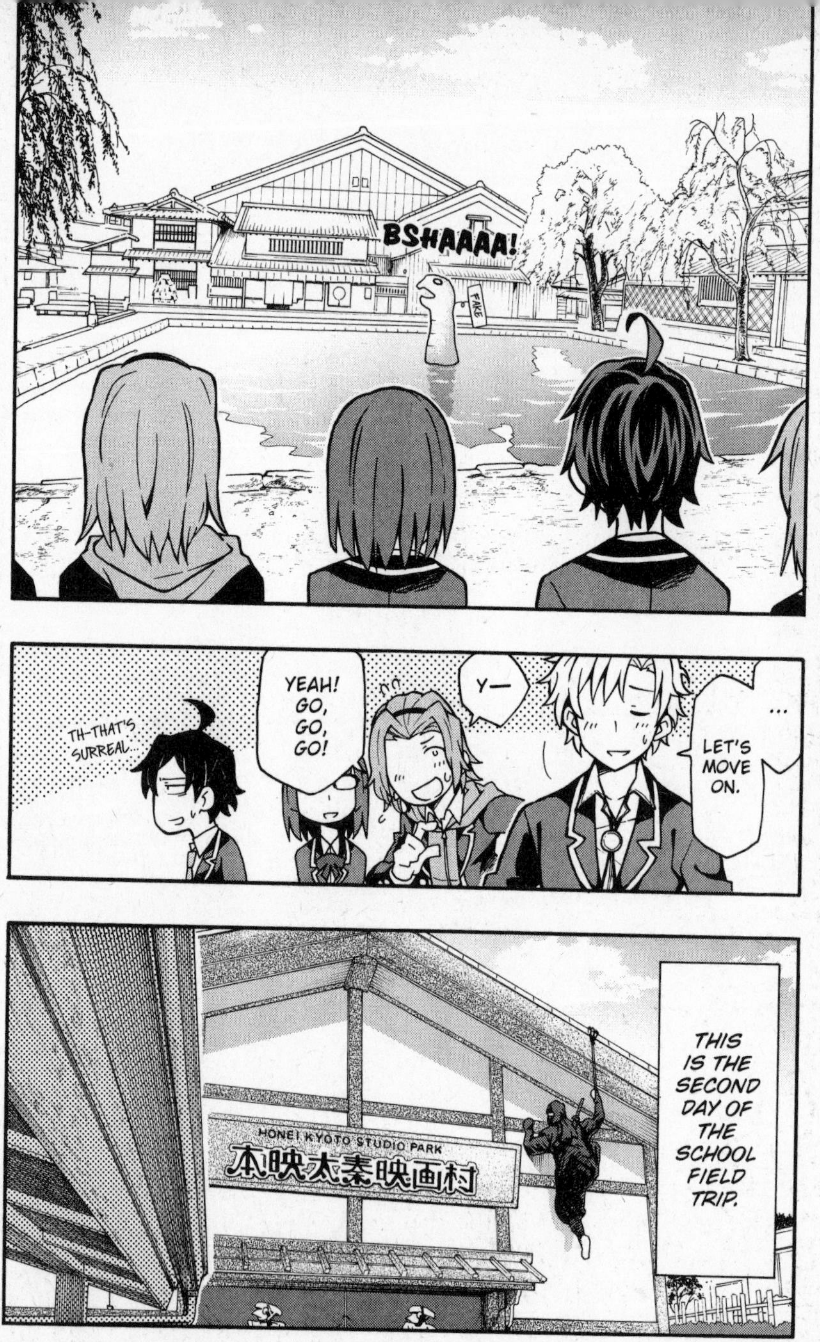
BSHAAAA!
FAKE
... LET'S MOVE ON.
Y—
YEAH! GO, GO, GO!
TH-THAT'S SURREAL...
THIS IS THE SECOND DAY OF THE SCHOOL FIELD TRIP.
HONEI KYOTO STUDIO PARK
本映太秦映画村

CHAPTER 52 ··· UNEXPECTEDLY, YUMIKO MIU RA IS ACTUALLY PAYING ATTENTION.

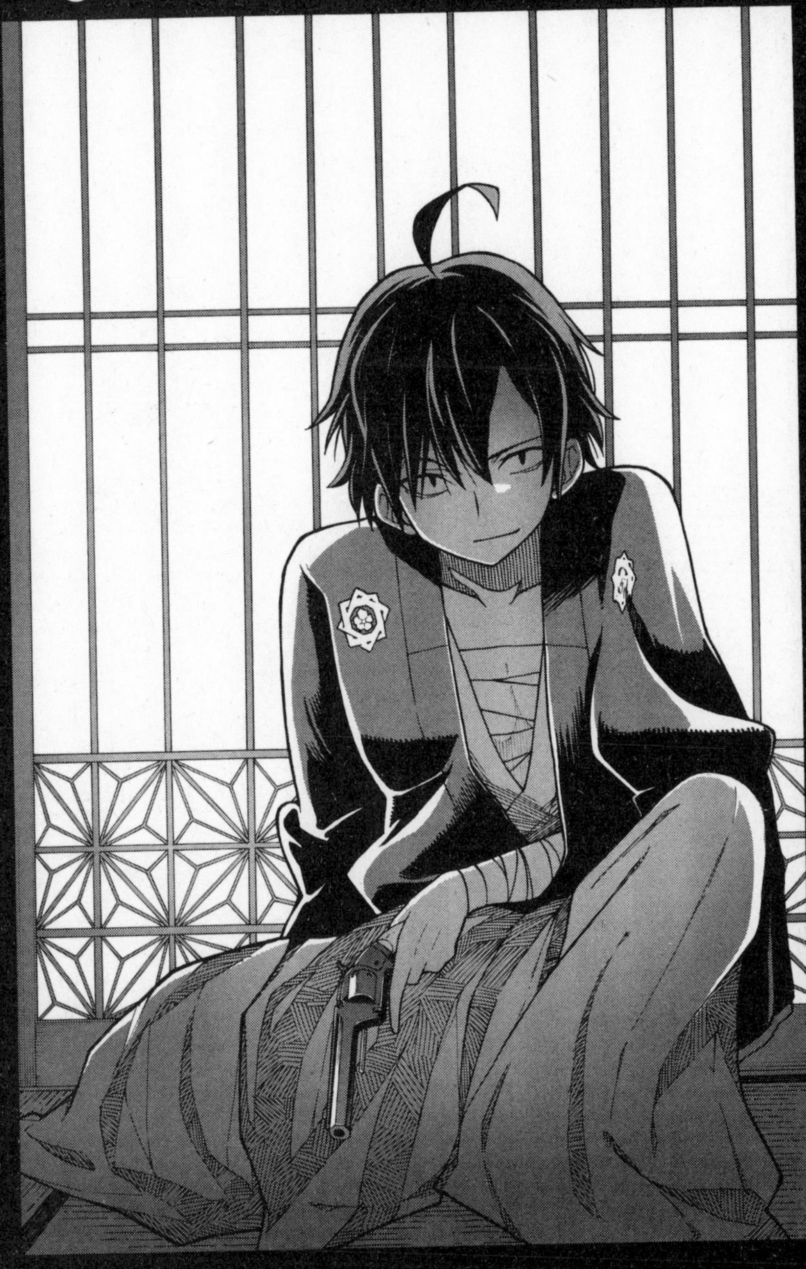

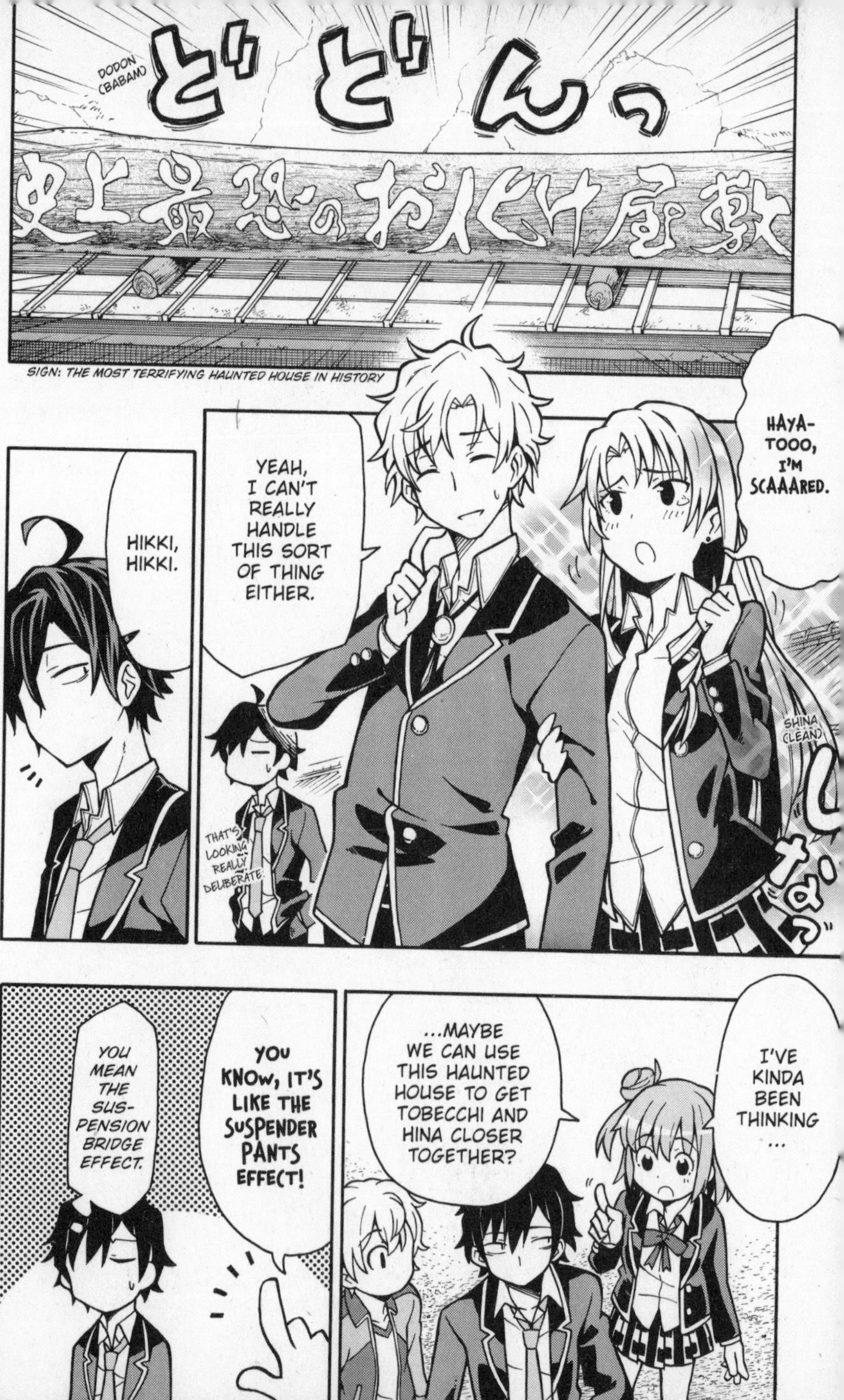
DODON (BABAM)
どどんっ
史上最恐のお化け屋敷
SIGN: THE MOST TERRIFYING HAUNTED HOUSE IN HISTORY
HAYA-TOOO, I'M SCAAARED.
SHINA (LEAN)
しなっ
YEAH, I CAN'T REALLY HANDLE THIS SORT OF THING EITHER.
THAT'S LOOKING REALLY DELIBERATE.
HIKKI, HIKKI.
I'VE KINDA BEEN THINKING...
...MAYBE WE CAN USE THIS HAUNTED HOUSE TO GET TOBECCHI AND HINA CLOSER TOGETHER?
YOU KNOW, IT'S LIKE THE SUSPENDER PANTS EFFECT!
YOU MEAN THE SUSPENSION BRIDGE EFFECT.

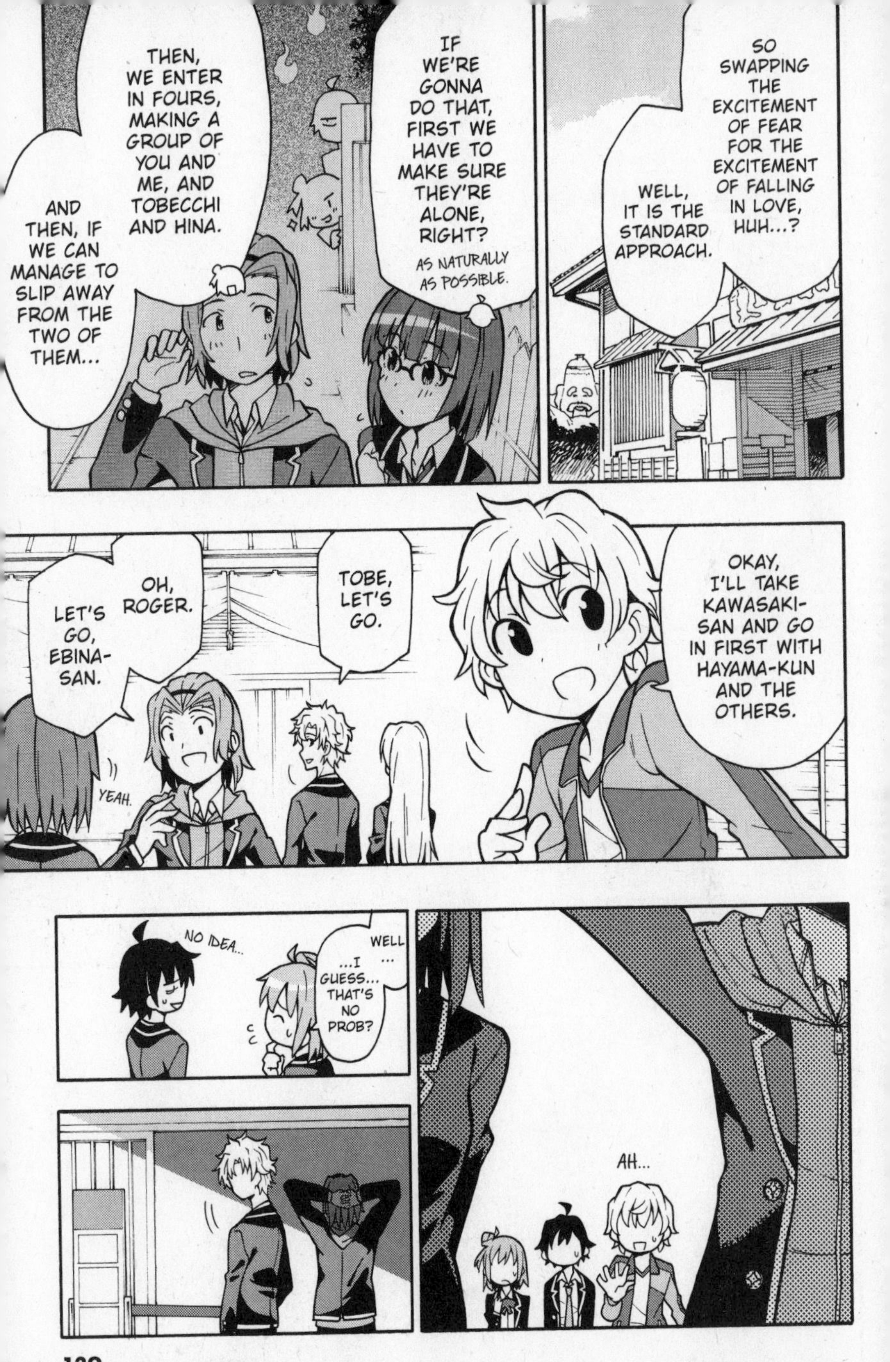
SO SWAPPING THE EXCITEMENT OF FEAR FOR THE EXCITEMENT OF FALLING IN LOVE, HUH...?
WELL, IT IS THE STANDARD APPROACH.
IF WE'RE GONNA DO THAT, FIRST WE HAVE TO MAKE SURE THEY'RE ALONE, RIGHT?
AS NATURALLY AS POSSIBLE.
THEN, WE ENTER IN FOURS, MAKING A GROUP OF YOU AND ME, AND TOBECCHI AND HINA.
AND THEN, IF WE CAN MANAGE TO SLIP AWAY FROM THE TWO OF THEM...
OKAY, I'LL TAKE KAWASAKI-SAN AND GO IN FIRST WITH HAYAMA-KUN AND THE OTHERS.
TOBE, LET'S GO.
OH, ROGER.
LET'S GO, EBINA-SAN.
YEAH.
AH...
WELL ... ...I GUESS... THAT'S NO PROB?
NO IDEA...

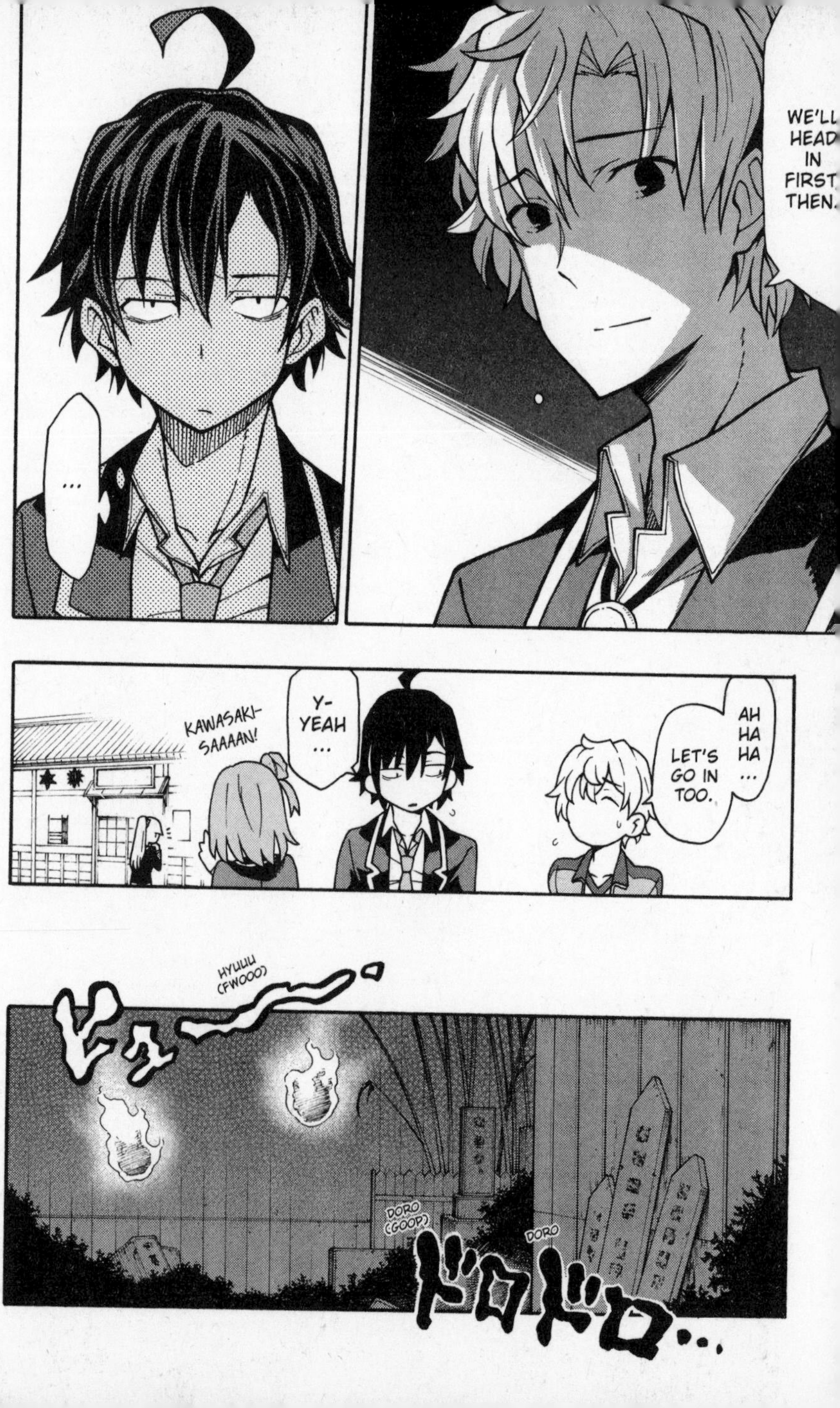
WE'LL HEAD IN FIRST THEN.
...
AH HA HA ... LET'S GO IN TOO.
Y-YEAH ...
KAWASAKI-SAAAAN!
HYUUU (FWOOO)
DORO (GOOP) DORO

I JUST HEARD A WEIRD CRY...!
DON'T YANK ON MY BLAZER...
IT'S QUITE ATMOSPHERIC, ISN'T IT?
I-I CAN'T REALLY HANDLE STUFF LIKE THIS...
GHOSTS AT A HAUNTED HOUSE AREN'T SCARY.
WHAT'S SCARY IS PEOPLE.
THERE HE GOES, BEING A SOUR-PUSS!
BUT IT KINDA MAKES YOU SEEM RELIABLE.
IN OTHER WORDS, IT'S SCARIEST WHEN ACTUAL PEOPLE DO THE SCARING.
BWAAAAGH!
BIKU (JUMP)
OR NOT!
NOT RELIABLE AT ALL!

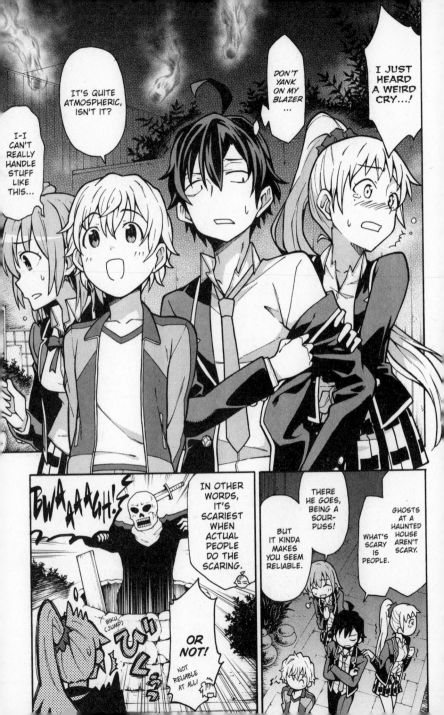

KAWASAKI-SAN, RUNNING IS DANGEROUS!

DA (DASH)

FULL SPRINT

OW!

ごちっ (GOCHI!) (BONK)

L-LET'S GO TOO...

WAAAIT!

ANYWAY, LET'S GO.

THEY'RE GONNA LEAVE US BEHIND.

ズ (SWF)

OW...

YEAH, THAT HURT LIKE HELL.

I'M SORRY. I DIDN'T HURT YOU, DID I?

HUH?
AH.
す
SU (SWIF)
THANKS.
!
GU (TUG)
ぐい
LET'S HURRY!

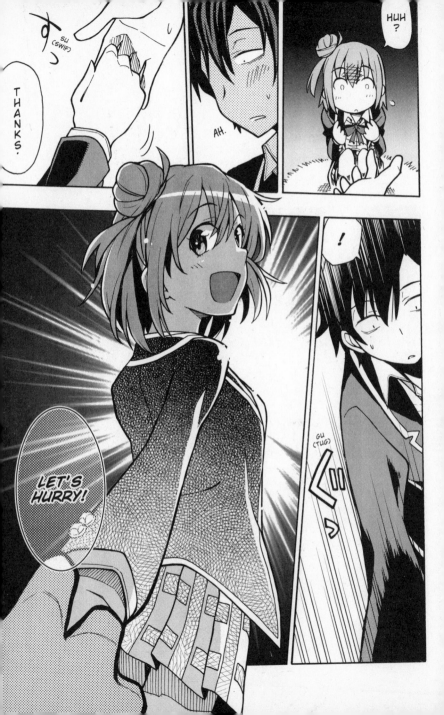

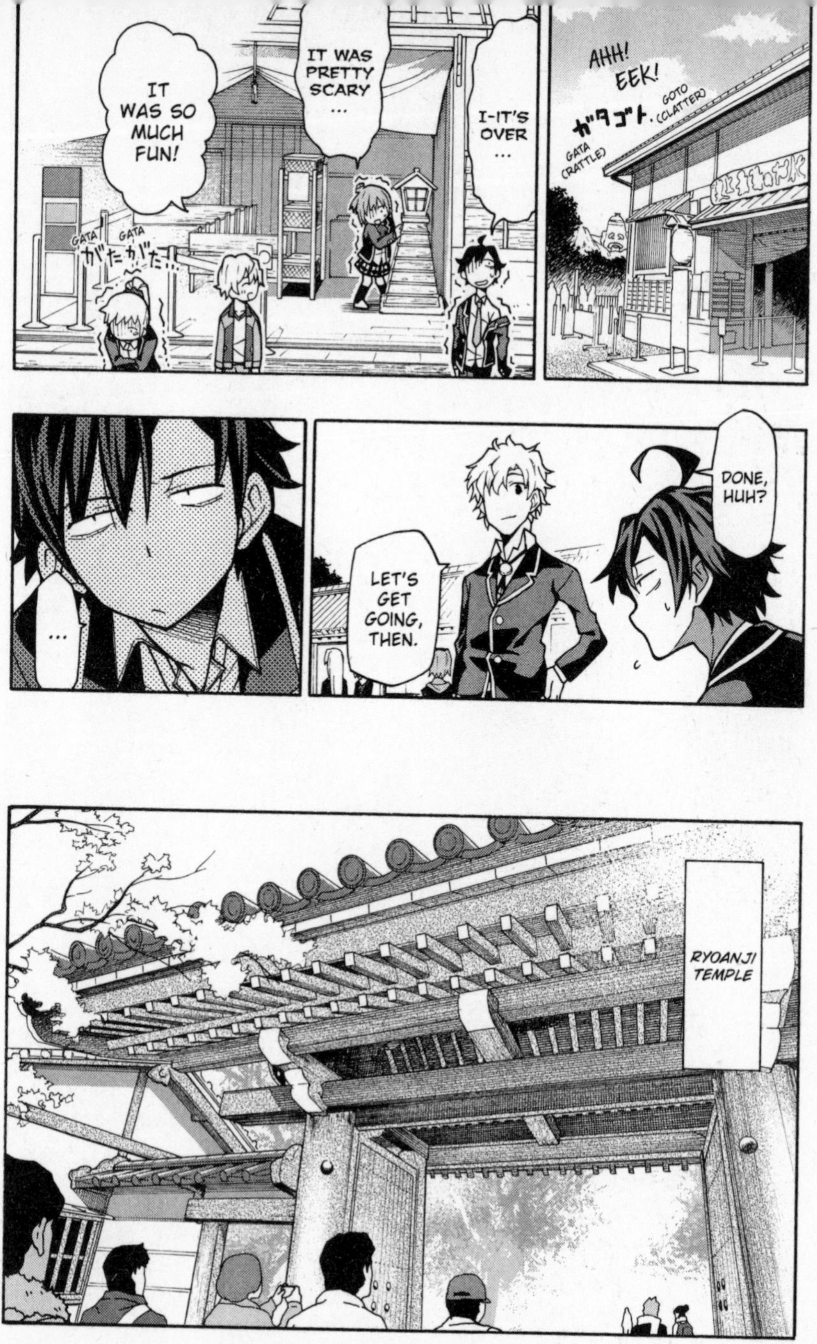
AHH!
EEK!
ガタゴト。
GATA (RATTLE)
GOTO (CLATTER)
I-IT'S OVER ...
IT WAS PRETTY SCARY ...
IT WAS SO MUCH FUN!
ガたガた…
GATA GATA
DONE, HUH?
LET'S GET GOING, THEN.
...
RYOANJI TEMPLE

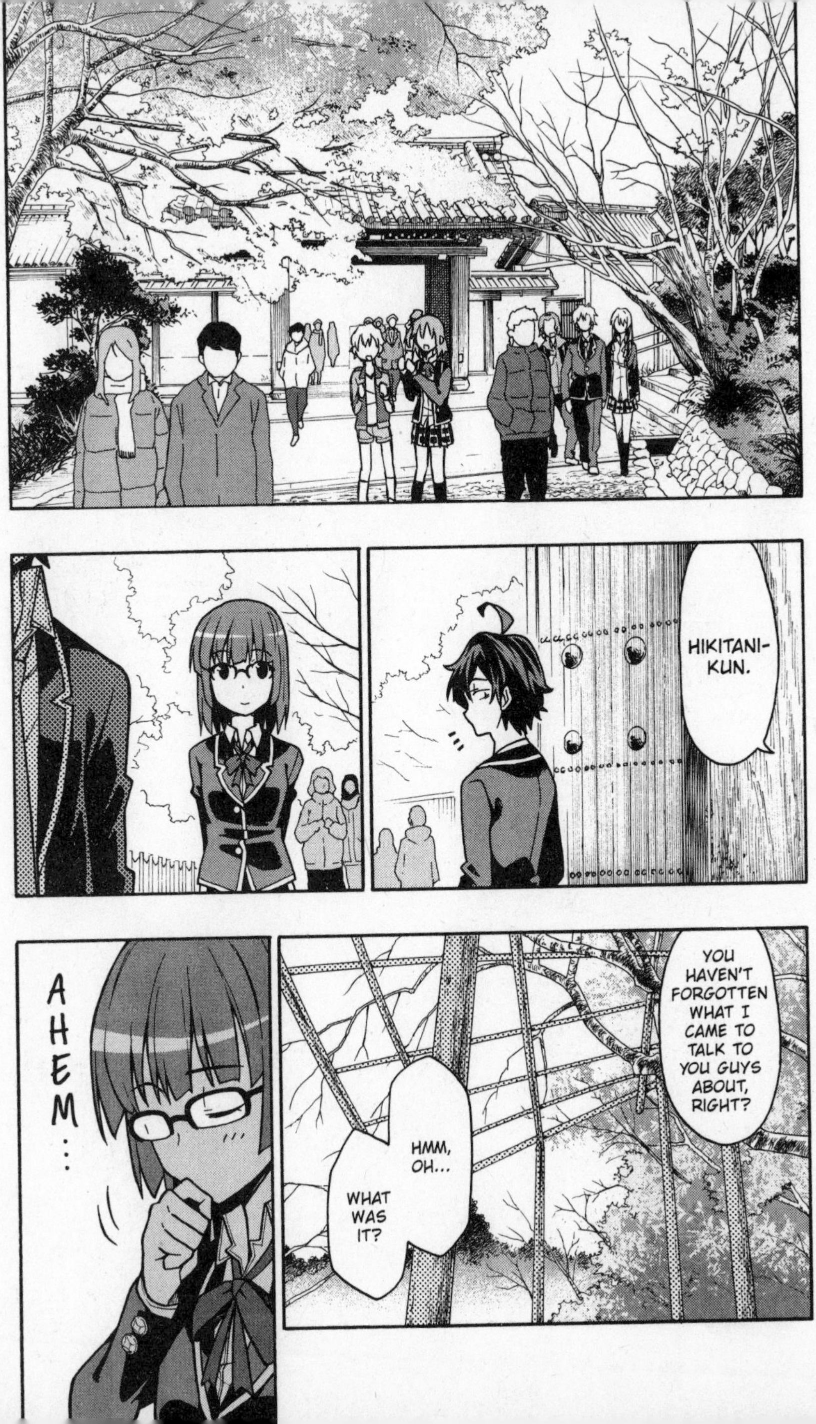
HIKITANI-KUN.
YOU HAVEN'T FORGOTTEN WHAT I CAME TO TALK TO YOU GUYS ABOUT, RIGHT?
HMM, OH...
WHAT WAS IT?
AHEM...

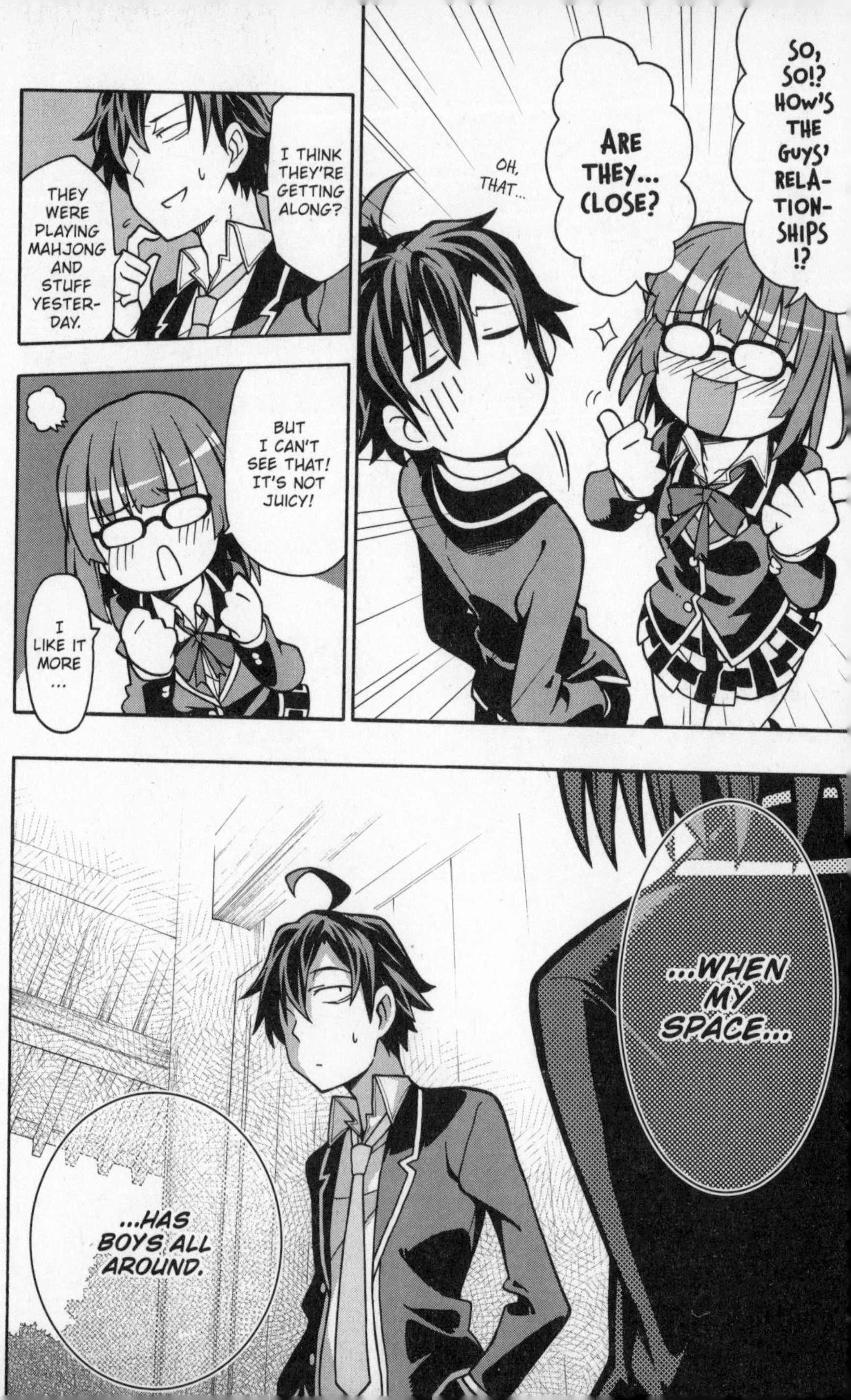
SO, SO!? HOW'S THE GUYS' RELATIONSHIPS!?
ARE THEY... CLOSE?
OH, THAT...
I THINK THEY'RE GETTING ALONG?
THEY WERE PLAYING MAHJONG AND STUFF YESTERDAY.
BUT I CAN'T SEE THAT! IT'S NOT JUICY!
I LIKE IT MORE ...
...WHEN MY SPACE...
...HAS BOYS ALL AROUND.

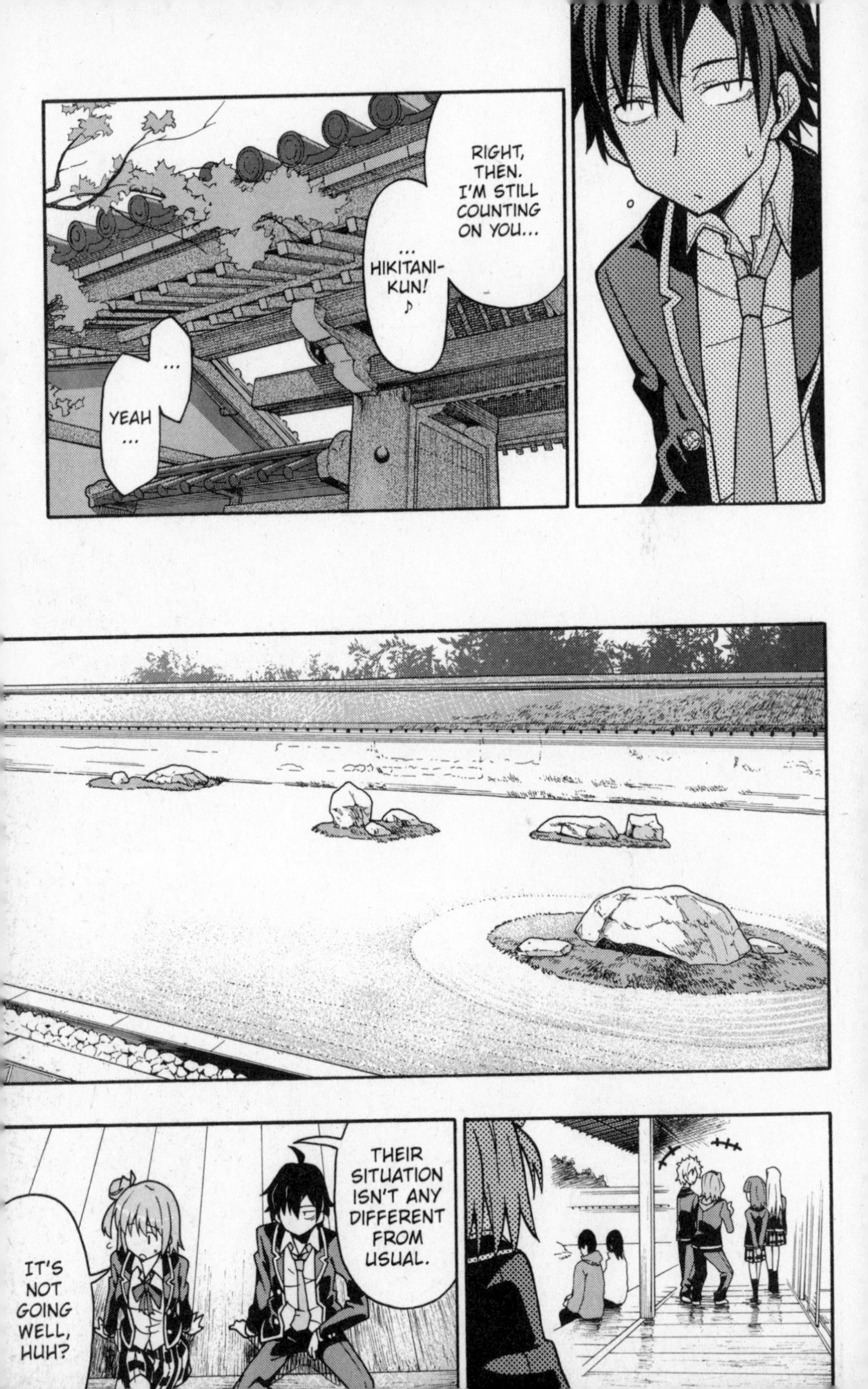
RIGHT, THEN. I'M STILL COUNTING ON YOU...
... HIKITANI-KUN! ♪
... YEAH ...
THEIR SITUATION ISN'T ANY DIFFERENT FROM USUAL.
IT'S NOT GOING WELL, HUH?

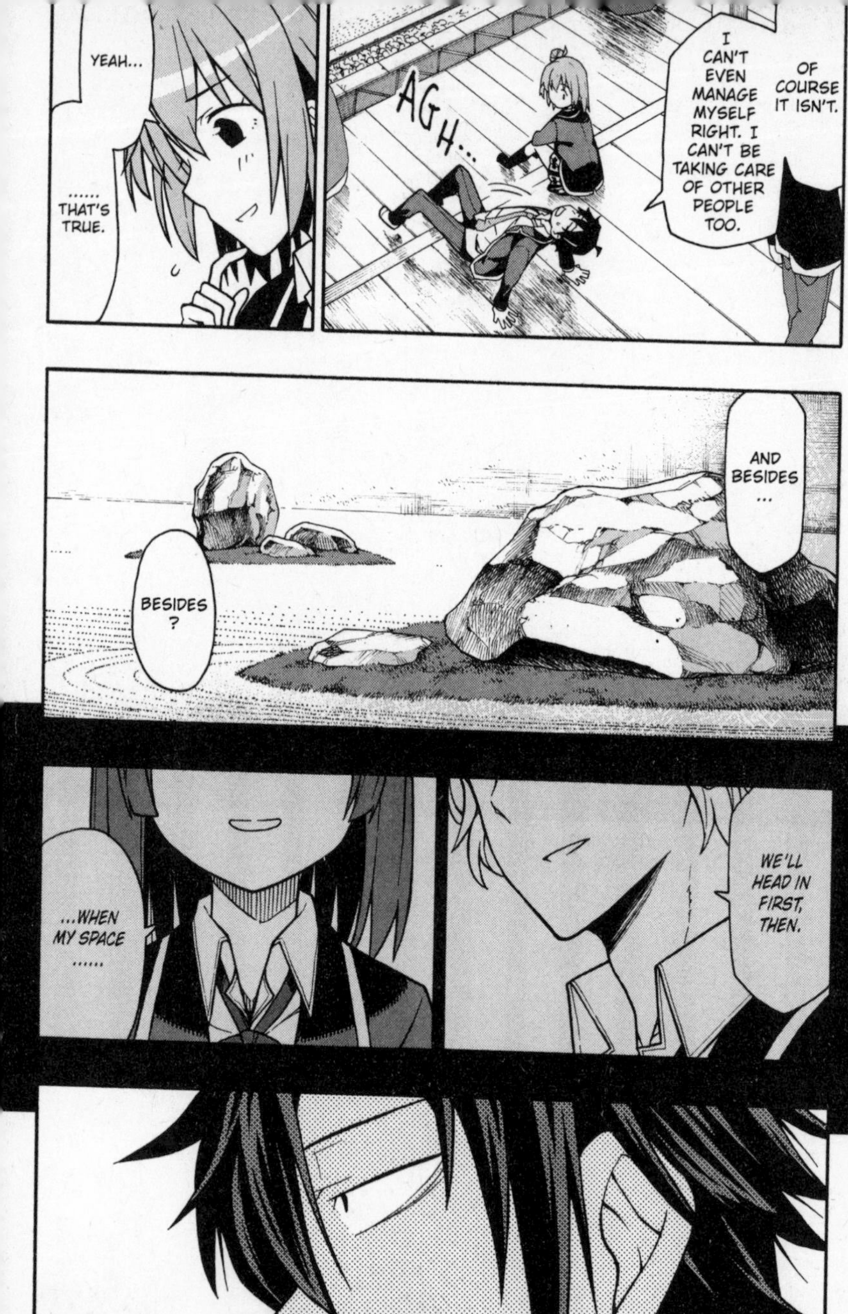
OF COURSE IT ISN'T.
I CAN'T EVEN MANAGE MYSELF RIGHT. I CAN'T BE TAKING CARE OF OTHER PEOPLE TOO.
AGH...
YEAH...
......THAT'S TRUE.
AND BESIDES...
BESIDES?
WE'LL HEAD IN FIRST, THEN.
...WHEN MY SPACE......

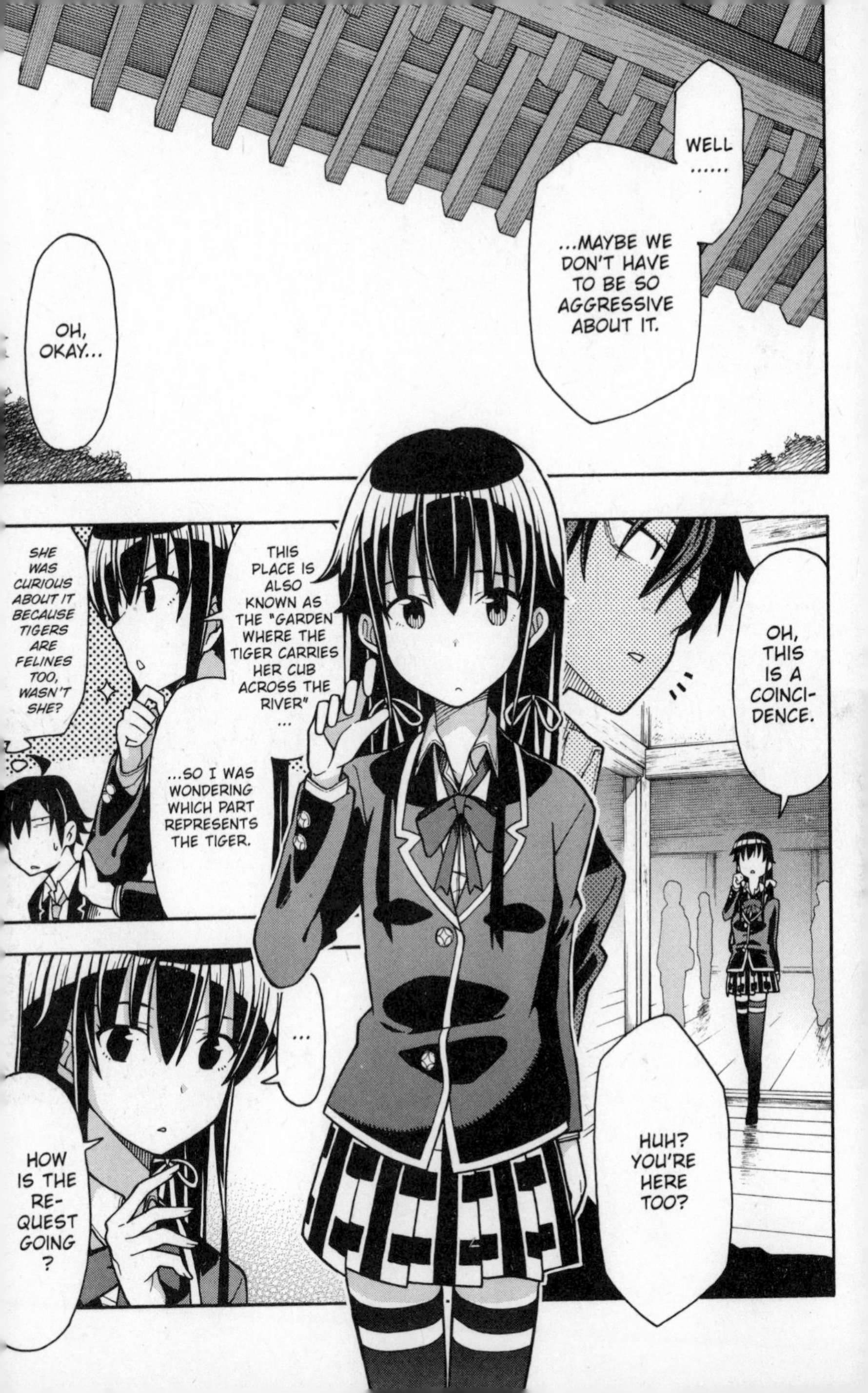
WELL ......
...MAYBE WE DON'T HAVE TO BE SO AGGRESSIVE ABOUT IT.
OH, OKAY...
OH, THIS IS A COINCIDENCE.
HUH? YOU'RE HERE TOO?
THIS PLACE IS ALSO KNOWN AS THE "GARDEN WHERE THE TIGER CARRIES HER CUB ACROSS THE RIVER" ...
...SO I WAS WONDERING WHICH PART REPRESENTS THE TIGER.
SHE WAS CURIOUS ABOUT IT BECAUSE TIGERS ARE FELINES TOO, WASN'T SHE?
...
HOW IS THE RE-QUEST GOING?

MAGAZINE: 100-PIECE, KYOTO IN FALL

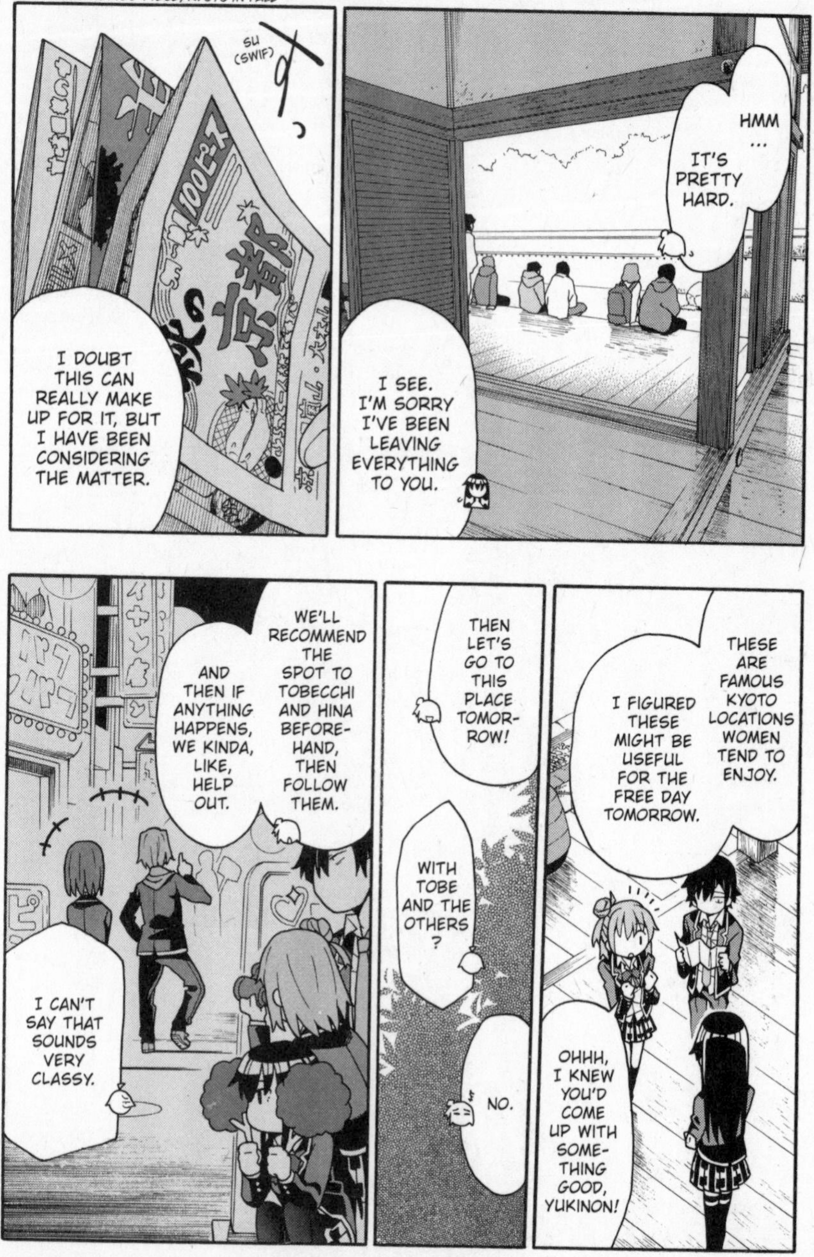
HMM ... IT'S PRETTY HARD.
I SEE. I'M SORRY I'VE BEEN LEAVING EVERYTHING TO YOU.
SU (SWIF)
100ピース
秋の京都
I DOUBT THIS CAN REALLY MAKE UP FOR IT, BUT I HAVE BEEN CONSIDERING THE MATTER.
THESE ARE FAMOUS KYOTO LOCATIONS WOMEN TEND TO ENJOY.
I FIGURED THESE MIGHT BE USEFUL FOR THE FREE DAY TOMORROW.
OHHH, I KNEW YOU'D COME UP WITH SOME-THING GOOD, YUKINON!
THEN LET'S GO TO THIS PLACE TOMOR-ROW!
WITH TOBE AND THE OTHERS ?
NO.
WE'LL RECOMMEND THE SPOT TO TOBECCHI AND HINA BEFORE-HAND, THEN FOLLOW THEM.
AND THEN IF ANYTHING HAPPENS, WE KINDA, LIKE, HELP OUT.
I CAN'T SAY THAT SOUNDS VERY CLASSY.

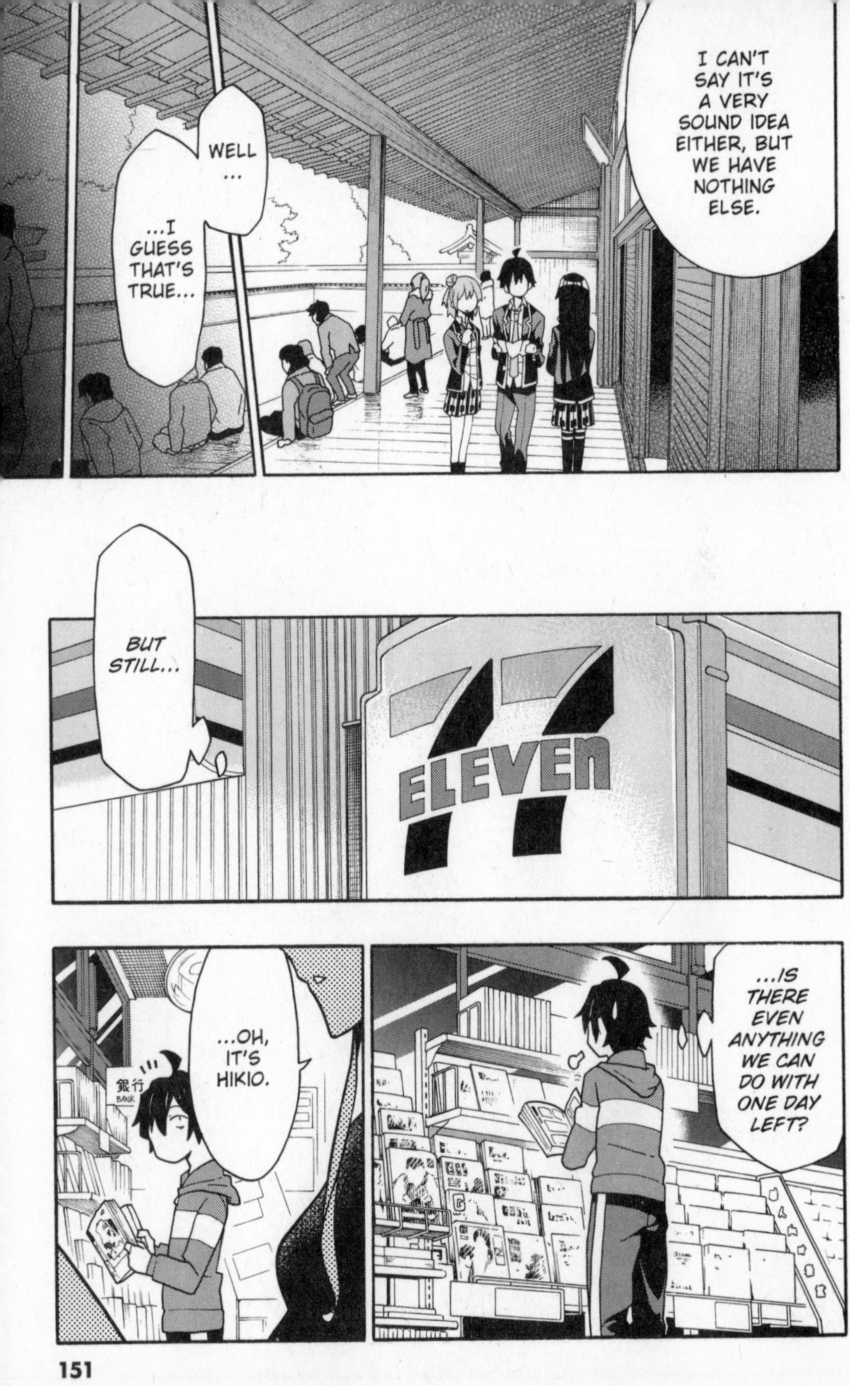
I CAN'T SAY IT'S A VERY SOUND IDEA EITHER, BUT WE HAVE NOTHING ELSE.
WELL...
...I GUESS THAT'S TRUE...
BUT STILL...
ELEVEN
...IS THERE EVEN ANYTHING WE CAN DO WITH ONE DAY LEFT?
...OH, IT'S HIKIO.
銀行
BANK

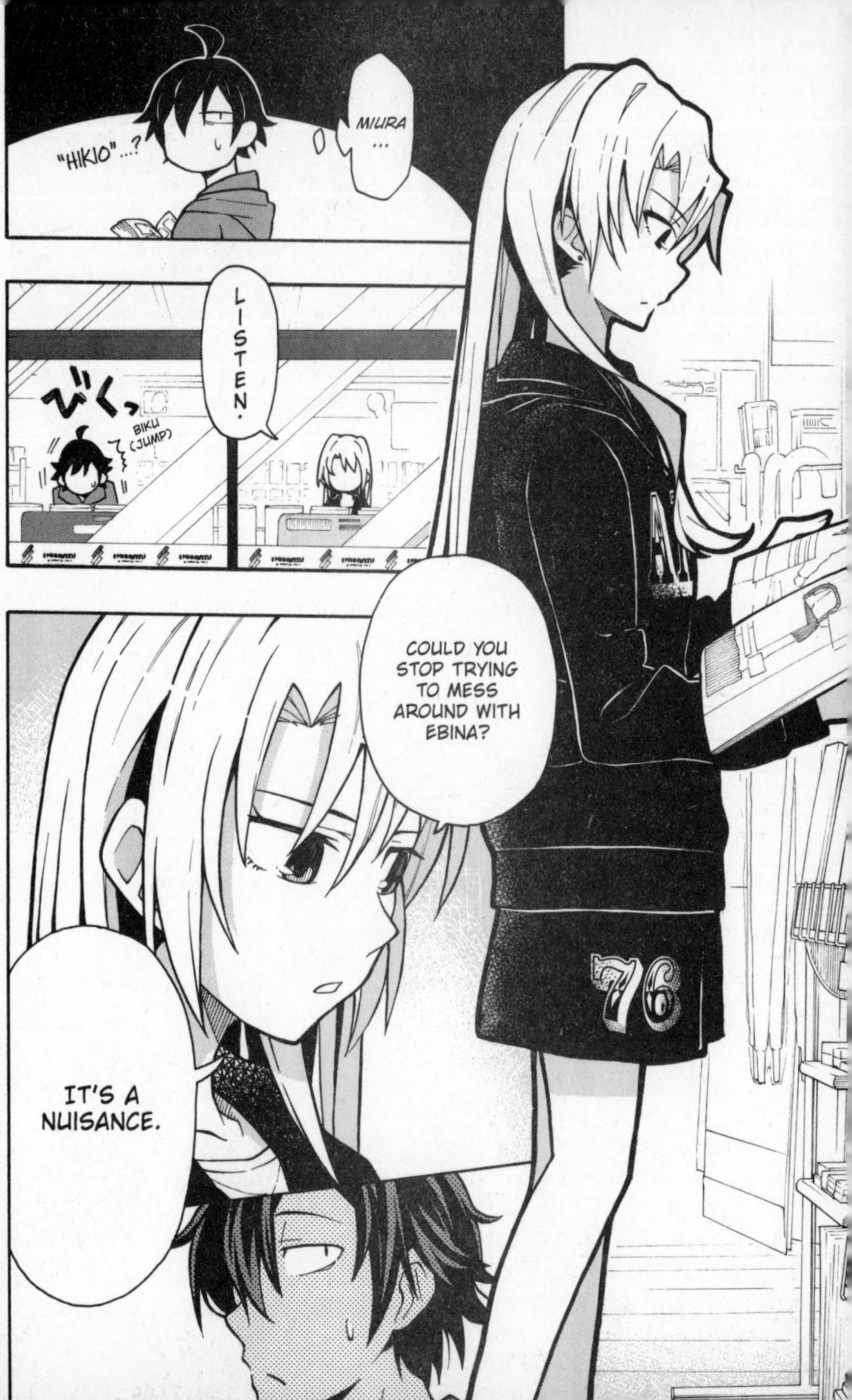

MIURA ...
"HIKIO"...?
LISTEN.
びくっ
BIKU (JUMP)
COULD YOU STOP TRYING TO MESS AROUND WITH EBINA?
IT'S A NUISANCE.

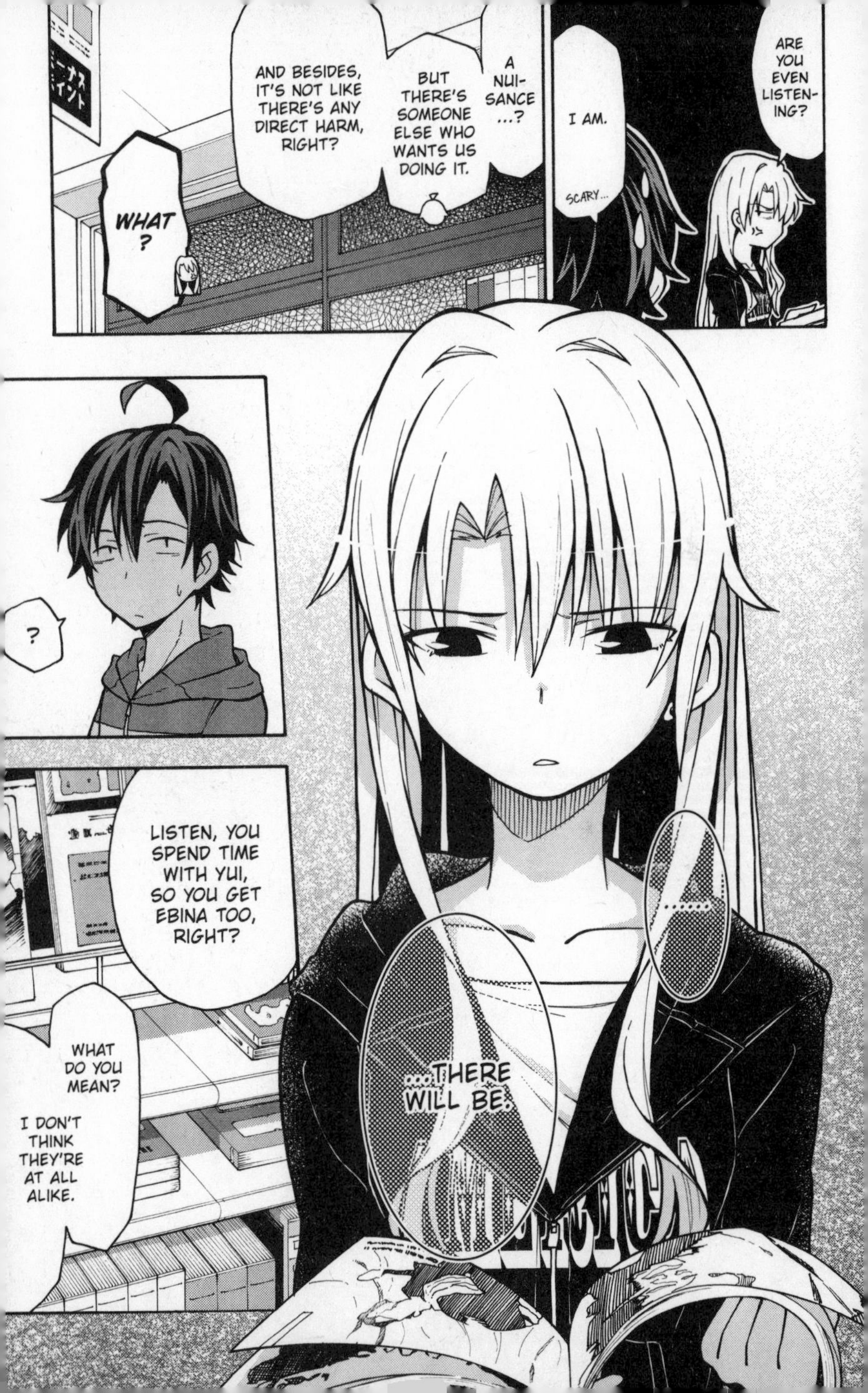
ARE YOU EVEN LISTENING?
I AM.
SCARY...
A NUISANCE...?
BUT THERE'S SOMEONE ELSE WHO WANTS US DOING IT.
AND BESIDES, IT'S NOT LIKE THERE'S ANY DIRECT HARM, RIGHT?
WHAT?
......
...THERE WILL BE.
?
LISTEN, YOU SPEND TIME WITH YUI, SO YOU GET EBINA TOO, RIGHT?
WHAT DO YOU MEAN?
I DON'T THINK THEY'RE AT ALL ALIKE.

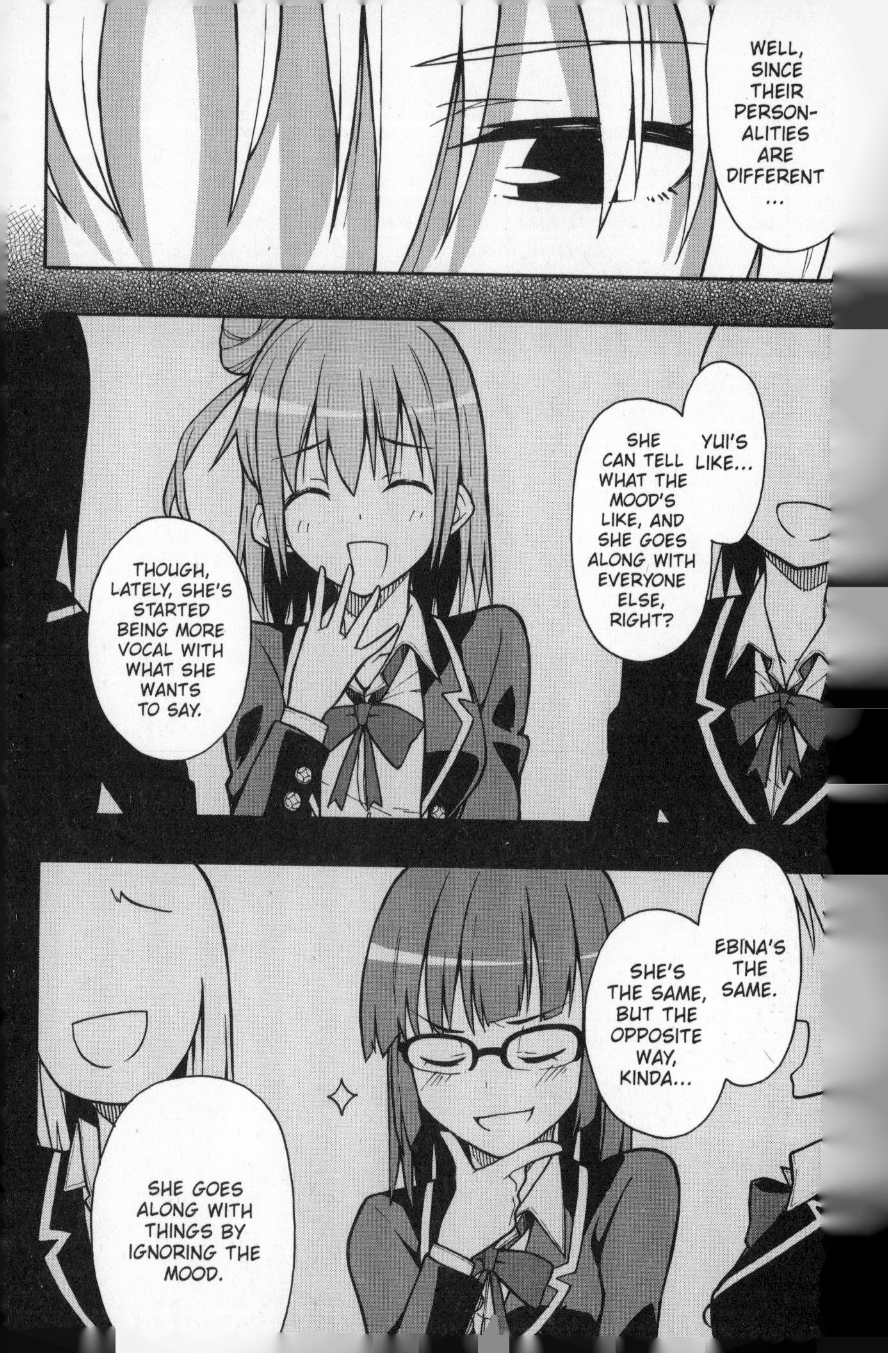
WELL, SINCE THEIR PERSONALITIES ARE DIFFERENT...
YUI'S LIKE...
SHE CAN TELL WHAT THE MOOD'S LIKE, AND SHE GOES ALONG WITH EVERYONE ELSE, RIGHT?
THOUGH, LATELY, SHE'S STARTED BEING MORE VOCAL WITH WHAT SHE WANTS TO SAY.
EBINA'S THE SAME.
SHE'S THE SAME, BUT THE OPPOSITE WAY, KINDA...
SHE GOES ALONG WITH THINGS BY IGNORING THE MOOD.

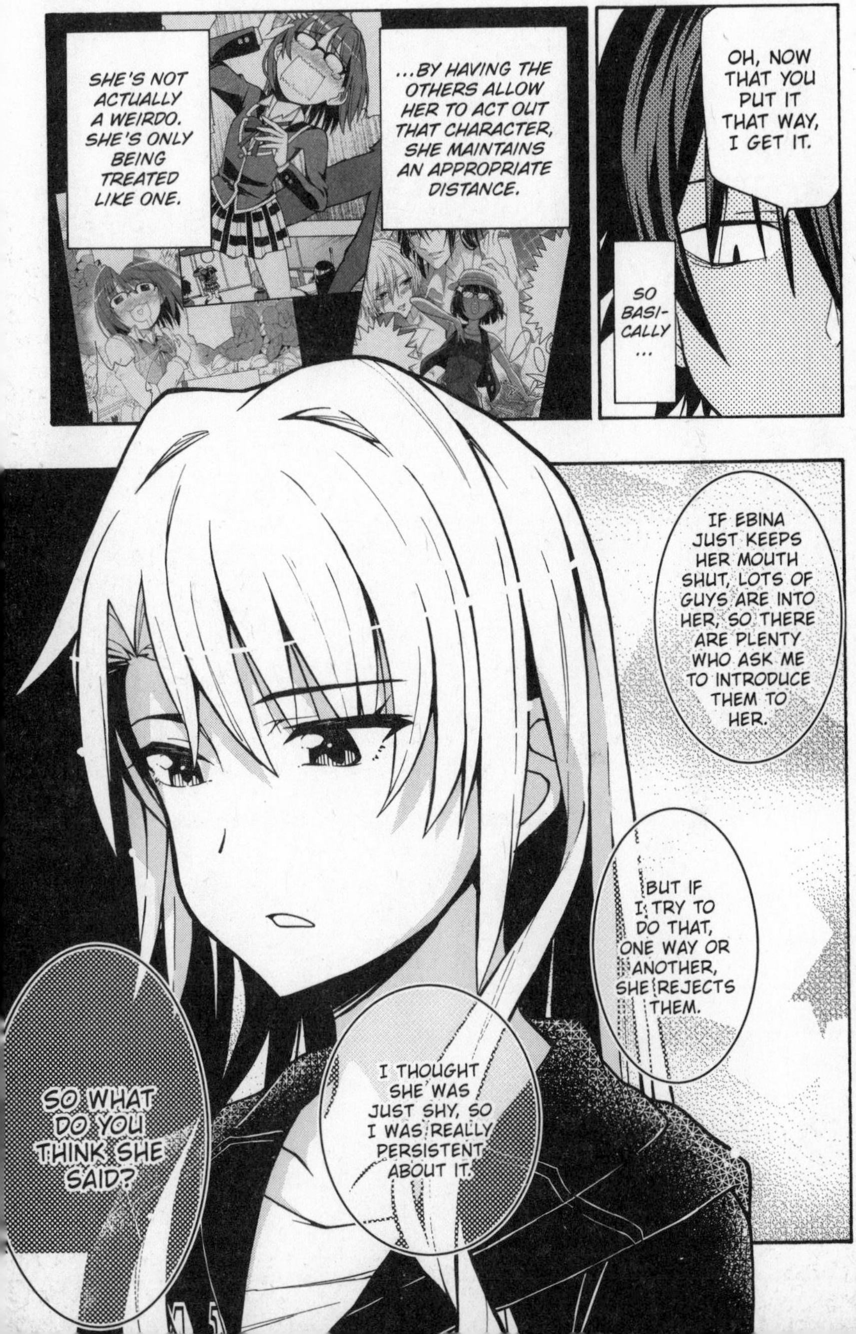
OH, NOW THAT YOU PUT IT THAT WAY, I GET IT.
SO BASI-CALLY...
SHE'S NOT ACTUALLY A WEIRDO. SHE'S ONLY BEING TREATED LIKE ONE.
...BY HAVING THE OTHERS ALLOW HER TO ACT OUT THAT CHARACTER, SHE MAINTAINS AN APPROPRIATE DISTANCE.
IF EBINA JUST KEEPS HER MOUTH SHUT, LOTS OF GUYS ARE INTO HER, SO THERE ARE PLENTY WHO ASK ME TO INTRODUCE THEM TO HER.
BUT IF I TRY TO DO THAT, ONE WAY OR ANOTHER, SHE REJECTS THEM.
I THOUGHT SHE WAS JUST SHY, SO I WAS REALLY PERSISTENT ABOUT IT.
SO WHAT DO YOU THINK SHE SAID?

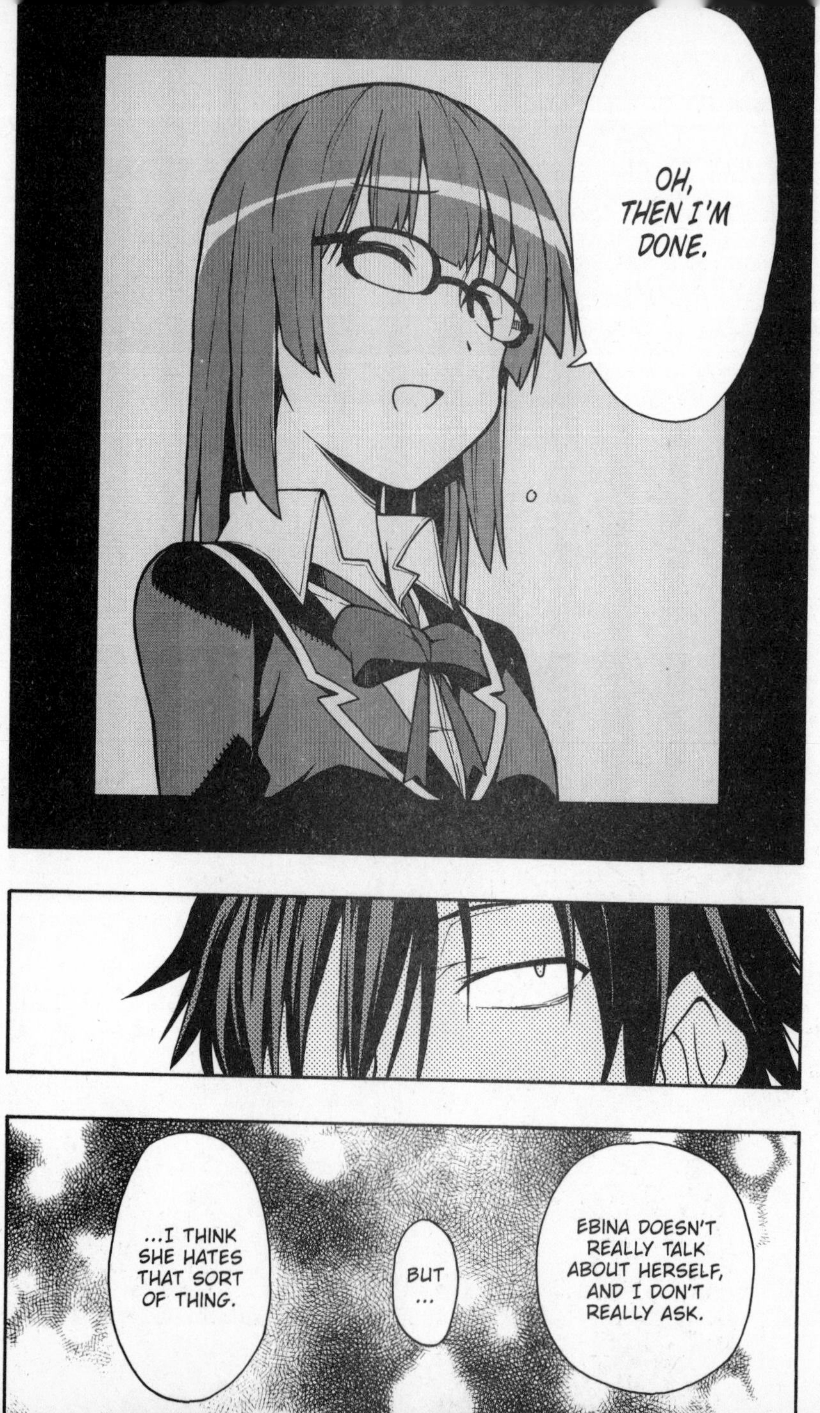
OH, THEN I'M DONE.
EBINA DOESN'T REALLY TALK ABOUT HERSELF, AND I DON'T REALLY ASK.
BUT...
...I THINK SHE HATES THAT SORT OF THING.

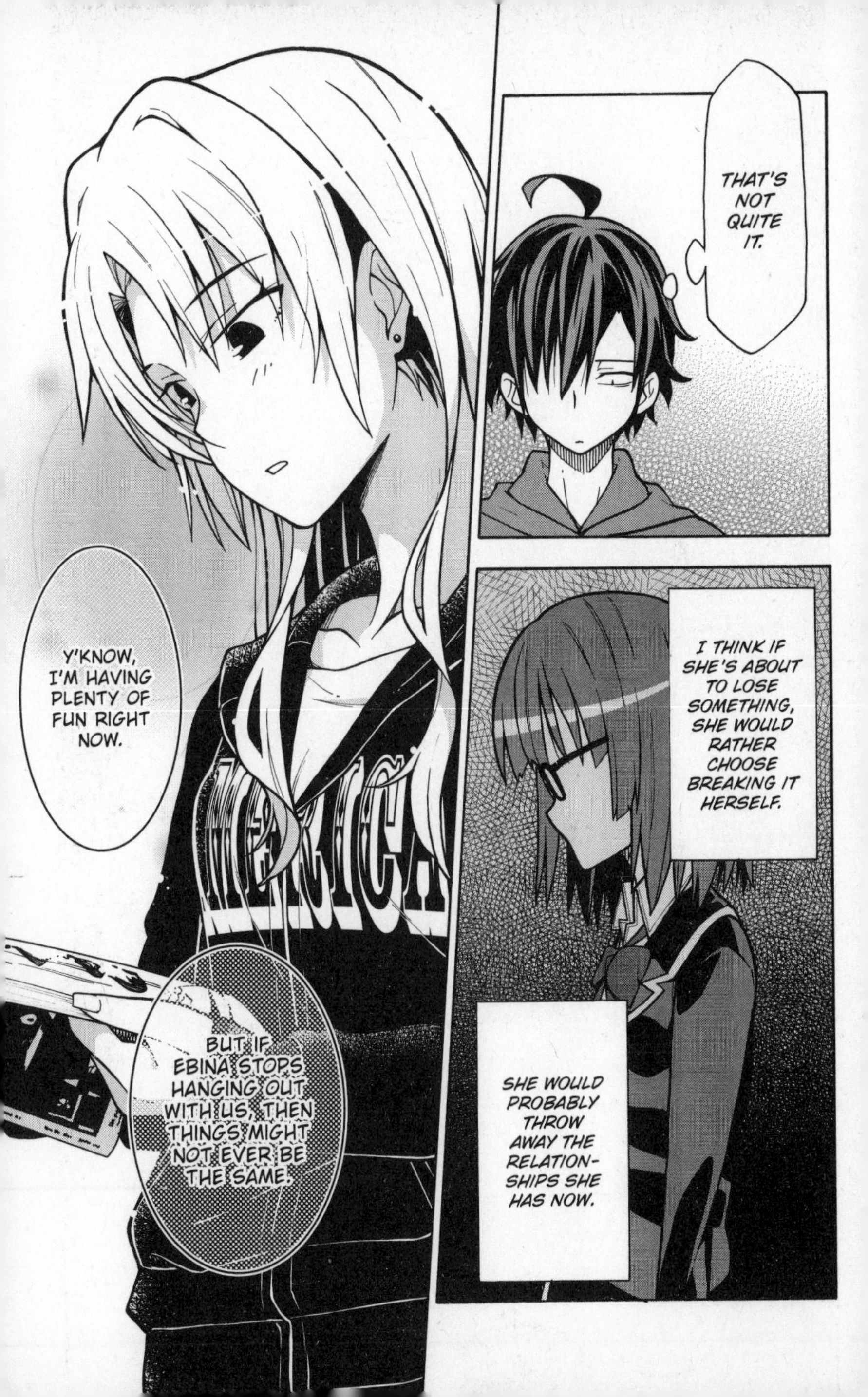
THAT'S NOT QUITE IT.
I THINK IF SHE'S ABOUT TO LOSE SOMETHING, SHE WOULD RATHER CHOOSE BREAKING IT HERSELF.
SHE WOULD PROBABLY THROW AWAY THE RELATION-SHIPS SHE HAS NOW.
Y'KNOW, I'M HAVING PLENTY OF FUN RIGHT NOW.
BUT IF EBINA STOPS HANGING OUT WITH US, THEN THINGS MIGHT NOT EVER BE THE SAME.

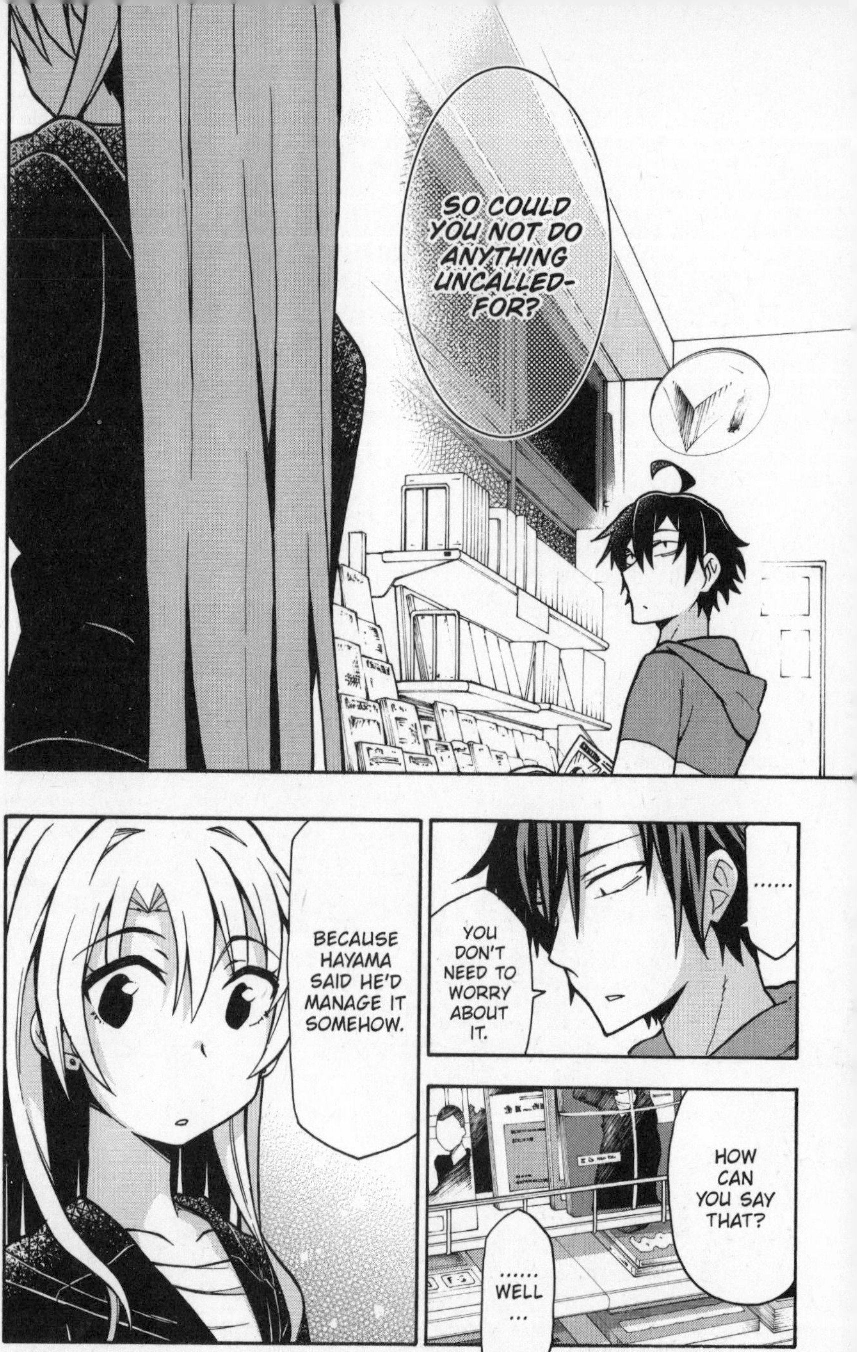
SO COULD YOU NOT DO ANYTHING UNCALLED-FOR?
......
YOU DON'T NEED TO WORRY ABOUT IT.
HOW CAN YOU SAY THAT?
......WELL ...
BECAUSE HAYAMA SAID HE'D MANAGE IT SOMEHOW.

WHAT THE HECK IS THAT?

HEH!

WELL, IF HAYATO SAYS SO, THEN WHATEVER.

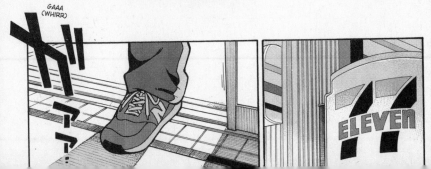

GAAA (WHIRR)

ELEVEN

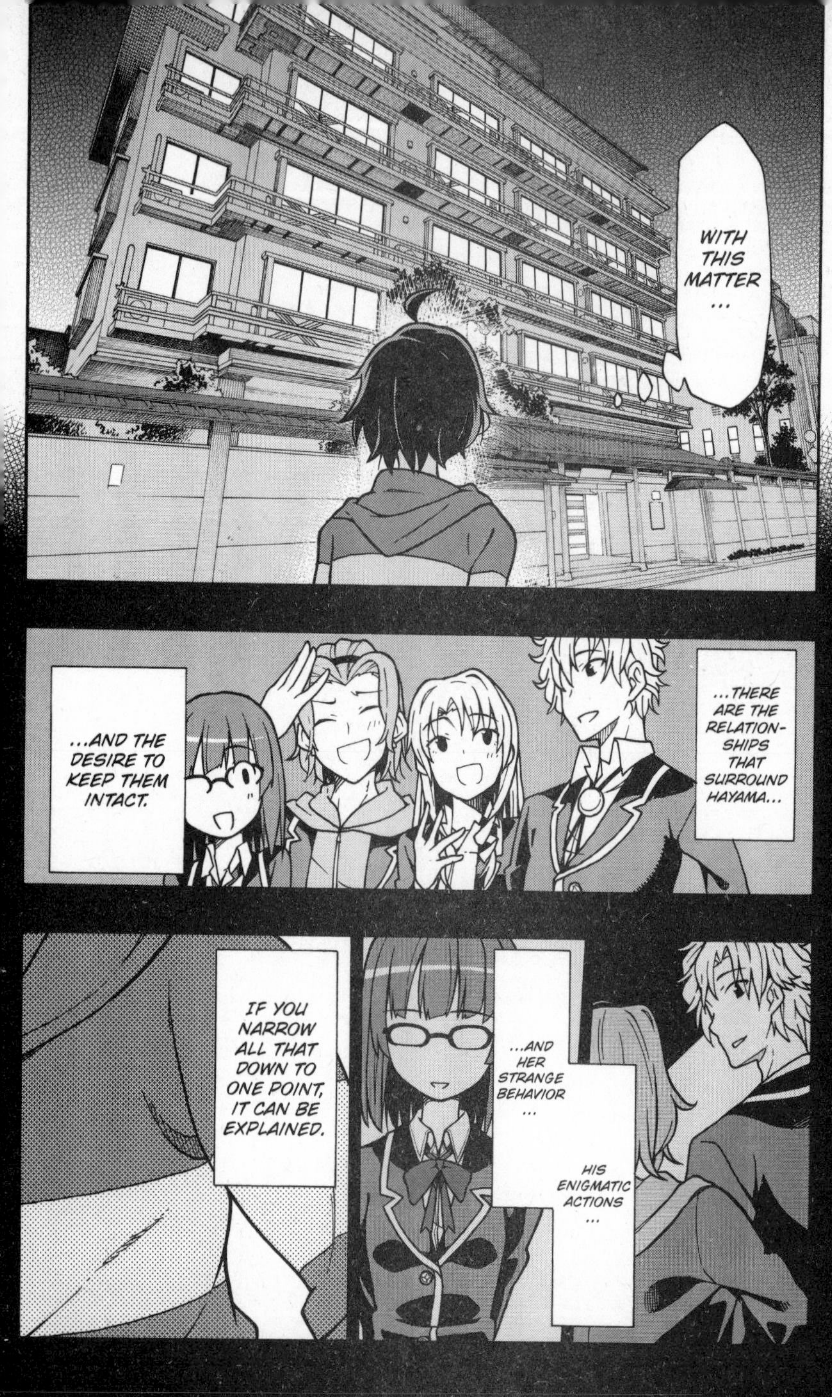
WITH THIS MATTER ...
...THERE ARE THE RELATIONSHIPS THAT SURROUND HAYAMA...
...AND THE DESIRE TO KEEP THEM INTACT.
HIS ENIGMATIC ACTIONS ...
...AND HER STRANGE BEHAVIOR ...
IF YOU NARROW ALL THAT DOWN TO ONE POINT, IT CAN BE EXPLAINED.

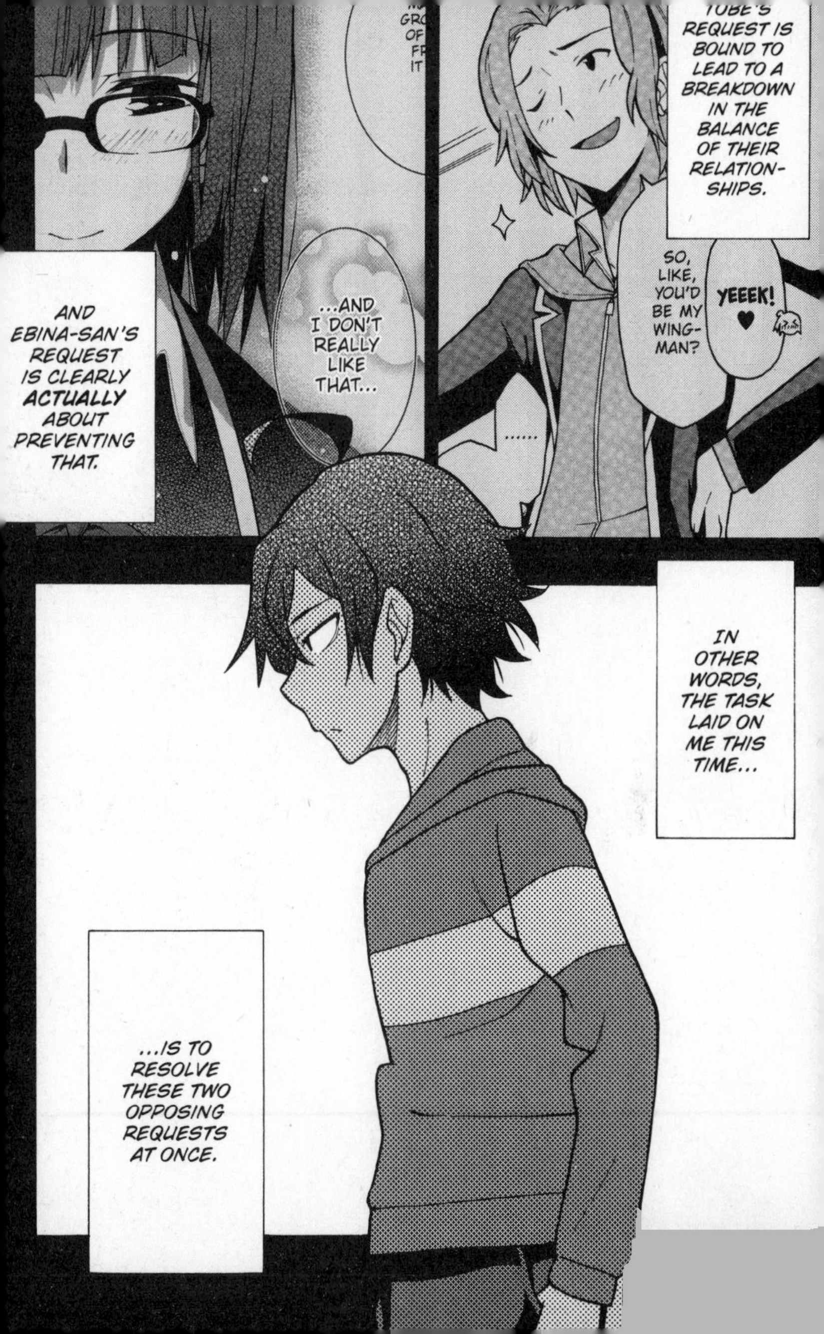
TOBE'S REQUEST IS BOUND TO LEAD TO A BREAKDOWN IN THE BALANCE OF THEIR RELATIONSHIPS.
YEEEK! ♥
SO, LIKE, YOU'D BE MY WING-MAN?
......
...AND I DON'T REALLY LIKE THAT...
AND EBINA-SAN'S REQUEST IS CLEARLY ACTUALLY ABOUT PREVENTING THAT.
IN OTHER WORDS, THE TASK LAID ON ME THIS TIME...
...IS TO RESOLVE THESE TWO OPPOSING REQUESTS AT ONCE.

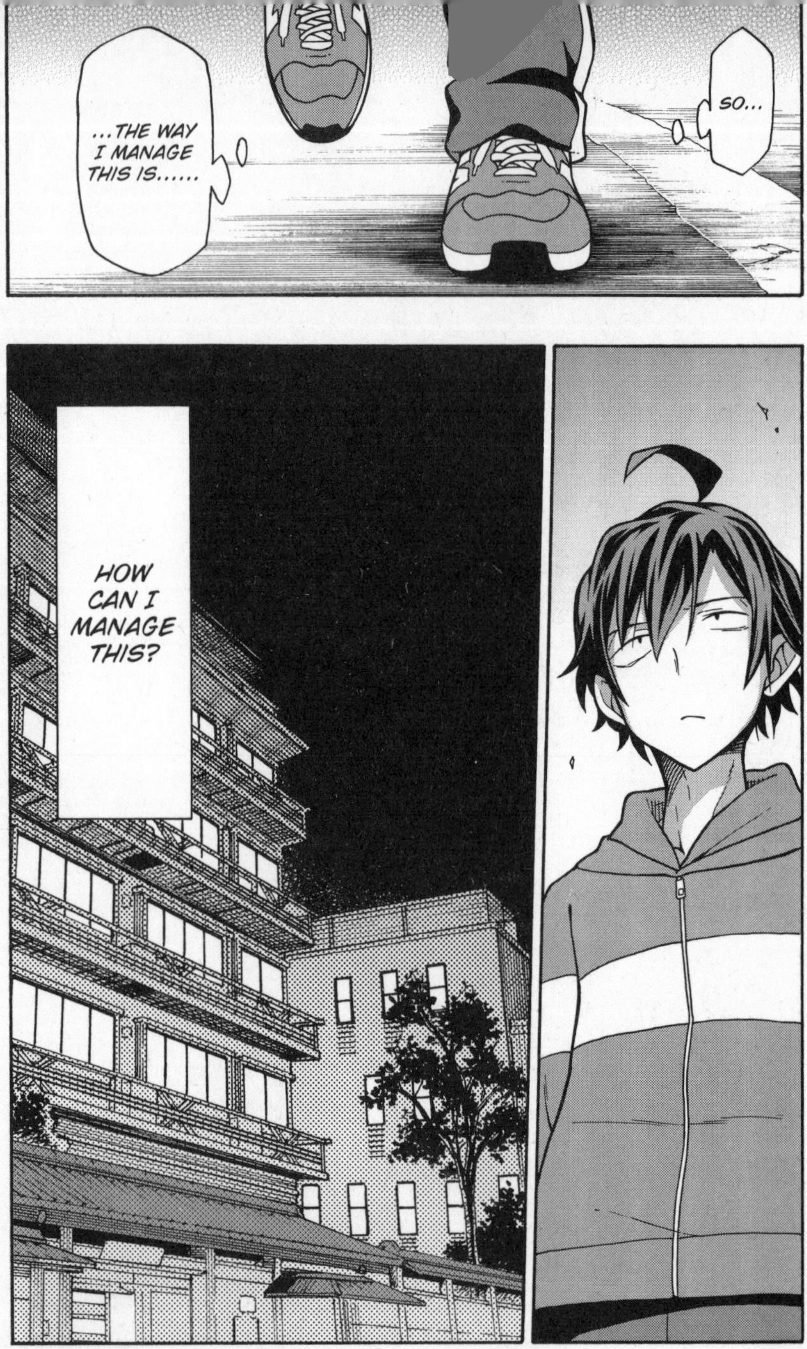
SO...
...THE WAY I MANAGE THIS IS......
HOW CAN I MANAGE THIS?

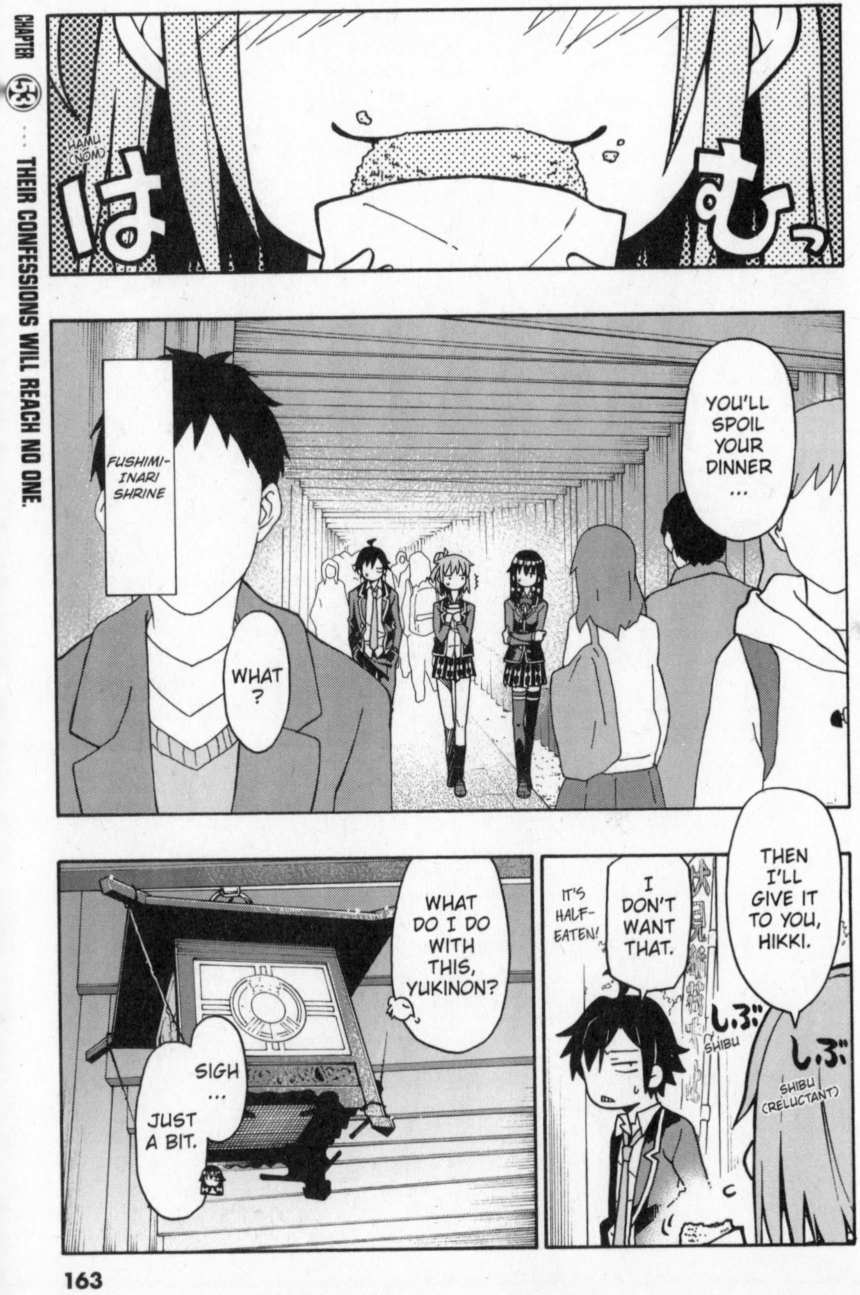
はむっ
HAMU (NOM)
YOU'LL SPOIL YOUR DINNER...
FUSHIMI-INARI SHRINE
WHAT?
THEN I'LL GIVE IT TO YOU, HIKKI.
しぶ
SHIBU (RELUCTANT)
I DON'T WANT THAT.
IT'S HALF-EATEN!
しぶ
SHIBU
WHAT DO I DO WITH THIS, YUKINON?
SIGH... JUST A BIT.

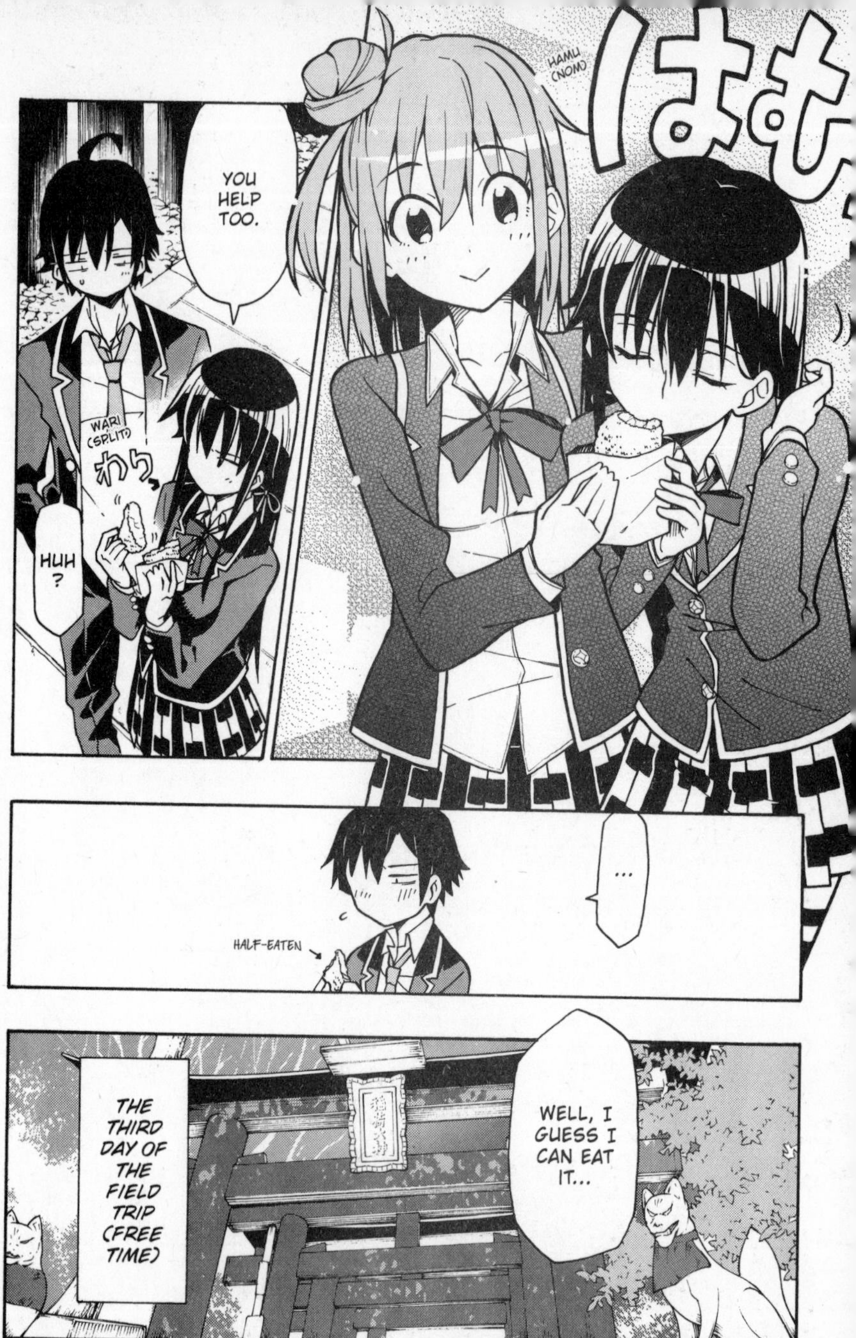
はむ
HAMU (NOM)
YOU HELP TOO.
WARI (SPLIT)
わり
HUH?
...
HALF-EATEN
WELL, I GUESS I CAN EAT IT...
THE THIRD DAY OF THE FIELD TRIP (FREE TIME)

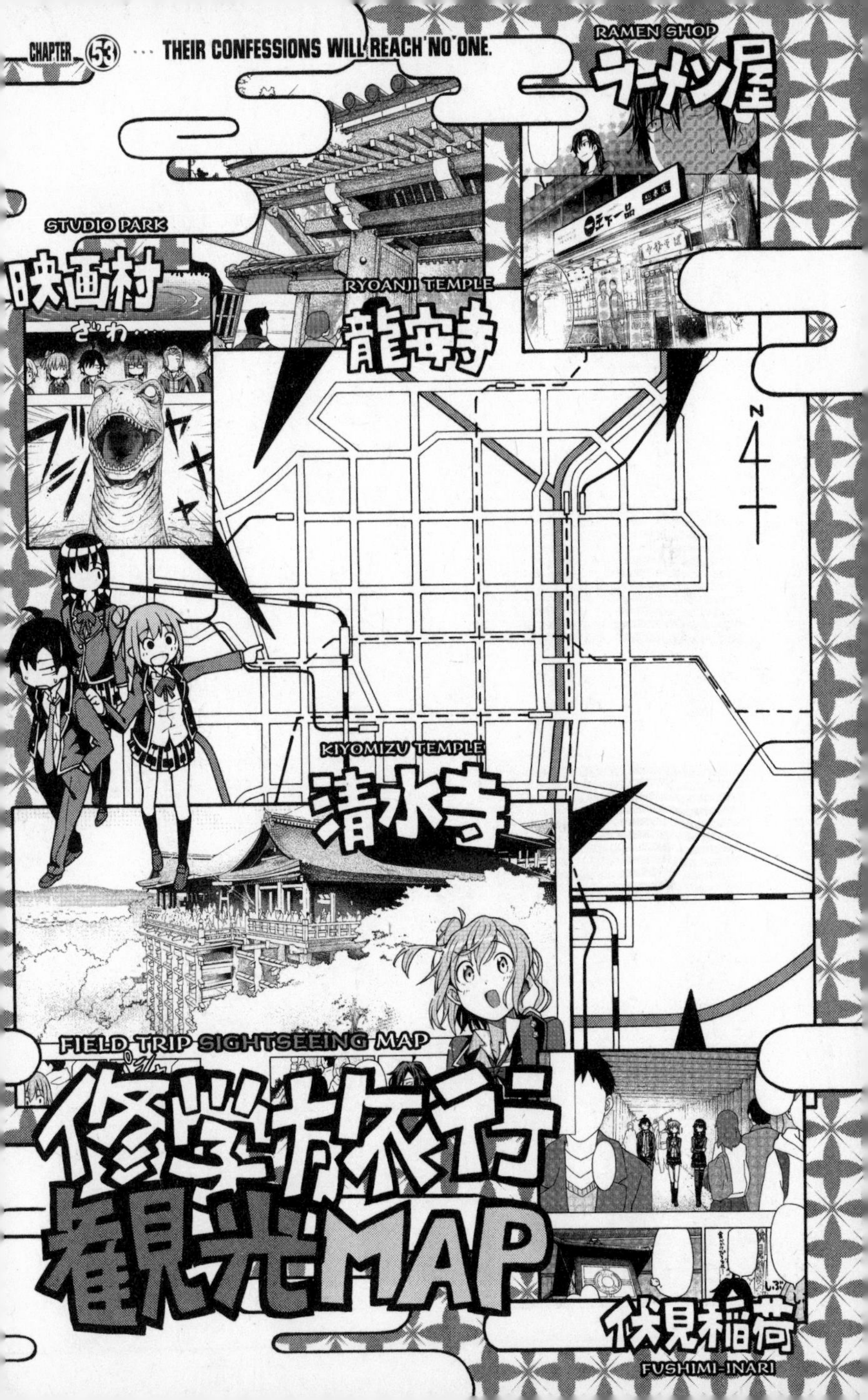
CHAPTER 53 ... THEIR CONFESSIONS WILL REACH NO ONE.
RAMEN SHOP
ラーメン屋
RYOANJI TEMPLE
龍安寺
STUDIO PARK
映画村
ざわ....
KIYOMIZU TEMPLE
清水寺
FIELD TRIP SIGHTSEEING MAP
修学旅行観光MAP
伏見稲荷
FUSHIMI-INARI

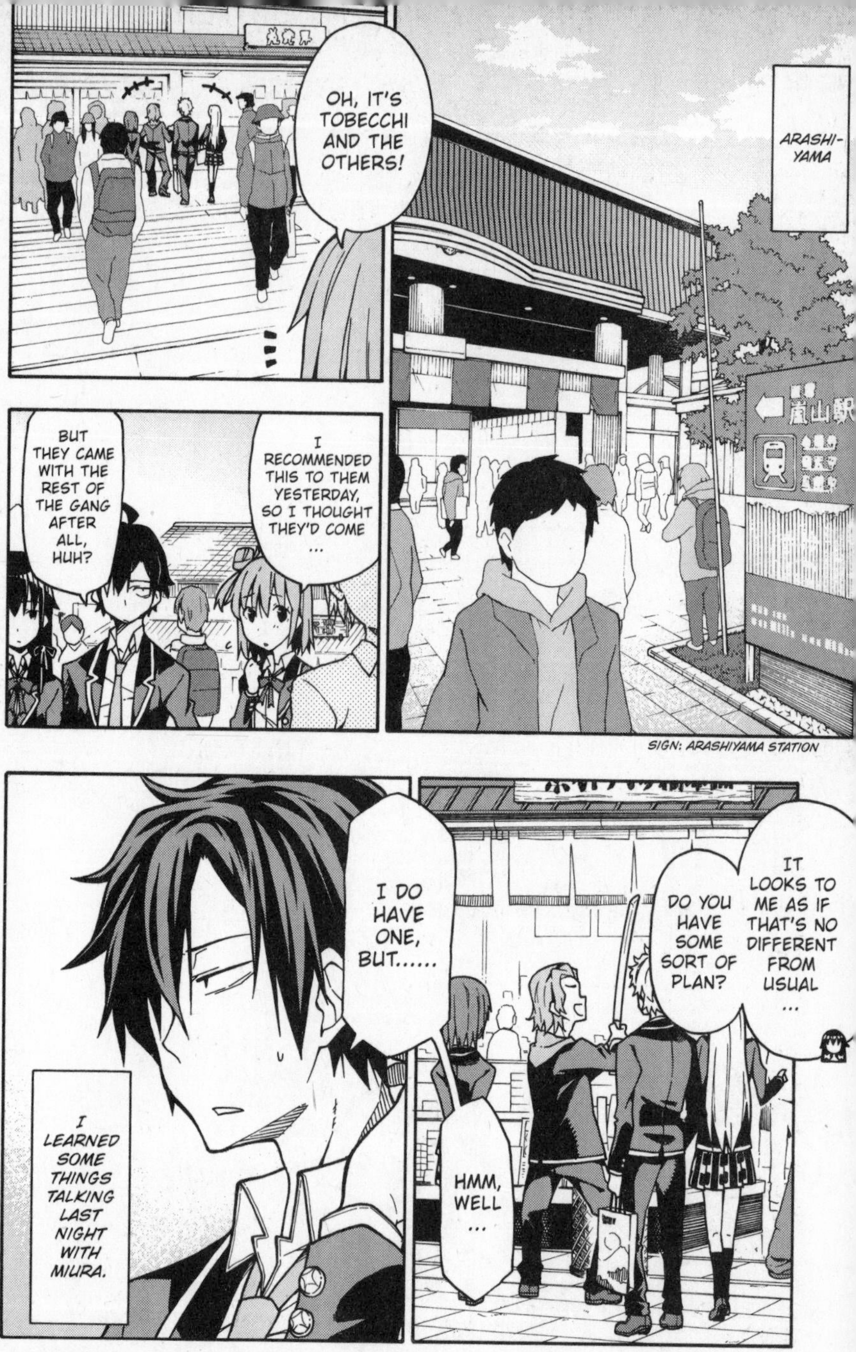
ARASHI-YAMA
SIGN: ARASHIYAMA STATION
OH, IT'S TOBECCHI AND THE OTHERS!
I RECOMMENDED THIS TO THEM YESTERDAY, SO I THOUGHT THEY'D COME ...
BUT THEY CAME WITH THE REST OF THE GANG AFTER ALL, HUH?
IT LOOKS TO ME AS IF THAT'S NO DIFFERENT FROM USUAL ...
DO YOU HAVE SOME SORT OF PLAN?
HMM, WELL ...
I DO HAVE ONE, BUT......
I LEARNED SOME THINGS TALKING LAST NIGHT WITH MIURA.

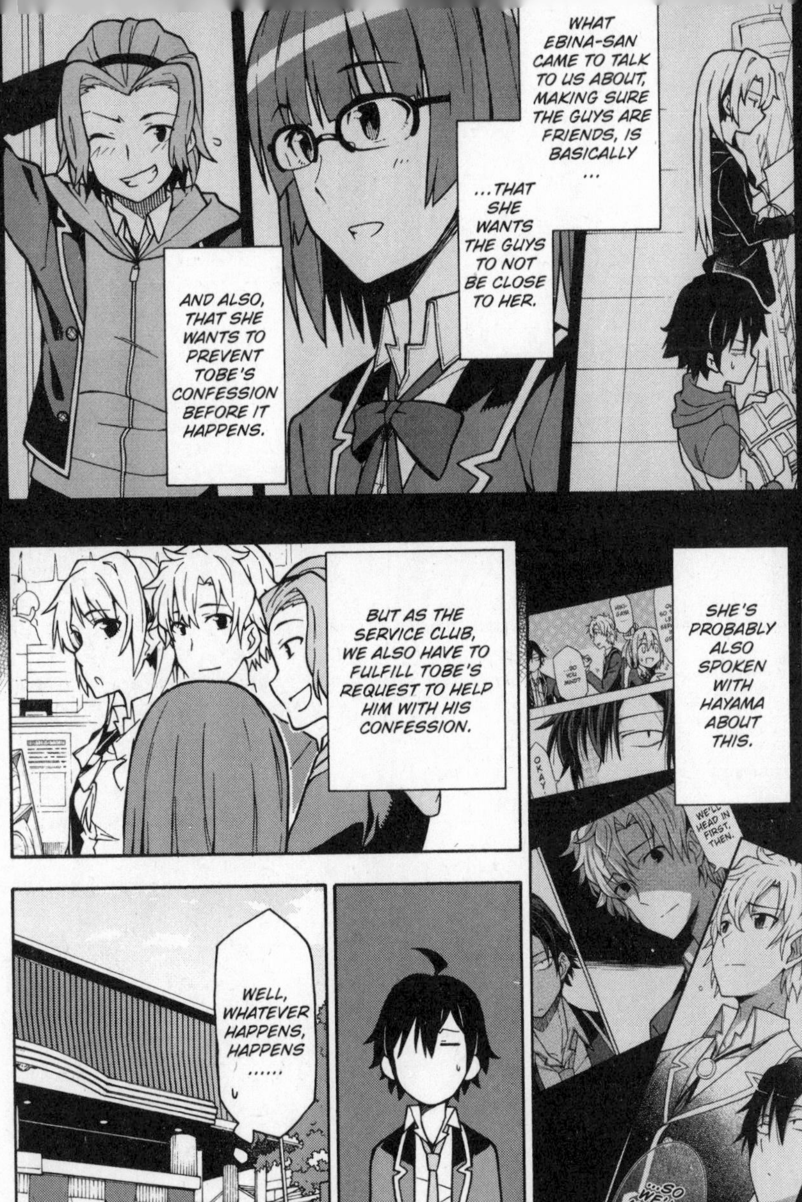

WHAT EBINA-SAN CAME TO TALK TO US ABOUT, MAKING SURE THE GUYS ARE FRIENDS, IS BASICALLY ...
...THAT SHE WANTS THE GUYS TO NOT BE CLOSE TO HER.
AND ALSO, THAT SHE WANTS TO PREVENT TOBE'S CONFESSION BEFORE IT HAPPENS.
SHE'S PROBABLY ALSO SPOKEN WITH HAYAMA ABOUT THIS.
OKAY
WE'LL HEAD IN FIRST, THEN.
...SO WE'LL MANAGE THAT
BUT AS THE SERVICE CLUB, WE ALSO HAVE TO FULFILL TOBE'S REQUEST TO HELP HIM WITH HIS CONFESSION.
WELL, WHATEVER HAPPENS, HAPPENS......

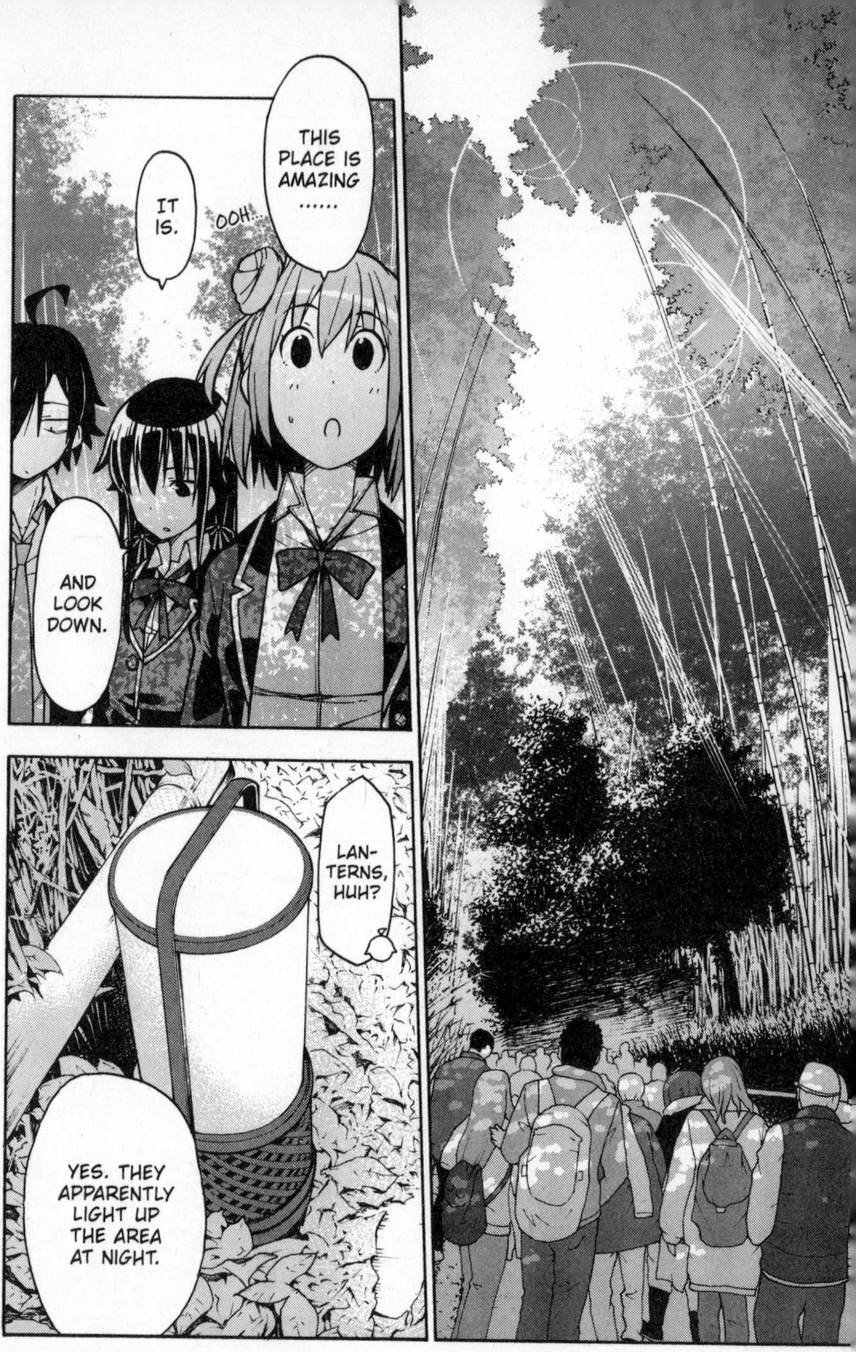
THIS PLACE IS AMAZING ......
OOH...
IT IS.
AND LOOK DOWN.
LAN-TERNS, HUH?
YES. THEY APPARENTLY LIGHT UP THE AREA AT NIGHT.

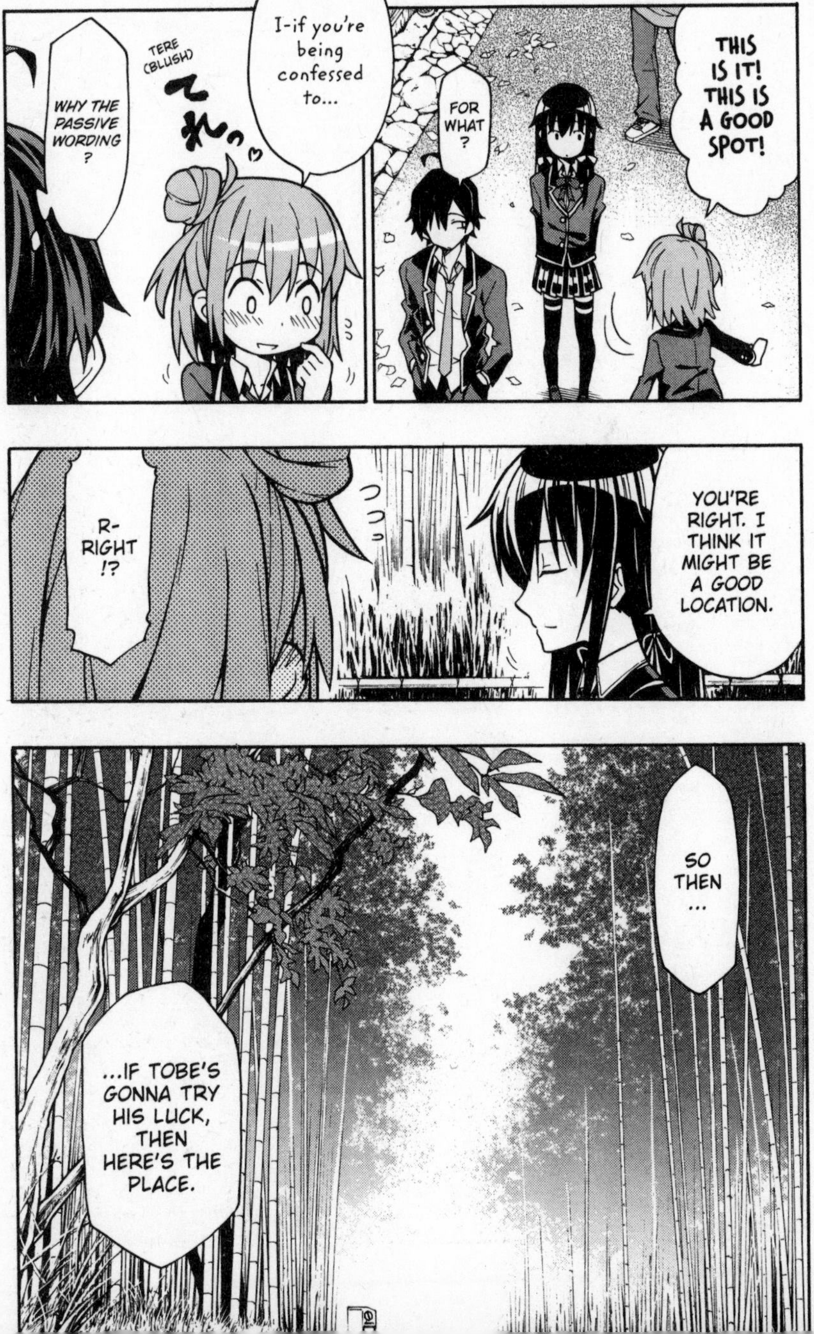
THIS IS IT! THIS IS A GOOD SPOT!
FOR WHAT?
I-if you're being confessed to...
TERE (BLUSH)
WHY THE PASSIVE WORDING?
YOU'RE RIGHT. I THINK IT MIGHT BE A GOOD LOCATION.
R-RIGHT!?
SO THEN...
...IF TOBE'S GONNA TRY HIS LUCK, THEN HERE'S THE PLACE.

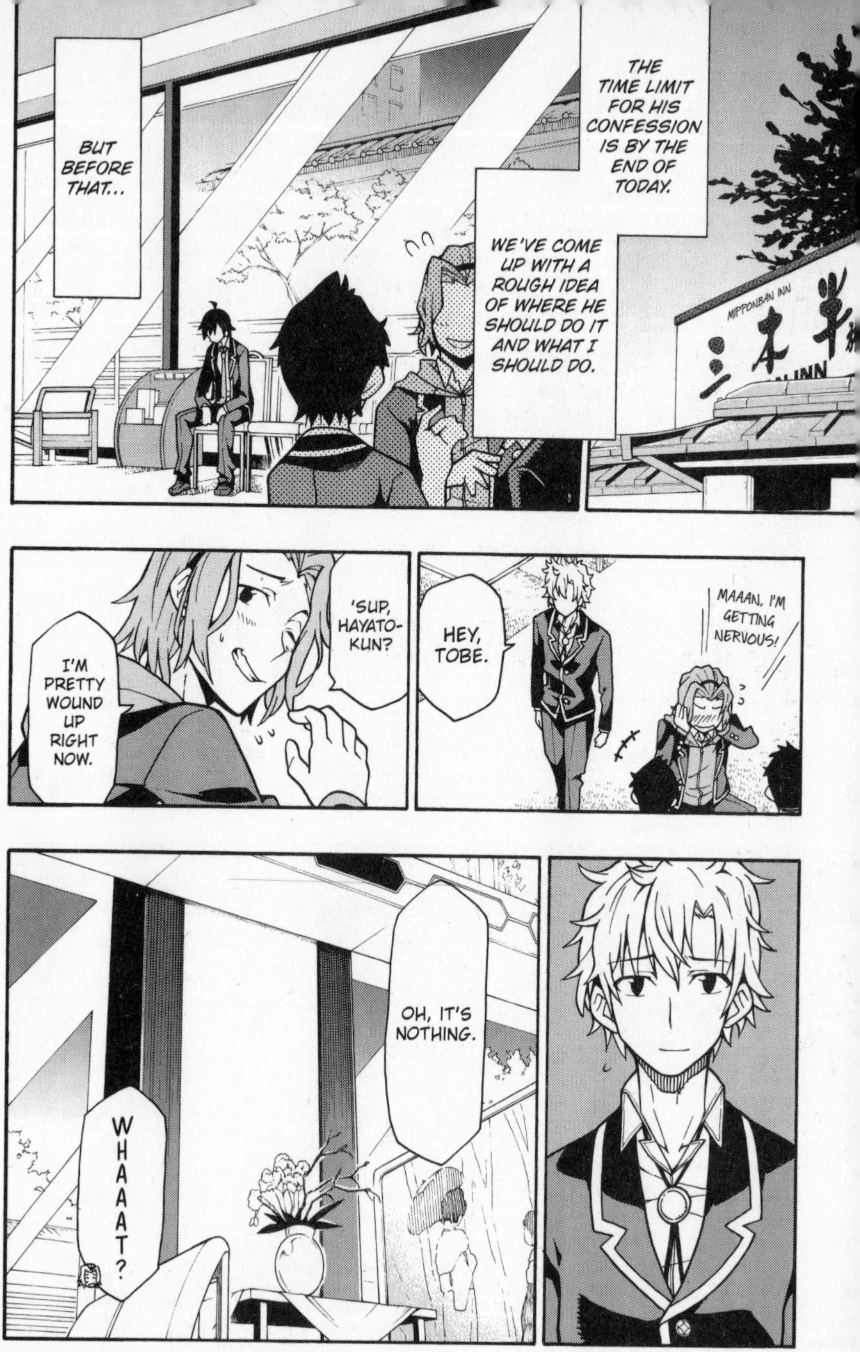
THE TIME LIMIT FOR HIS CONFESSION IS BY THE END OF TODAY.
WE'VE COME UP WITH A ROUGH IDEA OF WHERE HE SHOULD DO IT AND WHAT I SHOULD DO.
MIPPONBAN INN
BUT BEFORE THAT...
MAAAN, I'M GETTING NERVOUS!
HEY, TOBE.
'SUP, HAYATO-KUN?
I'M PRETTY WOUND UP RIGHT NOW.
OH, IT'S NOTHING.
WHAAAT?

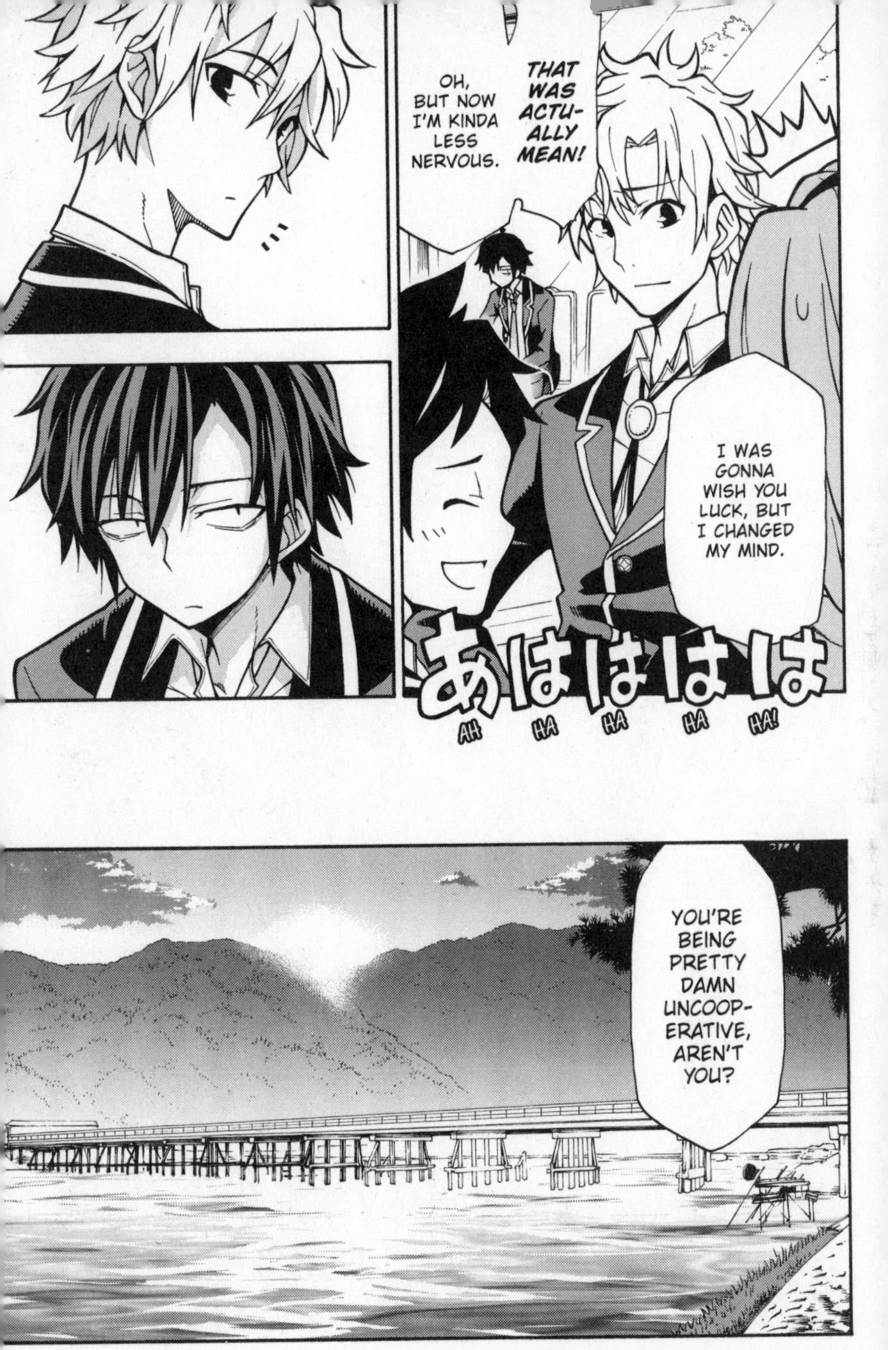
THAT WAS ACTU-ALLY MEAN!
OH, BUT NOW I'M KINDA LESS NERVOUS.
I WAS GONNA WISH YOU LUCK, BUT I CHANGED MY MIND.
あははははは
AH HA HA HA HA!
...
YOU'RE BEING PRETTY DAMN UNCOOP-ERATIVE, AREN'T YOU?

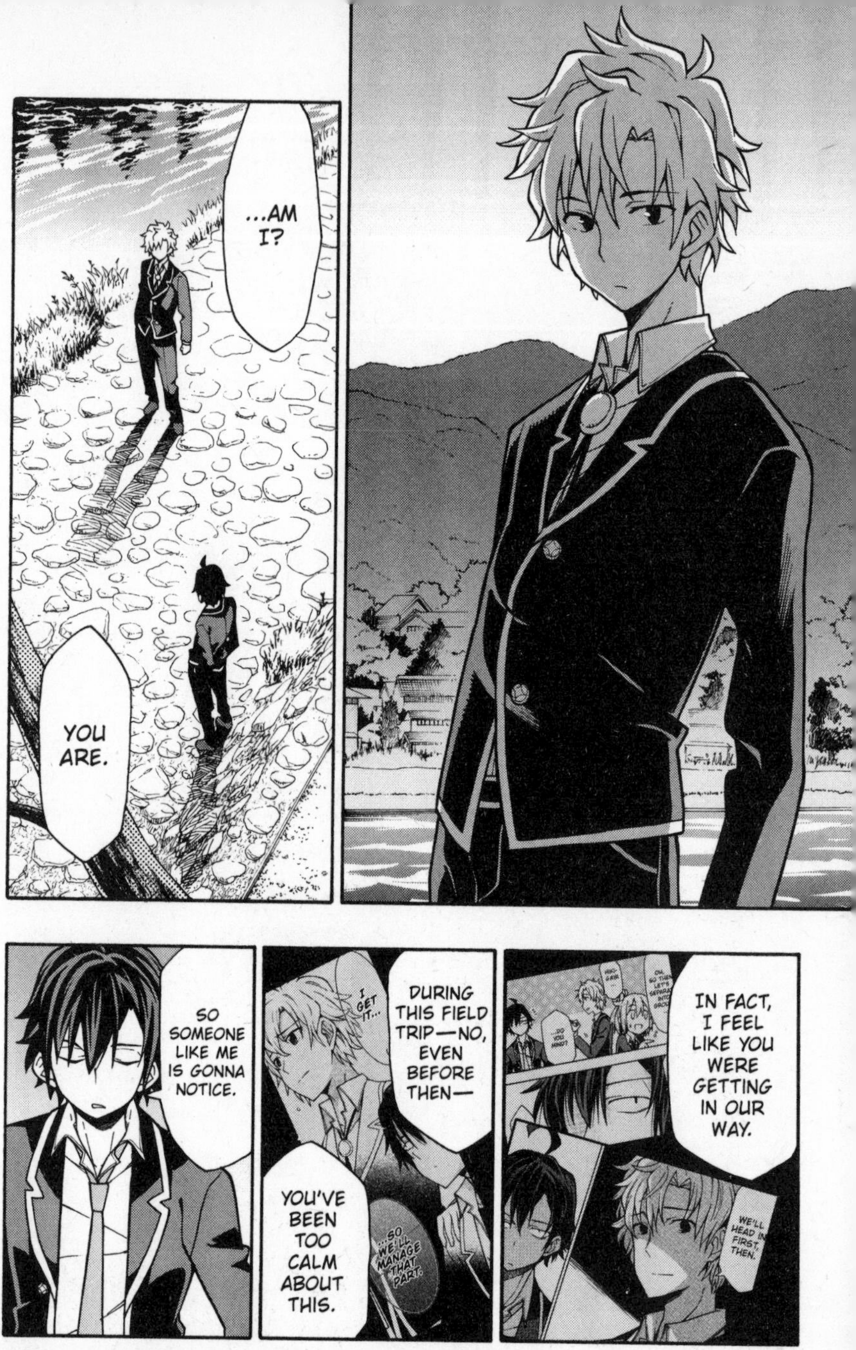
...AM I?
YOU ARE.
IN FACT, I FEEL LIKE YOU WERE GETTING IN OUR WAY.
HIKI-GAYA
...DO YOU MIND?
WE'LL HEAD IN FIRST, THEN.
DURING THIS FIELD TRIP—NO, EVEN BEFORE THEN—
I GET IT...
YOU'VE BEEN TOO CALM ABOUT THIS.
...SO WE'LL MANAGE THAT PART.
SO SOMEONE LIKE ME IS GONNA NOTICE.

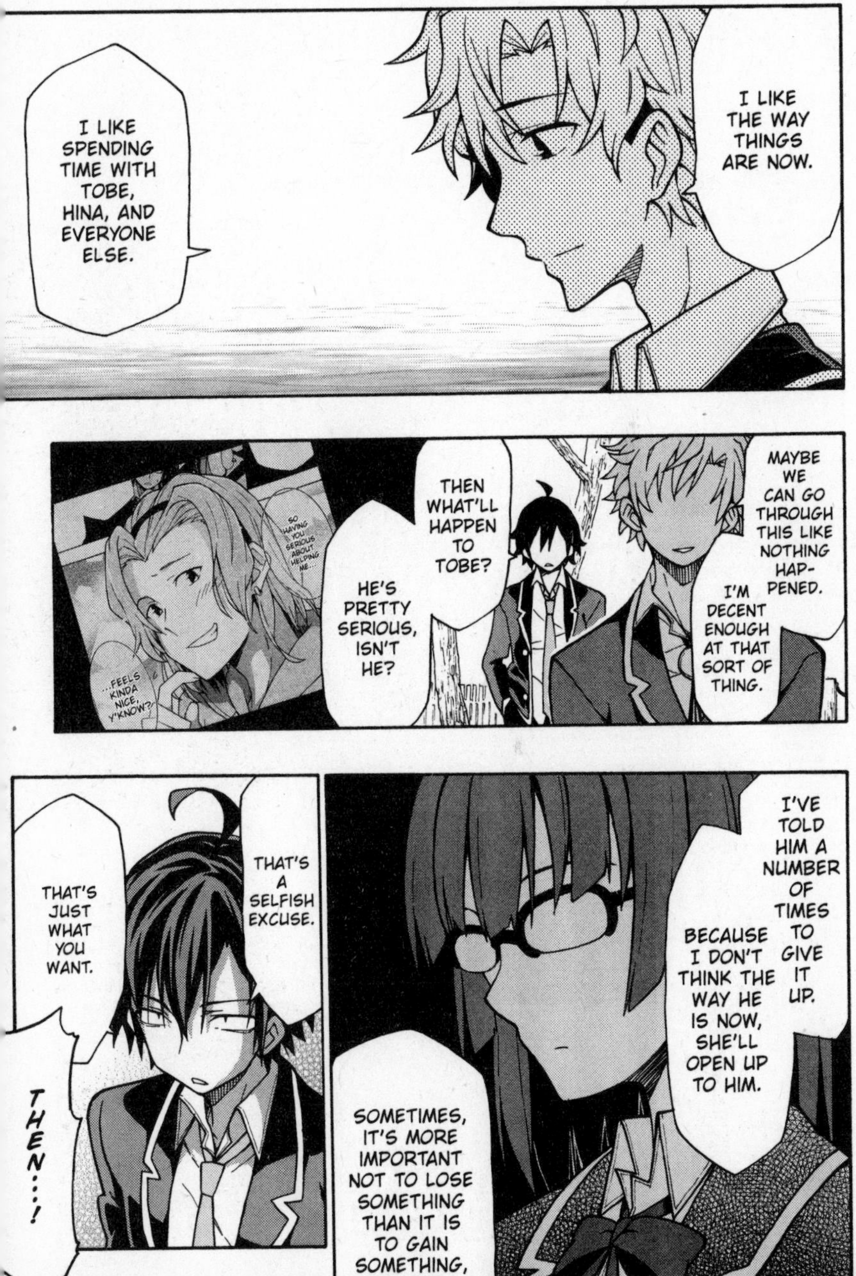
I LIKE THE WAY THINGS ARE NOW.
I LIKE SPENDING TIME WITH TOBE, HINA, AND EVERYONE ELSE.
MAYBE WE CAN GO THROUGH THIS LIKE NOTHING HAP-PENED.
I'M DECENT ENOUGH AT THAT SORT OF THING.
THEN WHAT'LL HAPPEN TO TOBE?
HE'S PRETTY SERIOUS, ISN'T HE?
SO HAVING YOU SERIOUS ABOUT HELPING ME...
...FEELS KINDA NICE, Y'KNOW?
I'VE TOLD HIM A NUMBER OF TIMES TO GIVE IT UP.
BECAUSE I DON'T THINK THE WAY HE IS NOW, SHE'LL OPEN UP TO HIM.
SOMETIMES, IT'S MORE IMPORTANT NOT TO LOSE SOMETHING THAN IT IS TO GAIN SOMETHING, RIGHT?
THAT'S A SELFISH EXCUSE.
THAT'S JUST WHAT YOU WANT.
THEN...!

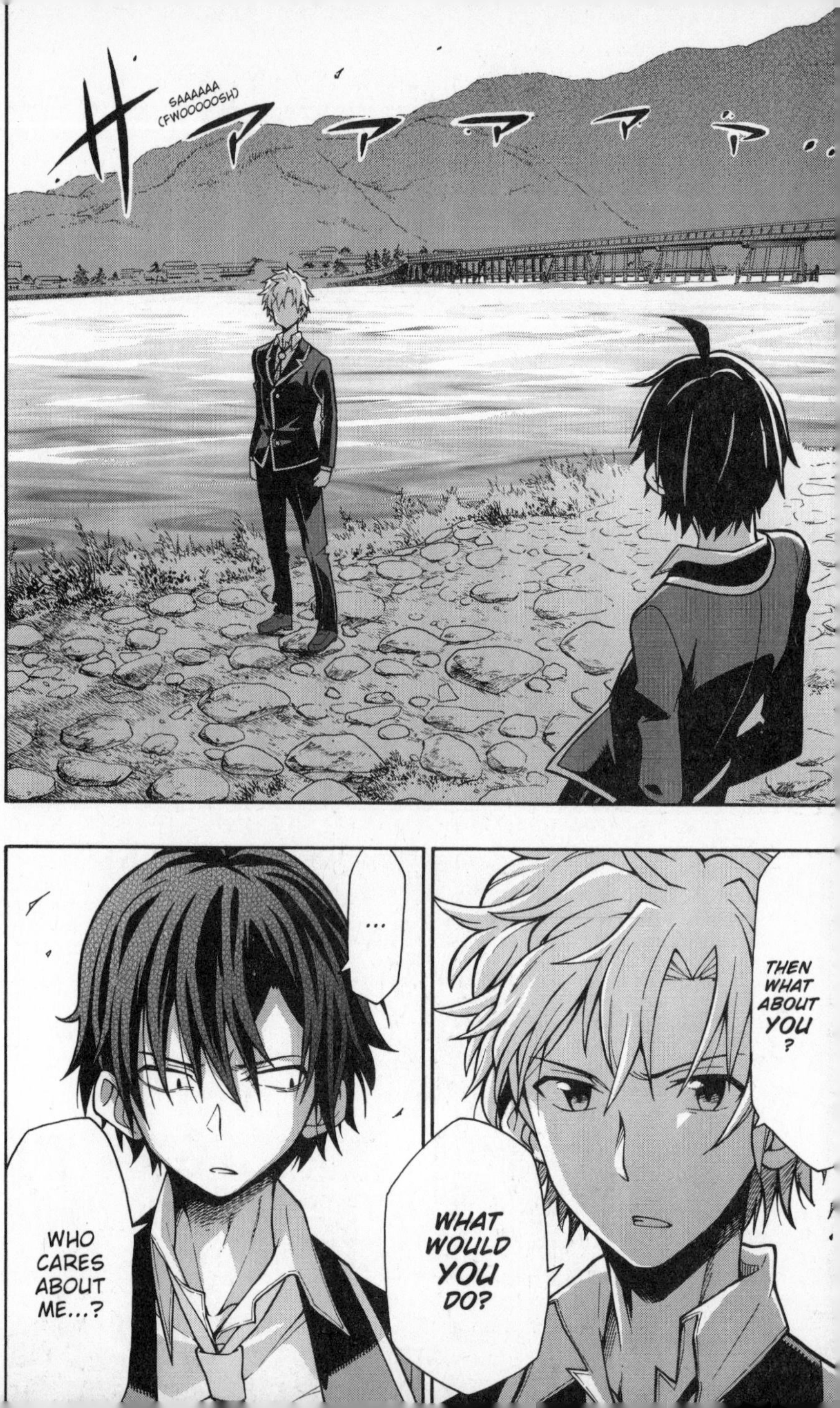
サァァァァ…
SAAAAAA
(FWOOOOOSH)
THEN WHAT ABOUT YOU?
WHAT WOULD YOU DO?
...
WHO CARES ABOUT ME...?

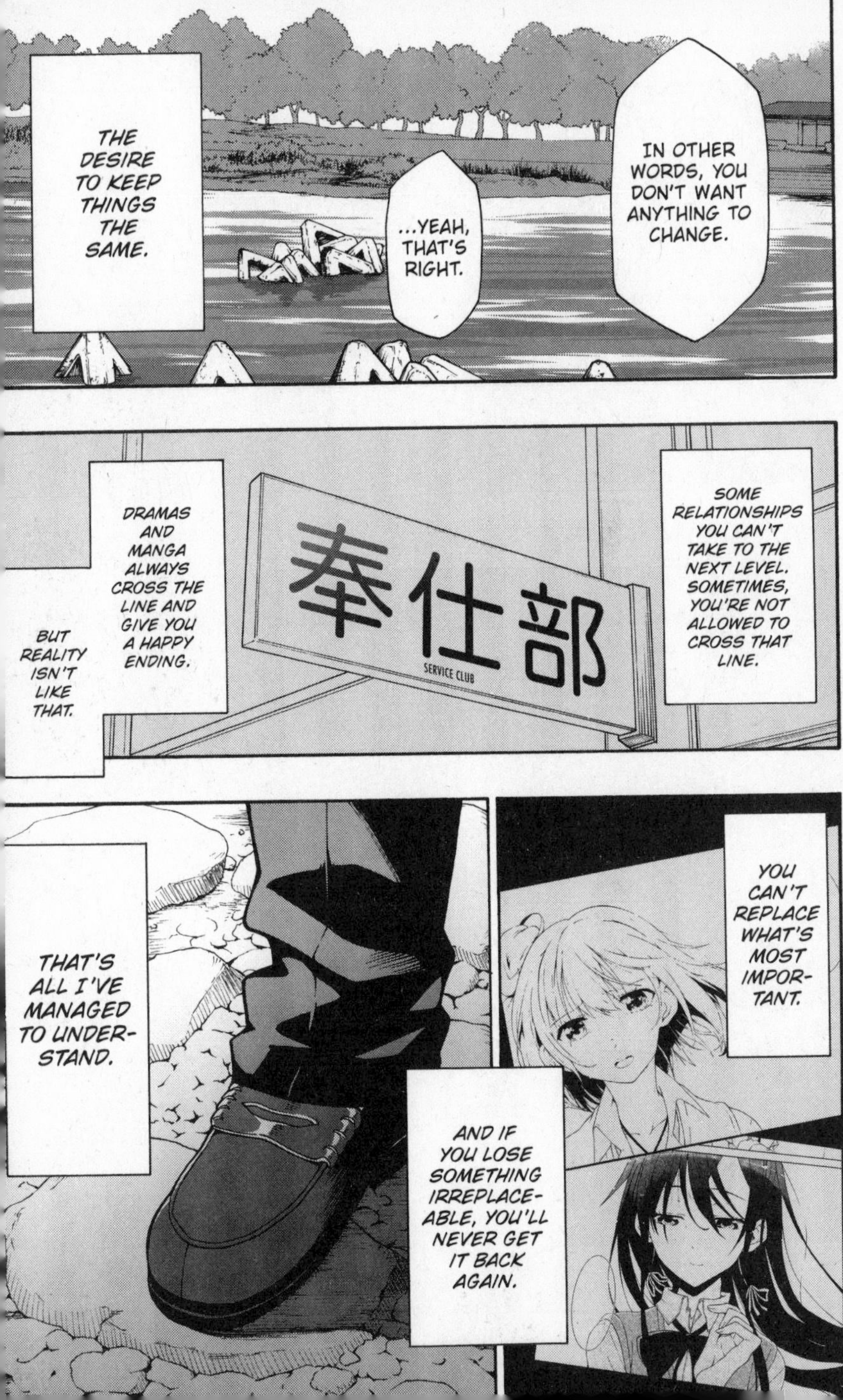
IN OTHER WORDS, YOU DON'T WANT ANYTHING TO CHANGE.
...YEAH, THAT'S RIGHT.
THE DESIRE TO KEEP THINGS THE SAME.
SOME RELATIONSHIPS YOU CAN'T TAKE TO THE NEXT LEVEL. SOMETIMES, YOU'RE NOT ALLOWED TO CROSS THAT LINE.
奉仕部
SERVICE CLUB
DRAMAS AND MANGA ALWAYS CROSS THE LINE AND GIVE YOU A HAPPY ENDING.
BUT REALITY ISN'T LIKE THAT.
YOU CAN'T REPLACE WHAT'S MOST IMPORTANT.
AND IF YOU LOSE SOMETHING IRREPLACEABLE, YOU'LL NEVER GET IT BACK AGAIN.
THAT'S ALL I'VE MANAGED TO UNDERSTAND.

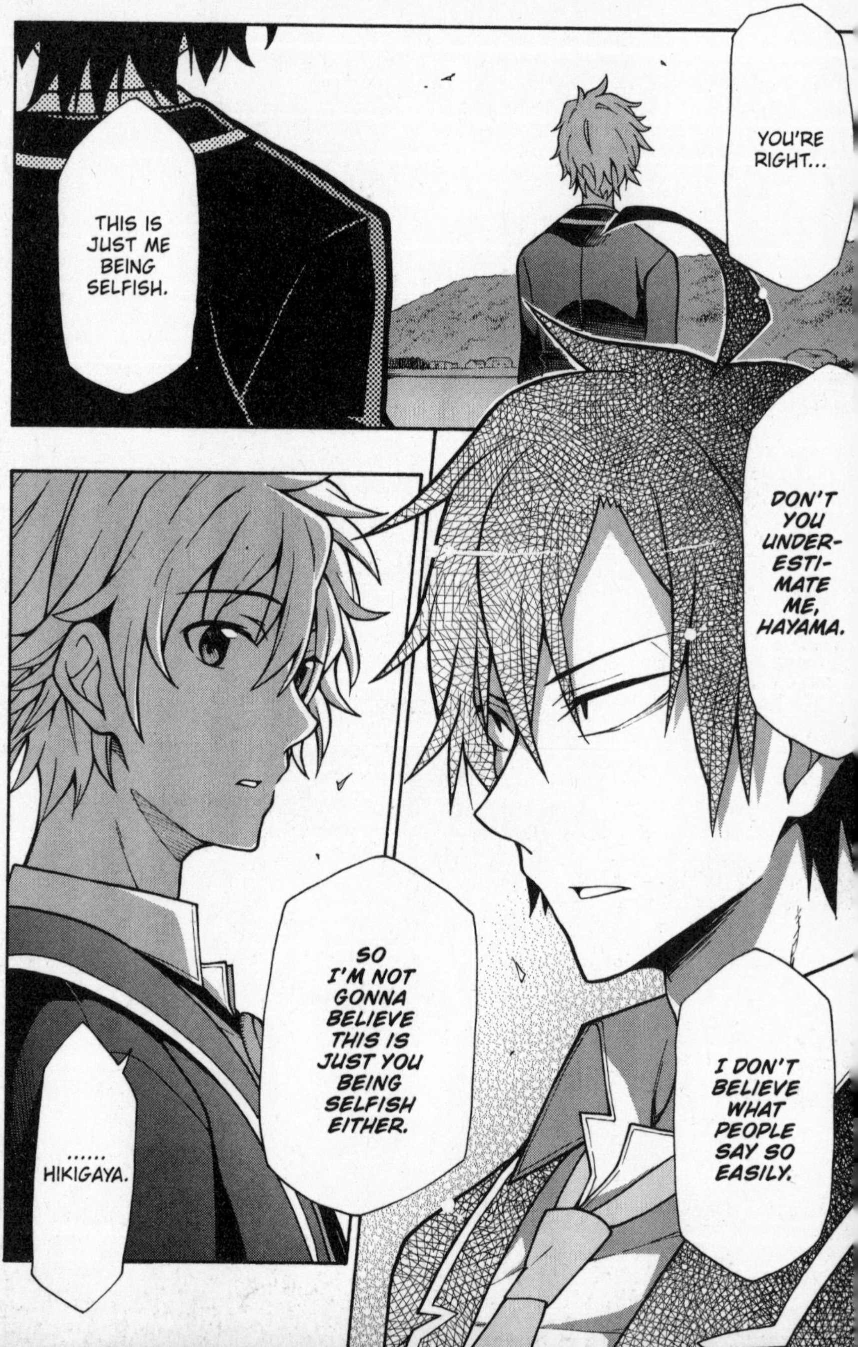
YOU'RE RIGHT...
THIS IS JUST ME BEING SELFISH.
DON'T YOU UNDER-ESTI-MATE ME, HAYAMA.
I DON'T BELIEVE WHAT PEOPLE SAY SO EASILY.
SO I'M NOT GONNA BELIEVE THIS IS JUST YOU BEING SELFISH EITHER.
...... HIKIGAYA.

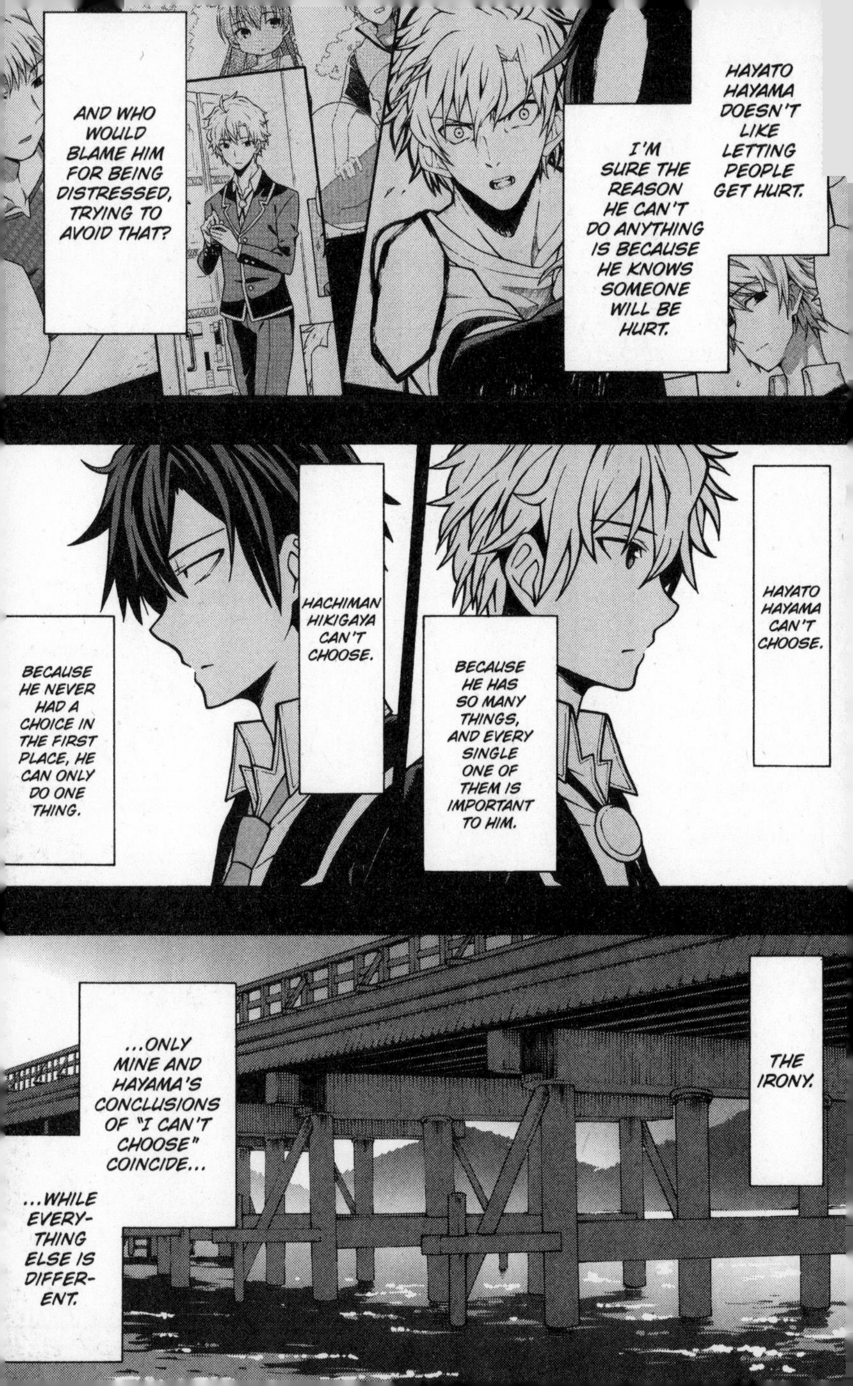
HAYATO HAYAMA DOESN'T LIKE LETTING PEOPLE GET HURT.
I'M SURE THE REASON HE CAN'T DO ANYTHING IS BECAUSE HE KNOWS SOMEONE WILL BE HURT.
AND WHO WOULD BLAME HIM FOR BEING DISTRESSED, TRYING TO AVOID THAT?
HAYATO HAYAMA CAN'T CHOOSE.
BECAUSE HE HAS SO MANY THINGS, AND EVERY SINGLE ONE OF THEM IS IMPORTANT TO HIM.
HACHIMAN HIKIGAYA CAN'T CHOOSE.
BECAUSE HE NEVER HAD A CHOICE IN THE FIRST PLACE, HE CAN ONLY DO ONE THING.
THE IRONY.
...ONLY MINE AND HAYAMA'S CONCLUSIONS OF "I CAN'T CHOOSE" COINCIDE...
...WHILE EVERY-THING ELSE IS DIFFER-ENT.

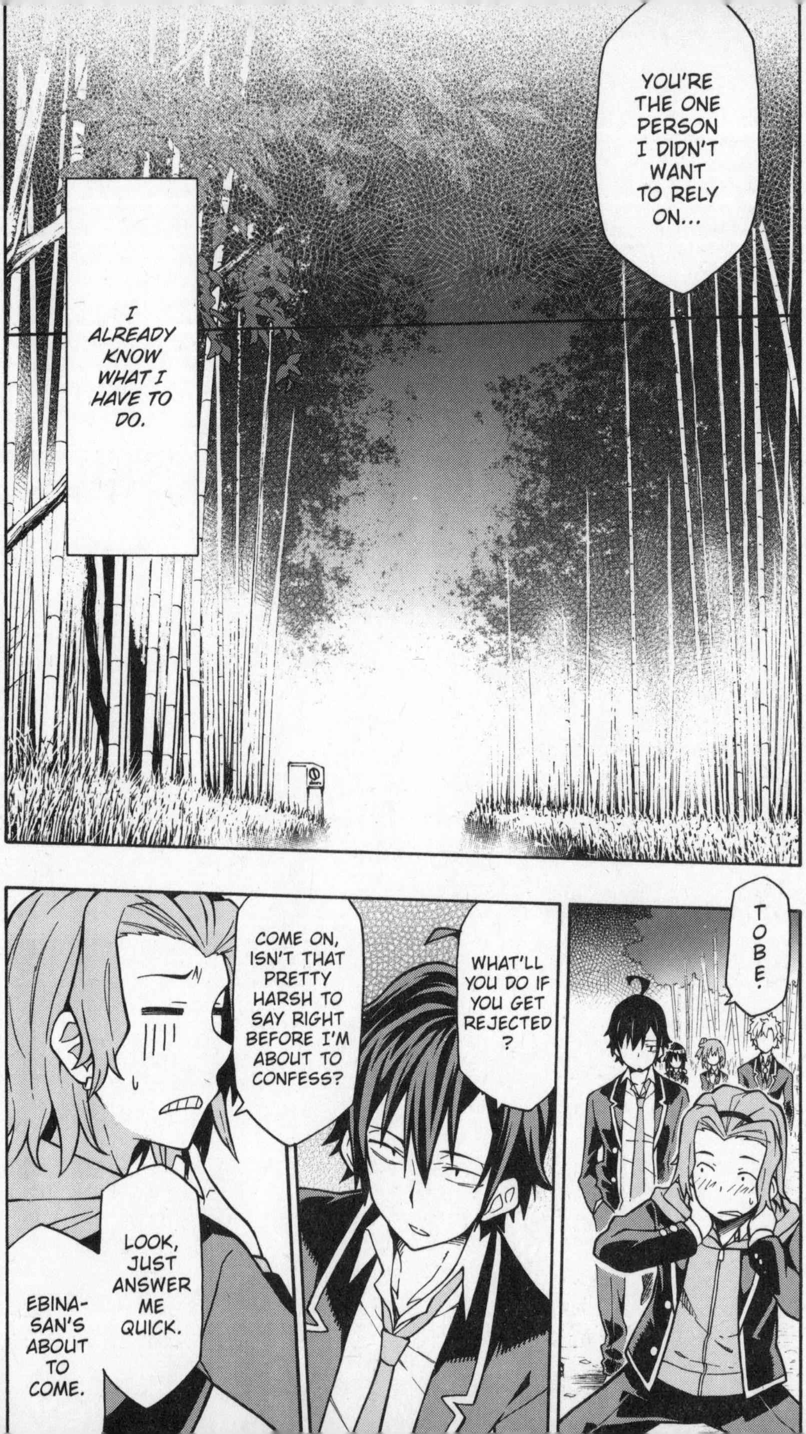
YOU'RE THE ONE PERSON I DIDN'T WANT TO RELY ON...
I ALREADY KNOW WHAT I HAVE TO DO.
TOBE.
WHAT'LL YOU DO IF YOU GET REJECTED?
COME ON, ISN'T THAT PRETTY HARSH TO SAY RIGHT BEFORE I'M ABOUT TO CONFESS?
LOOK, JUST ANSWER ME QUICK.
EBINA-SAN'S ABOUT TO COME.

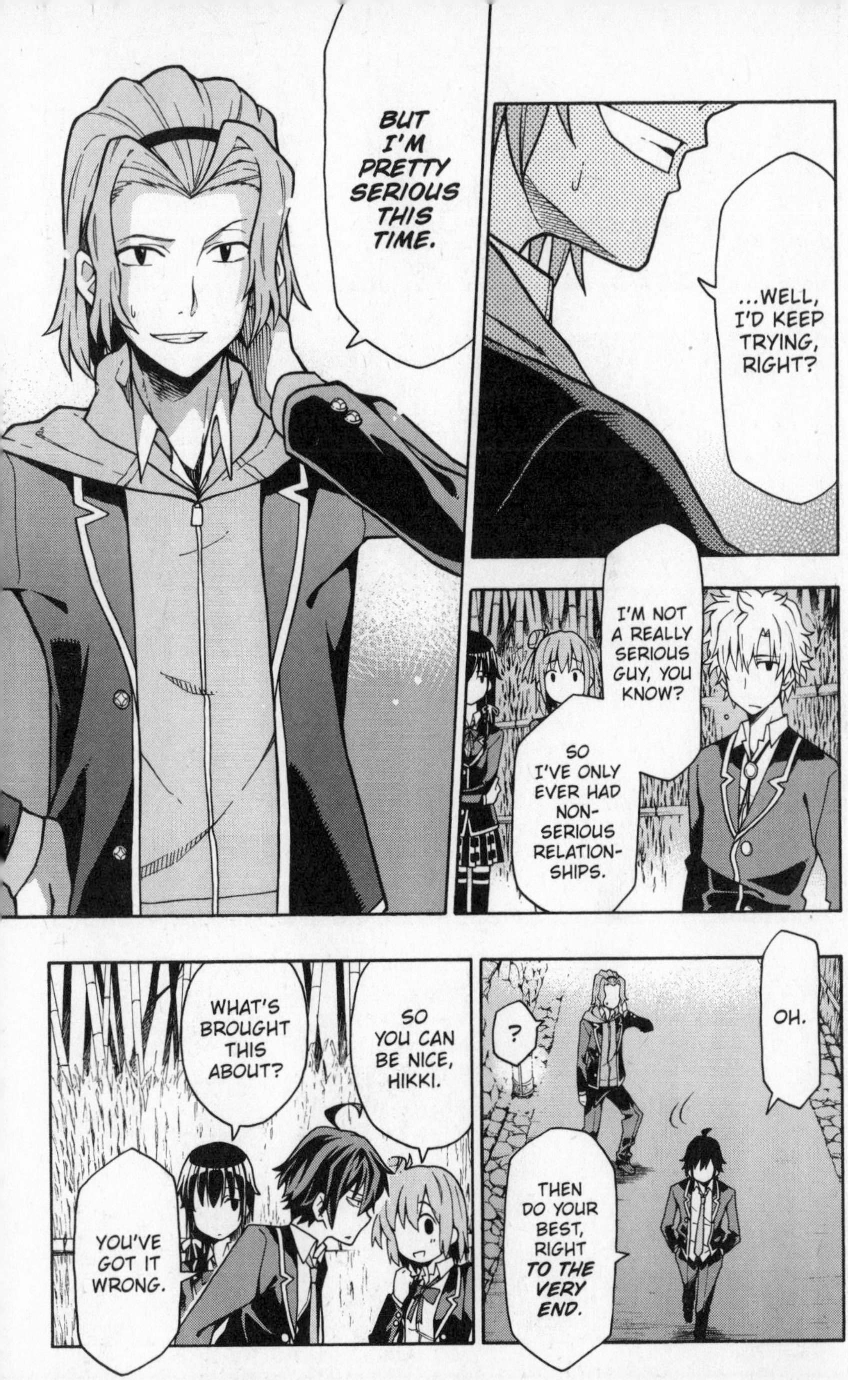
...WELL, I'D KEEP TRYING, RIGHT?
I'M NOT A REALLY SERIOUS GUY, YOU KNOW?
SO I'VE ONLY EVER HAD NON-SERIOUS RELATIONSHIPS.
BUT I'M PRETTY SERIOUS THIS TIME.
OH.
?
THEN DO YOUR BEST, RIGHT TO THE VERY END.
SO YOU CAN BE NICE, HIKKI.
WHAT'S BROUGHT THIS ABOUT?
YOU'VE GOT IT WRONG.

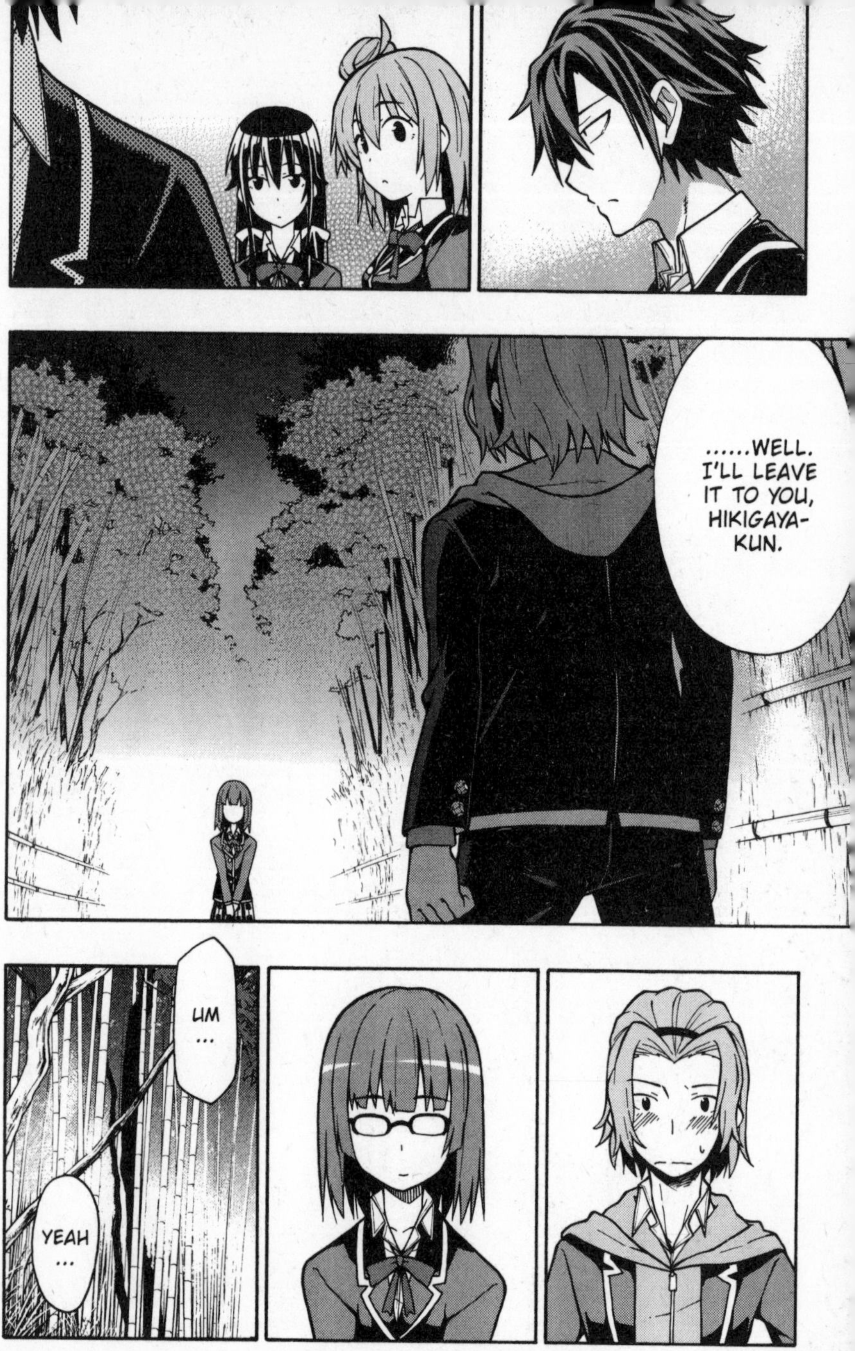
......WELL. I'LL LEAVE IT TO YOU, HIKIGAYA-KUN.
UM ...
YEAH ...

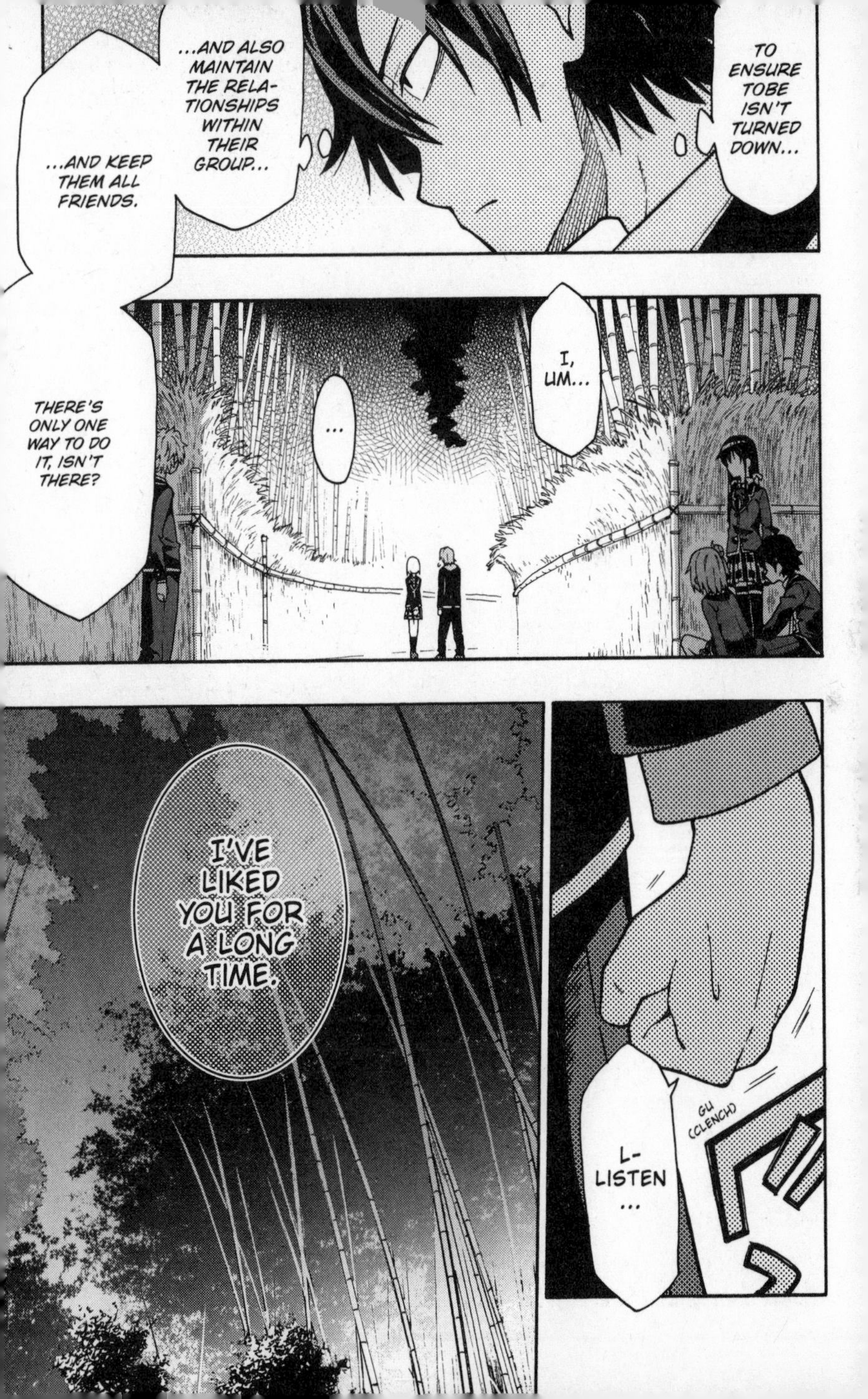
TO ENSURE TOBE ISN'T TURNED DOWN...
...AND ALSO MAINTAIN THE RELATIONSHIPS WITHIN THEIR GROUP...
...AND KEEP THEM ALL FRIENDS.
I, UM...
...
THERE'S ONLY ONE WAY TO DO IT, ISN'T THERE?
GU (CLENCH)
L-LISTEN...
I'VE LIKED YOU FOR A LONG TIME.

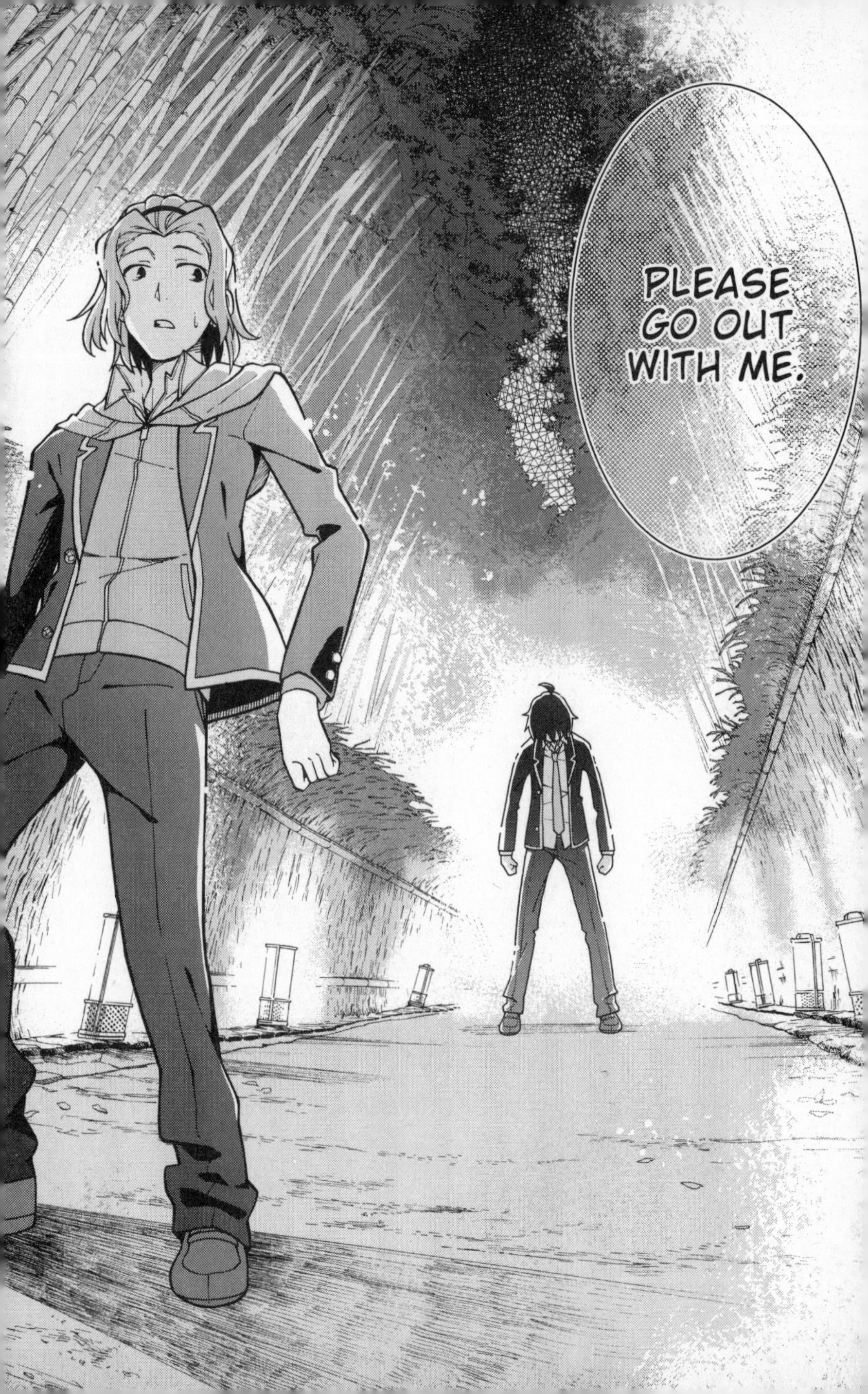
PLEASE GO OUT WITH ME.

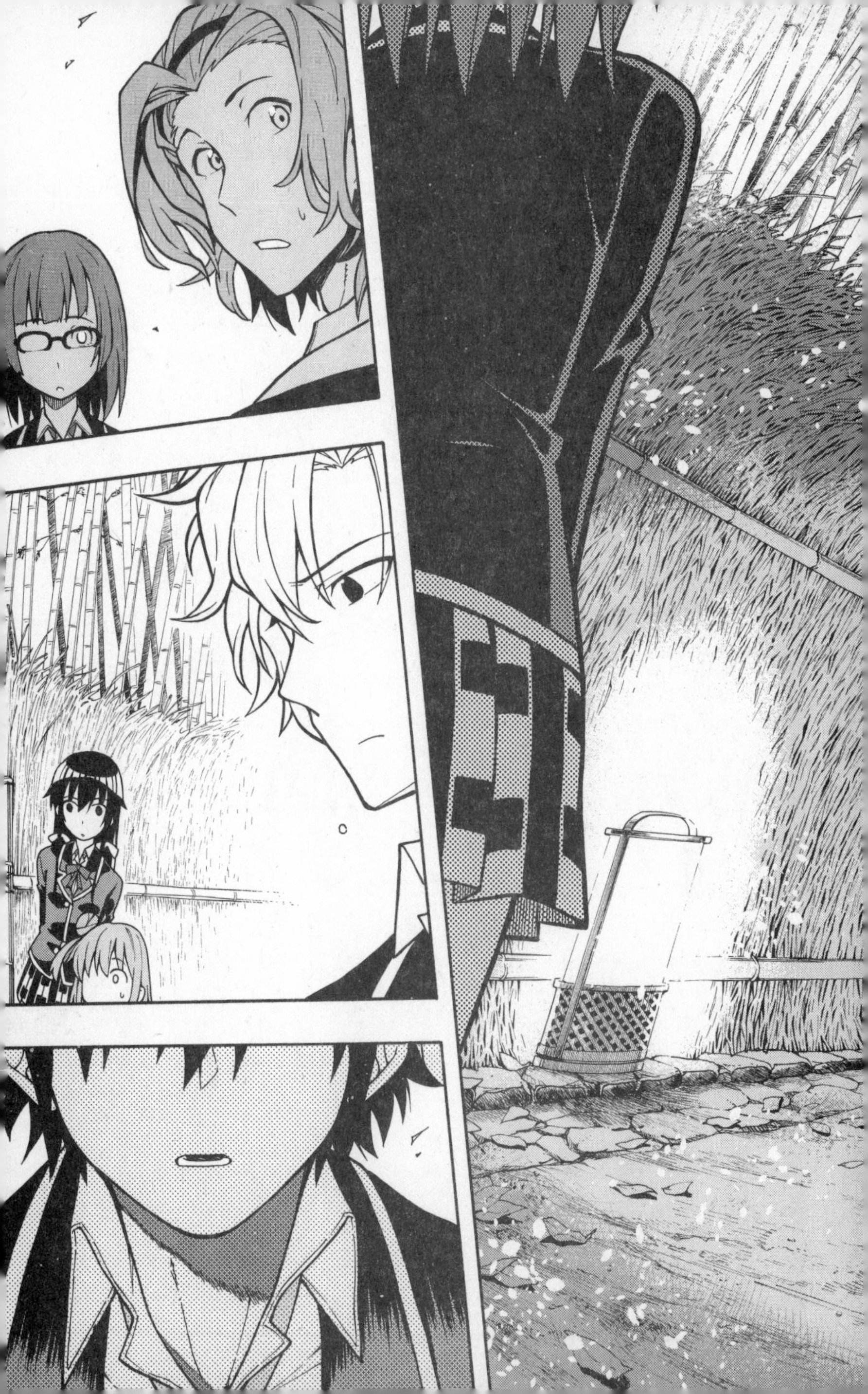

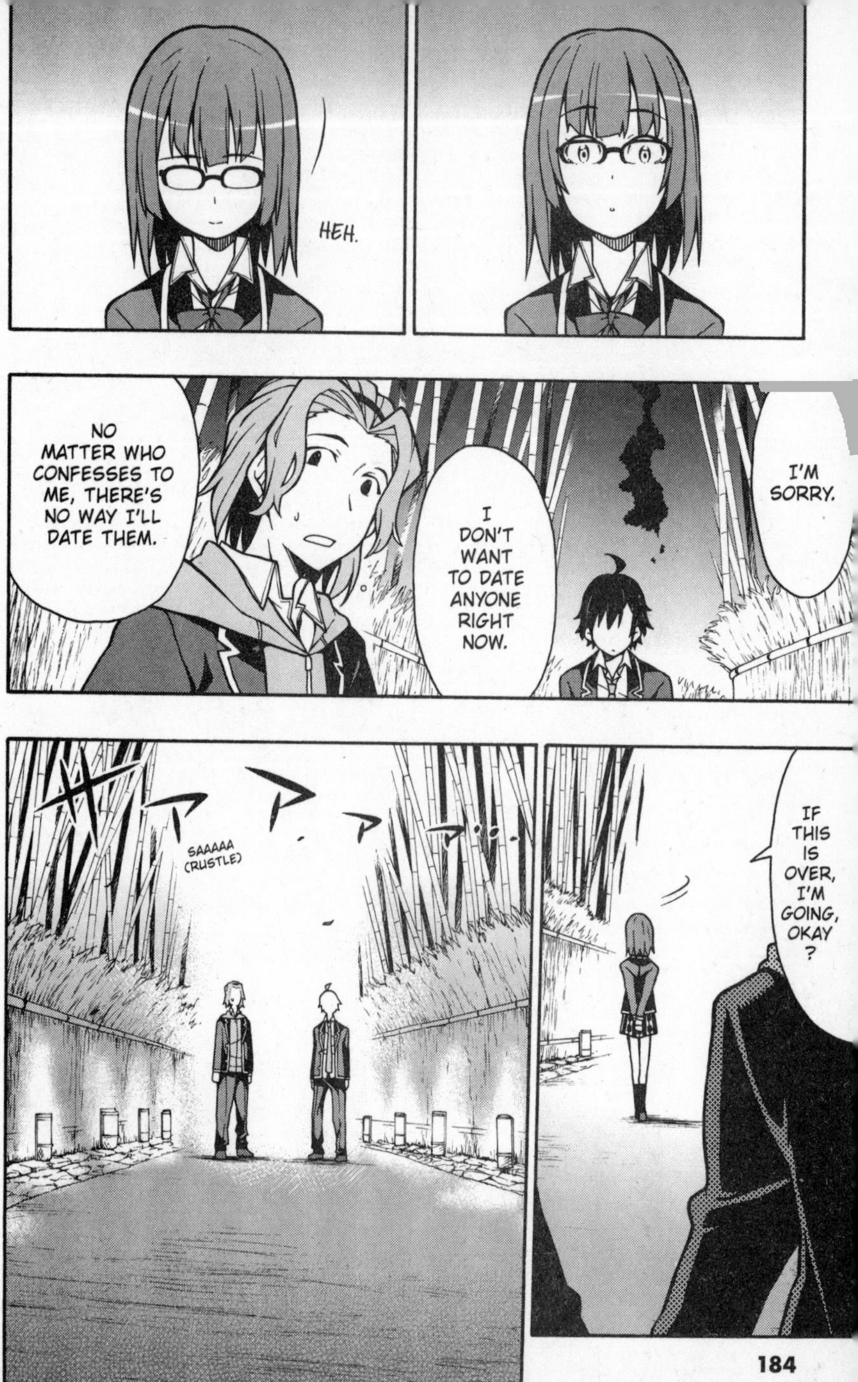
HEH.
I'M SORRY.
I DON'T WANT TO DATE ANYONE RIGHT NOW.
NO MATTER WHO CONFESSES TO ME, THERE'S NO WAY I'LL DATE THEM.
IF THIS IS OVER, I'M GOING, OKAY?
SAAAAA (RUSTLE)

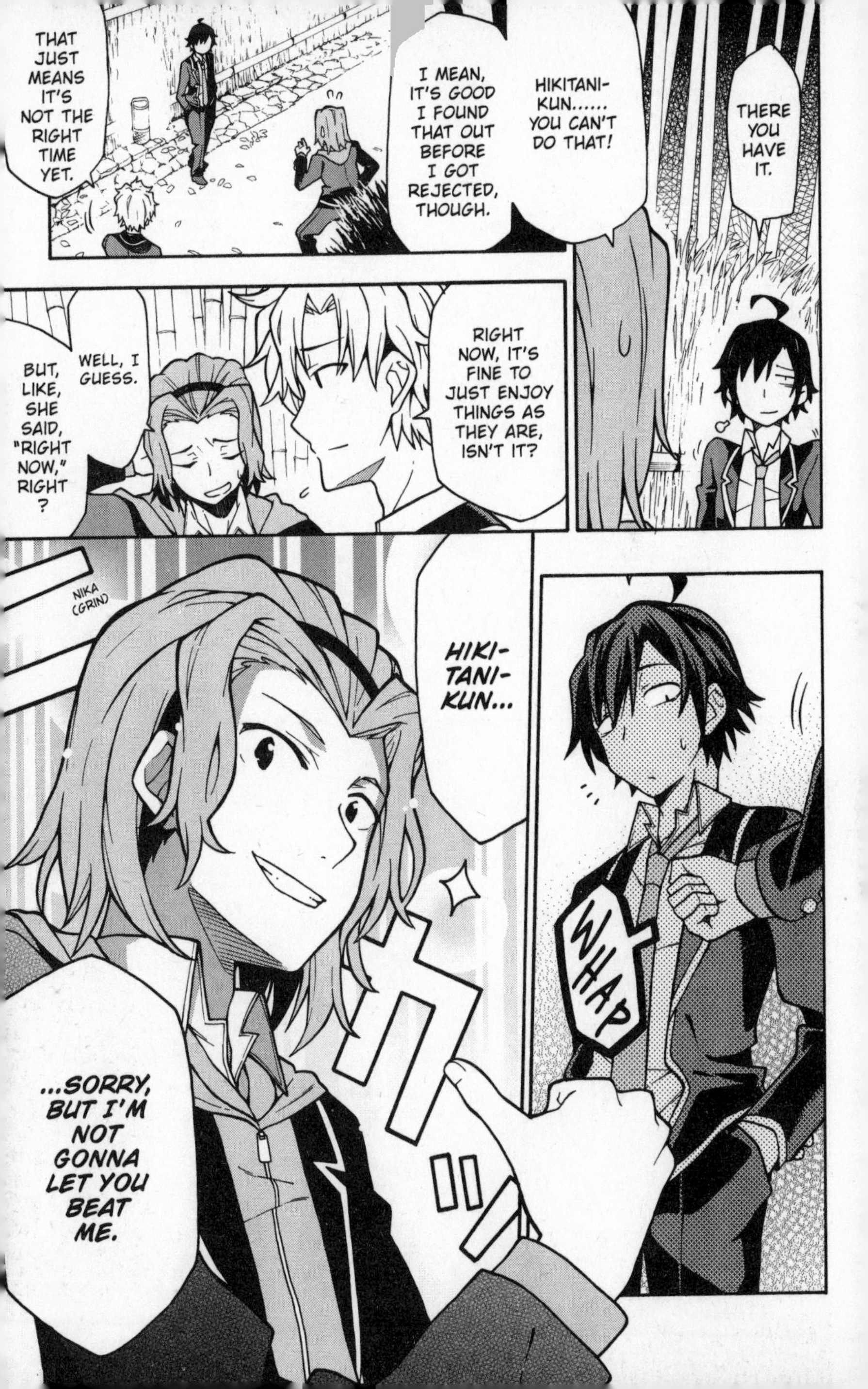
THERE YOU HAVE IT.
HIKITANI-KUN...... YOU CAN'T DO THAT!
I MEAN, IT'S GOOD I FOUND THAT OUT BEFORE I GOT REJECTED, THOUGH.
THAT JUST MEANS IT'S NOT THE RIGHT TIME YET.
RIGHT NOW, IT'S FINE TO JUST ENJOY THINGS AS THEY ARE, ISN'T IT?
WELL, I GUESS.
BUT, LIKE, SHE SAID, "RIGHT NOW," RIGHT?
WHAP
...
HIKI-TANI-KUN...
NIKA (GRIN)
...SORRY, BUT I'M NOT GONNA LET YOU BEAT ME.

I KNEW THAT WAS THE ONLY WAY YOU KNOW HOW TO HANDLE THINGS, BUT...

...I'M SORRY.

た っ
TA
(TROT)

DON'T APOLO-GIZE.

...

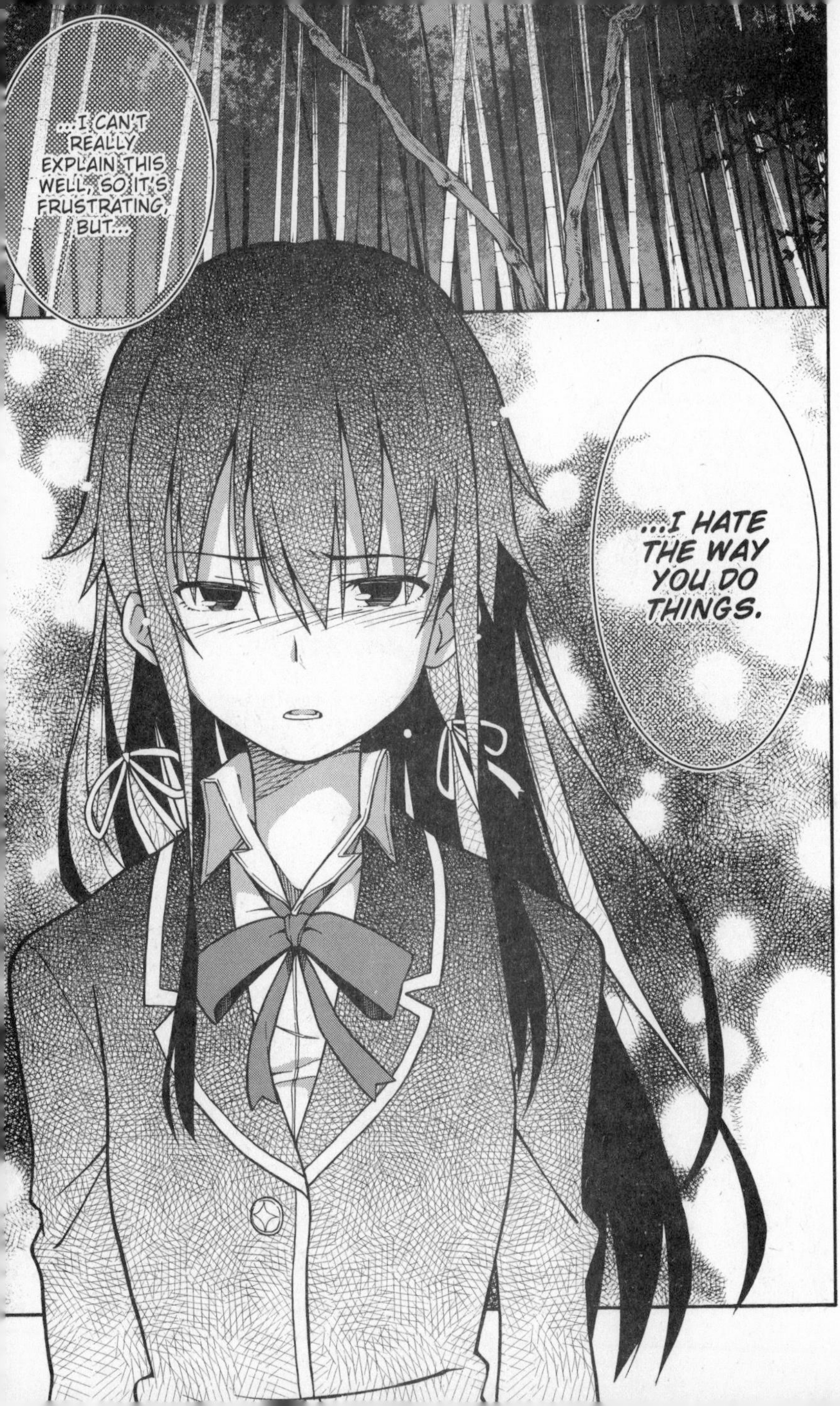
...I CAN'T REALLY EXPLAIN THIS WELL, SO IT'S FRUSTRATING, BUT...
...I HATE THE WAY YOU DO THINGS.

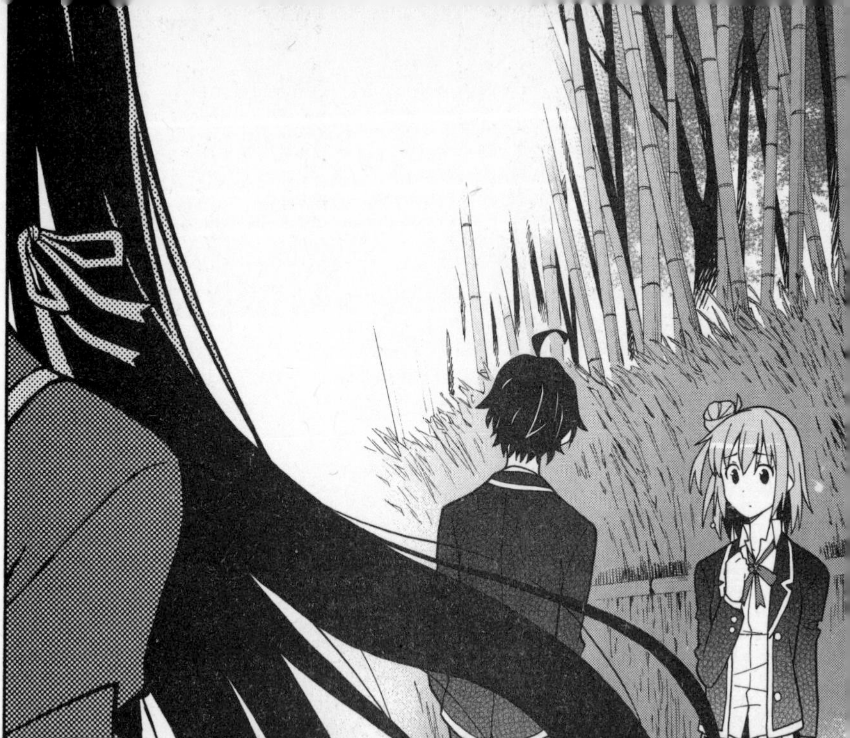

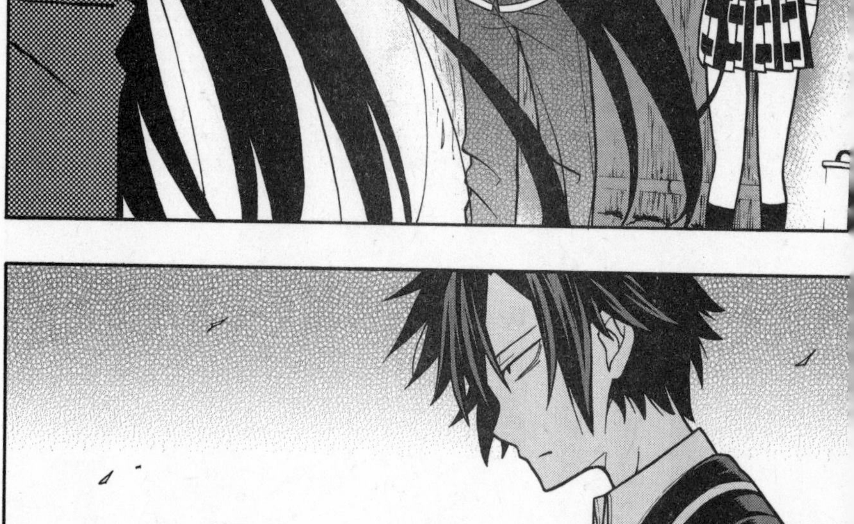

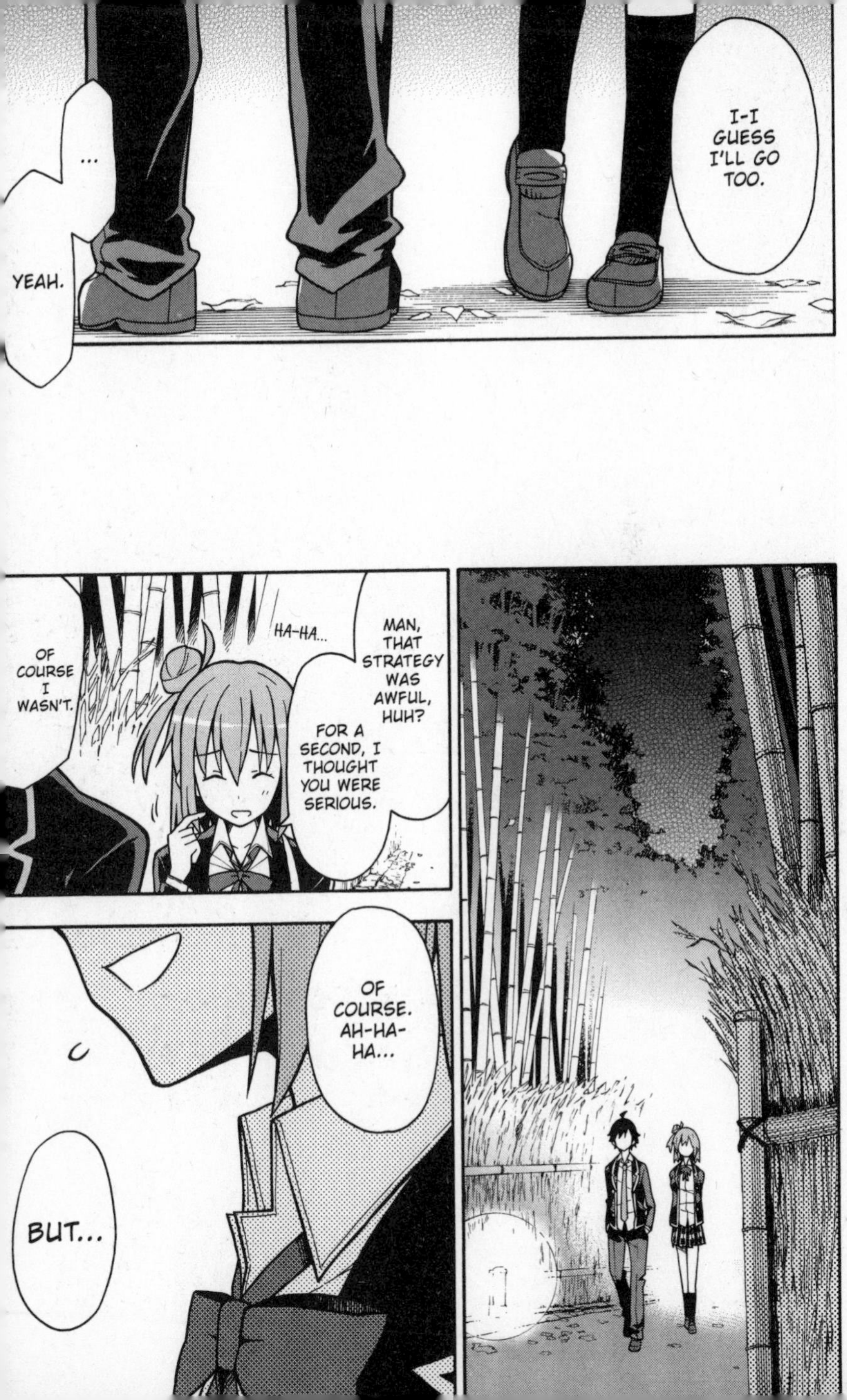
I-I GUESS I'LL GO TOO.
...
YEAH.
MAN, THAT STRATEGY WAS AWFUL, HUH?
HA-HA...
FOR A SECOND, I THOUGHT YOU WERE SERIOUS.
OF COURSE I WASN'T.
OF COURSE. AH-HA-HA...
BUT...

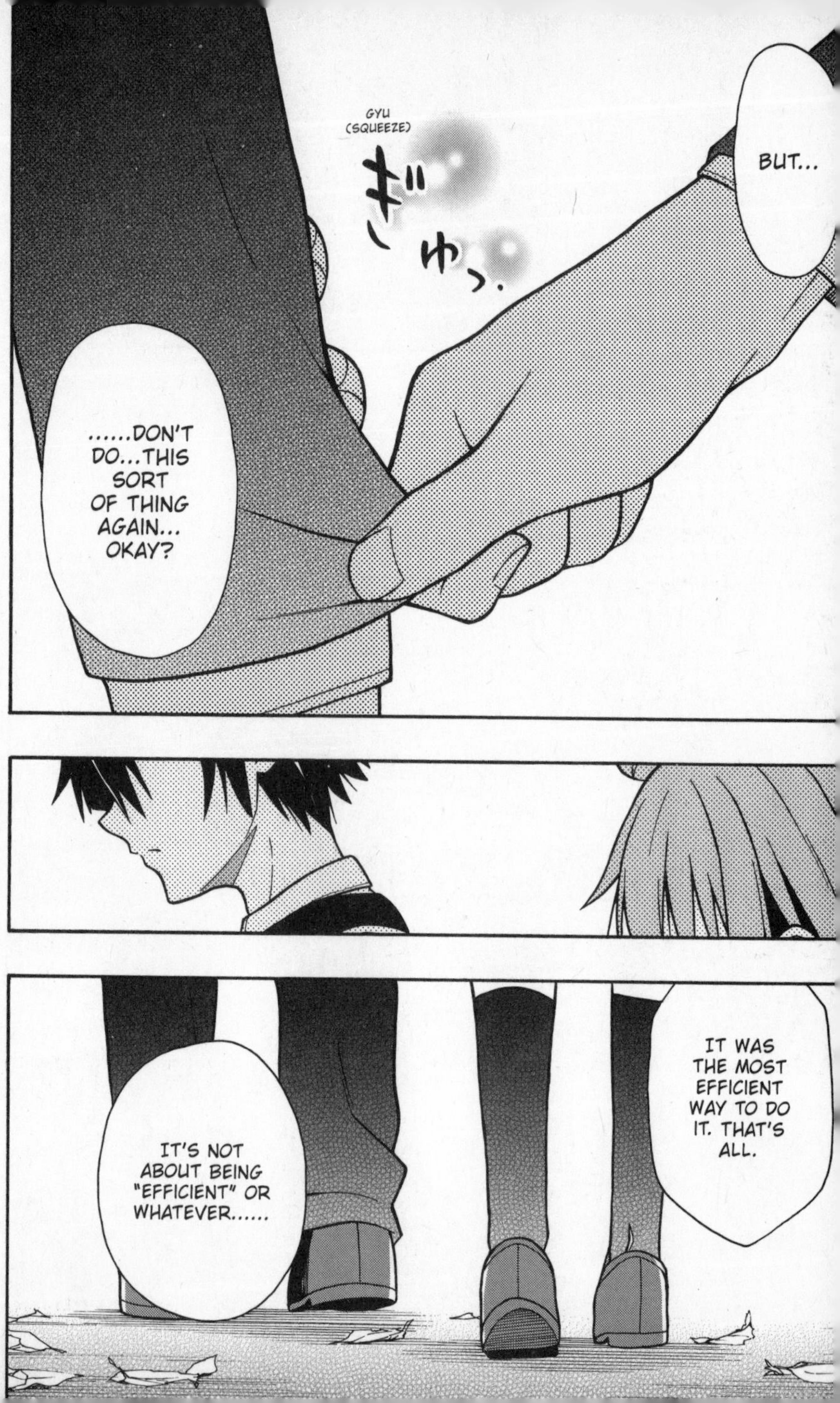
BUT...
GYU (SQUEEZE)
ぎゅっ
......DON'T DO...THIS SORT OF THING AGAIN... OKAY?
IT WAS THE MOST EFFICIENT WAY TO DO IT. THAT'S ALL.
IT'S NOT ABOUT BEING "EFFICIENT" OR WHATEVER......

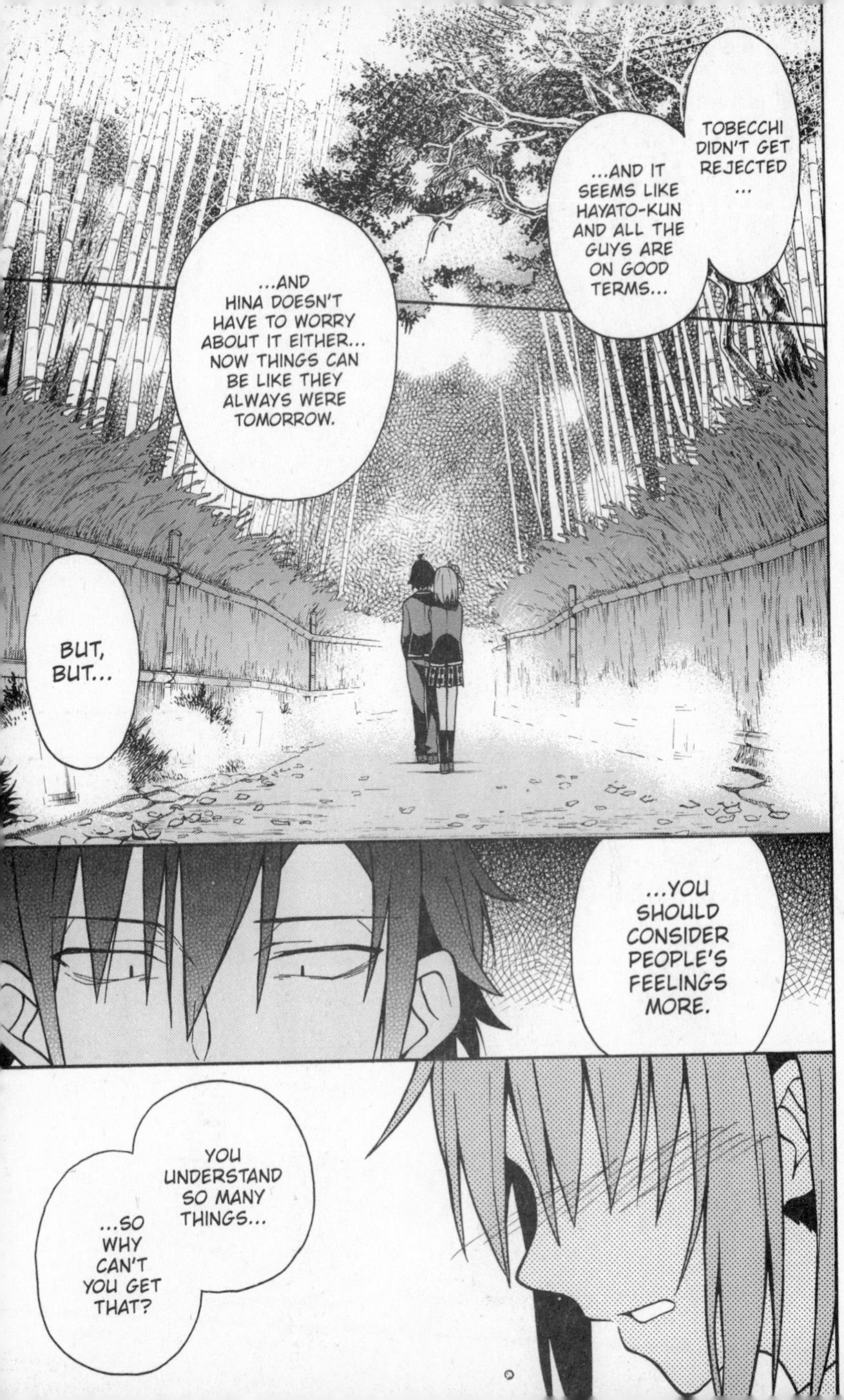
TOBECCHI DIDN'T GET REJECTED...
...AND IT SEEMS LIKE HAYATO-KUN AND ALL THE GUYS ARE ON GOOD TERMS...
...AND HINA DOESN'T HAVE TO WORRY ABOUT IT EITHER... NOW THINGS CAN BE LIKE THEY ALWAYS WERE TOMORROW.
BUT, BUT...
...YOU SHOULD CONSIDER PEOPLE'S FEELINGS MORE.
YOU UNDERSTAND SO MANY THINGS...
...SO WHY CAN'T YOU GET THAT?

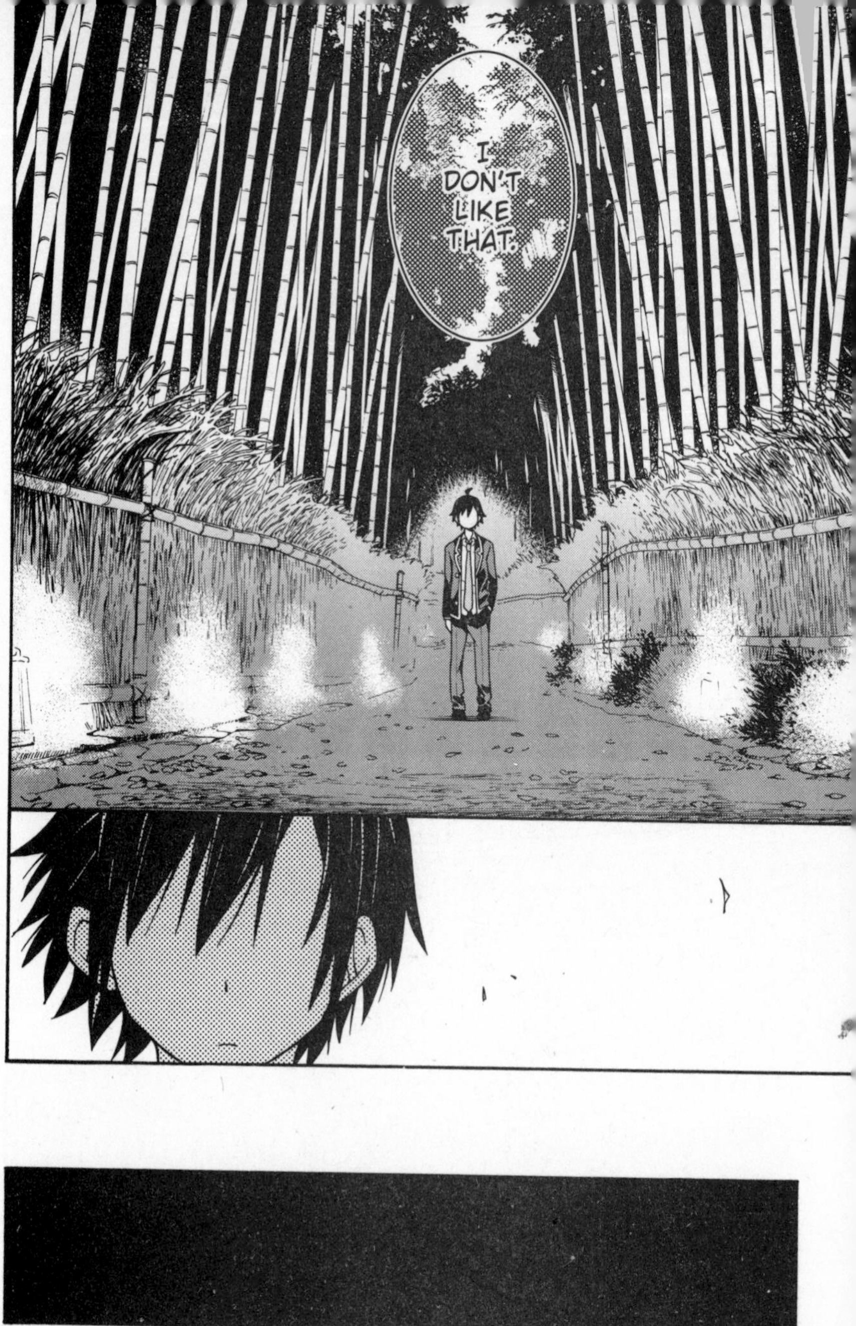
I DON'T LIKE THAT.

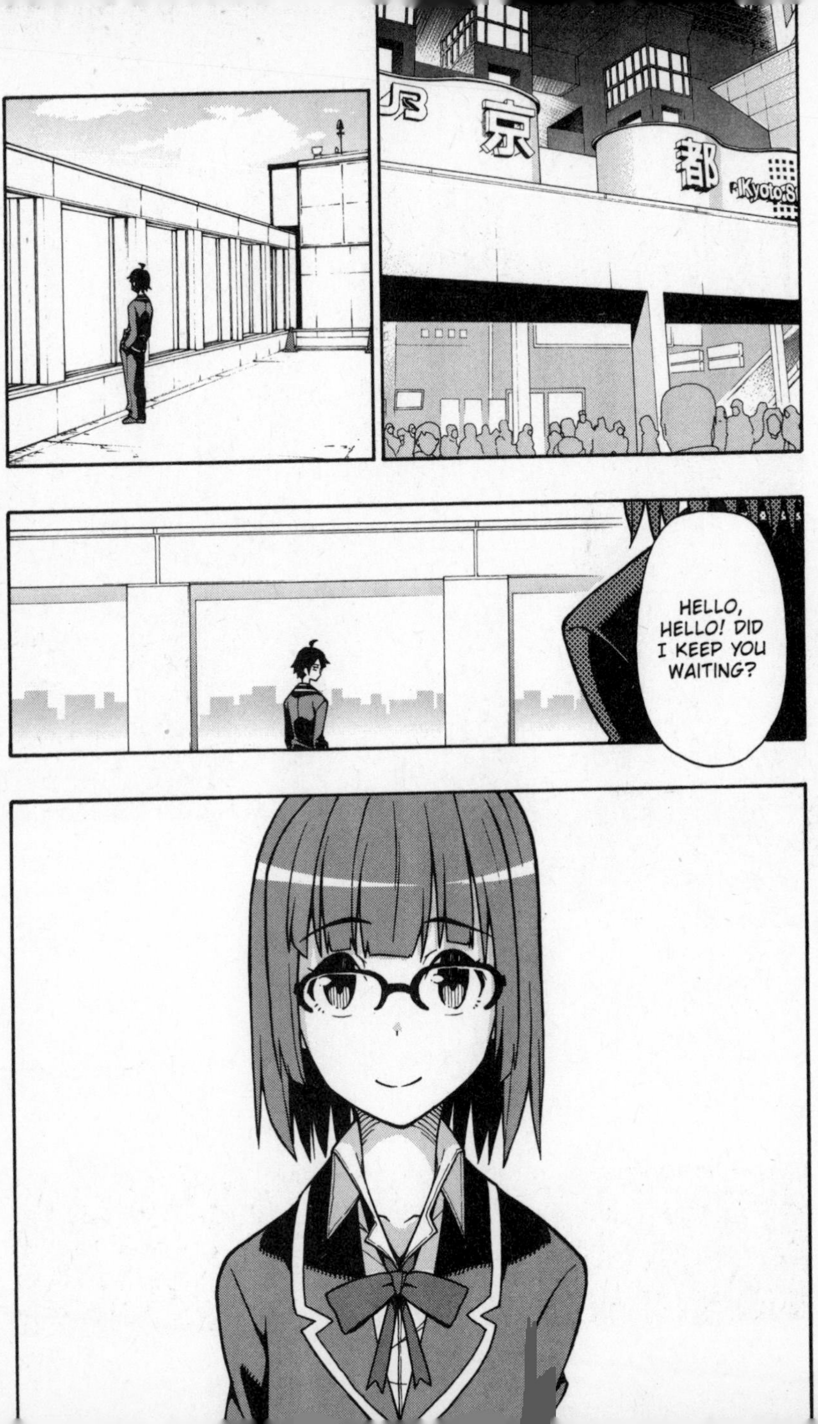
京
都
Kyoto St
HELLO, HELLO! DID I KEEP YOU WAITING?

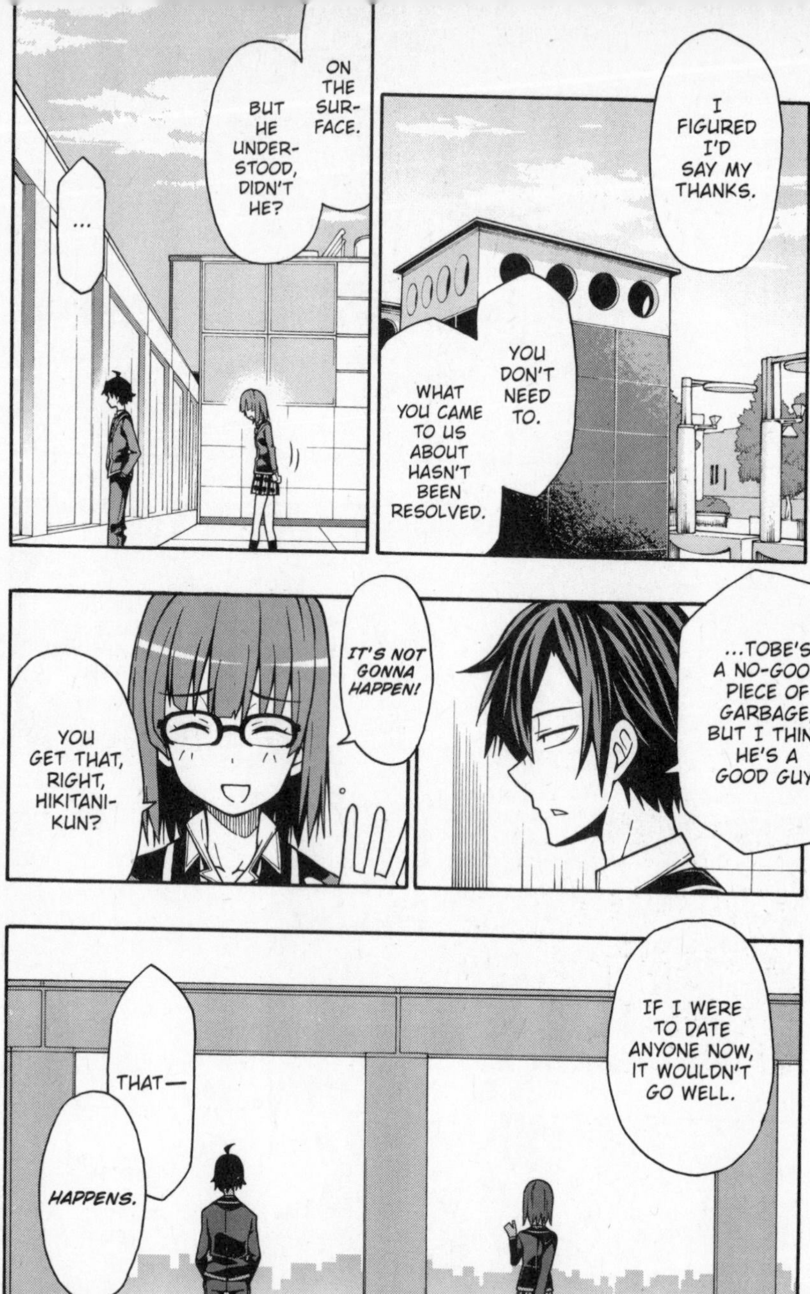
I FIGURED I'D SAY MY THANKS.
YOU DON'T NEED TO.
WHAT YOU CAME TO US ABOUT HASN'T BEEN RESOLVED.
ON THE SURFACE.
BUT HE UNDERSTOOD, DIDN'T HE?
...
...TOBE'S A NO-GOOD PIECE OF GARBAGE, BUT I THINK HE'S A GOOD GUY.
IT'S NOT GONNA HAPPEN!
YOU GET THAT, RIGHT, HIKITANI-KUN?
IF I WERE TO DATE ANYONE NOW, IT WOULDN'T GO WELL.
THAT—
HAPPENS.

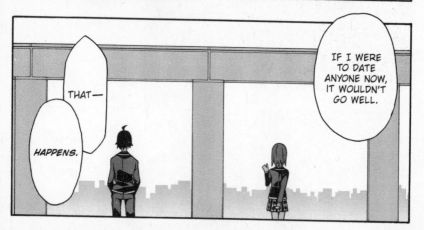

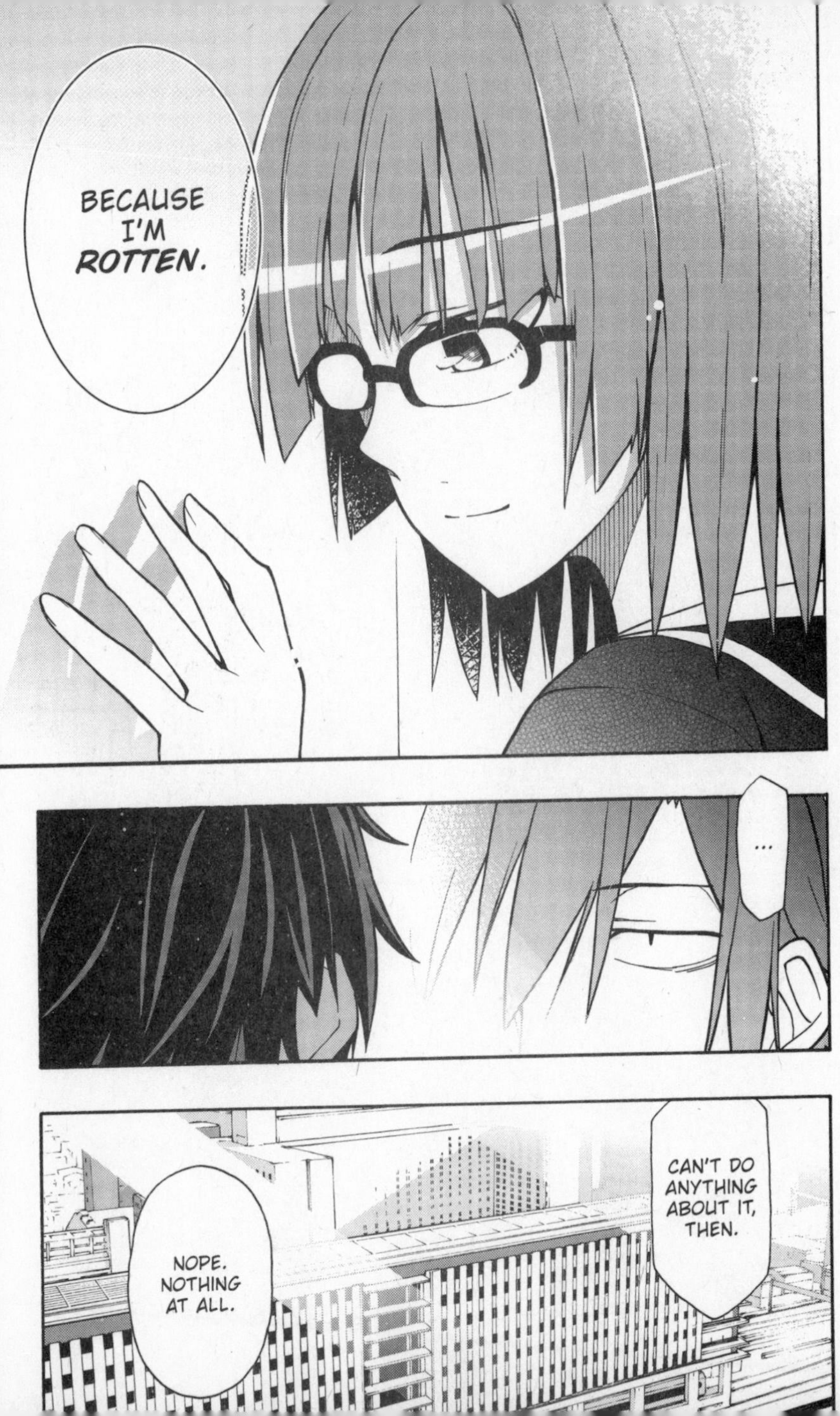
BECAUSE I'M *ROTTEN*.
...
CAN'T DO ANYTHING ABOUT IT, THEN.
NOPE. NOTHING AT ALL.

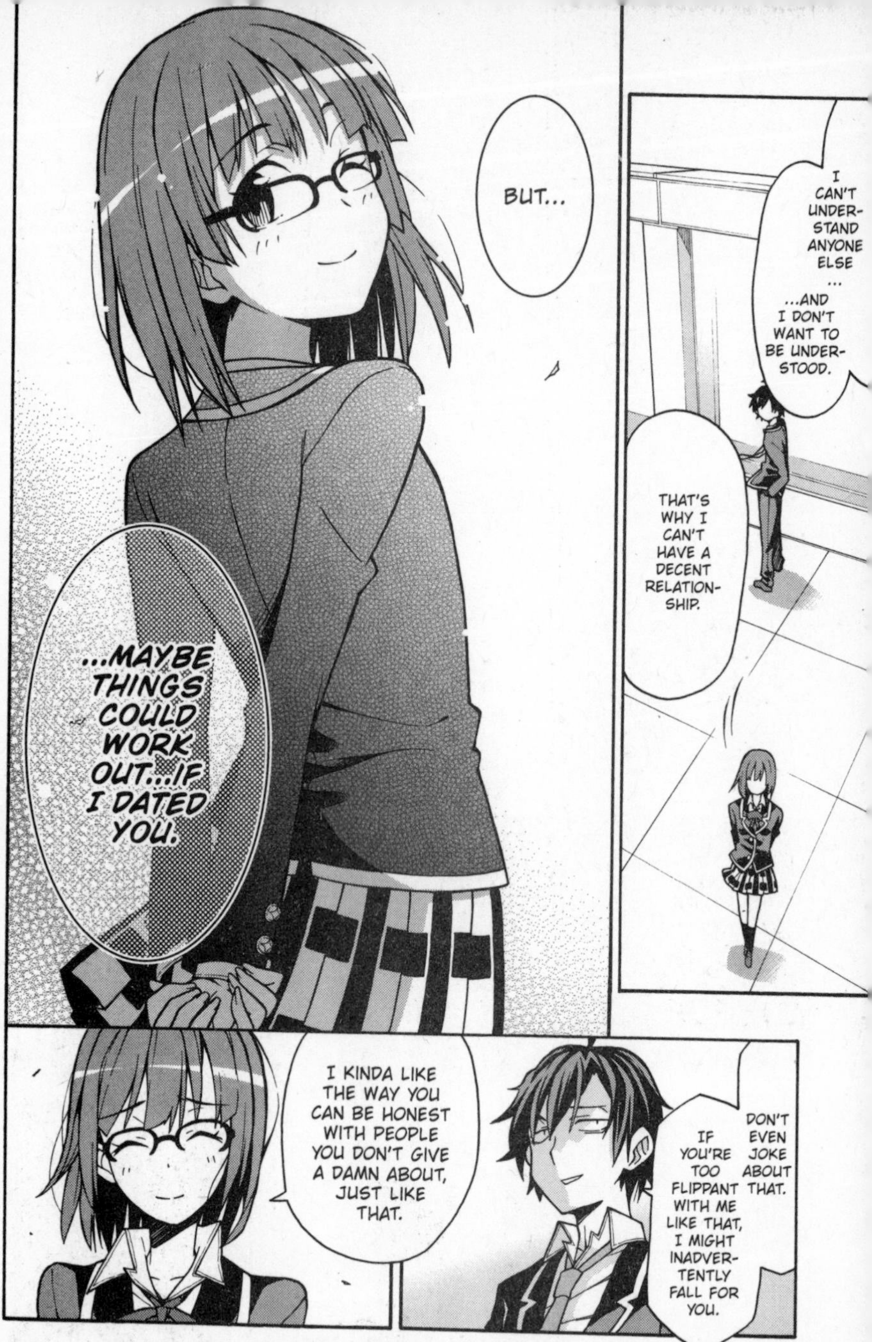
I CAN'T UNDERSTAND ANYONE ELSE ...
...AND I DON'T WANT TO BE UNDERSTOOD.
THAT'S WHY I CAN'T HAVE A DECENT RELATIONSHIP.
BUT...
...MAYBE THINGS COULD WORK OUT...IF I DATED YOU.
DON'T EVEN JOKE ABOUT THAT.
IF YOU'RE TOO FLIPPANT WITH ME LIKE THAT, I MIGHT INADVERTENTLY FALL FOR YOU.
I KINDA LIKE THE WAY YOU CAN BE HONEST WITH PEOPLE YOU DON'T GIVE A DAMN ABOUT, JUST LIKE THAT.

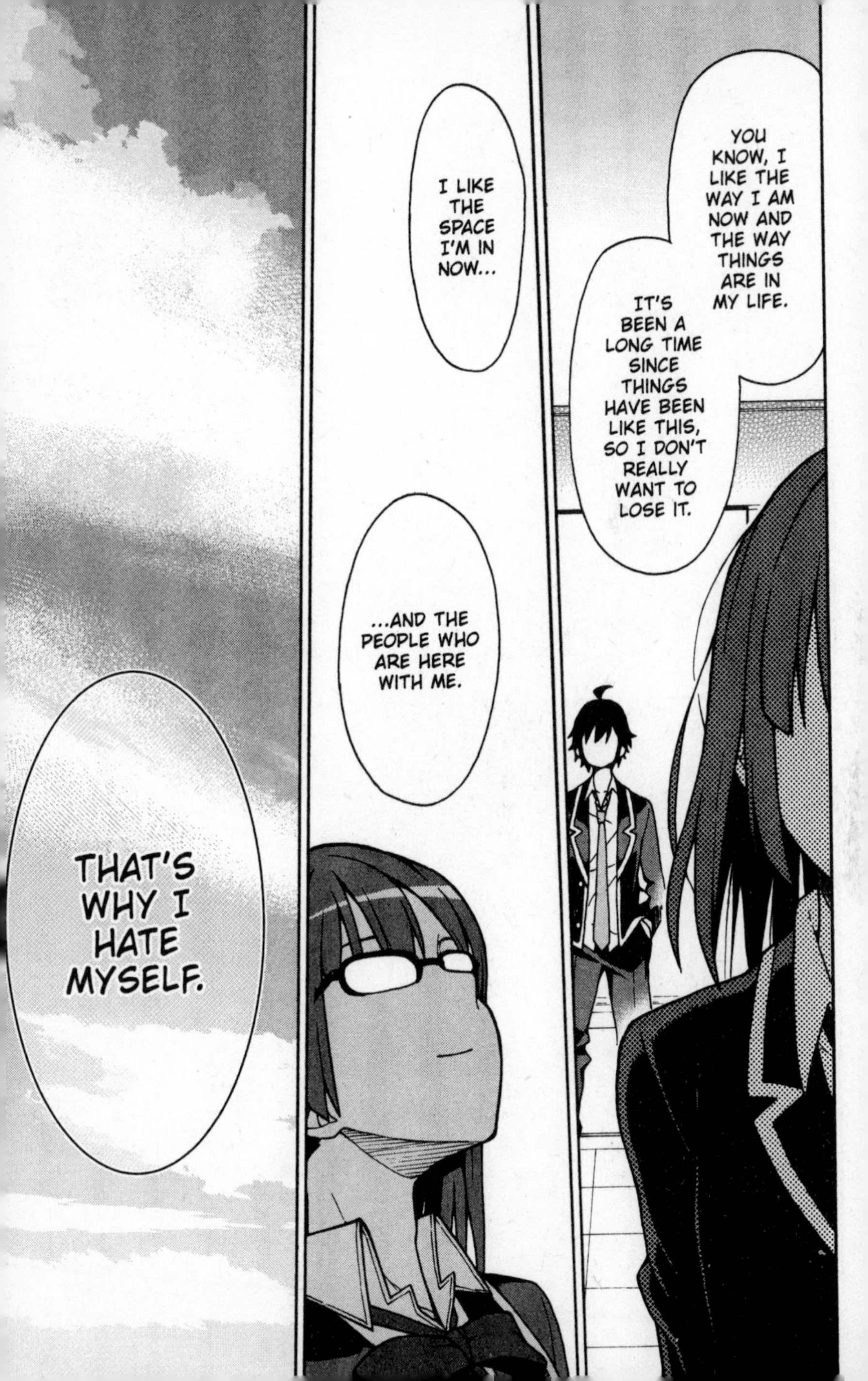
YOU KNOW, I LIKE THE WAY I AM NOW AND THE WAY THINGS ARE IN MY LIFE.
IT'S BEEN A LONG TIME SINCE THINGS HAVE BEEN LIKE THIS, SO I DON'T REALLY WANT TO LOSE IT.
I LIKE THE SPACE I'M IN NOW...
...AND THE PEOPLE WHO ARE HERE WITH ME.
THAT'S WHY I HATE MYSELF.

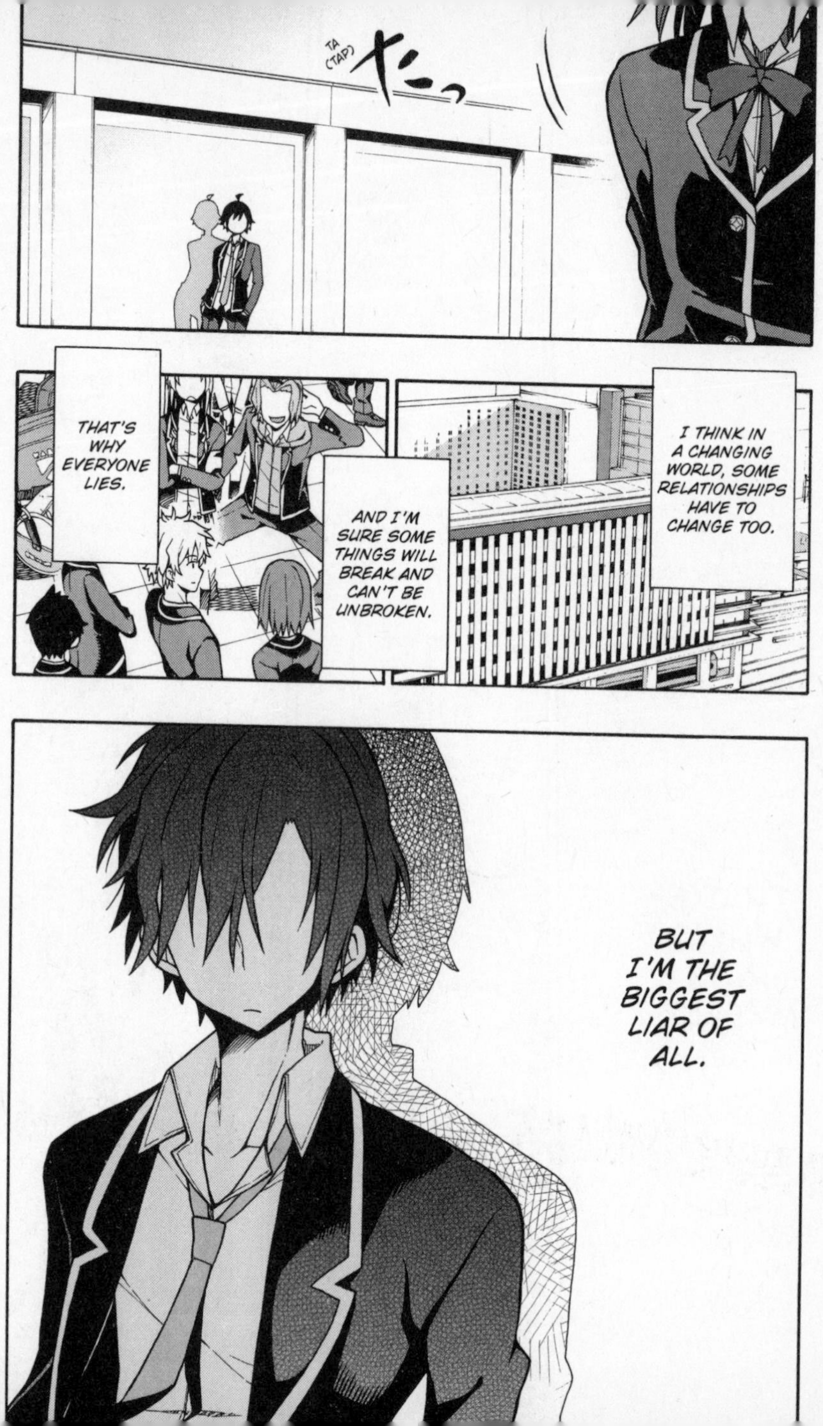
TA (TAP)
I THINK IN A CHANGING WORLD, SOME RELATIONSHIPS HAVE TO CHANGE TOO.
AND I'M SURE SOME THINGS WILL BREAK AND CAN'T BE UNBROKEN.
THAT'S WHY EVERYONE LIES.
BUT I'M THE BIGGEST LIAR OF ALL.

MY YOUTH ROMANTIC COMEDY IS WRONG, AS I EXPECTED

...To Be Continued.

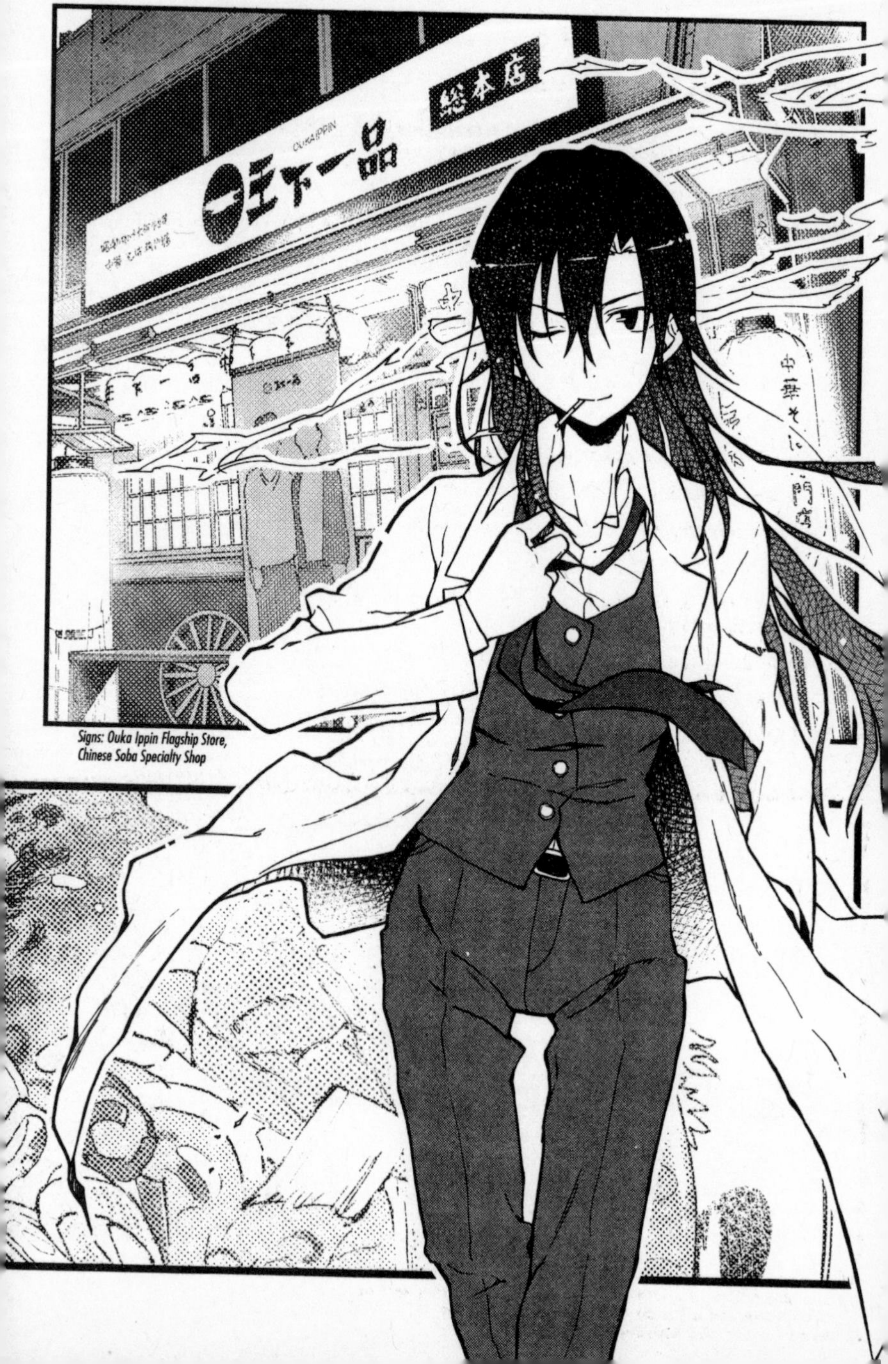
総本店
OUKA IPPIN
王下一品
中華そば
Signs: Ouka Ippin Flagship Store, Chinese Soba Specialty Shop

Do you know?

It's in Sakyo Ward in Kyoto, in Ichijoji.

Locally, Shirakawa Street is infamous for being the street of fashionable bastards. Perhaps this is because there's an arts school nearby, giving the whole area a strange subcultural aura, despite how it's fairly rural.

There, majestically, a single ramen shop stands tall.

It's a widely known fact that this shop, which bustles with students during the day and adult men at night, is a chain found all over the country.

But underestimate it not.

Though it's a national chain, this one was the very first store. In other words, it's no exaggeration to say that this is the Honnouji of Japan's ramen shops.

The flavor there is special.

Of particular note is their menu.

There is a special item on the menu you don't see in other stores or branches. It's called the "Street-Stand-Flavor Ramen."

Just the name alone is refreshing, isn't it? But its shining golden broth overturns the common sense of ramen.

An unusual small bowl sits beside the tables. Inside is Chinese chives dressed with chili pepper and sesame oil.

This brings the flavor of this ramen to even greater depths.

Don't spread this around, but this chive-dressed-with-chili-pepper mix originated at another shop in Kyoto, and you could say that it was stol...no, it was inspired by that item.

But right now, who cares about that?

When you come to Kyoto, try the "Street-Stand-Flavor Ramen with Extra-Extra Chives Combo."

You won't regret it. I guarantee it.

Acknowledgments: Wataru Watari-sensei, Ponkan⑧-sensei, The Gagaga Publishing editing department, The *Monthly Sunday GX* editing department, Chiba City Location Services-sama, Kyoto.
Assistants: Yamada-kun, Takahashi-kun, Sakurai-san.

CHAPTER 51.5 ··· KAKERU TOBE IS HOPELESSLY SHALLOW HERE TOO.

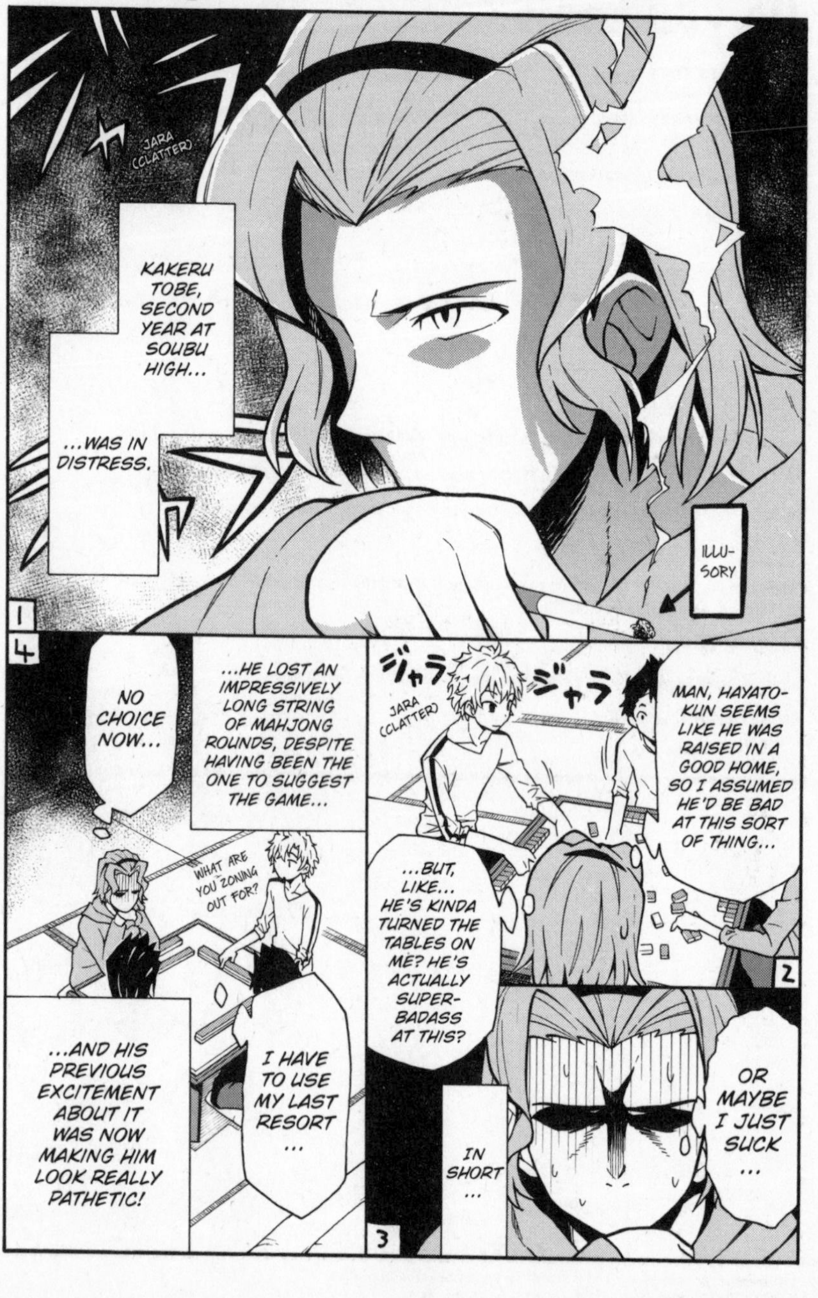
KAKERU TOBE, SECOND YEAR AT SOUBU HIGH...
...WAS IN DISTRESS.
JARA (CLATTER)
ILLUSORY
ジャラ
ジャラ
JARA (CLATTER)
MAN, HAYATO-KUN SEEMS LIKE HE WAS RAISED IN A GOOD HOME, SO I ASSUMED HE'D BE BAD AT THIS SORT OF THING...
...BUT, LIKE... HE'S KINDA TURNED THE TABLES ON ME? HE'S ACTUALLY SUPER-BADASS AT THIS?
OR MAYBE I JUST SUCK...
IN SHORT...
...HE LOST AN IMPRESSIVELY LONG STRING OF MAHJONG ROUNDS, DESPITE HAVING BEEN THE ONE TO SUGGEST THE GAME...
NO CHOICE NOW...
WHAT ARE YOU ZONING OUT FOR?
I HAVE TO USE MY LAST RESORT...
...AND HIS PREVIOUS EXCITEMENT ABOUT IT WAS NOW MAKING HIM LOOK REALLY PATHETIC!

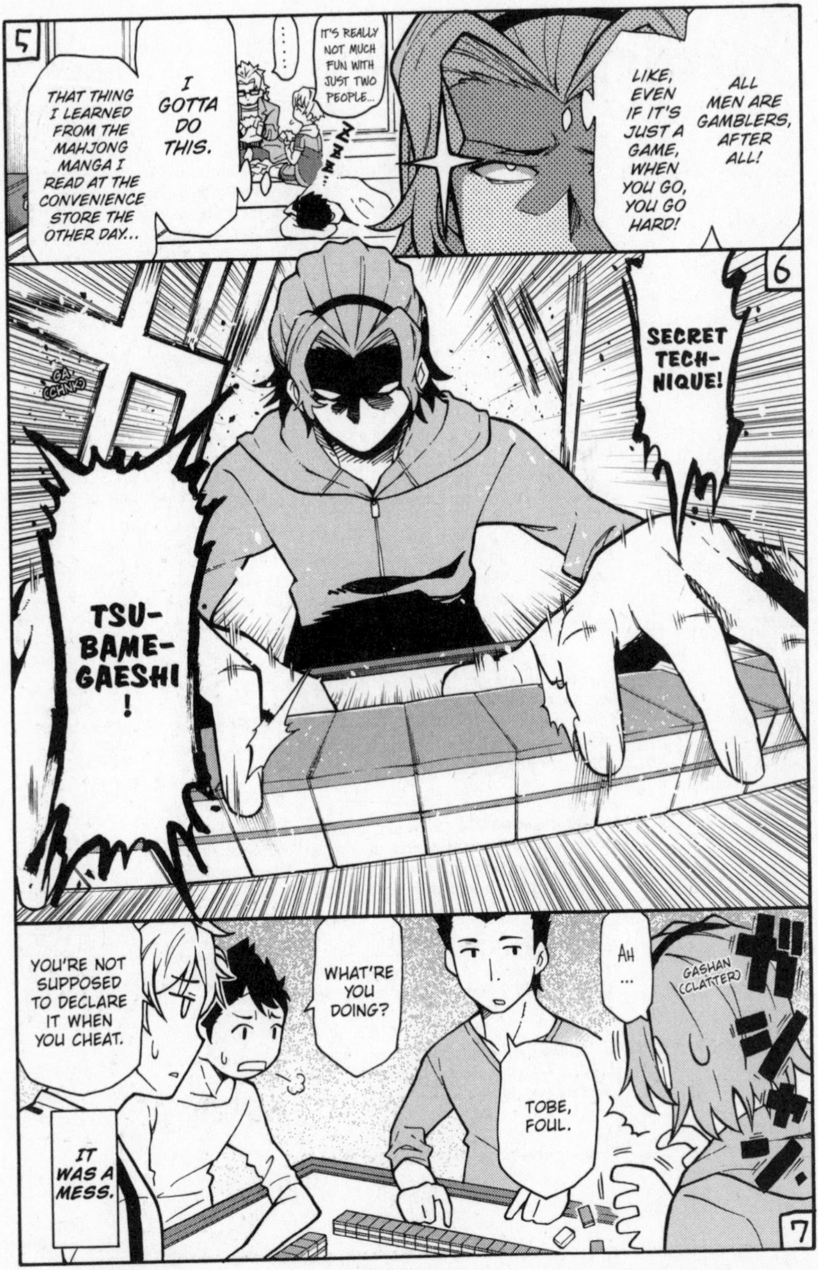
ALL MEN ARE GAMBLERS, AFTER ALL!
LIKE, EVEN IF IT'S JUST A GAME, WHEN YOU GO, YOU GO HARD!
IT'S REALLY NOT MUCH FUN WITH JUST TWO PEOPLE...
......
I GOTTA DO THIS.
THAT THING I LEARNED FROM THE MAHJONG MANGA I READ AT THE CONVENIENCE STORE THE OTHER DAY...
SECRET TECH-NIQUE!
GA (CHNK)
TSU-BAME-GAESHI!
GASHAN (CLATTER)
AH ...
TOBE, FOUL.
WHAT'RE YOU DOING?
YOU'RE NOT SUPPOSED TO DECLARE IT WHEN YOU CHEAT.
IT WAS A MESS.

THE END

TRANSLATION NOTES

Pages 40–41
The girls' **costumes** are based on the character Saber from the visual novel *Fate/stay night*. Rather than a name, "Saber" is a class of summoned servant in the Fate franchise, but it's generally accepted as referring to the blond, armored heroine of *Fate/stay night*. Because the servants are actually great heroes and warriors from across time, using titles such as Saber instead of their real names serves to obscure their identities and thus their strengths and weaknesses.

Page 42
"I just like it that way" is a quote from Ryoma Sengoku in the sentai series *Kamen Rider Gaim*. He's the scientist that came up with a belt that announces a transformation sequence in a rather unique-sounding way with a rather corny line.

Page 48
An **air throw** (*kuuki nage*) is a Judo technique that involves throwing the opponent with minimal contact.

Master Asia is an antagonist in the martial-arts giant-robot anime *G Gundam*, but he doesn't ever actually do an air throw.

Page 50
A *gakuran* is a traditional style of boys' school uniform derived from Prussian cadet uniforms. It's less common at more elite, modern Japanese schools (where a blazer is favored), but the military aesthetic makes it an appropriate costuming choice for this sort of competition.

Page 54
Guan Yu was a general in third-century China whose deeds have been lionized and fictionalized in the classic Chinese novel *Romance of the Three Kingdoms*. This novel has been very widely adapted into many different popular media, notably the Dynasty Warriors video game series.

Page 55
In the Japanese version, Ebina's play-by-play, instead of mentioning the white team **"trying to get on top of the opposing captain,"** has her emphasizing their "strong attack" (*tsuyoki seme*). This phrase is also the name of a boys' love character archetype and can also be translated as "aggressive top."

Page 56
"I have no regrets in life...!" are the famous last words of *Fist of the North Star* antagonist Raoh, who fires his remaining energy into the heavens to restore Earth's ability to sustain life. Zaimokuza's phrasing is slightly different, though.

Page 57
Stealth Hikki is a reference to "Stealth Momo," or Momoko Touyoko in the mahjong manga *Saki* by Ritz Kobayashi. She calls herself "Stealth Momo" because she is so ignored and unnoticed, her ability to blend into the scenery borders on the supernatural.

Page 71
Byaran is a reference to a real travel magazine called *Jyaran*.

Page 90
Buburu is a reference to the real travel magazine, *Rurubu*.

Todaiji Temple is a famous Buddhist temple in Nara prefecture.

Page 91
Arashiyama is a popular tourist area in west Kyoto city, while **Tofukuji Temple** is a large Zen temple in southeastern Kyoto. Both are staple spots for seeing the landscape and fall leaves.

Fushimi-Inari Shrine is a very popular shrine dedicated to Inari, god of rice. The shrine is most famous for its long row of red *torii* gates.

Power spots are thought to be sacred areas of high energy where one can feel at one with nature or be healed and refreshed spiritually. These locations are often popular with Japanese tourists, especially those who believe strongly in their effects.

Page 95
In Japanese, instead of **fu-jo-ho-ho**, Ebina laughs like *u-fu-fu-fu*, with each *fu* written with the character "rotten" from the word *fujoshi* (boys' love fangirl). Replacing *fu* syllables with the "rotten" character is a common sort of wordplay among *fujoshi*.

Page 101
In this picture, Yui is dressed in the uniform of the Shinsengumi, a special police force organized by the military government in the mid-nineteenth century, right before the revolution (Kyoto was the capital of Japan at this time). They're an oft-used subject in popular culture, especially in anime and manga.

Page 116
Mipponhan is a play on the name of a real *ryoukan* (traditional-style inn) in Kyoto city called Mikihan.

Page 117
WAX Coffee is a spoof of MAX Coffee, a Japanese coffee brand.

Page 124
Ouka Ippin is a play on the name of a real chain restaurant, Tenka Ippin.

Chinese soba is another term for ramen, owing to ramen's origins as a Japanese adaptation of a Chinese noodle dish.

Page 136
Honei Kyoto Studio Park is a spoof on Toei Kyoto Studio Park, a theme park modeled in the style of Edo-era Japan. Toei is a Japanese film, television, and animation company founded in 1948. In terms of anime, they're known for major titles such as *Dragon Ball, Sailor Moon, Mazinger Z, One Piece, PreCure, Slam Dunk*, and much more.

Page 137
In this illustration, Hachiman is dressed up like Ryouma Sakamoto, revolutionary of the nineteenth century and contemporary to the Shinsengumi (who Yui was cosplaying as in the previous chapter illustration). Notably, he was assassinated in Kyoto.

Page 138

In Japanese, Yui confuses **"suspension bridge effect"** (*tsuribashi kouka*) with "fishhook effect" (*tsuribari kouka*). The suspension bridge effect is the idea that a person standing on a precarious suspension bridge will feel an attraction to whomever they're with by confusing their fear with excitement toward that person.

Page 144

Ryoanji Temple is another zen temple, famous for its zen rock gardens. It's also a UNESCO World Heritage Site.

Page 195

"Rotten," here, is slang that refers to *fujoshi* (boys' love fangirls) and their hobbies, but it also seems to have a double meaning here, vaguely referring to something unpleasant about Ebina herself without being specific.

Page 201

Ichijoji is train station in Kyoto, the area of which is famous for having lots of ramen shops.

Honnouji Temple is a Nichiren Buddhist temple in Kyoto. It's most famous for being the site where Nobunaga Oda committed suicide. It's not the head temple of any Nichiren sects, however, making this a rather bad comparison.

Page 202

Tobe's pose, with a lit cigarette obscuring his mouth and an intense look in his eyes, is a reference to the mahjong manga *Naki no Ryuu*. Like most mahjong-themed Japanese comics, it involves lots of gambling and involvement with the *yakuza*. The main character, Ryuu, is known for being cool under pressure and stylishly defeating his opponents in mahjong.

Page 203

Tsubame-gaeshi ("swallow reversal") was originally a sword technique developed by Koujirou Sasaki (who famously died in a duel against Musashi Miyamoto) and is a popular name for special techniques, especially those that involve a swift hand. In this particular case, it refers to a cheat in mahjong where you slide the tiles in your hand into the stack in front of you and take a new hand of tiles. It's unclear as to what manga Tobe read exactly, but one especially famous series that features this move is *Tetsuya: The Man Called the Mahjong Saint*.

A foul in Japanese mahjong (*chonbo*) is anything that invalidates a hand and makes it so the owner can no longer win that round. This can be any number of errors, including drawing too many tiles, drawing too few, going out of turn, knocking over tiles, and more. Tobe here both accidentally scatters his tiles and declares his desire to cheat, making it a crystal-clear foul.

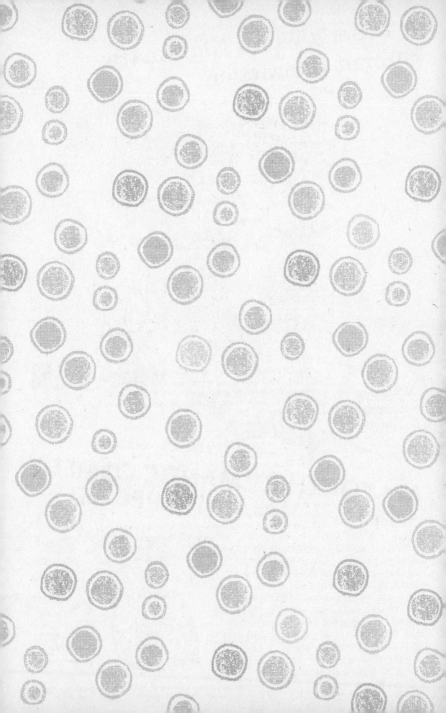

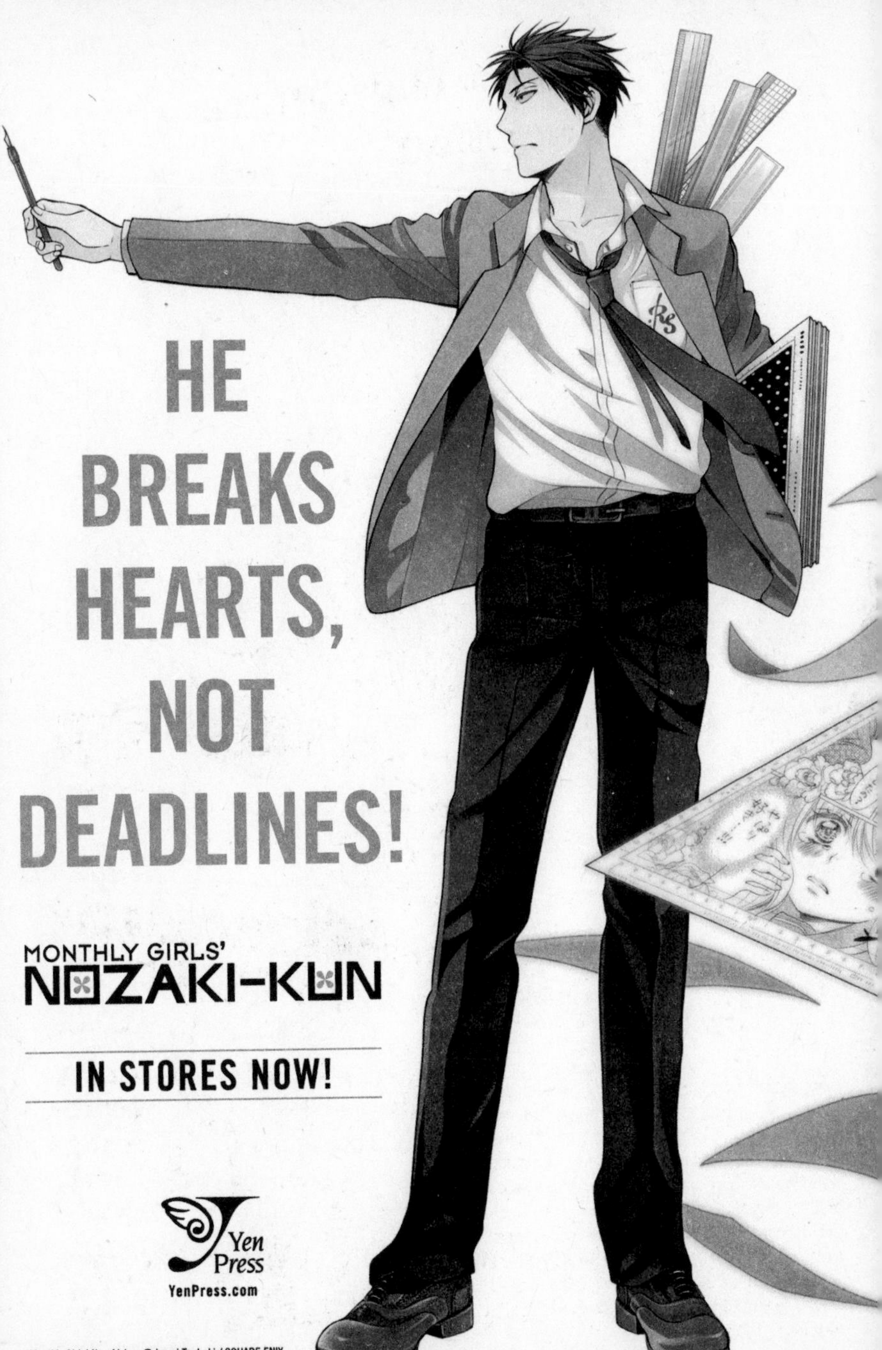
HE
BREAKS
HEARTS,
NOT
DEADLINES!
MONTHLY GIRLS'
NOZAKI-KUN
IN STORES NOW!
Yen
Press
YenPress.com

SOUL EATER

MY YOUTH ROMANTIC COMEDY IS WRONG, AS I EXPECTED @COMIC ❾

Original Story: Wataru Watari
Art: Naomichi Io
Character Design: Ponkan⑧
ORIGINAL COVER DESIGN/Hiroyuki KAWASOME (Graphio)

Translation: Jennifer Ward

Lettering: Bianca Pistillo

YAHARI ORE NO SEISHUN LOVE COME WA MACHIGATTEIRU. @COMIC Vol. 9 by Wataru WATARI, Naomichi IO, PONKAN⑧
© 2013 Wataru WATARI, Naomichi IO, PONKAN⑧
All rights reserved.
Original Japanese edition published by SHOGAKUKAN.
English translation rights arranged with SHOGAKUKAN through Tuttle-Mori Agency, Inc., Tokyo.

Yen Press
1290 Avenue of the Americas
New York, NY 10104

Visit us at yenpress.com
facebook.com/yenpress
twitter.com/yenpress
yenpress.tumblr.com
instagram.com/yenpress

First Yen Press Edition: December 2018

Yen Press is an imprint of Yen Press, LLC.
The Yen Press name and logo are trademarks of Yen Press, LLC.

Library of Congress Control Number: 2016931004

ISBN: 978-1-9753-8101-1

10 9 8 7 6 5 4 3 2 1

WOR

Printed in the United States of America